NATURAL LAW, LIBERALISM, AND MORALITY

D1546542

NATURAL LAW, LIBERALISM, AND MORALITY

Contemporary Essays

EDITED BY
ROBERT P. GEORGE

OXFORD
UNIVERSITY PRESS

*This book has been printed digitally and produced in a standard specification
in order to ensure its continuing availability*

OXFORD
UNIVERSITY PRESS

Great Clarendon Street, Oxford OX2 6DP

Oxford University Press is a department of the University of Oxford.
It furthers the University's objective of excellence in research, scholarship,
and education by publishing worldwide in

Oxford New York

Auckland Bangkok Buenos Aires Cape Town Chennai
Dar es Salaam Delhi Hong Kong Istanbul Karachi Kolkata
Kuala Lumpur Madrid Melbourne Mexico City Mumbai Nairobi
São Paulo Shanghai Singapore Taipei Tokyo Toronto

Oxford is a registered trade mark of Oxford University Press
in the UK and in certain other countries

Published in the United States
by Oxford University Press Inc., New York

ISBN 0-19-924300-X

PREFACE

Writing in 1953, Leo Strauss remarked on the polarized condition of moral, political, and legal philosophy in his time: 'Looking around us, we see two hostile camps, heavily fortified and guarded. One is occupied by liberals of various descriptions, the other by the Catholic and non-Catholic disciples of Thomas Aquinas.'[1] By 1980, John Finnis could assure his readers that 'things have changed during the past twenty-five years, and the debate need no longer be regarded as so polarized.'[2] Indeed, Finnis's own work, especially his path-breaking *Natural Law and Natural Rights*, not only dramatically revived the tradition of natural law theorizing, but has contributed to an unprecedented and highly fruitful engagement of natural law theory and philosophical liberalism in the second half of the 20th century. The purpose of the present collection of original essays by distinguished thinkers in both these traditions is to record and perhaps consolidate some of the progress that has been made as a result of this engagement and to push the debate forward on several fronts.

The volume opens fittingly with an important essay by Finnis defending the view that natural law political theory can and should accommodate the ideal of limited government. A standard liberal objection to Aristotelian and Thomistic political thought is that it licenses an excessively expansive and intrusive role for political authorities. Finnis argues that norms of natural law limit the scope and potential for intrusiveness of government in a variety of significant ways. Most notably, he suggests that a proper understanding of the common good of political society as instrumental, rather than intrinsic, places sharp limits on the authority of government to exercise moral supervision of the private and consensual activities of adult citizens. At the same time, Finnis rejects the strict libertarian claim that government cannot justly limit personal liberty for the sake of preserving the public moral environment which helps to shape people's lives and assists or hinders parents in their efforts to inculcate virtue in their children.

Responding to Finnis, Stephen Macedo places the focus on questions of sexual morality and public policy. While applauding Finnis's natural law defence of limited government, he contends that Finnis has too narrow a view of the possibilities of valuable and morally upright sexual relationships and forms of conduct. In particular, Macedo argues that Finnis's view of marriage as an inherently heterosexual institution is either

---

[1] Leo Strauss, *Natural Right and History* (University of Chicago Press, 1953), 7.
[2] John Finnis, *Natural Law and Natural Rights* (Clarendon Press, Oxford, 1980, 195), vi.

unsound, or, if sound, nevertheless inappropriate as a basis for law and public policy.[3] Appealing to John Rawls's doctrine of 'public reason', Macedo maintains that 'reasonably contestable comprehensive moral or religious claims,' such as those advanced by Finnis in defence of his view of marriage, cannot supply a valid basis for law and policy touching on basic questions of justice and individual rights—even if these claims are true. Finnis, of course, rejects the Rawlsian doctrine. His exchange with Macedo will give readers an understanding of the best arguments being developed by natural law theorists and philosophical liberals in the debate about the moral grounds of legislation.

What John Finnis has done for natural law theory, John Rawls has done for egalitarian liberalism. Interestingly, Rawls, like Finnis, has been challenged to show that his theory of political morality is consistent with limited government. Does Rawls's concern for equality license the state to act in ways that imperil important liberties? This question is vigorously debated by Michael Zuckert and Jeffrey Reiman. Zuckert contends that Rawlsian liberalism is, at best, helpless to provide principles to defend limited government in the face of demands for intrusions into private life for the sake of reducing social and economic inequalities. Reiman maintains that Rawls's *Political Liberalism* demonstrates that the practical arguments for the basic principles of justice Rawls identified in *A Theory of Justice* provide a sound basis for limited government.

This exchange is followed by a short essay by Michael Sandel which powerfully challenges the Rawlsian understanding of 'toleration' as a political virtue. Sandel's target is liberal, or 'non-judgemental', toleration which 'avoids passing moral judgement on the practices it permits'. He proposes as superior 'judgemental' toleration as exemplified in the work of Thomas Aquinas, among others. This non-liberal toleration 'assesses the moral worth' of acts such as abortion and homosexual conduct, 'and permits or restricts [them] according to the weight of those moral considerations in relation to competing moral and practical considerations'. According to Sandel, these competing conceptions of toleration are at the heart of the famous debates between Abraham Lincoln and Stephen Douglas about the restriction of slavery in the territories of the United States. Sandel argues that the superiority of Lincoln's position shows that 'judgemental toleration' may sometimes authorize intolerance—and that intolerance is sometimes, as in the case of slavery, fully justified.

---

[3] For a further elaboration of Macedo's critique of natural law theories of sexual morality, see 'Homosexuality and the Conservative Mind,' *Georgetown Law Journal* 84 (1995) 261–300; for a defence of traditional sexual morality and a critique of Macedo's view, see Robert P. George and Gerard V. Bradley, 'Marriage and the Liberal Imagination,' *id.*, pp. 301–20; also of interest: Hadley Arkes, 'Questions of Principle, Not Predictions: A Reply to Macedo,' *id.*, 321–7, and Stephen Macedo, 'Reply to Critics,' *id.*, pp. 329–37.

The toleration of putatively private wrongdoing is also at issue in a lively and illuminating exchange between Joseph Raz and Christopher Wolfe which immediately follows Sandel's essay. In his impressive 1986 book *The Morality of Freedom*, Raz defended a distinctive form of liberalism which combines 'perfectionism' (that is, the view that a principal objective of government is to help people to lead valuable and fulfilling lives) with a firm commitment to the 'harm principle', which excludes the use of coercion by government to protect or advance the moral well-being of those coerced. Critics—including the editor of the present volume—have expressed doubts about the ultimate compatibility of these beliefs. Here Raz advances a novel and highly interesting argument in defence of his 'perfectionist liberalism'. He claims that paternalistic coercion, even if undertaken for a good reason, can only be justified if it comes at the hands of someone reasonably trusted by the coerced. He maintains that moral coercion cannot be undertaken by governments, however, without undermining trust. Moreover, governments should treat people as full citizens; but full citizenship requires that a person reasonably be able to feel that his government considers his fate a matter of intrinsic value. Moral paternalism, in Raz's judgement, manifests a lack of respect that undermines full citizenship.

In reply, Wolfe contends that Raz has not shown that the criminalization and punishment of immoral conduct is inconsistent either with trust or with full citizenship. Raz's case is undercut, according to Wolfe, by a fact which Raz explicitly recognizes but whose implications he fails to see, namely, that it is not a *subjective* trust in government or a *subjective* sense of full citizenship that is required if paternalism is to be justified, but only government's giving *reasonable* grounds for trust or a citizen's having *reasonable* grounds to feel himself a full citizen. Wolfe argues that these are conditions which moral paternalism often meets.

Unsurprisingly, Raz and Wolfe differ not only about when and how morality can be legally enforced, but also about critical questions of what constitutes immoral conduct. In particular, they divide over the question whether homosexual conduct is immoral. In Raz's view, cultural disapproval of such conduct is a 'manifestation of bigotry [which], where officially sanctioned or socially widespread, condemns gay men and lesbians to second class status in their own society'. Wolfe infers from this that a Razian liberal state would force parents to tolerate active homosexuals (and homosexual activists) teaching in public schools and even private schools. The resistance of parents to such teaching—resistance which Wolfe maintains is a perfectly reasonable manifestation of parental concern for the formation of their children's moral ideas—is, he declares, 'intolerable in the liberal state'. Thus, Wolfe concludes, Raz's position 'involves a denial of very important freedoms', and, indeed, 'constitutes an invitation to liberal tyranny'. Obviously, there is much more to be said on both sides of the debate. As with the exchanges between Finnis and Macedo and Zuckert and Reiman, however, the essays by Raz and Wolfe put forward original and important arguments which anyone interested in natural law and liberalism will want to reflect upon carefully.

The essays by Randy E. Barnett and Walter Berns present sharply differing perspectives on the vexed question of whether, or when, it is legitimate for judges to appeal to non-textual principles of natural law and natural rights in constitutional cases. Barnett argues that the express terms of the Constitution of the United States themselves demand that its authoritative interpreters look beyond the text to a realm of unenumerated natural rights. 'The background natural rights of all persons require that a burden should be placed on those who seek to restrict liberty to justify their actions, rather than on the citizen to justify his freedom.' Berns explores the different conceptions of natural law and natural rights which scholars or various stripes have claimed to identify in the American constitutional scheme, sharply distinguishing the Lockean and Thomistic traditions. Contrary to the claims famously made by John Courtney Murray, Berns argues that American constitutionalism is Lockean, rather than Thomistic, in origin and shape. In this tradition, he maintains, we 'agree to surrender our natural rights or powers in exchange for the civil rights—or, in our case, the constitutional rights—not to be deprived of them without due process of law'. Appeals to a realm of natural law or natural rights beyond the Constitution have no place in this understanding. Judges who make such appeals violate, rather than vindicate, constitutional principle.

Lloyd Weinreb, who established himself as a thoughtful and sympathetic critic of natural law theory in his 1987 book *Natural Law and Justice*, takes the discussion well beyond the question of natural law's relevance to politics and adjudication. He asks the fundamental question whether natural law theory has anything to contribute to the elaboration and application of moral principles as such. His considered judgement is that it does not. He concludes, rather, that 'the proper place of natural law is not within moral debate but in defence of the moral point of view against skepticism or its modern counterpart, existentialism.' Theorists of natural law would be expected to object to Professor Weinreb's ascription to it of so limited a role, and Daniel Robinson, writing in reply, does not frustrate expectations. Robinson argues that Weinreb ought not to infer from uncertainty in the application of moral principles any similar uncertainty about the principles from which a sound application, however debatable, would derive its justification. Readers of various sympathies who are interested in theoretical questions regarding the foundations of moral judgement will find the exchange between Weinreb and Robinson instructive and, I suspect, thought-provoking.

Is belief in natural law ultimately a matter of religious faith? Liberal critics have sometimes suggested that it is. The leading figures in the tradition of natural law theory, however, have conceived the natural law as in principle accessible to unaided reason, even if many of its norms are buttressed and illumined by revelation. Still, most have been religious believers who suppose that the existence of God lends support to the objectivity of morality. Michael Moore, however, who is both a distinguished natural law theorist and something of a political liberal, believes that 'nothing exists answering to a personal conception of God'. In Moore's judgement, the non-existence of God is perfectly compatible with morality's objectivity. Indeed, in his contribution to the present volume, Moore argues that God's existence does not support the natural law theorist's case for moral objectivity and may, indeed, undermine it. 'The theist who grounds his ethics in his theism,' according to Moore, 'shares all the basic beliefs of the moral skeptic albeit such a theist seeks to save himself from skepticism with one last desperate manœuvre.' Moore suggests that the allegiance of such a theist to moral realism should be regarded 'with suspicion'.

Moore's challenging and provocative essay receives separate replies from J. L. A. Garcia and Charles Taliaferro, both of whom argue that God's existence is more than merely compatible with morality's objectivity. In Garcia's view, the God that is relevant to moral objectivity is not 'some divine Being with the attributes Moore assigns of being "a person-like . . . entity only with powers greater than those of ordinary persons," ' but rather, 'the God of Jews and Christians'. Garcia observes that 'the sort of story about God and God's relationship to humanity which most of the great natural law thinkers have accepted [is] the Biblical story'. He argues that this story helps to make sense of such features of morality as its paramountcy or 'overridingness' when the requirements of justice, for example, come into conflict with other important considerations (especially the avoidance of disaster).

Taliaferro, too, thinks that the God who is relevant to moral value and objectivity is no mere 'God of the philosophers', but is the ethically engaged God of Judaism, Christianity, and Islam. He asserts that 'theistic moral arguments *can* be constructed on the basis of a "non-ethical idea" of God,' but asks 'why should they be?' Responding to Moore's concerns that 'grounding moral objectivity on God's will allows for too much ontological precariousness and Divine whimsy,' Taliferro notes that 'for the theist in the classical tradition of Anselm and Aquinas, there is no metaphysical possibility that God does not exist, or that God would command or perform an evil act. God's essential goodness and existence is not a contingent affair.' Is belief in such a God reasonable? Taliaferro outlines a cosmological-ethical argument which, he maintains, when combined with teleological considerations and arguments from religious experience, 'make[s] theism more reasonable than its denial or agnosticism'.

Most of the essays collected in this volume were originally presented at a 1993 conference in Washington, D.C. sponsored by the American Public Philosophy Institute (APPI) with generous support from the Lynde and Harry Bradley Foundation. The APPI promotes discussion of natural law among representatives of different theoretical perspectives in the belief that natural law theory has something important to contribute to a wide range of public policy challenges.

R. P. G.
Princeton
1996

CONTENTS

List of Contributors   xii

1. Is Natural Law Theory Compatible with Limited Government?   1
   John Finnis

2. Against the Old Sexual Morality of the New Natural Law   27
   Stephen Macedo

3. 'Is Modern Liberalism Compatible with Limited Government?
   The Case of Rawls   49
   Michael P. Zuckert

4. John Rawls's New Conception of the Problem of Limited
   Government: Reply to Michael Zuckert   87
   Jeffrey Reiman

5. Judgemental Toleration   107
   Michael J. Sandel

6. Liberty and Trust   113
   Joseph Raz

7. Being Worthy of Trust: a Response to Joseph Raz   131
   Christopher Wolfe

8. Getting Normative: the Role of Natural Rights in
   Constitutional Adjudication   151
   Randy E. Barnett

9. The Illegitimacy of Appeals to Natural Law in Constitutional
   Interpretation   181
   Walter Berns

10. The Moral Point of View   195
    Lloyd L. Weinreb

11. Lloyd Weinreb's Problems with Natural Law   213
    Daniel N. Robinson

12. Good without God   221
    Michael S. Moore

13. 'Deus sive Natura': Must Natural Lawyers Choose?   271
    J. L. A. Garcia

14. God's Natural Laws   283
    Charles Taliaferro

Index   303

LIST OF CONTRIBUTORS

RANDY E. BARNETT is Austin B. Fletcher Professor of Law at Boston University and author of *The Rights Retained by the People: the History and Meaning of the Ninth Amendment*.

WALTER BERNS is John M. Olin Fellow at the American Enterprise Institute, and author of *The First Amendment and the Future of American Democracy*.

JOHN FINNIS is Professor of Law and Legal Philosophy at Oxford University and is also Biolchini Professor of Law at the University of Notre Dame. He is author of *Natural Law and Natural Rights*.

J. L. A. GARCIA is Professor of Philosophy at Boston College.

ROBERT P. GEORGE is McCormick Professor of Jurisprudence at Princeton University and author of *Making Men Moral: Civil Liberties and Public Morality*.

STEPHEN MACEDO is Laurence Rockefeller Professor of Politics at Princeton University.

MICHAEL S. MOORE is Leon Meltzer Professor of Law at the University of Pennsylvania and author of *Act and Crime: the Philosophy of Action and Its Implications for Criminal Law*.

JOSEPH RAZ is Professor of Philosophy of Law at Oxford University and Fellow of Balliol College, Oxford. He is the author of *The Morality of Freedom*.

JEFFREY H. REIMAN is William Fraser McDowell Professor of Philosophy at The American University and author of *Justice and Modern Moral Philosophy*.

DANIEL N. ROBINSON is Professor of Psychology at Georgetown University and author of *Aristotle's Psychology*.

MICHAEL SANDEL is Professor of Government at Harvard University and author of *Democracy's Discontent*.

CHARLES TALIAFERRO is Professor of Philosophy at St Olaf College and author of *Consciousness and the Mind of God*.

LLOYD L. WEINREB is Professor of Law at Harvard University and the author of *Natural Law and Justice*.

CHRISTOPHER WOLFE is Professor of Political Science at Marquette University, and the co-editor of *Liberalism at the Crossroads: An Introduction to Contemporary Liberal Political Theory and Its Critics*.

MICHAEL P. ZUCKERT is Professor of Political Science at the University of Notre Dame and author of *Natural Rights and the New Republicanism*.

1

Is Natural Law Theory Compatible with Limited Government?

JOHN FINNIS

In any sound theory of natural law, the authority of government is explained and justified as an authority limited by positive law (especially but not only constitutional law), by the moral principles and norms of justice which apply to all human action (whether private or public), and by the common good of political communities—a common good which I shall argue is inherently instrumental and therefore limited. If 'limited government' is not a term widely used in natural law theories, that is doubtless because it is so ambiguous. For the proper limits on government and political authority are quite various in their sources, as I have just indicated. Being 'limited' is only to a limited extent a desirable characteristic of government anyway: bad and powerful people and groups want government limited so that they can bully and exploit the weak, or simply enjoy their wealth untroubled by care for others. So 'limited' cannot be a framework term like 'just'.

The first theorist of government to articulate as a specific concept the desideratum that governmental authority/power be legally 'limited' seems to have been Thomas Aquinas. (However, these questions of priority are not to be taken too seriously.[1]) On the first substantive page of his commentary on Aristotle's *Politics*, Aquinas gives an explanation of the distinction, which Aristotle at that point draws but does not explain, between *political* and *regal* types of government or regimen. In 'regal' forms of government, says Aquinas, the rulers have plenary authority,[2] while in 'political' forms, their authority is 'limited [*coarctata*] in accordance with certain laws of the polity'.[3]

Why limit legally the authority of rulers? Well, Aquinas's uncompleted commentary ends before the passages where Aristotle discussed the desirability of a 'rule of laws and not of men'.[4] But in his commentary on Aristotle's *Ethics*, at the point in Book V where Aristotle briefly summarizes the merits of the rule of law,[5] Aquinas expands and perhaps deepens the summary a little: right government does not tolerate an unregulated rule by rulers ('rule of men'), but calls for rulers to be ruled by law, precisely because law is a dictate of *reason*, while what threatens to turn government into tyranny (rule in the interests of the rulers) is their human *passions*, inclining them to attribute to themselves more of the good things, and fewer of the bad things, than is their fair share. And the commentary on the *Politics* suggests another reason. 'Political [as opposed to despotic government] is the leadership of free and equal people; and so the roles of leader and led (ruler and ruled) are swapped about for the sake of equality, and many people get to be constituted ruler either in one position of responsibility or in a number of such positions.'[6] Such regular change overs in political office—standardly correlated with elections[7]—obviously need to be regulated by the laws which constitute (define) these offices; those who at any one time hold office accordingly do so 'according to law' (*secundum statuta*).[8] The guiding thought is: 'free and equal'. Indeed, in his own free-standing theological works Aquinas will say that the best arrangement of governmental authority (*optima ordinatio principum*) will include this, that 'everyone (*omnes*) shares in government, both in the sense that everyone is eligible to be one of the rulers, and in the sense that those who do rule are elected by everyone'.[9] And those who go beyond constitutional limits by enacting *ultra vires* laws are thereby acting unjustly;[10] their action is merely another way of getting more than their fair share (in this case, of authority, if of nothing else).

The account of the rationale and content of the *Rechtsstaat* or Rule of Law, and thus of the point and scope of the legal limits on government, has subsequently become ampler and more detailed. Suffice it to note that, like these early teachings of Aristotle and Aquinas, later accounts enriched by historical experience and the reflections of public lawyers properly pertain to natural law theory, in ways which I hope to make clearer in what follows.

II

Deeper and more demanding than any constitutional or other legal limits on governments are the moral principles and norms which natural law theory considers to be principles and norms of reason,[11] and which are limits, side-constraints, recognized in the conscientious deliberations of every decent person. The public responsibilities and authority of rulers do not exempt them from these limits:[12] no intentional killing of the innocent, no rape, no lies, no non-penal enslavement, and so forth.

The reassertion of the truths that there are indeed such limits on government, and that they can well be articulated in the relatively modern language of truly inviolable rights, is one of the principal teachings in the new encyclical *Veritatis Splendor*.[13] The justification of the traditional claim (reaffirmed in *Veritatis Splendor*) that these are truths which both pertain to revelation and are accessible to reason unaided by revelation would be matter for another treatise, or series of treatises.[14] Here I want merely to underline the importance for political theory of these unconditional, exceptionless limitations on government.

It may be appropriate to highlight the centrality of this point by recalling Strauss's explicit rejection of such limitations, in a passage surely central to his thought and perhaps to some of his influence. The passage occurs, fittingly enough, in the precisely central pages (pp. 160–162) of Strauss's (323 page) book, *Natural Right and History*, in the core of his discussion of the central (the Aristotelian) type among the 'three types of classic natural right teachings'.[15] The climax of this striking passage is the blunt assertion—*propria voce*—that, even (and precisely) for 'a decent society', in war '[t]here are *no limits* which can be defined in advance, there are no *assignable limits* to what might become just reprisals.'[16] Of course, many liberal politicians have acted upon such notions, for example in maintaining the strategic deterrent set up in the years when Strauss was (by unmistakably deliberate implication) articulating its supposed moral underpinnings (1949–53). Those politicians will not have thanked Strauss for going on to observe that these are teachings which cannot coherently be restricted to external affairs, and that the kind of 'suspension of rules of natural right' which he considers justified applies also to governmental dealings with 'subversive elements within society'.[17]

A natural law theory which rejects Strauss's defence of a right of governments *in extremis* to kill the innocent, and denies that it is better that one (innocent) man die (by such killing) than that the people perish, must undertake a radical critique of the assumptions about value, deliberation and choice which underlie every such consequentialism, utilitarianism, proportionalism, or situationism (labels to gesture towards a family of arguments many of which are hinted at or rapidly deployed in these remarkable pages of Strauss).[18] Such a critique must be open and public (as it is in the work of, say, Germain Grisez and others who have followed him in rethinking and developing the classic theory of natural law).[19] For a natural law theory of government certainly involves that, while governments rightly can have secrets and deliberate in deep secrecy, the moral principles by virtue of which they have authority to affect their subjects' deliberations, and which morally limit the exercise of their governmental powers, must all be publicly justifiable. Natural law theory explores, expounds, and explains the deep structure of morality, but morality is a matter of what reasons require, and reasons are inherently intelligible, shared, common.

III

The government of political communities is rationally limited not only by constitutional law and by the moral norms which limit every decent person's deliberation and choice, but also by the inherent limits of its general justifying aim, purpose or rationale. As Strauss observed in the passage I have recalled, that rationale is the common good of the political community. And that common good, as he did not observe, is (I shall argue) not basic, intrinsic, or constitutive, but rather, instrumental. How should it be explained?

Every community is constituted by the communication and co-operation among its members. To say that a community has a common good is simply to say that that communication and co-operation has a point which the members more or less concur in understanding, valuing, and pursuing. How does a critical political theory go about identifying, explaining, and showing to be fully reasonable, the various types of intelligible point or common good, and thus the various fully reasonable types of human community? It can do so only by going back to first principles. And the first principles of all deliberation, choice, and action are the basic *reasons for action*. What gives reason for action is always some intelligible benefit which could be attained or instantiated by successful action, such as: (1) *knowledge* (including aesthetic appreciation) or reality; (2) *skilful performance*, in work and play, for its own sake; (3) *bodily life* and the component aspects of its fullness: health, vigour and safety; (4) *friendship* or harmony and association between persons in its various forms and strengths; (5) the sexual association of a man and a woman which, though it essentially involves both friendship between the partners and the procreation and education of children by them, seems to have a point and shared benefit which is irreducible either to friendship or to life-in-its-transmission and therefore (as comparative anthropology confirms and Aristotle and the 'third founder' of Stoicism, Musonius Rufus came particularly close to articulating)[20] should be acknowledged to be a distinct basic human good, call it *marriage*, the *conjunctio* of man and woman which Aquinas speaks of when identifying the basic goods in his list of first practical principles; (6) the harmony between one's feelings and one's judgements (inner integrity), and between one's judgements and one's behaviour (authenticity), which we can call *practical reasonableness*; and (7) *harmony* with the widest reaches and *ultimate source* of all reality, including meaning and value. The propositions which pick out such basic human goods precisely as giving (underived, non-instrumental) reasons for action to instantiate those benefits, and for avoiding what threatens to destroy, damage or impede their instantiation, are propositions called by

Aquinas the first principles of natural law or, synonymously for him (if I dare to say so here), of natural right[21]—natural, not because they are principles deduced from some prior theoretical account of human nature, but rather because precisely by one's originally practical understanding of these aspects of human flourishing and fulfilment one comes both to realize (make actual in practice) and reflectively and theoretically to understand the nature of the sort of being (the human person, *homo*) who is fulfilled in these ways.[22]

With all this in mind, let me go back to the question of the basic types of *common* good and human community. There are three types of common good each of which provides the constitutive point of a distinctive type of community and directly instantiates a *basic* human good: (i) the affectionate mutual help and shared enjoyment of the friendship and *communio* of 'real friends'; (ii) the sharing of husband and wife in married life, united as complementary, bodily persons whose activities make them apt for parenthood—the *communio* of spouses and, if their marriage is fruitful, their children; (iii) the *communio* of religious believers co-operating in the devotion and service called for by what they believe to be the accessible truths about the ultimate source of meaning, value, and other realities, and about the ways in which human beings can be in harmony with that ultimate source. Other human communities have a common good which is instrumental rather than basic, though association and co-operation even when for an instrumental good (such as a business enterprise) have more than a merely instrumental character in as much as they instantiate the basic good of friendship in one or other of its central or non-central forms.

Thus the political community—properly understood as one of the forms of collaboration needed for the sake of the goods identified in the first principles of natural law—is a community co-operating in the service of a common good which is instrumental, not itself basic. True, it is a good which is 'great and godlike'[23] in its ambitious range: 'to secure the whole ensemble of material and other conditions, including forms of collaboration, that tend to favour, facilitate, and foster the realization by each individual [in that community] of his or her personal development'[24] (which will in each case include, constitutively, the flourishing of the family, friendship, and other communities to which that person belongs). True too, its proper range includes the regulation of friendships, marriage, families, and religious associations, as well as all the many organizations and associations which, like the state itself, have only an instrumental (e.g., an economic) common good. But such regulation of these associations should never (in the case of the associations with a non-instrumental common good) or only exceptionally (in the case of instrumental associations) be intended to take over the formation, direction, or management of these personal initiatives and interpersonal associations. Rather, its purpose must be to carry out a function which the Jesuit social theorists of the early twentieth century taught us to call subsidiarity (i.e., helping, from the Latin *subsidium*, help): the function[25] of assisting individuals and groups to co-ordinate their activities for the objectives and commitments they have chosen, and to do so in ways consistent with the other aspects of the common good of the political community, uniquely complex and far-reaching in its rationale and peculiarly demanding in its requirements of co-operation.[26]

The fundamentally instrumental character of the political common good is indicated by both parts of the Second Vatican Council's teaching about religious liberty, a teaching considered by the Council to be a matter of natural law (i.e., of 'reason itself'[27]). The *first* part of the teaching is that everyone has the right not to be coerced in matters of religious belief and practice. For, to know the truth about the ultimate matters compendiously called by the Council 'religious', and to adhere to and put into practice the truth one has come to know, is so significant a good and so basic a responsibility, and the attainment of that 'good of the human spirit'[28] is so inherently and non-substitutably a matter of *personal* assent and *conscientious* decision that, if a government intervenes coercively in people's search for true religious beliefs, or in people's expression of the beliefs they suppose true, it will harm those people and violate their dignity even when its intervention is based on the correct premise that their search has been negligently conducted and/or has led them into false beliefs. Religious acts, according to the Council, 'transcend' the sphere which is proper to government; government is to care for the temporal common good, and this includes [the subsidiary function of] acknowledging and fostering the religious life of its citizens; but governments have no responsibility or right to direct religious acts, and '*exceed their proper limits*' if they presume to do so.[29]

The *second* part of the Council's teaching concerns the proper restrictions on religious freedom, namely those restrictions which are

required for [i] the effective *protection of the rights* of all citizens and of their peaceful coexistence, [ii] a sufficient care for the authentic public peace of an ordered common life in true justice, and [iii] a proper upholding of *public morality*. All these factors constitute a fundamental part of the common good, and come under the notion of *ordre public.*[30]

Here too the political common good is presented as instrumental, serving the protection of human and legal rights, *public* peace and *public* morality—this last involving, the preservation of a social environment conducive to virtue. Government is precisely not presented here as dedicated to the coercive promotion of virtue and the repression of vice, as such, even though virtue (and vice) are of supreme and constitutive importance for the well-being (or otherwise) of individual persons and the worth (or otherwise) of their associations.

Is the Council's natural law theory right? Or should we rather adhere to the less complex view suggested by a quick reading of Aquinas's *On Government*, that government should command whatever leads people towards their ultimate (heavenly) end, forbid whatever deflects them from it, and coercively deter people from evil-doing and induce them to morally decent conduct?[31] Perhaps the most persuasive short statement of that teaching is still Aristotle's famous attack on theories which, like the sophist Lycophron's, treat the state as a mere mutual insurance arrangement.[32] But in two crucial respects, at least, Aristotle (and with him much of the tradition) has taken things too easily.

First: if the object, point or common good of the political community were indeed a self-sufficient life, and if self-sufficiency (*autarcheia*) were indeed what Aristotle defines it to be—a life lacking in nothing, of complete fulfilment[33]—then we would have to say that the political community has a point it cannot hope to achieve, a common good utterly beyond its reach. For subsequent philosophical reflection has confirmed what one might suspect from Aristotle's own manifest oscillation between different conceptions of *eudaimonia* (and thus of *autarcheia*), that integral human fulfilment is nothing less than the fulfilment of all human persons in all communities (in principle) and cannot be achieved in any community short of the heavenly kingdom, a community envisaged not by unaided reason (natural law theory) but only by virtue of divine revelation and attainable only by supernatural divine gift. To be sure, integral human fulfilment can and should be a conception central to a natural law theory of morality and thus of politics. For nothing less than integral human fulfilment, the fulfilment of all persons in all the basic human goods, answers to reason's full knowledge of, and the will's full interest in, the human good in which one can participate by action. And so the first principle of a sound morality must be as follows: in voluntarily acting for human goods and avoiding what is opposed to them, one ought to choose and will those and only those possibilities the willing of which are compatible with integral human fulfilment. To say that immorality is constituted by cutting back on or fettering reason by passions is equivalent to saying that the sway of feelings over reason constitutes immorality by deflecting one to objectives not in line with integral human fulfilment. This ideal community is thus the good will's most fundamental orientating ideal. But it is not, as early natural law theories such as Aristotle's prematurely proposed, the political community.

Secondly: when Aristotle speaks of 'making' people good, he constantly[34] uses the word *poiesis* which he has so often contrasted with *praxis* and reserved for techniques ('arts') of manipulating matter.[35] But helping citizens to choose and act in line with integral human fulfilment must involve something which goes beyond any art or technique. For only individual acting persons can by their own choices make themselves good or evil. Not that their life should or can be individualistic; their deliberating and choosing will be shaped, and helped or hindered, by the language of their culture, by their family, their friends, their associates and enemies, the customs of their communities, the laws of their polity, and by the impress of human influences of many kinds from beyond their homeland. Their choices will involve them in relationships just or unjust, generous or illiberal, vengeful or charitable, with other persons in all these communities. And as members of all these communities they have some responsibility to encourage their fellow members in morally good conduct and discourage them from morally bad conduct.

To be sure, the political community is a co-operation which undertakes the unique tasks of giving coercive protection to all individuals and lawful associations within its domain, and of securing an economic and cultural environment in which all these persons and groups can pursue their own proper good. To be sure, this common good of the political community makes it far more than a mere arrangement for 'preventing mutual injury and exchanging goods'. But it is one thing to maintain, as reason requires, that the political community's rationale requires that its public managing structure, the state, should deliberately and publicly identify, encourage, facilitate and support the truly worthwhile (including moral virtue), should deliberately and publicly identify, discourage and hinder the harmful and evil, and should by its criminal prohibitions and sanctions (as well as its other laws and policies) assist people with parental responsibilities to educate children and young people in virtue and to discourage their vices. It is another thing to maintain that that rationale requires or authorizes the state to direct people to virtue and deter them from vice by making even secret and truly consensual adult acts of vice a punishable offence against the state's laws. So a third way in which Aristotle takes things too easily is his slide from upholding government's responsibility to assist or substitute for the direct parental discipline of youth, to claiming that this responsibility continues, and in the same direct coercive form, 'to cover the whole of a lifetime, since most people obey necessity rather than argument, and punishments rather than the sense of what is truly worthwhile'.[36] There was a sound and important distinction of principle which the Supreme Court of the United States overlooked in moving from *Griswold* v. *Connecticut* 381 US 479 (1965) (*use* of contraceptives by spouses) to *Eisenstadt* v. *Baird* 405 US 438 (1970) (*public distribution* of contraceptives to *unmarried* people).[37] The truth and relevance of that distinction would be overlooked again if laws criminalizing private acts of sodomy between adults were to be struck down by the Court on any ground which would also constitutionally require the law to tolerate the advertising or marketing of homosexual services, the maintenance of places of resort for homosexual activity, or the promotion of homosexualist 'lifestyles' via education and public media of communication, or to recognize homosexual 'marriages' or permit the adoption of children by homosexually active people, and so forth.

IV

It is, I think, a mistake of method to frame one's political theory in terms of its 'liberal' or 'non-liberal' (or '[anti-]conservative' or '[non-]socialist' or '[anti-]capitalist') character. Fruitful inquiry in political theory asks and debates whether specified principles, norms, institutions, laws and practices are 'sound', 'true', 'good', 'reasonable', 'decent', 'just', 'fair', 'compatible with proper freedom', and the like—not whether they are liberal or incompatible with 'liberalism'.[38] Still, many who style their own thought 'liberal' offer to identify limits on government which go beyond those I have outlined above. So we can usefully ask whether these suggest a conception of limited government which natural law theory would be wrong to reject or overlook.

One proposal is that government not constrain liberty on the ground that one conception of what is good or right for individuals is superior to another. This proposal has been put forward by the later Rawls as appropriate for nearly-just, modern constitutional democracies such as he takes the United States to be. But this same, latter-day Rawls abstains from claiming that his theory is true, valid or sound; it is advanced instead as suitable to ensure stability and social unity from one generation to the next, by bringing about or maintaining an 'overlapping consensus' on certain constitutional principles (notably this one).[39] To claim validity or truth for his theory, or the principles it promotes, would be (Rawls claims) to violate the conditions of pluralism and (as other 'liberals' put it) 'neutrality' and to move from the proper domain of political theory and practice into the domain of private ideals and conceptions of the good—from public reasons for action to private reasons. Ronald Dworkin, on the other hand, has proposed that the requirement of government neutrality between conceptions of good and bad ways of life is an implication of a *true* political principle, that everyone is entitled to equal concern and respect.

Rawls's refusal to offer any further justification for these principles has attracted devastating criticism from Joseph Raz,[40] and others.[41] The essential point, in my opinion, is that any position like Rawls's postulates or presupposes an untenable distinction between public and private reasons for action, since like Rawls it will admit that in one's private deliberations, unlike public deliberations, one may and doubtless should be motivated by a conception of good and bad lives, a conception which one considers true. The untenability of this distinction is evident. For every political actor/agent is a human person or at least, in the case of the social acts of groups (states, corporations, teams . . .), has no existence apart from the personal acts of the people who are the group's leaders and/or other members. Each person's reasons for choosing to perform some political act must be, or at least be based upon, reasons which for that person are ultimate/basic (in need of no further, rationally motivating and thus justifying reason); and these reasons must all be consistent with the acting person's other reasons or principles of action. For one's public acts are at the same time one's private acts: they are part of one's one and only real life. One's engagement in a 'political' act must not be merely logically consistent with one's conception of a good and decent life; it must actually be rationally motivated by that conception (which after all can be nothing other than one's conception of what are good reasons for one's acting). So one's 'public' reasons for acting must also be one's 'private' reasons (though it does not follow that all one's reasons for action need be 'made public'). Moreover, political actions often have the gravest consequences both for the actor and for others; so, the public reasons are not good (adequate) reasons unless they justify the act, so to speak, all the way down, i.e., justify the actor in doing it. To postulate that political acts are all to be done for reasons publicly undiscussable ('private ideals') is to propose that the political order should refuse to offer its participants any good (adequate) reason for participating in it or for accepting the burdens of citizenship.

As for Dworkin's attempts to derive a constraint of neutrality from the 'principle of equal concern and respect', refutations of them are perhaps well enough known to need no repeating here.[42] A careful, fair, and decisive summation and development of these critiques can be found in Robert George's book, *Making Men Moral: Civil Liberties and Public Morality*.[43]

That enables me to turn, instead, to a proposal more recent and more cautious than either Rawls's or Dworkin's. Stephen Macedo rejects the claim that liberal justice is neutral among human goods or ways of life.[44] But government should do nothing disrespectful of its subjects, and respect for persons requires, he argues, that they be subjected to no constraint not publicly justifiable. 'People may rightly be coerced by the state only for certain limited reasons',[45] namely, public reasons—'reasons that all ought to be able to accept'.[46]

Thus stated, this is a limit which a natural law theorist will gladly accept. Natural law theory is nothing other than the account of all the reasons-for-action which people ought to be able to accept, precisely because these are good, valid, and sound as reasons. But Macedo, here following Rawls, proposes to interpret the limit differently: ." . . *public* moral justification . . . does not aim to identify what are simply the best reasons, where best is a function of only the quality of the reasons as reasons leaving aside the constraints of wide accessibility.[47] Now this is not a crude appeal to majority rule. It is intended as a substantive principle, limiting government action even where a majority support the action. For such a support is sometimes based not on reasons but on respect for tradition or mere uncritical *mores*. In such a case, despite the fact that a law or other governmental action has majority support and is, in truth, supported by the best reasons, the limit which Macedo proposes would be transgressed—and those subjected to the law would be treated without due respect—if the reasons supporting the action, though sound and true, involve 'very difficult forms of reasoning'.[48] The rational justification for the government's action must be 'accessible to people as we know them'.[49] But (he goes on) in a natural law theory such as Aquinas's or the new classical theory of Grisez, Boyle, Finnis, George and others, there is a gap between first principles and specific moral norms such as we find in the Decalogue, a logical space which must be filled by inferences *some* of which 'require a wisdom or reasonableness "not found in everyone or even in most people" '.[50] So, Macedo concludes, relevant parts of the natural law (even if true), or at least the inferences (even if sound) on which they depend, may be 'beyond the capacities of "most people" ' and therefore not proper grounds for law.[51]

But in fact these natural law theorists do not admit that the actual norms of the Decalogue, or even the inferences on which they rationally depend, are beyond the *capacities* of most people, or that they are inaccessible, or that they *cannot* be appreciated by most people. Macedo, throughout his work, ignores the distinction between native and formed capacity, between faculty and competence, i.e., the fact that I both *do* and *do not* have the capacity to speak Icelandic. And in each of the passages which Macedo implicitly relies upon, Aquinas says that the precepts of the Decalogue can be known from first principles with only a little reflection[52] and even ordinary folk can make the inference to them and see their point,[53] though it *can happen that* some people get confused about them;[54] *other* moral norms, inferable from the precepts of the Decalogue, are ones which *are known* (*cognoscuntur*)[55] by the wise rather than by others, who unlike the wise *do not* (not 'could not') diligently consider the relevant circumstances.[56] So, even on the face of the texts, there is no admission that the moral principles of the Decalogue are outside the domain of 'public justification' and public 'accessibility'.[57]

V

Macedo brings his proposed limit to bear on two main issues. The *first* is an embarrassing and difficult one to discuss, and that embarrassment turns out to be relevant to the political theoretical issue in more ways than one. For laws and public policies should indeed be based on reasons, not merely emotions, prejudices, and biases, and a subrational prejudice does not become a moral judgement merely by being labelled so. So if the promotion of certain types of conduct through, for example, educational facilities or legally supported domestic arrangements is deliberately discouraged by law (which will often have the side-effect of disadvantaging those who are ready and willing to engage in that sort of conduct), and if the decision to discourage that type of conduct is premised on the judgement that such conduct is morally deleterious and is thus a matter of legitimate concern in designing educational and socially supported domestic arrangements, then the law will be justified only if that adverse normative judgement is reasonable and not merely an expression of loathing. But Macedo's first issue is (as he frames it) homosexual conduct, and the discussion of that issue, indeed even private reflection upon it, is dogged by an embarrassment which renders most people more than usually inarticulate, and thus makes it more than usually difficult to differentiate between a reasonable though unarticulated judgement and a mere unthinking hostility.

So we are in a difficulty. On the one hand there is common sense wisdom, articulated in the second half of the first century AD by Musonius Rufus: 'One begins to lose one's hesitation to do disgraceful things when one loses one's hesitation to speak of them.'[58] On the other hand, a judgment like the judgment of the Court in *Bowers* v. *Hardwick*,[59] by its silence about why and in what respects homosexual conduct is bad, raises the suspicion that the laws on that matter (and even laws discouraging homosexual conduct in ways more in keeping with the state's subsidiary function) are grounded in subrational motivations.

Yet the fact is that many great philosophers—Socrates, Plato, and Aristotle—and other outstanding thinkers of classical antiquity rejected homosexual conduct.[60] Even those people inclined to it by their nature[61] viewed it as something degrading to the humanity of those who engage in it.[62] What is most striking about that rejection is not merely that it was the judgement of profoundly reflective thinkers untouched by the revealed teachings of the Old and New Covenants. It is that the judgement was reached very deliberately and carefully and, in the case at least of Socrates, Plato, and Aristotle reached in the midst of a distinctively homoerotic culture, and that its essential content was this: homosexual *conduct* (and indeed all extra-marital sexual gratification) is radically incapable of participating in, actualizing, the common good of friendship. Friends who engage in such conduct are following a natural impulse and doubtless often wish their genital conduct to be a good 'way to participate in the goods of intimate friendship'. But in supposing that it can in truth be that, they are deceiving themselves.

In his book, Macedo had put the opposing case like this: "[n]on-promiscuous homosexual relationships . . . also participate in real human goods (friendship, play, knowledge). And for those whose attractions nature has directed toward members of the same sex, homosexual love may be the best way to participate in the goods of intimate friendship".[63] So we must look more deeply into the foundations of the Socratic–Platonic judgement.

Here we can recall the reflections on marital communion in Musonius Rufus[64] and, a little later in the same generation, Plutarch.[65] And one could add Plato's identification of the work of Eros in the *Symposium* as paradigmatically that intercourse of man and woman which is a begetting and a divine thing.[66] These reflections become the more accessible to us if we set aside the long-dominant theological tradition whose dominance was inaugurated by Augustine's *De Bono Conjugali*. In this influential little treatise, Augustine taught that the marital good is an instrument good, in the service of the procreation and education of children so that the intrinsic, non-instrumental good of friendship will be promoted and realized by the propagation of the human race, and the intrinsic good of inner integration will be promoted and realized by the 'remedying' of the disordered desires of concupiscence.[67] Now, when considering sterile marriage, Augustine had identified a further good of marriage, the natural *societas* (companionship) of the two sexes.[68] Had he truly integrated this into his synthesis, he would have recognized that in sterile and fertile marriages alike, the communion, companionship, *societas* and *amicitia* of the spouses—their being married—is the very good of marriage, and is an intrinsic, basic human good, not merely instrumental to any other good. And this communion of married life, this integral amalgamation of the lives of the two persons (as Plutarch[69] put it before John Paul II[70]) has as its intrinsic elements, as essential parts of one and the same good, the *bona* and *fines* to which the theological tradition for a long time subordinated that communion. It took a long and gradual process of development of doctrine, through the *Roman Catechism* issued after the Council of Trent, the teachings of Pius XI and Pius XII, and eventually those of Vatican II— a process brilliantly illuminated in the new, second volume of Germain Grisez's masterly treatise on moral theology[71]—to bring the tradition to the position that procreation and children are neither the end (whether primary or secondary) to which marriage is instrumental (as Augustine taught), nor instrumental to the good of the spouses (as much secular and 'liberal Christian' thought supposes), but rather: parenthood and children and family are the intrinsic fulfilment of a communion which, because it is not merely instrumental, can exist and fulfil the spouses even if procreation happens to be impossible for them.

Now if marriage is a basic human good, there fall into place not only the elements of the classic philosophical judgements on non-marital sexual conduct but also the similar judgements reached about such conduct by decent people who cannot articulate explanatory premises for those judgements, which they reach rather by an insight into what is and what is not *consistent with* realities whose goodness they experience and understand at least sufficiently to will and choose. At the heart of the Platonic–Aristotelian and later ancient philosophical rejections of all homosexual conduct, and thus of the modern 'gay' ideology, are three fundamental theses: (i) the commitment of a man and woman to each other in the sexual union of marriage is intrinsically good and reasonable, and is incompatible with sexual relations outside marriage; (ii) homosexual acts are radically and peculiarly non-marital, and for that reason intrinsically unreasonable and unnatural; (iii) furthermore, according to Plato, if not Aristotle, homosexual acts have a special similarity to solitary masturbation, and both types of radically non-marital act are manifestly unworthy of the human being and immoral. These are the theses whose public accessibility and justifiability I wish to defend. Their defence will include an answer to the question I left hanging: why cannot non-marital friendship be promoted and expressed by sexual acts? Why is the attempt to express affection by orgasmic non-marital sex the pursuit of an illusion?

Plato's mature concern in the *Laws* for familiarity, affection, and love between spouses in a chastely exclusive marriage, Aristotle's representation of marriage as an intrinsically desirable friendship between quasi-equals, and as a state of life even more natural to human beings than political life,[72] and Musonius Rufus's conception of the inseparable double goods of marriage all find expression in Plutarch's celebration of marriage—as a union not of mere instinct but of reasonable love, and not merely for procreation but for mutual help, goodwill, and co-operation for their own sake.[73] Plutarch's severe critiques of homosexual conduct (and of the disparagement of women implicit in male homosexual ideology)[74] develop Plato's critique of homosexual and all other extra-marital sexual conduct. Like Musonius Rufus, Plutarch does so by bringing much closer to explicit articulation the following thought. Genital intercourse between spouses enables them to actualize and experience (and in that sense express) their marriage itself, a single reality with two blessings (children and mutual affection).[75] Non-marital intercourse, especially but not only homosexual, has no such point and therefore is unacceptable.

Underlying these rejections of extra-marital sex, and the judgement that such conduct is radically incapable of participating in, actualizing, the common good of friendship, is a thought which may be articulated as follows. The union of the reproductive organs of husband and wife really unites them biologically (and their biological reality is part of, not merely an instrument of, their *personal* reality). Reproduction is one function and so, in respect of that function, the spouses are indeed one reality, and their sexual union therefore can *actualize* and allow them to *experience* their *real common good*—their *marriage* with the two goods, parenthood and friendship, which are the parts of its wholeness as an intelligible common good even if, independently of what the spouses will, their capacity for biological parenthood will not be fulfilled in consequence of that act of genital union. But the common good of friends who are not and cannot be married (for example, man and man, man and boy, woman and woman) has nothing to do with their having children by each other, and their reproductive organs cannot make them a biological (and therefore personal) unit.[76] So their genital acts together cannot do what they may hope and imagine. Because their choice to activate their reproductive organs cannot be an actualizing and experiencing of the marital good—as marital intercourse can, even between spouses who happen to be sterile—it can do no more than provide each partner with an individual gratification. For want of a *common good* that could be actualized and experienced *by this bodily union*, that conduct involves the partners in treating their bodies as instruments to be used in the service of their consciously experiencing selves; their choice thus disintegrates each of them precisely as acting persons.[77]

Reality is known in judgement, not in emotion, and in reality, whatever the generous hopes and dreams with which some same-sex partners may surround their genital sexual acts, those acts cannot express or do more than is expressed or done if two strangers engage in such activity to give each other pleasure, or a prostitute gives pleasure to a client in return for money, or (say) a man masturbates to give himself a fantasy of more human relationships after a gruelling day on the assembly line. This is, I believe, the substance of Plato's judgement—in the *Gorgias* which is so important for political philosophy[78]—that there is no important distinction in essential moral worthlessness between solitary masturbation, being sodomized as a prostitute, and being sodomized for the pleasure of it.[79]

In short, sexual acts are not unitive in their significance unless they are marital (actualizing the all-level unity of marriage) and (since the common good of marriage has two aspects) they are not marital unless they have not only the generosity of acts of friendship but also the procreative significance, not necessarily of being intended to generate or capable in the circumstances of generating but at least of being, as human conduct, acts of the reproductive kind—actualizations, so far as the spouses then and there can, of the reproductive function in which they are biologically and thus personally one.

The ancient philosophers do not much discuss the case of sterile marriages, or the fact (well known to them) that for long periods of time (e.g., throughout pregnancy) the sexual acts of a married couple are naturally incapable of resulting in reproduction. They appear to take for granted what the subsequent Christian tradition certainly did, that such sterility does not render the conjugal sexual acts of the spouses non-marital. (Plutarch indicates that intercourse with a sterile spouse is a desirable mark of marital esteem and affection.[80]) For, a husband and wife who unite their reproductive organs in an act of sexual intercourse which, so far as they then can make it, is of a kind suitable for generation, do function as a biological (and thus personal) unit and thus can be actualizing and experiencing the two-in-one-flesh common good and reality of marriage, even when some biological condition happens to prevent that unity resulting in generation of a child. Their conduct thus differs radically from the acts of a husband and wife whose intercourse is masturbatory, for example sodomitic or by fellatio or coitus interruptus.[81] In law such acts do not consummate a marriage, because in reality (whatever the couple's illusions of intimacy and self-giving in such acts) they do not actualize the one-flesh, two-part marital good.

Does this account seek to 'make moral judgements based on natural facts'? Yes and no. No, in the sense that it does not seek to infer normative conclusions or theses from non-normative (natural-fact) premises. Nor does it appeal to any norm of the form 'Respect natural facts or natural functions'. But yes, it does apply the relevant practical reasons (especially that marriage and inner integrity are basic human goods) and moral principles (especially that one may never intend to destroy, damage, impede, or violate any basic human good, or prefer an illusory instantiation of a basic human good to a real instantiation of that or some other human good) to the realities of our constitution, intentions, and circumstances.

'Homosexual orientation', in one of the two main senses of that highly equivocal term, is the deliberate willingness to promote and engage in homosexual acts—the state of mind and will whose self-interpretation came to be expressed in the deplorable but helpfully revealing name 'gay'. This willingness treats human sexual capacities in a way which is deeply hostile to the self-understanding of those members of the community who are willing to commit themselves to real marriage in the understanding that its sexual joys are not mere instruments or accompaniments to, or mere compensations for, the accomplishment of marriage's responsibilities, but rather are the *actualizing and experiencing* of the intelligent commitment to share in those responsibilities. The 'gay' ideology treats sexual capacities, organs and acts as instruments to be put to whatever suits the purposes of the individual 'self' who has them, and so is radically inconsistent with the constitutive self-interpretative judgement of married people and their family, that adultery is *per se* (and not merely because it may involve deception), and in an important way, inconsistent with conjugal love. So a political community which judges that the stability and educative generosity of family life is one of the basic goods which political association itself exists to serve can rightly judge that it has a compelling interest in denying that 'gay lifestyles' are a valid, humanly acceptable choice and form of life, and in doing whatever it properly can, as a community with uniquely wide but still subsidiary functions, to discourage such conduct. This should not, I have argued, be done by way of a law of the type upheld in *Bowers* v. *Hardwick*, but rather by other legal arrangements supervising not the truly private conduct of adults but the *public realm or environment*. For that is (1) the environment or public realm in which young people (of whatever sexual inclination) are educated, (2) the context in which and by which everyone with responsibility for the wellbeing of young people is helped or hindered in assisting them to avoid bad forms of life, and (3) the milieu in which and by which all citizens are encouraged and helped, or discouraged and undermined, in their own resistance to being lured by temptation into falling away from their own aspirations to be people of integrated good character, autonomous, and self-controlled persons, rather than slaves to the passions.

VI

I have cut a long story rather short, partly because of the embarrassment which even tough Callicles felt in taking up such matters,[83] and partly because the second issue raised by Macedo is in itself more important. Macedo argues that governments should limit their protection of the unborn by a 'principled moderation' which demands that those with the best case should 'give something' to those who have put up a 'case that is very strong'. For, he says, '[t]here are . . . many reasonable arguments on both sides of the abortion debate . . . and it is easy to see how reasonable people can come down on either side . . . abortion . . . seems to come down to a fairly close call between two well-reasoned sets of arguments'.[84] But Macedo's proposal unreasonably assumes a dialectical symmetry which in reality does not hold. For if the better case is that what the abortions in dispute deliberately seek to kill are living human persons, then, however 'well-reasoned' the contrary arguments may be, it will be a grave wrong to the unborn that the right to deliberately kill them is the 'something' to be 'given' away to show our 'respect' for people who had denied the reality of the unborn's existence, nature and rights. But if the better case were some contrary (what?), then the loss of 'autonomy' or 'liberty' given away to honour the pro-life reasoners would involve no deliberate assault on mothers but merely an extension of those restrictions on intentionally destructive individual action which are the very first duty of government and the very basis of the common good. So there is no symmetry, and in this matter the responsibility of governments is to reach the right answer.

Indeed, a government which attends strictly to the arguments and is not distracted by the numbers and respectability of those who propose them, will find that (apart from the question whether killing is intended in cases where the pregnancy itself threatens the mother's life) the issue is not even a close call. Pro-choice arguments on abortion, however well-reasoned, nicely fit Macedo's description: arguments whose key premises are manifestations of prejudice (in this case, rationalizing the self-preference of men and women). They yield conclusions which, as he says about 'racism' and anti-Semitism, we should not wish to compromise with but should, as a community, approach 'with resoluteness rather than moderation'. For there are fundamental matters in which a sound theory of government is indeed incompatible with limitations based on an appeal to 'principled moderation' rather than to truth.

NOTES

1 It goes without saying that in so far as the concept of legal limitations on government is contained implicitly or virtually in Aristotle's conception of the rule of law, to that extent there is little original in Aquinas on this matter save the articulation of the term 'limited'.

2 See also *Summa Theologiae* I–II q. 105 a. 1 ad 2.

3 '. . . politicum autem regnum est quando ille qui praeest habet *potestatem coarctatam* secundum aliquas leges civitatis': Aquinas, *In libros Politicorum Aristotelis Expositio* I, 1 (Marietti ed., 1951, n. 13). In his *De Regno* , I, 6, Aquinas states that where one person is ruler, that person's power/authority should be 'limited' (*temperetur postestas*), lest it slide into tyranny (i.e., into government for private rather than common good). Aquinas's distinction between regal and political rule is enthusiastically taken up by Sir John Fortescue, *The Governance of England* (c. 1475), c. 1; likewise his *De Natura Legis Natural* ('On the nature of natural law') (c. 1462) c. 16; similarly his *De Laudibus Legum Angliae* ('In praise of the laws of England') (c. 1469) cc. 2–4. Thence it finds its way into Coke and the mainstream of English constitutional thought. The first editor of Sir John Fortescue's *Governance* (Lord Fortescue of Credan, when Solicitor-General to the Prince of Wales, in 1714) titled the work, 'The Difference Between an Absolute and Limited Monarchy'. In c. 1 of the *Governance*, as elsewhere in his writings on this theme, Fortescue appeals to the authority of Aquinas, explicitly to the *De Regno;* there is, however, no evidence that he read Aquinas's

commentary on the *Politics*: see Charles Plummer (ed.), *The Governance of England . . . by Sir John Fortescue . . .* (OUP, 1895) 172–3.

4 E.g., *Politics* III, 10: 1286a9, etc.

5 *Nicomachean Ethics* V, 6: 1134a35–b1.

6 Aquinas, *In libros Politicorum Aristotelis Expositio* I, 5 (Marietti ed., 1951, n. 90: 'politica est principatus *liberorum et aequalium*: unde commutantur personae principantes et subiectae propter aequalitatem, et constituuntur etiam plures principatus vel in uno vel in diversis officiis.'

7 Ibid. n. 152.

8 Ibid.

9 *Summa Theologiae* I–II, q. 105 a. 1c. On sharing in government as the essence of citizenship, see Aquinas, *In libros Politicorum Aristotelis Expositio* III, 1 (Marietti ed., 1951, n. 354).

10 This is one form of unjust law (and so more a matter of violence than of law properly understood): Aquinas, *Summa Theologiae* I–II q. 96 a. 4c.

11 See Plato, *Republic* IV, 444d; IX, 585–6 on acting according to reason and thus according to nature. More explicitly, Aquinas, *Summa Theologiae* I–II q. 71 a. 2c: 'The good of the human being is being in accord with reason, and human evil is being outside the order of reasonableness . . . So human virtue . . . is in accordance with human nature *just* in *so* far as it is in accordance with reason, and vice is contrary to human nature just in so far as it is contrary to the order of reasonableness.'

12 'When it is a matter of the moral norms prohibiting intrinsic evil, there are no privileges or exceptions for anyone. It makes no difference whether one is the master of the world or the "poorest of the poor" on the face of the earth. Before the demands of morality we are all absolutely equal': Encyclical Letter *Veritatis Splendor* Regarding Certain Fundamental Questions of the Church's Moral Teaching', dated 6 August 1993, s. 96. 'Intrinsic evil' has earlier in the document been explained as follows: 'acts which, in the Church's moral tradition, have been termed "intrinsically evil" (*intrinsece malum*) . . . are such always and per se, in other words, on account of their object, and quite apart from the ulterior intentions of the one acting and the circumstances': s. 80. The 'object' of an act had been explained as 'the proximate end of a deliberate decision which determines the act of willing on the part of the acting person': s. 78. An earlier, less precise statement: '[t]he same law of nature that governs the life and conduct of individuals must also regulate the relations of political communities with one another . . . Political leaders . . . are still bound by the natural law . . . and have no authority to depart from its slightest precepts': John XXIII, Encyclical *Pacem in Terris* (1963), part III, paras. 80–1. See Finnis, Boyle, and Grisez, *Nuclear Deterrence, Morality and Realism* (OUP, 1987), 205.

13 The treatment of inviolable human rights, based on the moral norms exceptionlessly prohibiting intrinsically evil kinds of act, centres on ss. 95–101 of *Veritatis Splendor*.

14 I have done something towards that project in the last four chapters of my book with Joseph Boyle and Germain Grisez, *Nuclear Deterrence, Morality and Realism* and in my little, more recent book *Moral Absolutes*. (Catholic University of America Press, 1991).

15 Leo Strauss, *Natural Right and History* (U. Chicago P., 1953), 146. Indeed, these and the other pages in question are from the book's *central* chapter, too, when we count the Introduction and the two demarcated halves of chs. V and VI respectively.

16 Ibid., 159–60 (emphasis added).

17 'But war casts its shadow on peace. The most just society cannot survive without "intelligence", i.e., espionage. Espionage is impossible without a suspension of certain rules of natural right. Considerations which apply to foreign enemies may well apply to subversive elements within society. Let us leave these sad exigencies covered with the veil with which they are justly covered.' Ibid., 160. In these and neighbouring pages Strauss is making the pleas which other philosophers and theologians have more carefully argued for: moral judgement has its truth only in and for 'particular situations'; in situations of 'conflict' (p. 159) one should decide by reference to a particular 'common good' which relativizes the principles of justice and suspends certain 'rules of natural right'; 'there is not a single [moral] rule, however basic, which is not subject to exception' (p. 160); and what matters in situations is not what one does but that one does it (unlike a Machiavellian *tout court*) with an *attitude* e.g., of 'reluctance' (p. 162).

18 A plea in mitigation of Strauss could fairly note that, when he wrote, the defenders of the 'Thomistic doctrince of natural right' which he was repudiating (see p. 163) in the passages above had scarcely undertaken that radical critique. Note also that although Strauss was professing to be finding 'a safe middle road between . . . Averroes and Thomas' (p. 159), his own views, starkly expressed on pp. 160–2, correspond most closely to 'the view characteristic of the *falasifa* (i.e., of the Islamic Aristotelians) as well as of the Jewish Aristotelians' (p. 158), namely, the view that what are presented in the Thomistic account of natural right (and indeed in a reading of Aristotle which Strauss fails to explore) as 'universally valid general rules' are in truth only generally valid—so that, as presented, without qualifications and exceptions, they are 'untrue . . . not natural right but conventional right' (p. 158). For the alternative reading of Aristotle, see John Finnis, *Moral Absolutes* , 31–41, 36.

19 See e.g., Grisez, 'Against Consequentialism' American J. Jurisprudence 23 (1978) 21–72; Finnis, Boyle, and Grisez, *Nuclear Deterrence, Morality and Realism*, pp. 238–72; Robert P. George, 'Does the "Incommensurability Thesis" Imperil Common Sense Moral Judgments?' American J. Jurisprudence 37 (1992) 185–95.

20 Everyone knows and few even profess to deny Aristotle's teaching that people are by nature social and indeed political animals. Many fewer seem aware of his teaching (*Nicomachean Ethics* VIII. 12: 1162a15–29) that people are by nature *even more primarily conjugal*.

21 *Summa Theologiae* I–II q. 94 aa. 2c, 3c.

22 On the fundamental but often overlooked Aristotelian and Thomistic methodological axiom, that natures are understood by understanding capacities, and capacities by understanding their actuations, and acts by understanding their objects (and on the basic human goods as the objects of acts of will), see John Finnis, *Fundamentals of Ethics* (Georgetown U.P., 1983), pp. 21–2. A further

methodological note may be in place. Although the worth of all these types of intrinsic benefit, of basic human goods, is obvious, a reflective account of them can and should be discursive and critical, assembling reminders of the experience, practices, and institutions which evidence the intelligibility and point of these forms of good, and defending the account against doubts and objections. For the inherent self-evident of some propositions does not preclude a rational defence of them; one argues for such a proposition dialectically, i.e., by relating it to other knowledge, and showing that denying it has rationally unacceptable consequences. Once again one can observe that when Strauss wrote, this work of argumentation and critical dialectic had been only patchily begun; but since then it has been essayed quite vigorously. See Grisez, Boyle, and Finnis, 'Practical Principles, Moral Truth and Ultimate Ends' *American J. Jurisprudence* 32 (1987) 99–148 and bibliography at pp. 148–51; Robert P. George, 'Recent Criticism of Natural Law Theory' *University of Chicago L. Rev.* 55 (1988) 1371–1429.

23 Aristotle, *Nicomachean Ethics* I, 1: 1094b9.

24 Finnis, *Natural Law and Natural Rights* (Clarendon Press, Oxford, 1980, 1995), p. 147. As I indicate, ibid., p. 160, this account of the common good of the political community is close to that worked out by French commentators on Aquinas in the early mid-twentieth century. A similar account was adopted by the Second Vatican Council: e.g., 'the sum of those conditions of social life which allow social groups and their individual members relatively thorough and ready access to their own fulfillment' (*Gaudium et Spes* [1965] para. 26; similarly, *Dignitatis Humanae* [1965] para. 6).

25 See Finnis, *Natural Law and Natural Rights* 146–7, 159.

26 Of course, the common good of the political community has important elements which are scarcely shared with any other community within the polity: for example, the restoration of justice by punishment of those who have offended against just laws; the coercive repelling and restraint of those whose conduct (including negligent omissions) unfairly threatens the interests of others, particularly those interests identified as moral ('human') or legal rights, and corresponding compulsory measures to secure restitution, compensation or reparation for violations of rights; the specifying and upholding of a system of holding or property rights which respects the various interests, immediate and vested or remote and contingent, which everyone has in each holding. But the fact that these and various other elements of the political common good are peculiar to the political community and the proper responsibility of its leaders, the government, in no way entails that these elements are basic human goods or that the political common good is other than in itself instrumental.

27 Declaration, *Dignitatis Humanae* para. 2. In the succeeding part, the Declaration treats the matter as one of divine revelation.

28 It is one of the *animi humani bona* mentioned in ibid., para. 1.

29 'Potestas igitur civilis, cuius finis proprius est bonum commune temporale curare, religiosam quidem civium vitam agnoscere eique favere debet, sed *limites suos excedere* dicenda est, si actus religiosos dirigere vel impedire praesumat': ibid., para. 3.

30 Ibid., para. 7. I use the French 'ordre public' to translate the Latin *ordinis publici*, for reasons explained in my *Natural Law and Natural Rights* p. 215.

31 *De Regno* c.14 (. . . *ab iniquitate coerceat et ad opera virtuosa inducat*). But in context, this and related passages in *De Regno* may be consistent with e.g. *Summa Theologiae* II–II q. 104 a. 5c which teaches that human government has no authority over people's minds and the interior motions of their wills. See Finnis, *Aquinas: Social, Political and Legal Theory* (Clarendon Press, 1997).

32 . . . the *polis* was formed not for the sake of life only but rather for the good life . . . and . . . its purpose is not [merely] for the sake of trade and business relations . . . any *polis* which is truly so called, and is not one merely in name, must have virtue/excellence as an object of its care [*peri aretes epimeles einai*: be solicitous about virtue]. Otherwise a *polis* sinks into a mere alliance, differing only in space from other forms of alliance where the members live at a distance from each other. Otherwise, too, the law becomes a mere social contract [*syntheke*: covenant] or (in the phrase of the sophist Lycophron) "a guarantor of justice as between one man and another"—instead of being,as it should be, such as will make ['*poiein*'] citizens good and just . . .' The *polis* is not merely a sharing of a common locality for the purpose of preventing mutual injury and exchanging goods. These are necessary preconditions of the existence of a *polis* . . . but a *polis* is a *communio* [*koinonia*] of clans [and neighbourhoods] in living well, with the object of a full and self-sufficient [*autarkous*] life . . . it must therefore be for the sake of truly good (*kalon*) actions, not of merely living together . . . Aristotle, *Politics* III. 5: 1280a32, a35, 1280b7–13, b30–31, b34, 1281a1–4.

33 Aristotle, *Nicomachean Ethics* I, 7: 1097b16–17. This, incidentally, differs widely from what Stephen Macedo, *Liberal Virtues* (Clarendon Press, Oxford, 1990), 215–17, means by 'an autarchic person'.

34 Apart from the passage just cited, see *Nicomachean Ethics* I, 10: 1099b32; II, 1: 1103b4; X, 9: 1180b24.

35 E.g., *Nicomachean Ethics* VI, 5: 1140a2; *Politics* I, 2: 1254a5.

36 *Nicomachean Ethics*, X. 9: 1180a1–3.

37 The law struck down in *Griswold* was the law forbidding use of contraceptives even by married persons; Griswold's conviction as an accessory to such use fell with the fall of the substantive law against the principals in such use. Very different, in principle, would have been a law directly forbidding Griswold's activities as a public promoter of contraceptive information and supplies. If U.S. constitutional law fails to recognize such distinctions, it shows its want of sound principle.

38 Inquiries framed in the latter way enmesh the would-be theorist in the shifting contingencies of political movements or programmes which, taken in their sequence since the term 'liberal' emerged in political use in the 1830s, having virtually nothing significant in common and, as movements, no principle for identifying a central case or focal sense. The only sensible way to deal with philosophical claims framed in terms of liberalism, liberal political institutions, etc., is to treat them as rhetorical code for 'sound', 'true', 'warranted', 'just', or the like; one translates accordingly and carries on with the consideration of the arguments or claims on their merits.

39 See the expository discussion of Rawls in Joseph Raz, 'Facing Diversity: The Case of Epistemic Diversity', *Philosophy & Public Affairs* 19 (1990) 3–46, p. 12.

40 Ibid. (the article also effectively criticizes the analogous proposals made by Thomas Nagel).

41 Macedo, *Liberal Virtues*, pp. 53, 55, 60–4.

42 To constrain people's actions on the ground that the conception of the good which (if they are done in good faith) those actions put into effect is a bad conception, may manifest not contempt but rather a sense of the equal worth and human dignity of those people; the outlawing of their conduct may be based simply on the judgement that they have seriously misconceived and are engaged in degrading human worth and dignity, including their own personal worth and dignity along with that of others who may be induced to share in or emulate their degradation. In no field of human discourse or practice should one equate judging persons mistaken (and acting on that judgement) with despising those persons or preferring those who share one's judgement. See Finnis, *Natural Law and Natural Rights*, pp. 221–3. After 1980 Dworkin revised his argument. Equality of concern and respect is violated whenever sacrifices or constraints are imposed on citizens in virtue of an argument they could not accept without abandoning their sense of their equal worth—for 'no self-respecting person who believes that a particular way to live is most valuable for him can accept that this way of life is base or degrading.' Ronald Dworkin, *A Matter of Principle* (Harvard U.P., 1985) 206. But this argument is as impotent as its forerunners. To forbid people's preferred conduct does not require them to 'accept an argument'. And if they did accept the argument on which the law is based, they would be accepting that their former preferences were indeed unworthy of them (or, if they had always recognized that, but had retained their preferences nonetheless, it would amount to an acknowledgment that they had been unconscientious). People can come to regret their previous views and conduct; so one must not identify persons (and their worth as human beings) with their current conception(s) of human good. In sum: either those whose preferred conduct is legally proscribed come to accept the concept of human worth on which the law is based, or they do not. If they do, there is no injury to their self-respect; they realize that they were in error, and may be glad of the assistance which compulsion lent to reform. (Think of drug addicts.) And if they do not come to accept the law's view, the law leaves their self-respect unaffected; they will regard the law, rightly or wrongly, as pitiably (and damagingly) mistaken in its conception of what is good for them. They may profoundly resent the law. What they cannot accurately think is that a law motivated by concern for the good, the worth and the dignity of everyone without exception, does not treat them as an equal. See Finnis, 'Kant v. Neo-Kantians' 87 Columbia Law Review 433, pp. 437–8 (1987).

43 George, *Making Men Moral: Civil Liberties and Public Morality* (Clarendon Press, Oxford, 1993) pp. 83–109.

44 *Liberal Virtues* p. 265.

45 Ibid., p. 263

46 Ibid., p. 195; cf. p. 41: 'that all reasonable people should be able to accept'.

47 Ibid., p. 50.

48 Ibid., p. 46; also p. 48 ('excessively subtle and complex forms of reasoning'),

pp. 63–4 ('too complex to be widely understood, or otherwise incapable of being widely appreciated by reasonable people').

49 Ibid., p. 43.

50 Ibid., p. 212; the internal quotation is from Finnis, 'Personal Integrity, Sexual Morality and Responsible Parenthood', *Rivista di Studi sulla Persona e la Famiglia: Anthropos* (now *Anthropotes*) 1 (1985) 43, p. 52, which in turn is citing and summarizing Aquinas, *Summa Theologiae* I–II q. 100 aa. 1c, 3c, 11c.

51 *Liberal Virtues*, p. 212.

52 Aquinas, *Summa Theologiae* I–II q. 100, a. 3c: 'modica consideratione'.

53 a. 11c: 'quorum rationem statim quilibet, etiam popularis, potest de facili videre'.

54 a. 11c: 'circa huiusmodi contingit judicium humanum perverti'.

55 a. 3c.

56 a. 1c: 'quas considerare diligenter non est cuiuslibet sed sapientum'.

57 Admittedly, large numbers of people can get confused even about one or another norm of the Decalogue, as (Aquinas remarks) the Germans encountered by Julius Caesar were morally confused about robbery. *Summa Theologiae* I–II q. 94 a. 4c. The conventions of a culture, reinforced by self-interest and a habit of following some passion, can obscure many people's understanding of a moral norm, deflecting rational inference by alluring images and by sophistical objections and rationalizations engendered by intelligence in the service of feeling. Moreover, what is principle and what is conclusion, and how they are related, can be outside the habits of reflection and powers of articulation of many who nonetheless, given time and skilful dialectic, could be brought to a reflective and articulate grasp of them.

58 See Musonius Rufus, Fragment 26, in Cora E. Lutz, 'Musonius Rufus "The Roman Socrates" ' 10 *Yale Classical Studies* (1947) 3 at 131.

59 106 S. Ct. 2841 (1986).

60 See Finnis, 'Law, Morality and "Sexual Orientation" ', 69 *Notre Dame Law Review* 1049 at 1055–63 (1994). In those pages will be found sufficient reason for treating with the greatest caution everything said in Martha C. Nussbaum, 'Platonic Love and Colorado Law', 80 *University of Virginia Law Review* 1515 (1994). Note in particular that the passages quoted by her from letters written to her by Sir Kenneth Dover and Anthony Price leave entirely intact the judgements of Dover and Price quoted and cited in my article, loc. cit. Indeed, passages quoted by her from these letters implicitly contradict statements made on oath by Professor Nussbaum herself, in Oct. 1993, in the circumstances described in my article. See also Robert P. George, ' "Shameless Acts" Revisited: Some Questions for Professor Nussbaum', *Academic Questions* 9 (1995) 24–32.

61 A case expressly envisaged by Aristotle, *Nicomachean Ethics* VII. 6: 1148b30.

62 Vlastos, *Platonic Studies* (Princeton U.P. 1973 / 1981) 25, citing Plato, *Phaedrus* 251A1 and *Laws* 636–7. Not all Vlastos's interpretations can be accepted, but this one is sound. See also Plato, *Republic* 403a–c; *Laws* 836–7, 840–1. For Musonius Rufus, see discourse XII in Cora E. Lutz, 'Musonius Rufus "The Roman Socrates" ', *Yale Classical Studies* 10 (1947) 3, pp. 84–9 (Greek / English), or A. J. Festugière, *Deux Prédicateurs de l'Antiquite': Teles et*

Musonius, pp. 94–5. For Plutarch, see his *Erotikos* (*Dialogue on Love*) 751c–d, 766e–771d.

63 *Liberal Virtues*, p. 211.
64 Discourses, XIIIA, XIIIB and XIV.
65 Plutarch, *Life of Solon* 20, 4; *Erotikos* 768–70.
66 *Symposium* 206c; see also the comments by R. E. Allen, *The Dialogues of Plato* vol. II, *The Symposium* (Yale U.P., 1991) 18. And see Plato, *Laws* 838–9, esp. 839b on familiarity and love between spouses in a chastely exclusive marriage.
67 *De Bono Conjugali* 9.9.
68 Ibid., 3.3.
69 *Erotikos* 769f.; *Conjugalia Praecepta* 142f.
70 Address to Young Married Couples at Taranto, Oct. 1989, quoted in Grisez, *Living a Christian Life* 571 at n. 46: '. . . a great project: *fusing* your persons to the point of becoming "one flesh" '.
71 Germain Grisez, *The Way of the Lord Jesus*, vol. 2, *Living a Christian Life* (Franciscan Press, Quincy 1993) 556–659.
72 *Ethics* VIII, 12: 1162a16–30; see also the probably pseudo-Aristotle, *Oeconomica* I, 3–4: 1343b12–1344a22; III.
73 Plutarch reads this conception back to the dawn of Athenian civilization and, doubtless anachronistically, ascribes it to the great original Athenian law-giver, Solon: marriage should be 'a union of life between man and woman for the delights of love and the getting of children': Plutarch, *Life of Solon* 20, 4. See also Plutarch, *Erotikos* 769: 'In the case of lawful wives, physical union is the beginning of friendship, a sharing, as it were, in great mysteries. Pleasure is short [or unimportant: *mikron*], but the respect and kindness and mutual affection and loyalty that daily spring from it convicts neither the Delphians of raving when they call Aphrodite "Harmony" nor Homer when he designates such a union "friendship". It also proves that Solon was a very experienced legislator of marriage laws. He prescribed that a man should consort with his wife not less than three times a month—not for the pleasure surely, but as cities renew their mutual agreements from time to time, just so he must have wished this to be a renewal of marriage and with such an act of tenderness to wipe out the complaints that accumulate from everyday living.'
74 See *Erotikos* 768D–770A.
75 Plutarch speaks of the union of husband and wife as an 'integral amalgamation' [*di' holon krasis*]: *Erotikos* 769F; *Conjugalia Praecepta* 142F.
76 Steven Macedo, 'The New Natural Lawyers', The Harvard Crimson, Oct. 28, 1993, writes: '[i]n effect, gays can have sex in a way that is open to procreation, and to new life. They can be, and many are, prepared to engage in the kind of loving relations that would result in procreation—were conditions different. Like sterile married couples, many would like nothing better.' Here fantasy has taken leave of reality. Anal or oral intercourse, whether between spouses or males, is no more a biological union 'open to procreation' than is intercourse with a goat by a shepherd who fantasizes about breeding a faun; each 'would' yield the desired mutant 'were conditions different'. Biological union between humans is the inseminatory union of male genital organ with female genital organ; in most circumstances it does not result in generation, but it is the behav-

iour that unites biologically because it is the behaviour which, as behaviour, is suitable for generation.

77 For the whole argument, see Grisez, *Living a Christian Life*, pp. 634–9, 648–54, 662–4.

78 *Gorgias*, pp. 494–5, especially pp. 494e1–5, 495b3.

79 A. W. Price, *Love and Friendship in Plato and Aristotle* (Clarendon Press, Oxford, 1989), pp. 223–35, esp. pp. 233, 235, concludes (despite Price's own regret) from a study of Plato's teachings on marital and non-marital sex that Plato had just about found his way to the understanding which Price finds articulated most notably, for modern times, by Paul VI in 1968 and after him by John Paul II.

80 Plutarch, *Life of Solon* 20, 3. The post-Christian moral philosophy of Kant identified the wrongfulness of masturbation and homosexual (and bestial) conduct as consisting in the instrumentalization of one's body, and thus ('since a person is an absolute unity') the 'wrong to humanity in our own person'. But Kant, though he emphasizes the equality of husband and wife (impossible in concubinage or more casual prostitution), did not integrate this insight with an understanding of marriage as a single two-part good involving, inseparably, friendship as well as procreation. Hence he was puzzled by the question why marital intercourse is right when the woman is pregnant or beyond the menopause. See Immanuel Kant, *The Metaphysics of Morals*, pp. 277–9, 220–2 ([1797] translated by Mary Gregor, C.U. Press, 1991, pp. 96–8, 220–2). (The deep source of his puzzlement is his refusal to allow intelligible goods any structural role in his ethics, a refusal which sets him against a classical moral philosophy such as Aristotle's, and indeed against any adequate theory of natural law, and in turn is connected with his dualistic separation of body from mind and body, a separation which conflicts with his own insight, just quoted, that the person is a real unity.)

81 Or deliberately contracepted, which I omit from the list in the text only because it would no doubt not now be accepted by secular civil law as preventing consummation—a failure of understanding. See also n. 35 above.

82 Macedo, loc. cit., 'All we can say is that conditions would have to be more radically different in the case of gay and lesbian couples than sterile married couples for new life to result from sex . . . but what is the moral force of that? The new natural law theory does not make moral judgements based on natural facts.' Macedo's phrase 'based on' equivocates between the first premises of normative arguments (which must be normative) and the other premise(s) (which can and normally should be factual and where appropriate can refer to natural facts such as that the human mouth is not a reproductive organ).

83 See *Gorgias*, p. 494e5.

84 *Liberal Virtues*, p. 72.

2

Against the Old Sexual Morality of the New Natural Law[1]

STEPHEN MACEDO

I. INTRODUCTION

It is said that when he was on his death-bed, W. C. Fields was seen by his daughter reading the Bible. Dumbfounded, she asked whether he had experienced a last minute conversion. 'No,' he replied, 'I'm just looking for loopholes.'

I hope that what follows is not the philosophical equivalent of looking for loopholes. I mean to take seriously the possibility that the new natural law's radical critique of contemporary sexual attitudes and conduct might be true. Consider Germain Grisez's challenge to the libertarianism which certainly characterizes an extreme form of liberalism that came to the fore in the 1960s:

The promoters of sexual liberation thought it would eliminate the pain of sexual frustration and make society as a whole more joyful. What has happened instead shows how wrong they were. The pain of sexual frustration is slight in comparison with the misery of abandoned women and unwanted children, of people lonely for lack of true marital intimacy, of those dying wretchedly from sexually transmitted disease. Moreover, unchastity's destructive effects on so many families impact on the wider society, whose stability depends on families . . . Boys and girls coming to maturity without a solid foundation in a stable family are ill prepared to assume adult social responsibilities.[2]

I do not believe that this is true—I feel sure that it is not the whole truth—but it may well represent an important and neglected part of the truth. Such charges need to be taken seriously, both on their own terms and as part of the broader conservative critique of the cultural changes accelerated by the sexual revolution of the 1960s.

The argument of this chapter is that while we should reject the sexual teachings of the new natural law—ably represented by John Finnis's important contribution to this volume—we also have something to learn from it. The natural lawyers are fundamentally right in their insistence that we must make value judgements in the realm of sexual morality.

They are also right, I believe, to insist on the continuing validity of important aspects of traditional morality, especially the value of married life. The new natural law goes badly wrong, however, in its very narrow view of the legitimate forms of sexual expression. In particular, I will argue, the new natural law's own moral stance, properly understood, provides grounds for affirming the good of sexual relationships between committed, loving homosexual partners, and for extending the institution of marriage to homosexuals.

I also mean this chapter to make a larger point about liberalism. Contrary to the suggestions of Michael Sandel and others, liberalism properly understood is not committed to a stance of neutrality on questions of the good life. There is no inconsistency between a robust commitment to liberalism (or perhaps I should say a commitment to a robust liberalism) and support for an institution such as marriage, which certainly expresses a judgement about better and worse lives. While liberal principles support a wide range of individual freedoms, they also allow space for political judgements to be made about better and worse ways of using our freedom. Public policies may encourage the better ways without coercing people or infringing on their basic rights.

The new natural lawyers correctly perceive that liberalism has less to do with neutrality than its critics allege. The natural lawyers are prepared to be judgemental, and liberal public policy can and should incorporate some of their judgements. Unfortunately, as we shall see in Parts III–V below, the natural law strictures about sexual morality are unreasonably narrow and arbitrary.

II. NATURAL LAW AND LIMITED GOVERNMENT

We can begin, however, by conceding that there are many ways in which natural law and limited government are compatible. Finnis points out in his contribution to this volume that natural lawyers have long affirmed the importance of such standard features of legally limited constitutional government as the rule of law and orderly rotation in office. Finnis also mentions the Second Vatican Council's momentous if somewhat belated embrace, in 1965, of a principled case for religious liberty, even for those with false beliefs. The Council allowed that the pursuit of religious truth is so 'inherently and inimitably a matter of *personal* assent and *conscientious* decision,' as Finnis puts it, that government intervention here both harms individuals and violates their dignity.[3] In these ways, and no doubt in many others, natural law theory endorses certain garden variety limits on government power.

There are also resources for limiting government power more specific to the natural law tradition: useful antidotes, for example, to civic republicanism and other doctrines that inflate the importance of political life. Natural lawyers emphasize the principle of subsidiarity, with its insistence that the state's function is instrumental with respect to those associations which directly promote basic human goods, such as the family, friendship, and religious communities. The state regulates and facilitates these associations but should not supplant them.[4] For the new natural lawyers, the goods of politics are instrumental rather than basic.

Finnis also describes the ideal community, 'the good will's most fundamental orienting ideal,' as one that transcends politics: it is 'nothing less than . . . the fulfilment of all persons in all the basic human goods'. The ideal community is not the political community, as Aristotle supposed, but rather the 'heavenly kingdom . . . attainable only by virtue of divine revelation'.[5] This too has the effect of putting politics in its place: as an affair about very important goods (peace, prosperity, freedom, order) but not about the whole good nor directly about the highest goods.

By emphasizing that politics is of essentially instrumental importance, and that the ideal community transcends what can be achieved in politics, natural law provides for a political moderation that may be lacking in theories sometimes more closely associated with liberal democracy. Totalistic democratic theories, such as that of John Dewey for example, posit political ends that embrace man's highest and most complete ideals, and encourage people to transfer all moral and religious aspirations onto the shared political project.[6] Concentrating moral energies in this way seems to me not only politically dangerous but a disservice to the complexity of the moral life. Finnis, in contrast, limits political aspirations, and insists that room be left for extra-political associations in which to pursue important parts of the good life, for Finnis the most important parts.

The new natural law certainly has resources for limiting political power. Indeed, in some respects its limitations are excessively strict. Finnis levels harsh criticisms at Leo Strauss for allowing that governments may sometimes do intrinsically nasty things when the safety of the whole people is at stake.[7] Strauss's sin is to have justified NATO's threat to use nuclear weapons against innocent civilians in order to deter aggression by Stalin's Soviet Union. Finnis argues, to the contrary, that the strategic deterrent (established around the time Strauss was writing *Natural Right and History*) was immoral.

Strauss was hardly eccentric in arguing that the normal rules of good conduct might justifiably be relaxed in extreme circumstances. Locke made similar allowances in his discussion of executive prerogative, and so have many other friends of limited government.[8] That a reasonably just nation like the United States might feel compelled to threaten innocent civilians to ward off an unjust and potentially devastating attack is deeply

unfortunate. It is also, it seems to me, clearly justifiable in some circumstances. What is unclear is how to justify the absolute prohibition on
threats against the innocent that Finnis espouses.

The new natural law's absolutism depends on the 'incommensurability
thesis', which holds that basic goods are plural, and that it is always wrong
to choose against basic goods. That values are plural is common ground
among many contemporary moral philosophers, including Isaiah Berlin,
Thomas Nagel, and Bernard Williams.[9] On this ground, one can agree
with the natural lawyers that utilitarians are wrong to posit a simple scale
according to which moral trade offs can be made in hard cases. Value pluralism does not, however, yield the new natural law's absolute prohibitions on choosing against basic goods—such as innocent life—no matter
what other values hang in the balance. It is a terrible thing to be forced to
threaten innocent lives in order to preserve ourselves from unjust aggression, as Strauss conceded. Catastrophic consequences do matter, however,
and they can matter enough to justify the sort of threat involved in the
nuclear deterrent posed by the United States.[10]

It is hard to see how one vindicates absolute prohibitions against the
kinds of threats involved in the strategic deterrent, unless one believes in
a providential deity who is prepared to sort out the consequences for us in
the end.[11] Absent such a faith, we should ourselves take the responsibility
for making hard trade offs, even though we cannot fully specify, aside
from particular decisions and circumstances, exactly how we do so, even
though we cannot define precisely in advance when it is justifiable to
break the normal moral rules and limits. If rule-like procedures were
available to us in hard cases the moral world would be simpler than it is.
As things stand (and as Strauss suggested, following Aristotle) the ultimate contours of moral rightness 'reside in concrete decisions rather than
in general rules'.[12] Neither utilitarian reductionism nor the absolutist
strictures of the new natural law are adequate to the complexity of the
moral realm.

There are, clearly, a number of reasons to think that contemporary natural law of the Finnis, Grisez, and George variety is not only compatible
with but supportive of various limitations on government power. This is
no great revelation. The important question is: how well does the new natural law view stack up against its rivals when it comes to justifying and
delimiting the proper role of government? Let us turn to the greatest point
of contention: the realm of personal privacy and sexual freedom.

III. SEXUAL MORALITY AND THE NEW NATURAL LAW

Finnis manages to blunt liberal objections to natural law teachings on sexuality by arguing that while 'public morality' is a legitimate political concern, this does not mean that government should promote virtue and punish vice 'as such'. Governments should maintain a 'social environment conducive to virtue,' not coercively deter evil-doing or legally mandate decent conduct.[13] Governments should not, that is, be especially concerned to punish private vices through the criminal law. With respect to homosexuality, for example, the law should not criminally prosecute homosexual acts among consenting adults committed in secret, but it should supervise 'the *public realm* or *environment*,' within which young and old are morally educated and encouraged toward good or bad lives. It should do this by 'denying that "gay lifestyles" are a valid, humanly acceptable choice and form of life, and in doing whatever it properly can . . . to discourage such conduct.'[14] Finnis suggests that the United States Supreme Court should have overturned the criminal prosecution of private homosexual acts in *Bowers* v. *Hardwick*, but only while distinguishing such permissibly private conduct from 'the advertising or marketing of homosexual services, the maintenance of places of resort for homosexual activity, or the promotion of homosexualist "lifestyles" '. The law should prohibit the public promotion and facilitation of homosexual activity, along with homosexual marriages and the 'adoption of children by homosexually active people'.[15]

In all this, Finnis advocates for society at large a stance not unlike the 'don't ask, don't tell' policy recently adopted for the military in the United States. The aim is to maintain a public, morally educative environment hospitable to what is deemed good conduct, not to engage in zealous witch-hunts against those who keep their homosexuality private. While it is all to the good that neither Professor Finnis nor the Clinton Administration advocates witch-hunts against homosexuals, we must pause before celebrating the proposed policies.

Finnis argues that natural law, properly understood, shows that homosexual acts are a distraction from the good life properly understood, and so should be discouraged by public policy. Given the tenor of recent discussions of homosexuality in American politics, it is worth noting at the outset that Finnis goes out of his way to distinguish his position from the narrow prejudice and mere 'disgust' which characterize much popular opposition to equal rights for gays and lesbians. Most significantly, neither Finnis or Grisez suggests that homosexual acts are unique in being distractions from real human goods, or in justly being subject to legal discouragement. Indeed, these new natural lawyers strikingly treated gay and lesbian sexual activity like most forms of heterosexual activity: just like all recreational sex, all sex outside of marriage, all contracepted sex and sex not open to the good of procreation, including all contracepted sex within a stable, permanent marriage.[16]

The new natural law's prohibitions on 'recreational' sexual activity are very broad, and are based on the contention that the only valuable sexual activity is activity that is open to procreation in heterosexual marriage. Openness to new life within stable, permanent marriage is what gives sex value and meaning: it is uniquely capable of making sex more than the mere use of bodies for pleasure.

The union of the reproductive organs of husband and wife really unites them biologically (and their biological reality is part of, not merely an instrument of, their *personal* reality). Reproduction is one function and so, in respect of that function, the spouses are indeed one reality, and their sexual union therefore can *actualize* and allow them to *experience* their *real common good—their marriage* with two goods, parenthood and friendship . . .[17]

For Finnis, Grisez, and other new natural lawyers, all non-procreative, recreational sex amounts the mere instrumentalization of bodies for mutual use and pleasure, all are the moral equivalent of mutual masturbation: simultaneous individual gratifications with no shared good in common.[18] This is as true of contracepted sex in marriage as it is of homosexual sodomy: all sex acts not open to procreation in marriage are incapable of participating in or expressing any shared goods such as friendship, and are not only valueless but distractions from real human goods.

Indeed, the case against recreational heterosexual sex may be even stronger than that against gay and lesbian sex. Uncontracepted heterosexual sex risks the great evil of bringing unwanted children into the world. Even when effectively contracepted, it is a choice against the great good of new life. Gay and lesbian sex does not share in either of these evils. Finnis and Grisez allow that people may be homosexual by nature, and so the goods of procreation and child rearing are not open to them.[19] Homosexual conduct is not, then, a choice against the great integrating goods of heterosexual marriage (as are wrongful heterosexual acts) because these goods are not open to gays and lesbians.

The wrongfulness of gay sex is merely its 'self-disintegrity': the purported failure to act in a way that is consistent with a desire for the real goods that homosexual couples may share in common, goods such as friendship and mutual helping. Real goods can be embodied in homosexual as well as heterosexual friendships, but sex only distracts from them. When sex is chosen it is as a source of 'subjective satisfactions' through the use and instrumentalization of each other's bodies.[20]

The foregoing analysis (which we can accept for the moment in order to consider its implications) casts a very interesting light on contemporary popular attitudes toward sexuality. Natural law analysis reveals the gross and unreflective arbitrariness of public policies and proposals that, in the name of family values, fix their scornful attention on gays and lesbians. There is a crisis of the family in America, but what could be easier in the face of rampant heterosexual promiscuity, premarital sex, teenage pregnancy, and sky-rocketing divorce rates than to fasten our attention on a long despised class of people who bear no children?

One might reply that nowhere is promiscuity greater than in the gay male population. This could be true, though I have no empirical evidence to support this assertion and Finnis cites none. Richard Posner (who has studied a wide range of evidence) argues that there may be natural grounds for supposing that homosexual male couples will tend, on average, to have a harder time than heterosexual couples maintaining long-term relationships (though he does not, so far as I can see, compare homosexual and sterile childless heterosexual couples).[21] Lesbian couples, on the other hand, are very stable. Supposing, as is possible, that lesbians have the lowest rates of infidelity, would we then be justified in establishing a three-tiered public moral pecking order with special honours for lesbian couples?

It would be hard to see how the mere fact (if it is one) that gay men have a harder time settling down in stable relationships could furnish a ground for discriminating against them. No doubt, there is promiscuity among gay men: too much, as elsewhere in society. Before we condemn these people we should consider how promiscuous men in general would be were their sexual desires not harnessed and controlled by their wives, children, and family life. If these inducements to stability were not available to heterosexual men—or imposed upon them as the case may be—how promiscuous would they be? So long as we refuse to extend to gay men the inducements to stability and self-control (such as marriage) available to heterosexuals, we should regard promiscuous gay men as victims of fate, circumstance, and public policy (at least in important part) rather than of any special moral depravity.

In any case, civilized societies have abandoned the notion of collective guilt. The fact is that not all homosexuals are promiscuous and not all promiscuous people are homosexual. If promiscuity is a social evil, let society oppose promiscuity wherever it appears. Indeed, if promiscuity is self-destructive and homosexual men are prone to it by nature, homosexuality might be regarded as a disability (albeit a fairly mild one). Rather than singling out people with this disability for special discrimination (something we do not normally regard as decent or proper) would it not be more honourable to try and improve these people's lives as best we can?

The great merit of the new natural law's position is its fair-mindedness and broad sweep. If Finnis, Grisez and others criticize those who would seek to 'normalize' homosexuality and equalize our legal treatment of it (as I would), he poses an even greater challenge to the *conventional wisdom* that would single out homosexuality as peculiarly perverse and 'unnatural'. Finnis shows that on reflection such attitudes embody a double standard of permissiveness toward straights and censoriousness toward gays engaging in acts that are essentially the same. For Finnis, the wrongness of homosexuality is captured by its similarity with much heterosexual activity: all sexual activity which is not between married couples and open to procreation shares with homosexuality the essential characteristics of masturbation, the use of bodies for mere physical pleasure, the disengagement of sexuality from real, shared goods. Contracepted sexual acts between happily married couples is essentially the same as homosexual sodomy.

An important implication of the foregoing account is that governments have just as much reason to act against all premarital and contracepted heterosexual sex as they do against homosexuality. The new natural law speaks in favour only of very broadly based public actions against sexual immorality in general: divorce, contraception, and all sex outside of marriage, along with homosexuality. A government that rejects natural law teachings with respect to illicit heterosexual activity thereby jettisons the only natural law grounds for passing laws that discriminate against homosexual conduct. This is a great—and I would have thought insuperable—obstacle to any state that would rely on natural law as a ground for prohibiting homosexual conduct but not contraception, extra-marital sex, and so on.

Now, a possible rejoinder would be that simply because some justifiable moral strictures (against heterosexuals) have been relaxed, that is no reason to relax them all. But it is a reason when the strictures arbitrarily maintained are directed against a long despised minority. It is a reason when the majority is unwilling to impose on itself constraints that it imposes on a discrete and insular minority like homosexuals. It is a reason when a small minority is selectively saddled with restrictions that should apply with the same force to the majority.

The argument so far has entertained a hypothetical, namely, the plausibility of the new natural law's sexual teaching. Now we must turn to the core issue: are there good reasons to confine valuable sexual activity as narrowly as the natural lawyers would have it?

As we have seen, Finnis and Grisez argue that homosexual sex acts lack the 'unitive' quality of sex open to procreation in marriage. The choice of gays and lesbians 'to activate their reproductive organs' (and the same goes for heterosexuals using contraception or engaging in sodomy or other deliberately non-procreative sex) 'cannot be an actualizing and experiencing of the marital good—as marital intercourse can, even between spouses who happen to be sterile—it can do no more than provide each partner with an individual gratification'.[22] Homosexual sex not only foregoes opportunities to participate in real goods, it positively undermines the goods that homosexual friends may share in their non-sexual relations: goodwill and affection can be expressed far more intelligibly and effectively by acts such as conversation, or mutually beneficial help in work, domestic tasks, etc. Those who openly proclaim their active homosexuality must be seen, Finnis concludes, as 'deeply hostile to the self-understanding of those members of the community who are willing to commit themselves to real marriage'.[23] Society should do what it can to discourage and stigmatize such conduct, short of criminalizing truly private acts.

What are we to make of all this? It seems quite wrong to say that the essential nature of non-procreative sexual acts engaged in by couples in committed relationships—or even by people who have recently fallen in love—is necessarily as private, incommunicable, and subjective, as Finnis and Grisez maintain. The new natural lawyers exaggerate the purely subjective, self-centred character of all non-procreative sexuality. And so, Finnis insists that 'whatever the generous hopes and dreams' of 'some same-sex partners,' their sexual acts

cannot express or do more than is expressed or done if two strangers engage in such activity to give each other pleasure, or a prostitute gives pleasures to a client in return for money, or (say) a man masturbates to give himself a fantasy of more human relationships after a gruelling day on the assembly line.[24]

Finnis's contention is that homosexual acts at their best (between loving couples in committed relationships) can express and embody nothing more than anonymous bathhouse sex, a quick trip to a prostitute, or masturbation. Is it even remotely plausible that there are no distinctions to be drawn here? And how can Finnis announce such confident and sweeping conclusions without any inquiry into the actual nature of homosexual relationships?

My guess is that most committed loving couples—whether gay or straight—are quite sensitive to the difference between loving sexual acts and mere mutual masturbation, and that they would regard the latter, with Finnis, as a real failure. Finnis is not all wrong: promiscuous, casual sex, engaged in with strangers may well have the valueless character he describes.

It is, however, simplistic and implausible to portray the essential nature of *every form* of non-procreative sexuality as no better than the *least valuable* form.

The great virtue of the new natural law's position on sexuality, I said above, is its fair-mindedness and broad sweep. While this is generally true, the position is plagued by a major and unexplained inconsistency. As we have seen, an essential condition of good sex for the new natural lawyers is the biological unity of heterosexual couples whose acts are open to procreation. And yet, Finnis and Grisez argue that sexual union within a *sterile* marriage has intrinsic value: 'marital union itself fulfills the spouses,' as Grisez puts it.[25] But as Andrew Koppelman asks, how can such a position be justified when the bodies of the elderly or sterile can form no 'single reproductive principle', no 'real unity'?[26] Sterile couples can only imitate the procreative act: there is for them no possibility of pro-creation. And yet, the new natural lawyers regard sex between involun-tarily sterile or elderly married couples as not only permissible but good.[27]

What is the point of sex in an infertile marriage? Not procreation: the partners know they are infertile. If they have sex, it is for pleasure and to express their love or friendship or some other shared good. It will be for precisely the same reasons that committed, loving gay couples have sex. Why are these good reasons for sterile or elderly married couples but not for gay and lesbian couples? And if, on the other hand, sex detracts from the real goods shared by homosexual couples, and indeed undermines their friendship, why is that not the case for infertile heterosexual couples as well? Why is not their experience of sexual intimacy as 'private and incommunicable' as that of gays?

How do we make sense of this rather glaring double standard? Perhaps because sterility is a condition beyond the control of couples rather than a choice? Because sterile heterosexual couples can do things that, were it not for conditions beyond their control, would result in procreation? But Grisez and Finnis allow that homosexuality is also an unchosen condition. So if the natural lawyers say that sterile heterosexual couples can have lov-ing sex that is good, why not gays and lesbians in committed relations?

For the natural lawyers, the presence of the appropriate, complemen-tary physical equipment is an essential condition of valuable sexual activ-ity. The problem for homosexuals and those using contraceptives is that 'their reproductive organs cannot make them a biological (and therefore personal) unit,' whereas sterile heterosexuals who 'unite their sexual organs in an act of sexual intercourse which, so far as they can make it, is of a kind suitable for generation, do function as a biological (and thus personal) unit,' and thus actualize and experience real goods in common.[28]

Of course, gays and lesbians do not have the physical equipment such that anyone could have children by doing what they can do in bed. They can, Finnis and Grisez repeatedly tell us, only imitate or fantasize the real procreative acts, and the real goods of marital sex. What the new natural lawyers fail to see is that exactly the same thing is true, albeit less vividly, of sterile married couples: their reproductive organs *do not unite them biologically*, they only appear to do so. Finnis simply denies this: sterile heterosexuals *can* be united biologically, he insists, because their equipment allows them 'to engage in the behaviour which, as behaviour, is suitable for generation'.[29]

Is sterile heterosexual intercourse 'as behaviour' suitable for generation? Pointing a gun at someone and pulling the trigger is behaviour that is suitable for murder. Are such acts still suitable for murder, and do they share murder's moral significance, if the gun is unloaded? If it is a water gun or a gun made of licorice? The National Rifle Association might have said, 'guns don't kill people, bullets kill people.'[30] Likewise, penises and vaginas don't unite biologically, sperm and eggs do (at least in a healthy uterus and under the right conditions). For the new natural lawyers, however, the crucial thing is penises and vaginas—whether they work or not!

Suppose one gay male has a sex-change operation (has his penis removed and a vagina installed). Is he then permitted on natural law grounds to have sex with another man? Or—leave aside the sex change operation—suppose a gay male eschews oral or anal sex in favour of intercrural sex (inserting the penis between the thighs of the partner) does this resemble sterile heterosexual behaviour closely enough to have 'procreative significance'?[31]

Is not all this a bit silly? Sex between sterile couples can in truth have no more 'procreative significance' than gay or lesbian sex. Sterile heterosexual sex has only the appearance but not the reality of biological unity. Finnis makes everything of the fact that heterosexual intercourse is in general the sort of behaviour appropriate to procreation. But such behaviour is not suitable for procreation in many cases and in some cases (the very old) it may bear less resemblance than gay sex to behaviour 'suitable for generation'.

Many classes of people cannot experience the good of procreation. All of these can only imitate 'procreative' relations as best they can (if imitating procreation is still a moral imperative for them, which is certainly questionable). It seems simply arbitrary to ascribe such overwhelming moral significance to brute facts of biology, especially when those brute facts represent appearances (of biological unity) rather than reality. Is this really the ground upon which to erect so crucial a moral distinction?

All this reveals a strange feature of the new natural law's version of teleological ethics, namely, its overbreadth. The new natural law asserts the *universal* validity of ends that are in general good for the species, even when those ends make no sense as applied to particular individuals.[32] Consider the analogy between sex and eating. We eat and have sex to sustain and reproduce human life, but also because both activities are also pleasurable in themselves, and especially when shared with others: social dining cements friendships, expresses affection, and so on. But suppose eating and nourishment are severed? Is eating for the same of mere pleasure unnatural or irrational? Koppelman suggests that chewing sugarless gum is to eating as masturbation is to sex. Is it immoral? Or as Andy Sabl has suggested to me, suppose a person lost his capacity to digest but not the capacity to eat. Nutrition could be delivered intravenously, but would it then be immoral to eat for the sake of pleasure, or perhaps for the sake of pleasure as well as the comradery of dining companions? Would it be incumbent on one in such a state to eat only a healthy, balanced diet, or would it be permissible to binge on chocolate to one's heart's content? Would it be necessary (as Sabl asks) 'to go on eating beets and tofu because this would be the kind of eating which, "as eating," is suitable for a human being' though useless to the digestively-impaired individual? A moral injunction of 'healthy' eating, in this case, would appear to make no sense, though it might provide psychological comfort.

Moral judgement on the new natural law view is a blunt instrument, inattentive to the good of those who differ from the majority of the species. Why should we be required to generalize—or over-generalize—our ethical judgements in this way?[33] In the political realm, of course, we have practical reasons—not a function of the pursuit of justice or rightness—to govern by general rules. We want to put people on notice as to what they must do to avoid running afoul of the law, and we simply lack the resources to decide each case on its individual merits. But why should our ethical judgements labour under such constraints?

The new natural law's moral injunctions are, in some respects too broad. The new natural law's account of valuable sexual activity is, in other ways, too narrow. The decisive feature of valuable sex on the natural lawyers' account is its openness to procreation and the great good of new life. Even accepting this questionable claim for the moment, we might say that gays and lesbians can, in effect, share the same openness to real goods beyond mere physical pleasure. In effect, gays can have sex in a way that is open to procreation, and to new life. They can be, and many are, prepared to engage in the kinds of loving relations that would result in procreation— were conditions different. Like sterile married couples, many would like nothing more than this. All we can say is that conditions would have to be more radically different in the case of gay and lesbian couples than sterile married couples for new life to result from sex . . . but what is the moral force of that? The new natural law does not make moral judgements based on natural facts. It is hard to see how this double standard can be reconciled within the new natural law framework.

For Finnis and Grisez everything turns on 'biological unity' and the 'organic complementarity' of men and women. Sodomy is an incomplete realization of the 'body's capacity'. All of this sounds perilously close to deriving an 'ought' from an 'is', or at least from certain selective 'is's': from the 'organic complementarity' of (some) heterosexuals, from the observation (reminiscent of the old natural law) that the male member and the female opening were obviously made for each other. Meanwhile, other 'natural facts' are simply left aside, such as the mutual attraction of homosexuals (why is homosexual activity an incomplete realization of the 'body's capacity' for one who is homosexual by nature, especially when compared with the celibacy the new natural lawyers would enjoin on homosexuals). If this is the real ground for the different treatment of infertile heterosexuals and homosexuals, then the much vaunted advances of the new natural law are a mirage.

Finnis ridicules the argument mentioned above (and made previously elsewhere[34]), namely, that gays and lesbians can have sex that is, in a sense, open to procreation. 'Here,' Finnis charges, 'fantasy has taken leave of reality. Anal or oral intercourse, whether between spouses or males, is no more a biological union "open to procreation" than is intercourse with a goat by a shepherd who fantasizes about breeding a faun.'[35] This is very clever but misses the point. The sterile heterosexual couple's 'openness to procreation' is as much a fantasy as that of Finnis's kinky shepherd. Sterile heterosexuals have as great a chance of breeding a child as the shepherd and his goat do a faun. Surely, the crucial thing about the loving sexual acts of sterile couples is not their openness to the sheer fantasy that their sexual acts are procreative, the crucial thing must be that their sex is open to goods such as friendship, mutual care, and so on. Surely, that is, their sterile union is valuable not because of goods that are absolutely *unavailable* to them and that they cannot share (procreation) but rather because of goods that they can attain and share (friendship, mutual help, etc.). Finnis's argument leads, absurdly, to the opposite conclusion.

The most that can be said for sterile heterosexual couples is that they can have loving sex in a way that is open to goods beyond mere physical gratification. All of the goods that can be shared by sterile heterosexuals can also be shared by committed homosexual couples. Homosexuals do not choose against the good of procreation any more than do the elderly or sterile. Finnis fails, therefore, to damage the conclusion that homosexuals can—every bit as much as sterile heterosexual couples—have sex that is open to goods beyond mere self-gratification.

The new natural law's sexual morality is caught in a bind of its own making. It does not want to describe the goods of sex purely in terms of procreation. It holds that sex is good within marriage (itself now considered a basic good), when sexual acts are open to new life: the good of new life must not be chosen against. So the circle of valuable sexuality is widened beyond the narrowly procreative, to bring in sterile and elderly couples. But how then can the circle exclude committed gay couples as well? The basis of the distinction drawn by new natural lawyers is the presence of a penis and vagina. But sterile non-working sexual organs that give only the appearance of biological unity cannot bear the weight of this important moral distinction. Finnis and Grisez mislocate the proper ground for drawing a distinction of moral goodness. The appropriate ground is the degree of mutual commitment and stable engagement in shared goods beyond the mere physical pleasures of sex.

The real point of a natural law prepared to endorse sex as a good in sterile unions must be that sex is a good so long as it is bound up in enduring intimacies, love, and shared commitments. Finnis and Grisez have broken the link between procreation and permissible sexual activity. That done, it is hard to fathom their continued insistence on the overwhelming moral significance of a biological complementarity that is necessary for procreation but that is not necessary for the other goods that sterile couples (and homosexuals) can share. It is absurd to allocate these valuable properties on the basis of irrelevant biological facts (non-working complementary organs). The attempt to ascribe value only to heterosexual couples fails.

The inconsistencies of the new natural law should not be allowed to obscure the valuable insight that sexual pleasure just for the sake of sexual pleasure—brute gratification—may well tend toward the masturbatory, and may well tend to undermine the reciprocity necessary to loving relations. We may well, therefore, have good reason to encourage people to integrate their sexual activities into stable commitments to monogamous relationships. All this is as true for homosexuals as it is for heterosexuals.

Finnis himself signals the failure of his argument by falling back on unsupported empirical generalizations about homosexual relationships. Homosexual acts are likened, as we have seen, to 'solitary masturbation', to sex between strangers, and to a quick trick with a prostitute.[36] No one remotely familiar with the variety of homosexual lives could engage in such gross generalizations, reminiscent of nothing so much as radical feminist Catherine Mackinnon's equation of all heterosexual sex with rape and violence against women.[37] Simplistic as they are, Finnis's generalizations are revealing. Given the implausibility of the insistence that biological complementarity is all important, Finnis must count on it being the case that homosexual relationships embody no real goods: none of the goods that might be shared by sterile heterosexuals. These sweeping generalizations are the only ground left to Finnis as a basis for condemning homosexual conduct as such. Homosexual conduct must be nothing more than solitary masturbation or sex with a prostitute, or else the new natural lawyers' wholesale condemnations make no sense. Heterosexual activity must be uniquely capable of expressing shared goods; otherwise, the radically different treatment of sterile heterosexuals and homosexuals hangs on nothing more than the all too obviously flawed biological complementarity argument.

Finnis provides no evidence whatsoever to support his account of the nature of homosexual intimacy: no reports or investigations into how homosexuals experience their sexual relations. Instead of evidence Finnis provides only offhanded references to 'the modern "gay" ideology', an ideology that 'treats sexual capacities, organs, and acts as instruments to be put to whatever suits the purposes of the individual "self" who has them'.[38] Here again, Finnis signals his argument's dependence on unexamined stereotype and over-generalization. Millions of homosexual lives and relationships are taken to be epitomized by a promiscuous, liberationist 'gay lifestyle', which rejects all sexual restraints and value judgements.[39] In the end, Finnis's argument boils down to nothing more than this stereotype, for it is the only ground that really could support his sweeping moral condemnations, rendered without regard for the complexity, ambiguity, or diversity of actual lives.

If the crude stereotype is not true then the new natural law's sexual teaching falls apart. Promiscuity is the core of the stereotype, so one might have thought that Finnis would at least say something about the apparently substantial differences in behaviour between gay males and lesbians. Richard Posner cites evidence showing that lesbians have quite stable relationships and have intercourse less frequently than heterosexual couples.[40] Even if one were to conclude—and this is certainly a point of scholarly controversy—that men tend by nature to be more promiscuous than women and that gay men will tend to have a more difficult time than heterosexuals settling down in stable relationships, we would still have to let lesbians off the hook.

Of course, as I have already said, a tendency toward promiscuity would hardly justify lumping all gay men and all homosexual conduct into one category, defined by the least admirable homosexual behaviour. Gay sex may tend toward the masturbatory and promiscuous somewhat more than heterosexual relationships (which may tend that way more than lesbian relationships). But what would we conclude from this? That homosexuality as such is to be condemned? Men tend to be more violent than women, but this does not justify the condemnation of men in general. It would be wrong to regard the essence of 'maleness' (or indeed, heterosexuality) as captured by its worst forms (domestic violence and rape). It is no better to characterize homosexuality in this way. We expect reasonable public policy not to condemn men as a class but to address the issue of domestic violence as such. With respect to sexuality we should, similarly, think seriously about working to curb promiscuity, whether gay or straight, and about how to elevate and stabilize sexual relationships in general. Relying on the stereotype of gay promiscuity is not only unjust to non-promiscuous gays but a serious impediment to sound policy.

The inconsistent treatment of sterile heterosexuals and homosexuals is the thread that unravels the new natural law's sexual teaching. The garment might be repaired, and the new natural law's position made consistent, either through exclusion or inclusion. The exclusive strategy would extend the category of valueless sexual activity to cover sex between elderly and sterile couples. The natural lawyers could save their proscriptions against homosexuality in this way by arguing that, like gays and lesbians, elderly couples can enjoy mutual helping and friendship, but sex adds nothing to these goods, indeed it distracts from and destroys them. Sex between elderly and infertile couples would no longer be morally permissible, and they would be denied the right to marry. It is surely the case that the vast majority of elderly couples marry, after all, with the expectation that they will not bear children: indeed, if they thought they might some would not get married. If the natural lawyers want to remain steadfast in their attitude toward gays, then public policy should deter fornication by the elderly, deny them the right to marry, prohibit the 'promotion, commendation, or facilitation' of sex among the elderly (though not, as with gays, criminalizing sexual acts committed by the elderly in secret), and otherwise drive elderly and sterile fornicators into the closet and underground, along with gays and lesbians. This path to consistency is not completely without precedent.[41]

There is, luckily, an alternative path to reasoned consistency, and that is to broaden the scope of legitimate sexuality to include committed gay couples. Given the implausibility of the new natural law's narrow analysis of the valuable forms of sexuality, the path of inclusion is surely to be preferred. As we have seen, the new natural lawyers have furnished no grounds for supposing that the goods shared by infertile and elderly couples cannot be shared by gays in committed relationships. They provide no reasonable grounds for regarding loving sex within committed relationships as morally equivalent to the most casual and promiscuous sex among strangers. The path of inclusion would acknowledge all this, and allow that even if being gay will be regarded by some (not completely without reason) as a kind of disability, it is no more so than infertility or age. Sexual activity within committed and loving relationships can, then, be endorsed as a genuine good for all.

The new natural law's position on sexual morality falls on two counts. It falls first because of its extremely narrow account of valuable sexuality (so deeply at odds with the judgements of virtually everyone outside the Catholic hierarchy): an account that is unreasonably reductionist and puritanical. Secondly, the new natural law fails to offer any rational ground for treating sex within sterile heterosexual marriages differently from sex within committed homosexual relationships. While broad and fair-minded in many respects, the new natural law's sexual teaching founders on an arbitrariness tailored to the interests of the heterosexual majority.

To reject Finnis's unreasonably narrow and (in part) arbitrarily defined strictures on sexuality does not require that one embrace a completely 'non-judgemental' attitude with respect to sexuality. There are reasonable elements within the natural law tradition that constitute good grounds for public measures to elevate and improve people's sexual lives, both for their own good and the good of society.

While rejecting Finnis's narrow prescriptions, we can still acknowledge that sexual desire can be a problem. There is something to the observation of Plato, Aristotle, and others that the relative intensity of the 'animal pleasures' means that most people will tend toward overdoing rather than undergoing not only sex but food, at least absent efforts at self-control and a well-developed character. Self-control and character development—crucial to a healthy and happy life—benefit greatly from social support, such as the inducements to stability that flow from the institution of marriage.[42]

Extending marriage to gays and lesbians is a way of allowing that the natural lawyers are not all wrong: promiscuous sex may well have the essentially masturbatory and distracting and valueless character that Finnis describes. We have legitimate public reasons to favour certain institutions that help order, stabilize and elevate sexual relations. But we should offer these inducements even-handedly to all whose real good can thereby be advanced: we offer them to the elderly and the sterile, to gays and lesbians, and not only to fertile heterosexuals. We provide everyone with help to stabilize and elevate their sexual relationships, and so to achieve the benefits that natural lawyers rightly claim for marriage. This allows us to accept and deploy a reasoned and defensible version of natural law.

IV. CONCLUSION: LIBERALISM, THE GOOD LIFE, AND ABORTION

We should reject the new natural law's narrow sexual teaching, but not its deeper conviction that we can make judgements about the good life, and that such judgements have a legitimate role to play in the public policy of the liberal state. Respect for individual choice and freedom is one central imperative of liberal politics, but it is far from exhausting the legitimate public policy aims of a liberal state. I have endorsed, for example, attaching benefits to the status of marriage on the ground that we have good reasons for encouraging people to settle down in long-term relationships. The vice of the new natural law's sexual teaching is not the wholesale illegitimacy of embodying reasonable, secular judgements about better and worse lives in public policy; it is, rather, the clear weakness of the substantive case with respect to sexual morality.

The best way of thinking about political power in a democratic constitutionalist regime such as ours is as the shared property of reasonable citizens, who should be able to offer one another reasons that can publicly be seen to be good to justify the use of that power.[43] Many natural law arguments (including those discussed above) are indeed acceptably public, as Finnis asserts: the reasons and evidence on which they are based are not overly complex or vague, and they can be shared openly with fellow citizens. The vice of the new natural law position described above is not its vagueness, complexity, or lack of public accessibility but, as we saw, its unreasonable narrowness and arbitrary extension. The new natural lawyers are right, therefore, to deny that liberalism is best identified with that straw man who is the principal exhibit and easy target of so many critics of liberalism, namely, neutralist liberalism.[44]

Rawls is nevertheless right, I think, to insist that we should avoid invoking reasonably contestable comprehensive moral and religious claims when fashioning the most basic principles that will inform the constitutional framework. This does not mean that Rawls—or liberalism properly understood—is similarly committed to excluding all such claims from politics as a whole. Though some of his critics have missed the point, Rawls develops his account of public reason as an appropriate basis for what he calls the 'basic structure' of society, not for politics as a whole.[45]

Even with respect to the 'basic structure' or the constitutional essentials, it would be a mistake to describe Rawls as committed to working without reference to human goods: he insists only that the conceptions of the good on which we rely when fashioning basic principles of justice should be widely acceptable to reasonable people. The constraints of wide acceptability may be, moreover, at lest somewhat relaxed with respect to mere policy questions that do not touch on fundamental rights and interests (just how much they are relaxed and in what way we need not consider here). Museums can be subsidized, the arts can be funded, marriage can be given a special status, and churches can be granted tax exemptions, even though all of these policies rest on judgements about human goods that are subject to reasonable disagreement. Marriage, museums, and many other policy issues, are not matters of basic justice. The sorts of arguments adduced in this chapter are (I believe) perfectly legitimate grounds for publicly supporting marriage within a liberal order: no one's fundamental liberties are at stake and the goods appealed to (such as the value of an institution that encourages stable intimate relationships), while perhaps contestable, do not depend on a particular, highly sectarian religious view or secular ideal of human perfection.

If public support for marriage is permissible in the liberal state, that support is also subject to principled constraints. The basic liberties of those who choose not to marry, for example, must not be infringed upon, and the opportunity to marry must be made fairly available to all who can benefit. Public officials including judges should, moreover, take special measures to insure that the good of marriage and other public goods are not unfairly denied to some groups who we know are often victims of long-standing prejudice and discrimination.

Public provision of a good, such as marriage, while within the realm of legislative discretion may not be provided on discriminatory grounds. On this score, unfortunately, public policy in the United States stands accused of injustice. It would not be a basic injustice if marriage were altogether abolished (though I believe that would be a bad thing), but it is a basic injustice (and one worthy of judicial remedy) that gays and lesbians are being denied the good of marriage on grounds of prejudice abetted by weak philosophical arguments.

A closing word about abortion, by way of place-holder, perhaps, for a more adequate discussion. Finnis takes issue with my argument that a principled case for compromise may exist on some issues, such as abortion, which are difficult precisely because one finds powerful moral considerations on both sides.[46] On such issues, I have suggested, it might be hasty to join Ronald Dworkin in concluding that the side with the strongest case has the right to win.[47] On a matter such as abortion, this conclusion would be simplistic: when there really are weighty arguments and reasons on both sides and not simply reasons that are strongly held) winning properly might require the law to acknowledge and express the fact that the 'losing' side was far from being all wrong.

On this basis, I have endorsed and continue to endorse attempts to fashion something like the sort of compromise that the Supreme Court allowed to stand in Pennsylvania.[48] One can argue about the propriety of state-mandated waiting periods or doctors' consultations for women who want abortions. Nevertheless, it seems to me that the law-makers ought to do something to express the fact that opponents of abortion have weighty and serious moral concerns on their side. Doing so expresses the virtue— too often neglected in this morally-charged area of our politics—of moderation and the good of comity.

Finnis is simply all too ready to characterize the arguments of his opponents in the abortion debate (the pro-choice side) as 'manifestations of prejudice'.[49] In this he is the mirror image of zealots on the pro-choice side who believe that concern for the human foetus in its early stages must reflect religious conviction or a lack of concern for women's freedom and equality. Zealots on both sides of the abortion debate view this area of moral world as too simple and stark. I admire Finnis's unflinching pursuit of the moral truth, and his transparent desire to get these difficult matters right. The sweep of his moral judgements, here as elsewhere, seem to me inadequate to the complexity of the moral world.

NOTES

1 My thanks to Andy Koppelman and Andy Sabl for their generous comments on earlier drafts.
2 Germain Grisez, *The Way of the Lord Jesus*, vol. 2, *Living a Christian Life* (Quincy, Ill., Franciscan Press, Quincy 1993), p. 662.
3 John Finnis, 'Natural Law and Limited Government', ch. 1, p. 6.
4 Ibid., pp. 5–6.
5 Ibid., p. 7.
6 For an uncharacteristically lucid statement of his position, see Dewey, *A Common Faith* (New Haven, Conn., Yale U.P., 1934).
7 Ch. 1, p.3.
8 *Second Treatise of Government*, ch. 14.
9 Isaiah Berlin, *Four Essays on Liberty* (Oxford, 1979), see the Introduction and 'Two Concepts of Liberty'; Thomas Nagel, 'The Fragmentation of Value', in *Moral Questions* (Cambridge, 1981); Bernard Williams, 'Conflicts of Values,' in *Moral Luck* (Cambridge, 1983).
10 At least so long as we faced an expansionist power such as the old Soviet Union, rightly characterized by President Reagan as an 'evil empire'.
11 As Russell Hittinger suggests in 'Does Natural Law require Theological Justification?', paper presented at the American Public Philosophy Institute Conference, 'Liberalism, Modernity and Natural Law', Washington, D.C. (Sept. 1993). A divinely-inspired teleology may be the only way to salvage the new natural law's sexual teaching.
12 Strauss, *Natural Right and History* (University of Chicago, 1953), p. 159, Strauss's critique of Thomism seems to me cogent, esp., pp. 162–3.
13 Ch. 1, p. 6.
14 Ibid., p. 17, *see also* pp. 8–9.
15 Ibid., p. 9.
16 See Grisez, pp. 653–4. Finnis's moral argument is replete with references to ancient authors which I will not take up here. A lively debate has developed on these matters, see Finnis, 'Law, Morality, and "Sexual Orientation"', Notre Dame University Law Review, v. 69 (1994) p. 1049, and Martha Nussbaum, 'Platonic Love and Colorado Law: The Relevance of Ancient Greek Norms to Modern Sexual Controversies', *Virginia Law Review*, v. 80, pp. 1515–1651 (1994).
17 Ch. 1, p. 15.
18 Ibid., pp. 13–16, for Grisez's elaborate account see *Living a Christian Life*, pp. 553–752.
19 Ch. 1, p. 12, Grisez, *Christian Life*, p. 653.
20 Grisez, pp. 653–4.
21 Richard Posner, *Sex and Reason* (Cambridge, Mass., Harvard U.P., 1992), p. 306, and see ch. 11 generally.

22 Ch. 1, p. 15.

23 Ibid., p. 16.

24 Ibid., p. 15.

25 Grisez, *Christian Life*, p. 573.

26 I have benefited from his development of this analogy in 'Homosexuality, Nature, and Morality', unpublished, and from his important work, *The Antidiscrimination Project* (Yale U.P., 1996).

27 Grisez, *Christian Life*, p. 572–3.

28 Ch. 1, pp. 15 and 16.

29 Ibid., n. 76.

30 I heard a stand-up comedian say this, but I cannot remember who. The analogy of sterility to unloaded guns is Koppelman's, 'Homosexuality'.

31 As in Finnis's insistence that good sex must have not only the 'generosity of acts of friendship but also the procreative significance,' Ch. 1, p. 15.

32 I am greatly indebted in this paragraph to a private communication from Sabl, 13 June 1994. See also Koppelman's 'Homosexuality'.

33 And of course, even our political judgements should be sensitive to false generalizations that ignore morally serious differences among people. I discuss these matters in 'The Rule of Law, Justice, and the Politics of Moderation'. *Nomos XXXVI: The Rule of Law* (New York U.P., 1994), pp. 148–77.

34 'The New Natural Lawyers', *Harvard Crimson*, 28 Oct., 1993.

35 Ch. 1, n. 76, p. 25.

36 Ch. 1, pp. 14–15.

37 See *Toward a Feminist Theory of the State* (Cambridge, Mass., Harvard U.P., 1989), p. 146 passim.

38 Ch. 1, pp. 14 and 16–7.

39 Ibid., pp. 16–17.

40 Posner, *Sex and Reason*, pp. 91–2.

41 Fustel de Coulange notes (as Sabl pointed out to me) that in some ancient cities it may have been obligatory for a man to divorce a wife who proved to be sterile, see *The Ancient City* (Johns Hopkins U.P., Baltimore, 1980). Philo of Alexandria condemned sex with an infertile partner (as Koppelman pointed out to me), likening it to copulation with a pig, see John Boswell, *Homosexuality, Christianity, and Social Tolerance* (University of Chicago Press, 1980), p. 148.

42 I have benefited from Andrew Sullivan's excellent 'Here Comes the Groom: A (Conservative) Case for Gay Marriage', *The New Republic*, 28 Aug. 1989, pp. 20, 22.

43 Which I argued in *Liberal Virtues: Citizenship, Virtue, and Community in Liberal Constitutionalism* (Oxford, Clarendon Press, 1990), mainly following Rawls, whose views have come together in *Political Liberalism* (Columbia, 1993).

44 See, for example, Michael Sandel's contribution to this volume, and his review of *Political Liberalism*, *Harvard Law Review*, vol. 107 (May 1994), pp. 1765–94. I criticize and reject neutralist liberalism in *Liberal Virtues*, pp. 67, 73–4, 260–3.

45 Rawls, *Political Liberalism*, p. 11. Sandel makes this mistake in his contribution to this volume.

46 *Liberal Virtues*, pp. 72–3.

47 See Ronald Dworkin, *Taking Rights Seriously* (Harvard U.P., 1977), and my discussion in *Liberal Virtues*, pp. 72–3, 84–95, and passim.
48 *Planned Parenthood of Southeastern Pennsylvania* v. *Casey* 112 S. Ct. 2791 (1992).
49 Ch. 1, p. 18.

3

Is Modern Liberalism Compatible with Limited Government? The Case of Rawls[1]

MICHAEL P. ZUCKERT

Contemporary liberalism differs not only from the various versions of natural law theory, but from liberalism in its original or classical form as well. Perhaps the most perspicuous way to characterize that difference is to say that contemporary liberalism is egalitarian to a much greater degree than classical liberalism was. The older liberalism, that of John Locke for example, was egalitarian to be sure, as in the affirmation of an original 'state of equality' and of equal natural rights, but contemporary egalitarian liberalism goes further in at least two respects. First, equal rights as such are insufficient; these are seen as (sometimes) merely formal, and as demanding supplementation by a concern for their equal effectiveness.[2] Thus an egalitarian liberal regime is not satisfied, for example, to decree formal equality of opportunity of all careers but acts to make the formal equality effective by, say, supplying education which can fit people to take advantage of formal opportunities. Secondly, egalitarian liberal regimes are those which are committed to (greater degrees of) equality in the distribution of resources of political power as good in itself or as a requirement of justice, and which thus enact policies aimed at achieving such (movement toward) equalization.[3]

In place of the egalitarianism of contemporary liberalism, the classical form puts central weight on liberty and hence on limited government. Thus liberalism frequently objected to natural law theory on the ground that the latter appears to mandate political action incompatible with limited government. The same objection is frequently raised against the egalitarian variety of liberalism: the establishment and maintenance of the kinds of equality sought require major intrusions by the state into the social, economic, and personal spheres of the community. As Robert Nozick, a recent partisan of classical liberalism, concisely put it, 'liberty upsets patterns'. Free actions produce unequal results, and if egalitarian liberalism requires equal or equalized distribution of resources, then, it would seem, limited government, that is to say, the respecting of a more or less large sphere of privacy and free action, stands in great tension with it.[4] The more we insist on equality beyond equality of rights, the more government must intrude in order to assure to existence of what does not arise or persist spontaneously.[5] Alexis de Tocqueville, in his provocative analysis of the great dangers facing modern egalitarian democracies, traced out the inherent dynamics of societies marked by a democratic or egalitarian social state as a source of inherent pressures toward larger, less limited, less free government. There is no need to recapitulate Tocqueville's complex and subtle argument. His chief point is that as human beings live in conditions of relative equality, the circumstances of their lives, the goals they come to seek, the type of people they come to be all converge on a steady drive for ever more centralized, more active, more intrusive government for the sake of supplying the security, uniformity, and equality that only a thoroughly regulated society can supply.[6]

Nonetheless, contemporary egalitarian liberals have also been at great pains to attempt to establish a form of egalitarian liberalism compatible with limited government, in part because of the sobering experience of the twentieth century's experiments in equalizing human beings.[7] This represents something of a new departure for theories animated pre-eminently by a drive toward equality. Thinkers like Rousseau and Marx, for somewhat different reasons to be sure, depreciated the kind of limitations and reservations the older, less egalitarian liberalism made on behalf of liberty or rights.[8] Even the more pragmatic liberalism that crystallized in the United States during the Progressive and New Deal eras was explicitly far more collectivist and far less sensitive to the requirements of limited government than the current liberal theorists.

Although many versions of egalitarian liberal theory have emerged in the past two decades, the thinker most responsible for the new theory is, without a doubt, John Rawls, on whom I will focus here.[9] In *A Theory of Justice*, Rawls devoted his considerable argumentative powers to attempting to establish the compatibility of egalitarian liberalism and limited government. However, the very features that were most essential to his effort to establish this compatibility were among the most contested aspects of his original theory. His new position, as outlined in *Political Liberalism*, ought to be seen in part as an effort to reformulate the theory so as to secure the compatibility he sought but failed to achieve originally. This most recent effort at establishing compatibility, while on the surface very promising, fails just as profoundly as his position in *A Theory of Justice*. Nonetheless, Rawls's failure does not of itself imply that an egalitarian liberalism compatible with limited government is unattainable; indeed he helps point the way toward what such a theory must be like.

I

> *He is the final builder of the total building,*
> *The final dreamer of the total dream.*
>
> Wallace Stevens, 'Sketch of the Ultimate Politician'

Rawls is a theorist of egalitarian liberalism, and proudly accepts the label (*PL*, pp. 6–7).[10] First, he is, generally speaking, unwilling to accept merely formal equality of rights (*TJ*, s. 12, p. 73; s. 32, p. 204; s. 38, p. 239; and esp. *PL*, VIII 7, pp. 325–7). Secondly, Rawls explicitly endorses a general principle of justice with a strong presumption favouring equality. 'All social values . . . are to be distributed equally unless an unequal distribution . . . is to everyone's advantage' (*TJ* s. 11, p. 62; cf. s. 26, pp. 150–1; and *PL*, VII 9, pp. 281–3). The 'unless' clause proves to be of very great importance in qualifying his commitment to pure equality, yet it is significant that the base line commitment, the standard from which departure must be justified is equal distribution.[11] Finally, the specific conception of distributive justice that Rawls endorses, the so-called Difference Principle, does require a more or less major redistribution of social resources in the direction of equalization.

At the same time that he clearly qualifies as a partisan of egalitarian liberalism, he also aims at limited government. He affirms the rule of law and understands it in terms very similar to those characteristic of the precedent liberal tradition in its concern for limited government (cf. *TJ*, s. 38, pp. 240–1). He also takes for granted the institutions of majority rule, and thus of citizen control of government officials (e.g., *TJ*, s. 54, pp. 356–62). Moreover, both these procedural elements of limited government are supplemented by important substantive principles. In at least three other key places Rawls builds in considerations and principles sensitive to, and apparently productive of, limited government. The first concerns the purported ends of political life. He holds justice to be 'the first virtue of social institutions,' and justice, he holds, is built on the 'priority of the right to the good'. Thus he declares his theory 'deontological', for it 'does not interpret the right as maximizing the good' (*TJ*, s. 1, p. 3; s. 6, pp. 30–1). Since government does not aim to achieve some notion or other of the good, or of the good life, just social life is compatible with a wide variety of independently and individually chosen goods.[12] He thus understands political life to be limited in its ends compared to political thinkers like Aristotle or the natural law tradition: not to foster virtue, but to secure only the terms of fair social co-operation. In this respect, Rawls follows on the notion of limited ends that came into political philosophy with liberalism.[13]

Rawls's commitment to limited government also appears more concretely and positively in his two principles of justice themselves. The first principle directly establishes the place of liberty in his scheme: 'each person is to have an equal right to the most extensive basic liberty compatible with a similar liberty for others.' This 'basic liberty' includes such things as 'political liberty, . . . freedom of speech and assembly, . . . liberty of conscience, freedom of the person along with the right to hold personal property; and freedom from arbitrary arrest and seizure' (*TJ*, s. 11, pp. 60–1). As the list of liberties makes clear, Rawls has in mind the kind of citizen rights embodied in the American Bill of Rights and enforced by the United States Supreme Court, the very rights in terms of which limited government is normally described. Liberty so understood has priority over other political principles. 'A departure from the institution of equal liberty cannot be justified by, or compensated for, by greater social and economic advantages' (*TJ*, s. 11, p. 61). Rawls thus does not depreciate the relative importance of what leftist political traditions have derisively labelled 'bourgeois liberties'.[14]

Finally, Rawls also makes room for limited government in his second principle of justice, providing for 'fair equality of opportunity' and his well-known Difference Principle. Both parts of the second principle empower a limited but real freedom of sway for liberty to pursue one's own course and reap some of the differential rewards thereof. Moreover, the second principle aims to achieve its egalitarian mandate through a lesser rather than a greater sort of governmental intrusion. Since inequality in itself is not held to be offensive to justice, but only inequalities which are not to the benefit of all, those natural differences among persons which exist are allowed some immunity from the constant and pervasive rectification which a thoroughly egalitarian regime would require. Constant suppression of the results of unequal faculties, efforts, and so on is not necessary, but only a certain redistribution of material goods, largely accomplishable through the public taxing and funding mechanism (for details, see *TJ*, s. 42).

Given Rawls's serious effort to reconcile liberty and equality, or limited government and egalitarianism, it is easy enough to understand how Rawls's effort has achieved so much acclaim, and aroused so much interest. In a word, Rawls does seem 'the ultimate politician', or the teacher of the ultimate politician.

II

> *I heard two workers say, 'this chaos*
> *will soon be ended.*
>
> *This chaos will not be ended,*
> *The red and blue house blended,*
>
> *Not ended, never and never ended . . .*
> >   Wallace Stevens, 'Idiom of the Hero'

Despite all the acclaim and attention it has received, Rawls's *A Theory of Justice* has also come in for its share of highly charged criticism, especially of the three features identified above that effectuate Rawls's accommodation with limited government. My point in reviewing these criticisms is to show how vulnerable these three features of *A Theory of Justice* have been shown to be.[15] This in turn lends credibility to my suggestion that Rawls's post-*Theory* turn to a different kind of theory of justice represents an effort to redeem the enterprise of an egalitarian liberalism securely at peace with limited government.[16]

The Difference Principle

The Difference Principle is probably the signature doctrine of the Rawls of *A Theory of Justice*. In holding that no inequalities of resources are justifiable unless they work to make the worst off in society better off than they would be without the inequalities, Rawls propounds both his most novel and his most controversial conclusion. Although thinkers on both left and right have objected to the Difference Principle, either for allowing too much inequality, or for tying it to the fate of the least well-off, I will not dwell on these somewhat external and politically inspired criticisms.[17] Rather, I wish to bring out some of the more theoretical difficulties posed by the Difference Principle within Rawls's own scheme of thought.

The charge is that the Difference Principle contradicts two of the chief grounding thoughts, or foundational principles on which Rawls constructs his theory. These principles are foundational in that they precede and shape the better known, more formal features of the Rawlsian construct, such as the Original Position and the rational choice of the two principles of justice behind the Veil of Ignorance.[18] The first of these primitive or foundational principles might be called the Anti-utilitarian Principle; the second, the Demand of Justice.

Rawls takes utilitarianism to hold that 'society is rightly ordered, and therefore just, when its major institutions are arranged so as to achieve the greatest net balance of satisfaction summed over all the individuals belonging to it' (*TJ*, s. 5, p. 22). Such a view, Rawls believes, 'does not take seriously the distinction between persons' in its apparent willingness to trade off the agony of some against the pleasure of others (*TJ*, s. 5, p. 27). In this it is proceeding contrary both to the empirical fact that human individuals are the reality, society a construct, and to the moral fact that we have an 'intuitive conviction', or a 'considered moral judgment' of the 'primacy of justice', which finds 'an inviolability founded on justice' in each person 'that even the welfare of society as a whole cannot override' (*TJ*, s. 1, pp. 3–4). The greater good of some or even of the whole cannot outweigh sacrifices imposed on others. This intuition of 'the inviolability of each individual,' is what we are dubbing the Anti-utilitarian Principle.

Rawls also makes a foundational appeal to a Demand of Justice, which is an essentially negative insight: justice cannot be the rewarding of un-deserved inequalities, or more broadly, of undeserved qualities. This prin-ciple has great critical bite for Rawls because, he asserts, 'no one deserved his place in the distribution of native endowments,' any more than he can claim credit for those 'fortunate family and social circumstances', which support the 'superior character' which in turn supports 'effort' (*TJ*, s. 17, p. 104). Therefore, justice cannot be what modern liberalism believes, the rewarding of achievement based on natural talent and effort. Rawls's point is quite radical. What one is due cannot rest on any of the natural, social, or other proscribed bases of desert.[19]

The conjunction of the two foundational principles produces the fol-lowing theory which Rawls propounds: the generation of principles of justice via a 'performance' undertaken within specially constrained cir-cumstances. Since the utilitarians fail to pay sufficient attention to the indi-vidual's claims, then the remedy is to give each individual a voice. All must agree to the principles of justice, and since they are allowed to act in a self-interested way, none will accept any principle which might sacrifice him or her to others or to the whole (*TJ*, s. 3, p. 14).[20] Yet Rawls needs to combine the self-assertion of self-interested actors, which guarantees one side of justice (the inviolable claims of the individual), with the disinter-estedness required to satisfy the other side (the rightful claims of others). Disinterestedness and non-arbitrariness are satisfied by building into the performance constraints on deliberation responsive to the Demand of Justice. The chief constraints are those Rawls identifies with the Veil of Ignorance, developed in response to a decision 'to look for a conception of justice that nullifies the accidents of natural endowment and the contin-gencies of social circumstance (and psychological make-up) as counters in the quest for political and economic advantage'. Those 'accidents' and 'contingencies' are to be 'nullified' in the Original Position in that the veil of ignorance guarantees that no contractor can make any decisions taking account of any of these things.[21]

It has been much debated whether the performance as thus defined and constrained can indeed produce an agreement on, or a rational choice for, Rawls's two principles of justice, but more fundamentally, even if it can do so, those principles, or at least the Difference Principle, cannot satisfy the primary or foundational moral insights on which the entire edifice is con-structed. On the one hand, the Difference Principle runs afoul of the Anti-utilitarian Principle. At times Rawls formulates his Difference Principle as a way of treating the morally arbitrary 'distribution of natural talents as a common asset' according to which the less favoured derive (some of) the benefit from the natural and acquired talents, abilities, and efforts of the more favoured, on the model, perhaps, of a fair exchange (*TJ*, s. 17, p. 102).[22] Nozick, among others, has pointedly brought out the problem here:

People will differ in how they view regarding natural talents as a common asset. Some will complain, echoing Rawls against utilitarianism, that this 'does not take seriously the distinction between persons'; and they will wonder whether any reconstruction of [the Kantian imperative not to treat others as means] that treats people's abilities and talents as resources for others can be adequate.[23]

Rawls's Difference Principle no better satisfies his second foundational insight, the Demand of Justice. Rawls's principle, while not directly rewarding 'chance' or 'arbitrary' factors like 'natural endowment or effort', nonetheless, preserves rather than nullifies inequalities which benefit the least advantaged, that is, those inequalities which are productive of more goods and from which the least advantaged benefit by getting some share. Rawls ties the differential reward to the differential social contribution, but what is it after all which allows the more favoured to make their greater contributions? Surely, it is the very natural endowment and effort which Rawls has thrown overboard as morally otiose prizes in the natural and social lottery.[24] To reward the greater contribution is in fact to reward the 'undeserved' bases of those contributions, and thus to violate the Demand of Justice.[25] The Difference Principle, therefore, cannot quality as just under Rawls's own specification of the requirements a valid or acceptable principle of justice must meet.[26]

The First Principle

The First Principle has three features. The representative person in the Original Position would select a distribution rule for basic rights and liberties such that this class of primary social goods is (a) to be distributed equally, meaning that 'the liberties of equal citizenship must be the same for each member of society'; (b) to be as extensive as possible taken as a whole system of liberty, 'assuming that their extensions can be measured'; and (c) to have priority over the other primary social goods once a certain minimal level of wealth or economic development prevails (*TJ*, s. 26, pp. 151–2; s. 82, p. 542). This last means that 'a basic liberty covered by the First Principle can be limited only for the sake of liberty itself, that is, only to insure that the same liberty or a different basic liberty is properly protected and to adjust the one system of liberty in the best way' (*TJ*, s. 32, p. 204; s. 39, pp. 244–50). We can refer to these three features of the First Principle in brief as the requirements of the equality, extensitivity and priority of liberty.

For our theme of egalitarianism and limited government, the third dimension of the First Principle, the priority of liberty, is most important, but it has proved extremely vulnerable to criticism. In post-*Theory* writings Rawls has more or less conceded the force of the objections raised by H. L. A. Hart, which can be recapitulated briefly as follows. (*PL*, s. VIII, pp. 289–91). The core of Rawls's argument for the priority of liberty in the *Original Position* lies in the thought that 'as the conditions of civilization improve, the marginal significance for our good of further economic and social advantages diminishes relative to the interests of liberty, which become stronger as the conditions for the exercise of the equal freedoms are more fully realized' (*TJ*, s. 82, p. 542). Persons in the Original Position, recognizing or predicting this fact about themselves 'in the real world' will find it rational, Rawls believes, to adopt the priority rule for the First Principle. Hart objects, first, to the form of the argument. If indeed the representative persons do or will prefer liberty to increases in wealth or other primary goods, then they can perfectly well embody that in their own policy. Unless they are tempted to do otherwise, there is no need for a rule of justice to constrain them. Or, if they are tempted to trade liberty for wealth, then, Hart replies, 'it is not obvious . . . why it is rational for men to impose on themselves a restriction against doing something they may want to do at some stage . . . because at a later stage . . . they would not want to do it'.[27] That is, the priority rule is either superfluous or it is irrational.

Hart raises a yet more fundamental objection: 'the parties in the original position, ignorant as they are of the character and strength of their desires, just cannot give any determinate answers' to the sort of question to which the priority of liberty is an answer.[28] Robert Paul Wolff restates more or less the same point: there are plans of life within which Rawls's priority principle makes a great deal of sense, 'but there are other plans of life, equally rational' for which it does not. Without knowledge of their specific plans of life, parties in the Original Position would lack any basis for judging which stance toward the basic liberties would be most rational for them. (Consider also Scanlon's reasonable point that Rawls's 'marginal value' argument applies better to certain of the basic liberties than to others and indeed hardly seems to apply to some at all).[29]

Moreover, Hart shows that it is hardly rational to agree to limit liberty solely for the sake of liberty, and never for the sake of welfare. Many of the regulations and restrictions of liberty that we find perfectly acceptable can hardly be described as being for the sake of liberty. 'Laws restraining libel or slander, or publications grossly infringing privacy, or restrictions on the use of private property (e.g., automobiles) designed to protect the environment and general social amenities . . . are commonly accepted as trade-offs not of liberty, but of liberty for protection from harm or loss of amenities or other elements of real utility.'[30] Rational deliberators in the Original

Position would notice this fact and would not adopt Rawls's priority rule.[31]

Hart concludes, therefore, and Rawls later concedes the point, that for these various reasons Rawls's argument from the marginal value of liberty cannot succeed in establishing the priority of liberty. With the collapse of that principle falls the second of Rawls's two pillars purportedly harmonizing egalitarian liberalism and limited government.

The Right and the Good

Two decades of intense critical scrutiny have also revealed the unsatisfactory character of Rawls's doctrine of the good, the third pillar of his synthesis of egalitarian liberalism and limited government. The chief brunt of Rawls's reflections on the good is to show that justice (or right) is (relatively) independent of the good. Yet the good features in Rawls's theory in three places. (1) In setting up the Original Position Rawls stipulates that the actors know that they (or their principals) have some determinate conception of the good or other, but they do not know what it is. They know *that*, but not *what*. (2) However, since Rawls sets up the Original Position as a situation where the principles of justice emerge from a self-interested and rational choice by agents seeking their own good, he must fit them with some relatively determinate notion of the good in terms of which they can choose. This, of course, is the function of the primary goods. Primary goods 'are things which it is supposed a rational man wants whatever else he wants' (*TJ*, s. 15, p. 92). Or, as Rawls puts it yet more concisely, 'these goods normally have a use whatever a person's rational plan of life' (*TJ*, s. 11, p. 62; cf. s. 63, p. 411). The primary goods are in this sense neutral among the various conceptions of good human beings may have, but of which the abstract persons in the Original Position are ignorant. (3) Rawls maintains that in the actual deliberation over principles of justice in the Original Position all teleological doctrines would be rejected, among which would be the doctrine Rawls calls Perfectionism, or the 'realization of human excellence', a particularly important version of the doctrine of the human good.[32] (cf. *TJ*, s. 50)

Each of the three parts of his treatment of the good is beset with difficulties not satisfactorily resolved in *A Theory of Justice*. This is true of even the apparently most straightforward of the three, the argument for the rejection of Perfectionism in the Original Position. That argument is certainly simple: parties in the Original Position know 'that', but not 'what' with regard to their conceptions of the good. Any agreement on a perfectionist doctrine threatens the conception of the good they may have. 'Thus it seems that the only understanding that the persons in the original position can reach is that everyone should have the greatest equal liberty consistent with a similar liberty for others. They cannot risk their freedom by authorizing a standard of value to define what is to be maximized by a teleological principle of justice' (*TJ*, s. 50, pp. 327–8).

However, whatever Rawls may think, there is no reason the parties in the Original Position should be debarred from deliberating about the good just because they are ignorant of their own conceptions. What makes Rawls's argument even appear to work is his stipulation that the parties 'are assumed to be committed to different conceptions of the good and they think that they are entitled to press their claims on one another to further their separate aims'. In effect, this means that conceptions of the good are declared out-of-bounds from the outset; the parties are defined to be unwilling to put at risk their (potential) conceptions of the good. But this stipulation is surely not an evident part of the Original Position. Rawls's anti-perfectionist argument does not succeed, therefore, in carving out a sphere of autonomy and privacy on behalf of limited government.

Rawls's argument also fails at the next crucial step, for the primary goods in terms of which the parties choose cannot be defined so as to possess the required neutrality between ultimate conceptions of the good.[33] The original Position brackets all conceptions of the good equally, and is not in its very structure to favour or disfavour any. If indeed the conception of primary goods is genuinely open-ended, then it is highly unlikely that any list of means is in fact all-purpose for all conceptions of the good or equally so, in any case. For example, the primary goods and the motives posited for agents in the Original Position favour acquisitive over ascetic conceptions of the good, materialistic over spiritual, Locke over Thoreau or Mother Theresa.[34] The set-up of the Original Position, moreover, is biased against expensive life plans, and against persons with special needs, for it fails to take account of the fact that the same amount of some primary good goes much further toward satisfying some conceptions of a good life (Thoreau's) than some others (Donald Trump's).[35]

Rawls disarmingly, although quietly, anticipates these objections when he qualifies his description of the primary goods with terms like 'generally' or 'normally'. Even if he is generally or normally correct, however, that does not excuse the biasing that occurs in the way he has set up the Original Position. It is not supposed to prejudge any conceptions of the good. The cumulative weight of Rawls's own concessions and the critics' powerful rejoinders show that, as presented in *A Theory of Justice*, the 'thin theory of the good' does not succeed.[36]

Rawls is driven to the 'thin theory' because of his more fundamental commitment to veiling or disregarding substantive ('thick') conceptions of the good in the Original Position. Representative persons behind the veil of ignorance know *that* they have some conception of the good, but not *what* it is. An early and powerful critique of *A Theory of Justice* by Thomas

Nagel has brought out how genuinely problematical this part of Rawls's treatment of the good is also. Nagel addresses Rawls's explicit defence for omitting the *whats* from the Original Position. According to that defence, parties behind the Veil of Ignorance are denied knowledge of 'things that are irrelevant from the standpoint of justice' (*TJ*, s. 4, p. 18). Rawls's most general way of capturing the moral imperative that leads him to shroud the *what* is his notion of fairness: 'the principles of justice are agreed to in an initial situation that is fair . . .' (*TJ*, s. 3, p. 12). Fairness seems to mean, in the first instance, impartial or disinterested ('un-self-preferring'). 'It should be impossible to tailor principles to the circumstances of one's own case,' which one cannot do if one is ignorant of the circumstances of one's own case, including one's own aims, goals, and evaluations (*TJ*, s. 4, p. 18). In the Original Position, then, 'no one is in a position to tailor principles to his advantage' (*TJ*, s. 24, p. 139; cf. s. 25, p. 148).[37]

Nagel points out, however, that '[i]t seems odd to regard [knowledge of the what] as morally irrelevant from the standpoint of justice. If someone favors certain principles because of his conception of the good, he will not be seeking special advantages for himself so long as he does not know who in the society he is. Rather, he will be opting for principles that advance the good for everyone, as defined by that conception.' Similarly, William Galston concludes 'there is no reason to believe that impartiality requires ignorance'. Agreement arrived at when the parties know even their own conceptions of the good are not necessarily biased.

Suppose . . . that individuals are asked to agree on principles governing the relation between church and state. Rawls grants them the knowledge that they differ profoundly in religious belief. But how will the situation differ if, instead of this general knowledge, each individual knows what his or her beliefs are? For as long as unanimity is required, each individual can block an outcome adverse to his or her convictions. Quickly the group will realize that its alternatives reduce to no agreement and some form of toleration for all religions.[38]

Much in *A Theory of Justice* hangs on Rawls's specific treatment of knowledge of the good in the Original Position, but as these critiques make clear, this is another part of the system where he has failed to make a compelling case for the line of argument he has followed.[39]

The Three Pillars

What then of egalitarian liberalism and limited government? Rawls begins, it will be recalled, with a presumption favouring equality as the just rule, but he qualifies that presumption in three important places in his overall theory the Difference Principle, the Priority of Liberty, and the Priority of Right over Good. Each sets a limitation on the commitment to equality in a Rawlsean society; each thereby opens up space for liberty, for realms of private action immune from or resistant to governmental control. Each, in a word, is part of his programme for reconciling limited government with (qualified) egalitarian liberalism.

The Difference Principle gives legitimacy and reward for differential endowment, effort, and application. It does not point toward constant rectification of inequalities introduced by nature, or chance, as a full blown egalitarianism would seem to require. Under the Difference Principle there is no, or little, temptation to engage in the egalitarian policy of 'mowing down the tall grasses'. However, since the Difference Principle is insupportable on Rawlsian grounds, then the default doctrine appears to be that presumption of equality with which Rawls began, an egalitarianism with ambiguous relations at best to limited government. Likewise, the failure of the Rawlsean argument for the limited-government-preserving aspects of the First Principle leaves him with his strong presumptive identification of justice with equality, and no special protection for liberties against public policies aimed at effectuating a public good understood in terms of equality.

Rawls's commitment to the priority of right over good was also meant to be a support for limited government. Conceptions of the good are matters for the citizens themselves; government has no business fostering one or another of these, except in so far as the principles of right demand it. In the event, however, the Rawlsean theory of the good is far less formidable a bulwark for limited government or liberty than it first appears. His argument fails in its first task of ruling out of court perfectionist political aims. Moreover, his theory that the *that* of conceptions of the good have moral significance, but the *whats* do not, leads to a real depreciation in importance of actual goods sought. It turns out they have no independent force against the public principles of right, the way, for example, Lockean rights do. In Rawls's scheme, however, the priority of right over good turns out not to be so much an insulation of private liberty against state intrusion, as a warrant for the overriding of private liberty by public right. Thus Rawls endorses admittedly uncertain amounts of 'tutelary' intrusions in the name of justice in order to produce citizens who favour the principles of justice over their own conceptions of the good.[40]

The anti-limited government implications of Rawls's position appear to go even further, not only allowing intrusions in the name of right, but perhaps requiring them as well. One component of right is the duty to esteem others and their conceptions of the good, no matter what these are, or how objectionable one may find them. Again, Rawls is exceedingly vague on how far this duty extends and on what measures would be justified in order to enforce it. We might speculate, for example, that laws forbidding disparaging remarks addressed to racial or sexual minorities would be legitimate under this rule, especially if we recall that the priority of liberty is quite untenable in the theory as developed. Perhaps even more stringent measures would be licit. Citizens have a right not only to forbearance from contemptuous comments, but to something more than 'indifference', to 'esteem', or 'respect'. Rawls nowhere states clearly what this might include, but he seems to mean that one who makes it his good to count blades of grass has a right to the encouragement and support of her fellows as much as someone who devotes himself to, say, explicating the principles of justice (*TJ*, s. 65, pp. 432–3; 51, p. 338). Are those who cannot bring themselves to agree that this is a worthy human life to be 're-educated' until they can find a way to admire those who devote themselves to counting blades of grass?[41] No doubt Rawls would bridle at such suggestions, but it is not clear that he has any particular authority over the application of his principles.[42]

III

> *The imperfect is our paradise.*
> *Note that, in this bitterness, delight,*
> *Since the imperfect is so hot in us,*
> *Lies in flawed words and stubborn sounds.*
> Wallace Stevens, 'The Poems of our Climate'

Almost twenty years after *A Theory of Justice* was published Rawls published his new and long awaited treatise, *Political Liberalism*. The relationship between the Rawls of *A Theory of Justice* (hereafter Rawls I) and the Rawls of *Political Liberalism* (hereafter Rawls II) is sure to be hotly debated for many years to come; here I wish to offer a reading of the new Rawlsean theory as an effort to remedy the failure of Rawls I to secure the sought after harmonization of egalitarian liberalism and limited government.

Rawls II persists in his allegiance to that project. He reaffirms equality as the presumptive rule for the distribution of social goods. That is to say, *Political Liberalism* proceeds via an 'implicit reference to equal division as a benchmark' (*PL*, I.3.2, p. 17). He again emphasizes the inadequacy of merely formal rights; he reaffirms his two principles of justice, the second principle's requirement of *fair* equality of opportunity and the first principle's requirement of the fair value of political liberties. (*PL*, VIII.7, p. 327). If anything, Rawls II is more strongly committed to the fair value of political liberty and the compensating policies that must be enacted (e.g., public financing of campaigns, campaign expenditure limits) than Rawls I was (cf. *TJ*, s. 36, pp. 224–5). As he says in summary statement, 'I presuppose . . . the same egalitarian conception of justice as before' (*PL*, I.1.2, pp. 6–7; also cf. p. xvi: 'the structure and content of *Theory* . . . remains substantially the same').

Rawls II is no less devoted to limited government. He defines his entire project once again as the attempt to discover 'principles of justice to realize the values of liberty and equality' (*PL*, I.1.1, p. 5). He affirms the desirability of protecting individuals and associations 'from the intrusions of government and from other powerful associations' (*PL*, VI.3.2, p. 221, n. 8). Far more explicitly than in *A Theory of Justice*, Rawls II rejects a communitarian approach to politics 'because, among other things, it leads to the systematic denial of basic liberties and may allow the oppressive use of the government's monopoly of (legal) force' (*PL*, IV.3.3, p. 146, n. 13).

Indeed, the themes of protection of liberty and limited government take on substantially greater importance in *Political Liberalism* than in *A Theory of Justice*. This is signalled in part by the appearance of a new theme: Rawls now clearly conceives the state as a coercive apparatus. 'Political power is always coercive power backed by the government's use of sanctions' (*PL*, IV.1.2, p. 136; cf. II.4.1, p. 68). Thus Rawls II develops a new theory of legitimacy, emphasizing the boundaries of legitimate state coercion (cf. *PL*, I.6.2, p. 37; II.3.2, p. 60; 3.4, p. 62; III.8.1, p. 125; IV.1.4, pp. 138, 140; VI.2.1, p. 217). With the recognition of those boundaries comes, of course, a heightened dedication to limited government.

Between *A Theory of Justice* and *Political Liberalism* the problem of limited government has become more urgent for Rawls. The most obvious or surface reason for this is a certain practical difficulty that he claims inspired the shift from *A Theory of Justice* to *Political Liberalism*: 'A modern democratic society is characterized not simply by a pluralism of comprehensive religious, philosophical, and moral doctrines but by a pluralism of incompatible but reasonable doctrines. No one of those doctrines is affirmed by citizens generally' (*PL*, p. xvi). Nor can we expect any one to be so affirmed. Yet *A Theory of Justice* presented a doctrine of justice that Rawls expected to become the one accepted doctrine (cf. *PL*, p. xvi). *Political Liberalism* seeks the appropriate response to the fact of irremediable pluralism, which, Rawls 'assumes', is 'the inevitable result of the exercise of human reason within the framework of free institutions' (*PL*, p. xvi; I, p. 4). Rawls's acceptance of this pluralism of ultimate views does not bespeak skepticism on his part about the possibilities of genuine knowledge regarding the good life and morality, or their religious and philosophical groundings. He 'does not question that many political and moral judgements . . . are correct . . . Nor does [he] question the possible truth of affirmations of faith' (*PL*, II.3.5, p. 63; cf. IV.4.1, p. 154).

Inevitable pluralism resets rather on 'recognition of the practical impossibility of reaching reasonable and workable political agreement in judgment on the truth of comprehensive doctrines' (*PL*, II.3.5, p. 63). There are certain 'burdens of judgment', unnecessary to detail here, which strongly predispose freely thinking human beings to differ in their understandings of the large religious, philosophical, and moral questions that face humanity. It is, Rawls concludes, perfectly reasonable that there should be such disagreement, and would be, therefore, most unreasonable to expect others to conform to one's own comprehensive view of the good[43] (cf. *PL*, II.2, pp. 54–8). Since the existence and acceptance of such pluralism is reasonable, impositions of authority to overcome it are illegitimate. 'Those who insist, when fundamental political questions are at stake, on what they take as true but others do not, seem to others simply to insist on their own beliefs when they have the political power to do so' (*PL*, II.3.3, p. 61; cf. I.6.2, p. 37). Because he appreciates the inevitability of pluralism he clings ever more fiercely to the desideratum of limited government.

Thus Rawls II joins a bevy of thinkers who have retreated from what Alasdair McIntyre has called the 'enlightenment project'.[44] That project had two dimensions: (a) the claim that foundational truth regarding moral and political matters is accessible to the human mind, and (b) that this rational truth can serve as the basis for society. Rawls's challenge to this project is less far-reaching than that of, say, Richard Rorty, for he does not, on the face of it, deny the first enlightenment claim, but he does reject the second, whereas Rorty rejects the first and therewith the second as well (*PL*, p. xviii). In a way, Rawls's stance is far more reminiscent of the seemingly very distant political thinker, Leo Strauss, who, like Rawls, rejects the second but not the first enlightenment claim. Political society, says Strauss, remains irremediably the Platonic cave. The comparison with Strauss is highly instructive, for it brings into the light the non-evident inference Rawls draws from his own insight into the inevitable failure of the enlightenment project. Strauss reasons that if the open, free society can never produce the rational society, then political life cannot proceed on the basis of the enlightenment commitments to an open and free society. In the light of Strauss's conclusions, Rawls's tack seems genuinely paradoxical: despite the failure of the open and free society to produce the rational results originally projected for it (by Rawls himself, among others) Rawls commits yet more firmly to the open and free society.[45]

Inspired by his insight into inevitable pluralism, Rawls recasts the aim or purpose of his theorizing. The aim of *A Theory of Justice* was to present a philosophical doctrine of justice, built upon the contractarian tradition, as a position superior to the then dominant approach, utilitarianism. However, the aim of *Political Liberalism* is more immediately practical, 'to resolve the impasse in the democratic tradition' or 'in our recent political history' (*PL*, VIII.9, p. 338; 14, p. 368). The impasse cannot be broken by following the strategy of *A Theory of Justice*, that is, by adumbrating a doctrine of justice at the same level as those doctrines which have produced the impasse. He must proceed on the basis of accepting the pluralism and thus, in a way, accepting the impasse. His solution to this paradoxical task is the distinction between two types of concepts of justice, political and comprehensive.

Comprehensive doctrines are more familiar to us, for they are the kind of 'religious, philosophical, and moral doctrines' that citizens typically hold and that moral theorists typically propound (*PL*, p. xvi). They are comprehensive in that they relate to a very wide range of moral and political phenomena (*PL*, I.2.2., p. 13). 'Religious and philosophical doctrines express views of the world and of our life with one another, severally and collectively, as a whole' (*PL*, II.2.4, p. 58). Moreover, comprehensive doctrines appeal for their validity to what Rawls loosely calls 'metaphysics', which seems to include appeals to such disparate things as 'specific metaphysical or epistemological doctrines' and to the kind of deep faith commitments one finds in religious believers. (*PL*, I.4.4, p. 10, cf. I.5.1, p. 29, n. 31). Comprehensive conceptions appeal to what we might be tempted to call ultimate truths of philosophy or religion.

A political conception of justice differs from a comprehensive conception of justice, first, in that its subject matter is limited in scope to the political realm, to what Rawls I and Rawls II both call 'the basic structure of society', defined as 'a society's main political, social, and economic institutions' (*PL*, I.2.1, p. 11; cf. *PL*, VI.4.1, p. 223). Many important moral matters thus lie outside its coverage. It is also 'free-standing' in that 'it is neither presented as, nor as derived from . . . comprehensive doctrines' (*PL*, I.2.2, p. 12). It is 'presented independently of any wider comprehensive religious or philosophic doctrine' (*PL*, VI.4.1, p. 223). It thus 'offers no specific metaphysical or epistemological doctrine beyond what is implied by the political conception itself,' (*PL*, I.1.4, p. 10). It aims to be more or less neutral in derivation among all the various comprehensive doctrines to which citizens adhere in society. This is the quality which promises a way beyond the 'impasse' by which Rawls II is so impressed; neither originating in any of these, nor making any judgements about the truth or value of any, the political concept aims to find its ground completely independently of the various conflicting comprehensive doctrines. A political conception thus is a second order doctrine, as opposed to comprehensive first order doctrines. Like the theory of religious toleration, which takes as its point of departure an analogous impasse of religious doctrines, a political conception is not a set of commitments at the same level as the competing comprehensive doctrines.

If the political conception is foreclosed from appealing to any comprehensive doctrine, or from being itself a comprehensive doctrine, then the question necessarily arises, to what can it appeal? Can we generate a conception of justice merely from the fact of impasse? Is it enough to 'agree to disagree'? Rawls thinks not, for he seeks a theory of a genuinely moral character, which a mere *modus vivendi* does not provide (cf. esp. *PL*, IV.3.4, pp. 147–9).[46] Moreover, he still seeks the same sort of 'thick theory of justice' he had presented in *A Theory of Justice* and an 'agreement to disagree' is not substantive enough to produce such a theory.

Rawls thus includes a third element in his notion of a political conception. 'The content . . . of a political conception of justice . . . is expressed in terms of certain fundamental ideas seen as implicit in the public political culture of a democratic society' (*PL*, I.2.3, p. 13; cf. *PL*, VI.4.1, p. 223). Rather than looking to the kind of ultimate truths about 'Humanity, God and Nature' proclaimed within one or another of the comprehensive doctrines, Rawls instead 'starts from within a certain political tradition' (*PL*, I.2.3, p. 14). This way of generating content for a political conception coheres with the original inspiration for the turn to political conceptions:

Justice as fairness aims at uncovering a public basis of justification on questions of political justice given the fact of reasonable pluralism. Since justification is addressed to others, it proceeds from what is, or can be, held in common; and so we begin from shared fundamental ideas implicit in the public political culture in the hope of developing from them a political conception that can gain free and reasoned agreement in judgment (*PL*, III.2.2, pp. 100–1).

The chief task then is to see how Rawls uses the appeal to the culture to reconceive the main outlines of his theory of justice, and in so doing attempts again to reconcile egalitarian liberalism and limited government. Perhaps the most important fact to keep in mind when attempting to grasp *Political Liberalism* is that Rawls is looking to justify the same ultimate results as in *A Theory of Justice*, the same (more or less) two principles and their derivation in the Original Position. Yet the arguments producing these results are quite different.

We can limit ourselves to noting briefly five of the elements of Rawls's new system: these, it turns out, will prove of most relevance to the three pillars. First, Rawls II deploys new foundational principles for developing the Original Position. Secondly, he deploys a new theory of primary goods, much less vulnerable to the criticisms centred on violations of neutrality in the thin theory of the good. Thirdly, he derives the Difference Principle differently and insulates it against the dissolving power of both the two foundational principles as in *A Theory of Justice*. Fourthly, he derives the priority of liberty, i.e., the First Principle, in rather a different way, again less vulnerable to the critique recounted above. Finally, pervading the whole, is a new way of relating the good to the right, on the one hand, and to freedom, on the other.

The Original Position

The Original Position in *A Theory of Justice* owes its existence and character to two 'foundational principles': the Anti-utilitarian Principle and the

Demand of Justice. The new Rawls breaks with this approach. The raw materials for his new model of the Original Position are supplied by reference to ideas derived from or implicit in the public political culture of modern democratic, constitutional societies. There are three steps to Rawls's argument here. First, he develops a conception of society as a 'fair system of cooperation', a conception ostensibly derived from or implicit in the public culture itself. From that he derives an idea of the person as a citizen of that society. Then, he develops the Original Position so that it 'models' the various elements of these 'fundamental ideas'.

'*The* fundamental organizing idea of justice as fairness . . . is that of society as a fair system of cooperation.' The 'terms of cooperation' are 'fair' in that 'each participant may reasonably accept' them, 'provided that everyone else likewise accepts them' (*PL*, I.3.1–2, pp. 16–17, emphasis added). He 'takes this idea to be implicit in the public culture of a democratic society,' because 'in their political thought, and in their discussion of political questions, citizens do not view the social order as a fixed natural order, or as an institutional hierarchy justified by religious or aristocratic values' (*PL*, I.3.1, p. 15). That it is not seen as a 'fixed order' implies, I take it, that citizens in fact look at society in terms of standards according to which society can be judged worthy of adherence or not on the basis of principles not 'fixed' in advance by nature or God, and thus not consigning persons to social duties and political subordination independently of their own ability to rationally accept their social role.[47]

From among all the possible ways of thinking about human nature, Rawls 'adopts a conception of the person to go with this idea . . . of society as a fair system of cooperation over time.' 'Beginning with the ancient world, the concept of the person has been understood, in both philosophy and law, as the concept of someone who can take part in, or who can play a role in, social life . . . Thus we say that a person is someone who can be a citizen' (*PL*, I.3.3, p. 18). If Rawls's history is supposed to matter at all, then this is very poor history. If anything is true of both philosophy and law for most of the period 'beginning with the ancient world', it is that a distinction between person and citizen was drawn. The list of philosophers who reject the identification Rawls affirms includes almost the entire roster of historical political philosophers, and the historical law of slavery, to mention perhaps the most extreme case, understood slaves as persons, but surely not as citizens. But Rawls makes a more discriminating subsequent appeal to 'the tradition of democratic thought'. Within that tradition 'we think of citizens as free and equal persons' (*PL*, I.3.3, pp. 18–19). This is a far more plausible claim, to be sure. That the democratic tradition conceives of persons as free and equal gives some specification to the fairness of the fair system of co-operation, and to the fullness in the notion of persons or citizens as 'full participants' in that system.

Persons are not only held to be free and equal, but to them are attributed 'two moral powers, . . . namely, a capacity for a sense of justice and a capacity for a conception of the good' (*PL*, I.3.3, p. 19). Rawls is very clear that these moral powers are 'an attribution' (*PL*, VIII.3, p. 301), which I take it means they are not derived directly by reference to the democratic political culture. The attribution seems to be a logical requirement of 'the capacity for social cooperation' in a society understood as a fair system of co-operation (ibid.). As an inference from the public conception of society and of a person as a full participant therein, the idea of the person as possessor of the two moral powers is entirely a 'political conception of the person', in which no 'metaphysical doctrine of the person is pre-supposed' (*PL*, I.5.1, p. 29; cf. I.4.5, p. 27; III.2.2, p. 100). The two moral powers are also described by Rawls as the 'reasonable' and 'the rational', corresponding to the capacity for a sense of justice, and for a conception of the good, respectively (*PL*, cf. II, pp. 45–54; III.3.3, p. 104). With that terminology in place, we now arrive at Rawls's most common formulation of 'the fundamental idea' of his system: 'society as a fair system of cooperation between free and equal citizens as reasonable and rational.' (*PL*, III.8.1, p. 126; cf. III, intro., p. 90; III.4.1, p. 107).

Rawls never supplies a completed derivation for the two powers, but his thought must be something like the following. If persons are 'fully participating members in a fair cooperative system,' they must have the capacity to co-operate fairly, that is, to follow the rules that specify fair co-operation. They must, then, have a capacity for justice, for that is what justice is. Likewise, if society is a fair system of co-operation, its fairness must be a function of how each member of it derives benefit from it. But in order to derive benefit, each member must have some good in terms of which benefit is assessed (*PL*, I.3.2, p. 16). Rawls assumes this good is properly stated in terms of a conception of the good, held or formed by each person. Therefore, the idea of society Rawls deploys implies the moral power of being capable of having or formulating a conception of the good.

The two moral powers stand to *Political Liberalism* as the two foundational principles stand to *A Theory of Justice*. That is to say, 'the form of procedure,' i.e., the derivation of principles of justice through an agreement reached in the Original Position, 'and its more particular features,' i.e., the Veil of Ignorance, etc., 'are drawn from the conceptions of citizens and of a well-ordered society,' i.e., a society the basic structure of which conforms to the principles of justice so generated (*PL*, III.3.2, p. 103). 'The procedure' of the theory 'is simply laid out using as starting points the basic conceptions of society and person . . .' (*PL*, III.3.3, p. 104).

The overall goal of the Original Position remains, as it was in *A Theory of Justice*, to 'model what we regard . . . as fair conditions under which the representatives of free and equal citizens are to specify the terms of social cooperation' (*PL*, I.4.3, pp. 25–6). Rawls shows how 'citizens' moral powers of the reasonable and the rational are modelled in the original position' to determine the most significant features of the latter (*PL*, II., intro., p. 48). The persons or representatives themselves model the moral power of rationality: 'we suppose that the parties represent citizens regarded as having at any given time a determinate conception of the good, that is, a conception specified by certain definite final ends, attachments, and loyalties to particular persons and institutions, and interpreted in the light of some comprehensive religious, philosophical, or moral doctrine' (*PL*, II.5.2, p. 74). As we will see, because of the other moral power, agents in the Original Position are denied knowledge of 'the content of these determinate conceptions' (ibid.). Thus far, the representative in Rawls II's Original Position is indistinguishable from that in Rawls I's: it knows *that* but not *what*.

But under the guidance of the new conceptualization in *Political Liberalism*, the agents model the moral power of rationality in additional ways as well. In addition to knowing that they have substantive ends attached to some (unknown) comprehensive conception of the good, agents in the Original Position also know of themselves in terms of their existence as political persons, and thus of the necessity for their possession of the two moral powers. The 'adequate development and full exercise' of those moral powers becomes an additional end for their rationality (ibid.). That is to say, the development and exercise of their capacity for justice, and the development and expression of the capacity 'to form, to revise and rationally to pursue a conception of the good' are taken into account in the Rawls II Original Position. One important result of that, again going beyond anything explicitly stipulated in *A Theory of Justice*, is that 'they . . . have a third higher-order interest to guide them, for they must try to adopt principles of justice' that 'allow for possible changes of mind and conversions from one comprehensive conception to another' (ibid.).

The other power, the 'citizen's capacity for a sense of justice, is modelled within the procedure itself by such features as the reasonable condition of symmetry (or equality) in which the representatives are situated as well as by the limits on information expressed by the Veil of Ignorance' (*PL*, III.3.3, p. 104). Instead of laying out the features of the Veil of Ignorance in terms of the Demand of Justice as in *A Theory of Justice*, Rawls II appeals to 'the fundamental idea of equality as found in the public political culture of a democratic society'. In the performance Rawls II is staging, the aim is to generate rules governing citizenship. But the citizens in a democratic society are regarded as equal to each other, and thus the process which is to generate the rules of fair co-operation among them must treat them all as equals, which is to say, must not give to any of them special advantages at this stage which will skew the rules of justice in such a way as may specially favour them, or the causes they prefer. Symmetry means precisely this situation of 'no advantage'. Rawls thus concludes that all matters that might advantage any are to be left out of account. (*PL*, I.4.2, p. 23; cf. p. 24). 'Features relating to social position, native endowment, and historical accident, as well as to the content of persons' determinate conceptions of the good, are irrelevant, *politically speaking*, and hence placed behind the Veil of Ignorance' (*PL*, II.6.3, p. 79, emphasis added). Notice that Rawls makes no reference here to theories of desert of any sort; despite the fact that *A Theory of Justice* attempted to move away from a desert-based notion of justice, in fact it depended on a very strong theory about desert, or rather about what was not deserved, as embodied in the Demand of Justice. This theory of (non)desert is apparently an expression of a comprehensive conception and finds no explicit place in *Political Liberalism*.[48]

Primary Goods

Rawls still functionally requires the primary goods, because he still requires choosing principles of justice in terms of benefits or goods of the agent choosing, and he still veils the determinate conceptions of good. The new theory of primary goods is the first place where we can see the effectiveness of the new political or constructivist approach in countering the most telling critiques of *A Theory of Justice*. The new treatment of primary goods is marked by an explicit rejection of his earlier approach:

What are to count as primary goods is not decided by asking what general means are essential for achieving the final ends which a comprehensive empirical or historical survey might show that people usually or normally have in common. There may be few if any, such ends; and those there are may not serve the purposes of a conception of justice (*PL*, VIII. 4, p. 308; cf. I.6.4, p. 31).

The primary goods are most definitely not to be seen as 'all-purpose goods' no matter what one's conception of the good; the primary goods must rather be envisioned in a way specifically to 'serve the purposes of a conception of justice,' which means the list is to be drawn up 'only in the light of a conception of the person given in advance' (*PL*, I.6.4, p. 39; VIII.4, p. 308). 'The thought is not that primary goods are fair to comprehensive conceptions of the good associated with such doctrines . . ., but rather fair to free and equal citizens as those persons who have those conceptions' (*PL*, I.6.4, p. 40; cf. *PL*, V.3.2, p. 180).

The list of primary goods is thus 'worked out' in terms of 'what citizens need and require when they are regarded as free and equal persons and as normal and fully cooperating members of society' (*PL*, V.3.1, p. 178). The 'basis' of primary goods is a 'conception of citizens' needs that, is, of persons' needs as citizens' (*PL*, V.3.2, p. 179; cf. III.8, p. 332). The primary

goods constitute a 'political understanding of what is to be publicly recognized as citizens' needs and *hence* as advantageous to all' (ibid., emphasis added). Thus, 'primary goods are clearly not anyone's idea of the basic
values of human life and *must not be so understood*, however essential their
possession. We say instead that, given the political conception of citizens,
primary goods specify that their needs are part of what their good is as citizens when questions of justice arise' (*PL*, V.4.1.2, p. 188, emphasis added).

Rawls proceeds to list more or less the same set of primary goods as in
A Theory of Justice, but now he breaks them down more precisely into different categories of goods which he connects explicitly to various aspects
of the two moral powers of persons. There are five such classes of primary
goods: (1) The 'basic liberties', including freedom of thought and liberty of
conscience, 'are the background institutional conditions necessary for the
development and the full and informed exercise of the two moral powers'.
(2) The 'opportunities' (freedom of movement and free choice of occupa-
tion) 'allow the pursuit of diverse final ends and give effect to a decision
to revise and change them, if we so desire'. (3) 'Powers and prerogatives
of offices and positions . . . give scope to various self-governing and social
capacities of the self,' while (4) 'income and wealth are needed to achieve
directly or indirectly a wide range of ends, whatever they happen to be.'[49]
Finally, (5) '[t]he social bases of self-respect . . . are morally essential if citizens are to have a lively sense of their own worth as persons and to be able
to develop and exercise their moral powers and to advance their aims with
self-confidence' (*PL*, VIII.4, pp. 308–9). One could wish for a more strenu-
ous effort by Rawls to link the primary goods to the two powers, but it is
clear in any case that he is taking quite a different approach to them from
the one in *A Theory of Justice*. Since he no longer aims at the kind of neutrality he did at first, it does not appear to be so debilitating to his position
that he fails to achieve it. Thus his new conception of primary goods
enables him to evade some of the most obvious of the critiques raised
against *A Theory of Justice*. For example, no longer claiming that primary
goods are to serve equally well all comprehensive conceptions of the good,
he easily parries the objections raised by Sen and Arrow that he discrimi-
nates against more expensive 'life-plans' (*PL*, V.3.3, pp. 182–3).

The Difference Principle

The significant shift from *A Theory of Justice* to *Political Liberalism* leaves the
Difference Principle on much more solid ground. The chief problem with
the Difference Principle in *A Theory of Justice* was its inability to satisfy
either of the two foundational principles. But *Political Liberalism* deploys
neither of these. The two moral powers, which replace the two foundational principles, do not conflict in as clear-cut a way with the Difference

Principle as did their counterparts in *A Theory of Justice*, if they conflict at all. (In part, however, this is because the two moral powers are much more vague and less hard-edged than the foundational principles.)

In accordance with the new grounding of the Difference Principle in the two moral powers, Rawls tends to speak quite differently of it when he does speak of it. (It must be noted that it has far less prominence for Rawls II than it had for Rawls I.[50] This diminished status for the Difference Principle coheres with the shift away from the Demand of Justice, which had such a formative role on Rawls's thinking in *A Theory of Justice*.) When speaking of the Difference Principle, he refrains (mostly) from the language of 'undeserving' and a general concern for equality, but instead connects it to his political conception of citizenship. Justice 'requires measures . . . to assure that the basic needs of all citizens can be met so that they can take part in political and social life.' This language of needs is something of a new departure for Rawls, but he carefully distinguishes it from a general needs-based approach to justice. 'The idea is not that of satisfying needs as opposed to mere desires and wants; nor is it that of redistribution in favor of greater equality. The [idea] is rather that below a certain level of material and social well-being, and of training and education, people simply cannot take part in society as citizens, much less as equal citizens' (*PL*, IV.7.3, p. 166; cf. the suggestive comment at I.7.2, p. 42 and esp. VI.5.3, pp. 228–9).[51] All of this is to say that Rawls appears to have reformulated the substructure of his position so as to avoid the deadly conflict between the foundation and the edifice of *A Theory of Justice*. Other things equal, Rawls's new position leaves standing the Difference Principle, that important pillar of his attempted harmonization of egalitarian liberalism and limited government.

The First Principle

He begins, is new discussion of the First Principle by conceding *A Theory of Justice* had a 'gap', an insufficient presentation of 'the grounds upon which the parties in the original position accept the first principle of justice and agree to the priority of its basic liberties' (*PL*, VIII.3, p. 299). The introduction of the two moral powers makes the behaviour of parties in the Original Position far more complex than it was in *A Theory of Justice*, for now there are 'three kinds of considerations the parties must distinguish when they deliberate . . .'; (1) and (2) are considerations relating to 'the development and the full and informed exercise of the two moral powers, each power giving rise to considerations of a distinct kind'; and (3) 'considerations relating to a person's determinate conception of the good' (*PL*, VIII.4, p. 310). *A Theory of Justice* in effect only incorporated the last of these, and from it alone the equality and priority of liberty cannot be derived.

Although Rawls II makes a half-hearted effort to derive the priority of liberty from the third ground, it is apparent that this still cannot succeed without the buttressing supplied by the reasons connected more specifically to the two moral powers. He attempts this derivation in relation to a liberty that might seem especially easy for him, liberty of conscience. Persons in the Original Position know they have some conception of the good about which they might care very much, but the content and social predominance of which they do not know. Under those conditions,

they cannot take chances by permitting a lesser liberty of conscience for minority religions, say, on the possibility that those they represent espouse a majority or dominant religion and will therefore have an even greater liberty. For it may also happen that these persons belong to a minority faith and may suffer accordingly (*PL*, VIII.5, p. 311).

The argument fails for at least two good reasons. First, some reasoner like Plato, Hobbes, Rousseau, or Durkheim, might say that social cohesion, from which he and all members of society would benefit, requires more or less unity of religious views (or at least of public religious professions) in a society, and therefore it would be rational not to affirm liberty of conscience. Moreover, another type of reasoner might judge it worth the risk to reject liberty of conscience, thinking it a good enough gamble to take that he would end up in the majority. The old charge that Rawls illicitly builds risk-aversion into his system remains potent.

In order to respond to the latter kind of deliberator, and in order to show that he has no special commitments to risk aversion, Rawls replies that gambling would be ruled out under the hypothesis of the situation. 'If the parties were to gamble in this way, they would show that they did not take the religious, philosophical, or moral convictions of persons seriously and in effect, did not know what a religious, philosophical, or moral conviction was' (ibid.). One can imagine John Calvin, or a person in the Original Position who thinks he might be John Calvin 'on the other side' replying to Rawls: 'For shame, Professor Rawls. Is a bit of threat to your comfort and safety all it takes to scare you off your "convictions"? Better to call them whims or fancies. How can you dishonour the divine truth, sir, by mandating public indifference to it? It would be bad, very bad if others imposed their errors on us, but better to suffer for the truth than be indifferent to it. Do you men of Harvard know nothing of truth? Martin Luther said, "Here I stand, I can do no other." He knew the princes of church and state would give him no peace, no rest, yet he stood. And you Harvard philosophers, what do you say? "Here I sit. I dare do no more!" '

With this chiding, Rawls I would slink away as quietly as possible, but Rawls II has an answer. The agents are also united explicitly around the two moral powers, including the 'capacity to form, to revise, and rationally to pursue a determinate conception of the good' (*PL*, VIII.5, p. 312). Here Rawls makes explicit what was required all along to make his argument for the priority of liberty go through. Not merely do agents in the Original Position conceive themselves as persons with (unknown) conceptions of the good, but they also consider themselves as possessing 'the capacity for a conception of the good'. They know, that is, that no existing conception of the good is necessarily final for them, and that the most important thing, more important than the pursuit of any given conception of the good they might have, is the power to reconsider, refine, or even form new conceptions of the good. Thus, they are likely to give a privileged place to those powers or rights which allow this sovereign stance toward their own goods. The focus on the political person and its moral powers brings explicitly into the Original Position the kind of freedom Rawls was assuming at some level in *A Theory of Justice*, but not deploying in the deliberations on justice.

The parties in the Original Position are also oriented toward the other moral power, the capacity for a conception of justice, or 'reasonableness'. They can, and Rawls maintains they will, rationally take this power into consideration when they deliberate on principles of justice. 'Reasonable persons', says Rawls, 'desire for its own sake a social world in which they, as free and equal, can cooperate with others on terms all can accept' (*PL*, II.1.1, p. 50). So far as actions in the Original Position are reasonable in this sense, it is easy to see that Calvin's approach would not be accepted in the Original Position, for he rejects the kind of reciprocity this moral power implies. Rawls argues that the rational deliberators will indeed appeal to the principle of reasonableness, because, in a variety of complicated ways, it is a solid means to their determinate conception of the good. Just to mention one of Rawls's several points here. Even though the Original Position is defined in such a way that agents are not permitted to 'invoke reasons founded on regarding the development and exercise of this capacity as part of a person's determinate conception of the good,' (for this moral power is modelled in the constraints imposed in the Original Position, not in the motives of the actors), yet they can appeal to reasonableness as a means. Rawls maintains they will do so, and the priority of the basic liberties will appear to them an important part of this appeal. To cite only one of Rawls's many arguments on this score, he argues that it is a 'great advantage to everyone's conception of the good' to have a 'just and stable scheme of cooperation', Therefore, the second moral power and the principle of reciprocity embodying it becomes eligible as means to this 'just and stable scheme' (cf. *PL*, VIII.6, pp. 315–24).

Again, Rawls has shored up the case for one of his three pillars, for, granting him his two powers and the Original Position as constructed on their basis, his case for the First Principle and the Priority of Liberty is much stronger than he left it in *A Theory of Justice*, precisely because the two moral powers are posited as containing the very considerations, the absence of which prevented the argument in *A Theory of Justice* from going through.

The Right and the Good

Just as Rawls's new approach incorporating the two moral powers gives him better purchase on the priority of liberty, so it does the same for the problem of perfectionism. In *A Theory of Justice* the argument against perfectionism failed in just the same way as did the argument for the priority of liberty; in *Political Liberalism* it succeeds in the same way as the argument for the priority of liberty. Just as the moral power of rationality gives weight to liberty by bringing to the fore the capacity to revise and even entirely shift conceptions of the good, so it tilts things against perfectionism. The moral power of rationality gives the agents in the Original Position a certain distance from their actual and existing conceptions of the good, whatever these might be, and forecloses them from being so committed to any view of the good that they would choose to make its achievement the object of their social life. Likewise, their other moral power, their reasonableness, more or less directly builds into the foundations of the system, and therewith into the deliberations in the Original Position, the Rawlsian claims about inevitable pluralism of views of the good, and the moral bearing of this fact. To be reasonable in Rawls's sense means to possess 'the willingness to recognize the burdens of judgement and to accept their consequences for the use of public reason in directing the legitimate exercise of political power in a constitutional regime' (*PL*, I.2.1, p. 54). Now, as we have just seen, even though reasonableness is not directly modelled in the Original Position via the motivational assumptions for agents, nonetheless Rawls makes a plausible if not overwhelming case that rational agents there will see the development of a conception of justice as rational, and therewith accept the rationality of being reasonable. So far as this is true, they will not accept perfectionist standards, for these contradict, or at least stand in great tension with, the approach to inevitable pluralism built into the concept of reasonableness. (On anti-perfectionism as more loosely connected to the political character of justice in *Political Liberalism*, see V.5.4, pp. 194–5).

The other, and I think ultimately more critical issue in *A Theory of Justice* concerned the place Rawls gave to the good in the structure of the Original Position: the parties know *that*, but not *what*. The political conception takes as its point of departure the idea of inevitable pluralism, which gives a direct political rendering of the Rawlsian practice of modelling the *that* but not the *what* in the Original Position, and thus frees the theory from dependence on questionable or incomplete metaphysics. The *that* but not the *what* in Rawls II models not the nature of the human self, but the pluralism of modern free society. For purposes of a political conception we must accept the fact that the *that* is politically relevant, but the *whats* cannot be in the same way, that is, they cannot be the basis for fair co-operation, and therefore cannot be constitutive in any way for justice in a modern society. Thus Rawls elegantly, and far more simply than in *A Theory of Justice*, generates a rationale for this so critical part of his procedure.[52]

IV

> *O thin men of Haddam*
> *Why do you imagine golden birds?*
> *Do you not see how the blackbird*
> *Walks around the feet*
> *Of the women about you?*
> Wallace Stevens, 'Thirteen Ways of Looking at a Blackbird'

What then of egalitarian liberalism and limited government? On the basis of so much of *Political Liberalism* as we have so far looked into, it looks good. Rawls's three pillars do not fall because of structural incompatibilities with other elements of his edifice. Yet there are at least three aspects of *Political Liberalism* we have thus far ignored that lead to a much less optimistic conclusion. The first difficulty centres on the effort to generate a new type of political theory. Rawls's turn to a political conception is motivated by an appreciation of the 'burdens of judgment' which make it unlikely and even unreasonable for any doctrine of the comprehensive type to win sufficiently wide acceptance so as to be able to shape a society's basic institutions. Yet why should the burdens of judgement not be as serious a problem for a political conception as for a first order comprehensive doctrine? That Rawls labels it differently does not mean that all the uncertainties of the operation of human reason will not have precisely the same effect on second order as on first order doctrines. (He concedes there will be an indefinite number of political conceptions, and that any one of them 'often allows more than one reasonable answer to any particular question' (*PL*, VI.7.1, p. 240, cf. *PL*, VI.4–5, p. 227). This problem seems especially serious, for Rawls is asking people to engage in a very sophisticated intellectual feat to set aside their comprehensive conceptions of the good, enter into the thinking characteristic of his political conception, and then find a way to hold the two together, the political conception now a 'module' within the previously held conceptions (*PL*, I.2.2, p. 12). So far as the failure due to the burdens of judgement speaks against theories of the traditional sort, so it does against Rawls's political conception.

Rawls's most general answer to the problem of how political liberalism can be expected to avoid falling before the burdens of judgement rests on the fact that it is built up on the basis of ideas (somehow) present in the reigning political culture, that he is appealing, in some sense, to ideas all or most already (somehow) accept. Thus the political conceptions would seem to avoid the shoals of the burdens of judgement in a way that comprehensive doctrines do not. This reply points to the second major difficulty in Rawls's new theory: to what extent has he indeed built on foundations supplied by 'ideas within the public political culture'?

I have a simple point to make here. The political culture does not supply sufficiently determinate ideas on which Rawls can build, and he compensates for (and conceals) this difficulty by smuggling into his new theory conceptions taken over from his old theory. These conceptions are neither adequately defended within the new theory, nor are they without their old destructive effects. Rawls begins his construction with 'ideas' allegedly taken over from the political tradition of liberal democracy. He means 'idea' to cover 'both concepts and conceptions', a distinction familiar from *A Theory of Justice*. 'Roughly, the concept is the meaning of a term, while a particular conception includes as well the principles required to apply it' (*PL*, I.2.3, p. 14, n. 15). He illustrates the difference in terms of 'justice'. The concept 'means, say, that [an] institution makes no arbitrary distinctions between persons in assigning basic rights and duties.' The conception fills in the specifics: what kind of distinctions are arbitrary? What rights and duties are basic? As Rawls indicates, people may agree about the concept and yet strongly disagree about the conception, as seems indeed to be the case with justice.

This distinction between concept and conception helps clarify the logic of what might otherwise appear to be Rawls's puzzling enterprise of appealing to the tradition, the culture, and its contents in order to break the impasse within the tradition and the culture. If he can find a level of agreement beneath the disagreement, or implicit somehow in the practices and commitments of citizens, then he might be able to use an appeal to the culture at one level to resolve disagreements at another. The distinction between concept and conception, making available to him a solid way of thinking about different levels of agreement and disagreement, would seem a key part of the apparatus needed to engage in this effort.

There remain, nevertheless, two great flaws in what he has done. The first is on the order of 'The dog that didn't bark.' The way he has set up his new theory imposes on him the imperative to trace with care the movement from practices and ideas in the culture to ideas within his theory. With regard to this part of his task, Rawls surely does not bark; he barely whimpers. He should specify how we identify the basic ideas (concepts or conception) in a political culture; he should specify how he has selected these ideas as the basic ones from among the many possible ways of characterizing the tradition. Where is a nuanced awareness, much less a presentation, of the political ideas of the thinkers we might identify as authoritative or representative within the political culture? A few off-hand references to Lincoln do not substitute for a real knowledge of Lincoln, Jefferson, the *Federalist*, Herbert Croly, Franklin D. Roosevelt, John F. Kennedy, Reinhold Niebuhr, and others whom we might take to have voiced the aspirations and meanings of the tradition qua tradition. If these modes of grasping the tradition are too vulgar, shallow, or empirical for philosophy, then where is the analysis needed to bring out what is deeply 'implicit in the culture' in its practices or 'values'? Assuming that Rawls's approach has any merit for moral and political philosophy, it requires a much better execution than it has received here (cf. *PL*, VI.4.5, p. 227).

Rawls seeks an agreement beneath or implicit within the disagreement in the culture upon which he can then build in order to overcome the disagreement. He finds such an agreement in the ideas of society as a fair system of co-operation, and of citizens as free and equal. From these ideas, as we have seen, he derives his two moral powers, and thence the chief features of the ornate apparatus of the Original Position. Rawls has gone astray, however, in that he has perceived an agreement at the level of concept, i.e., on such general matters as the freedom and equality of persons, which he has attempted to interpret as an agreement at the level of conception. Or, to put it another way, the agreements and practices to which he points in the culture do not exist at the level of specificity or with the content that he gives them when he brings them into his theory.

The idea of equality within the public political culture is used to lay out the structural constraints embedded in the Original Position, in particular the Veil of Ignorance. There is indeed widespread agreement within the culture that citizens are equal, that all, for example, have or should have equal rights. Yet there is also a wide range of disagreement over what about persons makes them equal, and over what the claim of equality entitles them to. Moreover, in American society, at least, the acceptance of the equality of persons is accompanied with a concomitant acceptance of important inequalities, which most Americans accept as legitimate as well. If anything, there is an agreement that there are limits to the equality of results required by the equality of persons.[53] For example, in a recent dispute concerning streaming (or tracking) in the Alexandria, Virginia, public schools, even the advocates of a no-streaming system insisted on the legitimacy and appropriateness of treating students differently (unequally) in relation to (some of) the respects in which they were equal.

Even they reaffirmed the importance of special instruction and opportunities for 'gifted and talented' students.

Nonetheless, when Rawls brings the agreement on the concept of equality into his system he treats it as if it were an agreement on a conception. He leaps, for instance, from the notion of equality to the veiling of 'features relating to social position, native endowment, and historical accident, as well as to the content of persons' determinate conceptions of the good' in his set-up of the Original Position. This is meant 'to model . . . the fundamental idea of equality as found in the public political culture' (*PL*, II.6.3, p. 79). It does not do that, but models one possible conception of the concept of equality, one that goes well beyond the concept on which there is in fact agreement to a conception on which there is not. This shift from concept to conception is simply arbitrary and illegitimate within the terms of Rawls's own thought.[54]

Actually, it is not arbitrary. Rawls has derived the content from his previous system; the notion of equality he deploys here is an inexplicit and undefended version of the old Demand of Justice. Yet the Demand of Justice has no legitimate place in *Political Liberalism*, relating as it does to a comprehensive moral philosophy; moreover, to the extent that *Political Liberalism* implicitly depends on the Demand of Justice, once again it has its old dissolving power. On the surface *Political Liberalism* appears more solid, but not far beneath the surface are the old shoals.[55]

There is a third important general problem in Rawls's new approach which can be stated very briefly. The approach via ideas in the political culture runs more afoul than most moral theories of the is-ought problem. Even assuming that Rawls can find ideas, concepts, or conceptions within the public culture on which he could rear his mighty leviathan, wherein lies the moral quality that gives them their rightness? *A Theory of Justice* had dealt with this in an ingenious if not entirely successful manner in the theory of moral theory and justification Rawls developed there. As he claimed, echoing Hume, moral theory is rather like other types of theory, a systematization and clarification of our moral capacity. The data from which such systematization proceeds are the 'considered moral judgments' that we do in fact make.

Ultimately, this theory of moral theory fails because Rawls is unable to identify the source of the ought, or of moral claim, but this failing is far more severe in *Political Liberalism*. The failing shows up, for example, in the derivation of the two moral powers. The first moral power is 'the capacity for a sense of justice'. Rawls finds this idea implicit in the public culture. Apart from the fact that Rawls leaves it very vague, let us grant that there is such an idea embedded or implicit in the culture. What follows from it as an ought? Does it follow that one ought to be just because one can be just, because there is a widespread or implicit idea that one can be just, because social practices assume or imply some general level of just behaviour? The problem can be seen if we think of a dialogue between Rawls and Thrasymachus or Callicles, or between Rawls and David Hume. The problem is not only that Rawls cannot get such a specific theory of justice as fairness from such a general thing as the capacity for a sense of justice, but that even if he could, it wouldn't be a real *theory* of justice, that is, a theory with moral bite, which is what Rawls is seeking.[56]

What then of egalitarian liberalism and limited government? It now appears that Rawls's apparent success in *Political Liberalism* was due to a series of patches he sewed over the bare spots in *A Theory of Justice*. These patches, cut for the moment's need, lacked texture and heft, and soon fell off, revealing the same bare spots as in *A Theory of Justice*.

Yet Rawls's double failure should not lead to the conclusion that no successful theory harmonizing egalitarianism and libertarianism is possible. Surely this examination of Rawls's two monumental efforts has not established that. Indeed, the inquiry into Rawls's efforts has helped point toward what such a reconciling theory must be like. On the positive side, Rawls makes clear that something like his three pillars are necessary constituent elements of any theory that could successfully reconcile egalitarian liberalism and limited government. This is not to say that the three pillars necessarily, or even probably, should appear in just the form they do in Rawls. Yet something like the Difference Principle, by which I mean a *tempered* principle of egalitarian claims to distribution must be part of any such theory. If there is no egalitarian-leaning principle of just distribution, then it will not qualify as an egalitarian liberalism. If that egalitarian principle is not tempered, it will be very unlikely to support a securely limited government, securely protecting a sphere of liberty. Likewise, Rawls's second pillar, explicit protection for liberty with some insulation of liberty claims from general claims for welfare or the common good is also necessary. Otherwise, the claims of public welfare too easily override the claims of limited government. A solid theory of limited government, in other words, needs a place for a theory of rights. Finally, Rawls points to the need for a tempered role for the good in a liberal theory. He has not made the case that the good has no place, or has only a strictly derivative and secondary place, but he has shown that a too perfectionist doctrine on the one hand, or a too needs-based doctrine on the other, overrides limited government.

Rawls also shows us what we must avoid. He goes most astray in two places in his theory: first, in the extremely negative insight about claims or rights that is embodied in his Demand of Justice and less openly in *Political Liberalism*'s construal of equality, and secondly in his theory of the moral irrelevance of the good. The former proves to be disabling of any and all justice claims, as the failures of his ingenious efforts to generate such claims despite the Demand of Justice reveal. The lesson Rawls's failure here holds for us is not merely the negative one, to avoid his Demand of Justice, but the more positive one that a successful theory must discern a ground of right, or a ground of claim. This can be done either in a theory of the teleological or of the deontological sort. Rawls was foreclosed from the one by his radical and disabling theory of the good; he was foreclosed from the other by his radical and dissolving theory of desert. At bottom, the problem behind both these aspects of Rawls's thought was his search for, and failure to find the 'morally relevant', or the source of moral claim. The approach he took to this question was by no means evident or necessary, and his failure proves little about the impossibility of ultimate success. Indeed, several authors represented in this very volume have arguably put forward more promising, more successful theories reconciling egalitarian liberalism and limited government than that titan of our age, John Rawls.

NOTES

1 This chapter was written during a period of residence as Visiting Scholar at the Social Philosophy and Policy Center, Bowling Green, Ohio. The author wishes to thank the directors of the Center for their support, and, of course, to absolve them of all responsibility for the views expressed here.

2 See, e.g., Kai Nielsen, *Equality and Liberty, A Defense of Radical Egalitarianism* (Totowa, N.J., 1985), pp. 5–6.

3 Ibid., pp. 7–8.

4 Robert Nozick, *Anarchy, State and Utopia* (New York, 1974), 160.

5 See Daniel Bell, 'On Meritocracy and Equality', *The Public Interest* 29 (Autumn, 1972), pp. 29–68.

6 See Alexis de Tocqueville, *Democracy in America*, ed. J. P. Mayer (New York, 1969), vol. II, part IV.

7 Consider, e.g., Jeffrey Reiman, *Justice and Modern Moral Philosophy* (New Haven, 1990); Ronald Dworkin, *Taking Rights Seriously* (Cambridge, Mass., 1977).

8 See Alan Buchanan, *Marx and Justice: The Radical Critique of Liberalism* (Totowa, N.J., 1982), ch. 4.

9 Cf. Thomas Nagel, *Equality and Partiality* (New York, 1991), v: Rawls 'changed the subject.'

10 I am leaving references to Rawls's two main books in the text. *A Theory of Justice* (*TJ*) (Cambridge, Mass., 1972); *Political Liberalism* (*PL*) (New York, 1993). I will reply to as many of Jeffrey Reiman's arguments as I conveniently can in the notes. I will restrict myself to responding to what he says regarding 'Rawls's letter and spirit' and not follow him when he gives 'Rawlsian inspired' rather than 'Rawlsian' arguments. This is not to say his Rawlsian inspired arguments are unworthy of serious reflection; considerations of space foreclose my doing

so here, however. See Jeffrey Reiman, 'John Rawls' New Conception of the Problem of Limited Government: Reply to Michael Zuckert,' in this volume.

11 Cf. Nagel, *Equality and Partiality*, pp. 63–74; Nielsen, *Equality and Liberty*, pp. 48–53.

12 Cf. Gerald Dworkin, 'Non-Neutral Principles, in *Reading Rawls*, Norman Daniels, (ed.) (New York, 1975); David A. J. Richards, *Toleration and the Constitution* (New York and Oxford, 1986); William A. Galston, *Liberal Purposes* (Cambridge, 1991), pp 79–162.

13 Galston, *Liberal Purposes*, ch. 1.

14 For the recent restatement of these charges by the Italian Marxist Galvano della Volpe, see J. Q. Merquior, *Liberalism Old and New* (Boston, 1991), pp. 143–4.

15 In light of Reiman's reply, I'd like to reiterate that I am not so much putting forward my critique of *TJ* here, but recapitulating widespread and widely (although not universally) accepted criticisms of *TJ*.

16 Reiman, 'Rawls' New Conception', rightly identifies the difference between our readings of the relation between *TJ* and *PL*. He claims 'the arguments of *TJ* are presupposed by *PL*.' Rawls himself is quite ambiguous on this question, but when the day is done, it is difficult to see how *PL* can presuppose the arguments of *TJ* for *TJ* is what Rawls calls a comprehensive conception and *PL* a political conception. (On the distinction, see below, Part II.) It is definitive of a political conception that it cannot rest on a comprehensive conception. Therefore *PL* cannot, in any strong sense, 'presuppose the arguments of *TJ*'.

17 Representative critiques along those lines from Rawls's left: Nielson, *Equality and Liberty*; Brian Barry, *The Liberal Theory of Justice* (Oxford, 1973); Robert Paul Wolff, *Understanding Rawls* (Princeton, 1977); from Rawls's right: Robert Nozick, *Anarchy*; Bell, 'On Meritocracy'.

18 For a more complete explication of the two foundational principles and of their role in *TJ*, see Michael P. Zuckert, 'Liberalism and Nihilism: Contemporary Constrained Performance Theories of Justice', *Constitutional Commentary* 2 (Summer, 1985), pp. 593–5. For a parallel treatment of 'foundational principles' of ethics, see Nagel, *Equality and Partiality*, 15.

19 Cf. Jeffrey Paul and Fred D. Miller, Jr., 'Communitarian and Liberal Theories of the Good', *Review of Metaphysics* 43 (June 1990), pp. 803–30.

20 Thus Richard Rorty and Thomas Scanlon are off the mark in suggesting Rawls could do without self-interested actors in the Original Position. See Richard Rorty, *Objectivity, Relativism, and Truth* (Cambridge, 1991), 184; T. M. Scanlon, 'Contractualism and Utilitarianism', Bernard Williams and Amartya Sen (ed.) (Cambridge, 1982).

21 Cf Nozick, *Anarchy*, 215–16; T. M. Scanlon, 'Rawls's Theory of Justice' in *Reading Rawls*, pp. 204–5; Zuckert, 'Liberalism and Nihilism', pp. 394–5.

22 Michael P. Zuckert, 'Justice Deserted: A Critique of Rawls's *A Theory of Justice*', *Polity*, 13 (1981), pp. 466–83; Scanlon, 'Rawls's Theory', 204; Michael J. Sandel, *Liberalism and the Limits of Justice* (Cambridge, 1982), pp. 66–72; Jeffrey Reiman, 'Rawls's New Conception', claims Rawls 'in no way assumes the strange doctrine that natural talents are a common asset'. Rawls, however, says '[w]e see then that the difference principle represents, in effect, an agreement to regard the distribution of natural talents as a common asset and to share the benefits

of this distribution whatever it turns out to be.' (*TJ*, s. 17, p. 101). That Rawls does not develop or endorse every possible implication of a common asset view, as Reiman points out, does not imply that his difference principle does not involve acceptance of the common asset view. Reiman's distinction between talents and rewards to talents requires a good deal more argumentation than he provides in order to support his sweeping conclusion that 'rewards to talent' simply 'belong to the rest of society'. In any case, this appears a 'Rawlsian inspired' rather than a Rawlsian argument.

23 Nozick, *Anarchy*, p. 228; cf. Scanlon, 'Rawls's Theory', pp. 198–9; Sandel, *Liberalism*, pp. 77–9, 100–3; Paul and Miller, 'Communitarianism', 819–20, 823; John Rawls, 'Fairness to Goodness', *Philosophical Review*, 841 (Oct. 1975), pp. 540–5.

24 Cf. Victor Gourevitch, 'Rawls on Justice', *Review of Metaphysics* 28 (March 1975), pp. 507–10.

25 For Rawlsian testimony to the general bearing of arguments of this form, see Rawls, 'Fairness', 537; on the continuing role of endowment and motivation in Rawls's 'well-ordered society', see *TJ*, s. 46, p. 301; for a counter-argument, see *TJ*, s. 17, pp. 101–4; Sandel, pp. 70–2. Reiman claims this argument rests on 'a simple logical error'. I have addressed this notion in my 'Justice Deserted', pp. 478–80, to which I refer the reader. It is fairly clear, I think, that the connection between differential reward and the proscribed bases of desert is a very different and a great deal more intimate than the example Reiman provides about perspiration and effort. Reiman's reformulation in terms of 'contributions' does not work for Rawls, as is apparent in his rejection of 'liberal equality' as an acceptable principle of justice. See *TJ*, s. 12, pp. 72–5.

26 For a more nuanced discussion of the failure of the Difference Principle, see Zuckert, 'Justice Deserted'; also Paul and Miller, 'Communitarianism', 823. Reiman makes a series of important points regarding what he takes to be a 'philosophic error' in my account of Rawls's Demand of Justice. His chief point is that 'desert is a derivative rather than a primitive moral notion,' and thus that I misapply or weigh too heavily the Demand of Justice or, perhaps, that I am incorrect in attributing this Demand to Rawls at all. I have several points to make in turn: 1) most importantly, I have presented a fairly long answer to the general argument Reiman makes regarding the role of desert in my 'Justice Deserted', pp. 479–81; 2) I agree with Reiman that as I read Rawls, he is 'saddled with a truly impossible doctrine'. See 'Justice Deserted', pp. 475–8 for an account of how he might be led to make his 'impossible' argument. If, as I argue below, Rawls has made a mistake here, I still show that this was not a merely foolish or unintelligent point; 3) Reiman asserts that 'Rawls is not claiming that more talented people cannot deserve greater rewards', but this contradicts many statements by Rawls himself. E.g., 'distributive shares . . . decided by the outcome of the natural lottery [are] arbitrary from a moral perspective. There is no more reason to permit the distribution of income and wealth to be settled by the distribution of natural assets than by historical and social fortune,' (*TJ*, s. 12, p. 74). Rawls also speaks of his 'conception of justice' as one that 'nullifies the accidents of natural endowments . . . as counters in the quest for political and economic advantage,' for those 'accidents' are 'arbitrary from a moral

point of view,' (*TJ*, s. 3, p. 15); 4) the core of the difference between Reiman and myself regarding the Demand of Justice lies in his view that for Rawls 'desert is [simply] derivative from a conception of justice,' that is to say, posterior to the formulation of the principles of justice, while I hold that Rawls deploys a negative conception of desert at the outset (the Demand of Justice) that in turn leads to the result Reiman correctly identifies regarding positive desert within Rawls's system. For further discussion, see my 'Liberalism and Nihilism', pp. 393–5.

27 H. L. A. Hart, 'Rawls on Liberty and Its Priority', in *Reading Rawls*, 250–2.

28 Ibid., 252.

29 Wolff, *Understanding Rawls*, p. 93; cf. Hart, 'Rawls on Liberty', p. 249; Scanlon, 'Rawls's Theory', p. 185.

30 Hart, 'Rawls on Liberty', p. 245.

31 Consider also Sanlon's argument, 'Rawls's Theory', pp. 183–4, on liberty and common interest in relation to *TJ* s. 16, p. 97.

32 John Finnis, *Natural Law and Natural Rights* (Oxford, 1980), represents a fine example of the kind of theory Rawls is not developing, deriving right from good, and understanding good in a perfectionist manner. (See esp. ch. VIII).

33 The issue of neutrality is a complex and often confusing one in Rawls; it is sometimes thought that it requires principles of justice neutral among all conceptions of the good, and that he fails to achieve such neutrality. This is for the most part a misplaced criticism, however. For discussion see Galston, *Liberal Purposes*, chs. 4 and 6; Buchanan, *Marx and Justice*, pp. 142–4; David L. Schaefer, *Justice of Tyranny*? (Port Washington, NY, 1979).

34 Cf. Barry, *Liberal Theory*, p. 26; Schaefer, *Justice or Tyranny*, pp. 30–7; Sandel, *Liberalism and the Limits of Justice*, 27; Paul and Miller, 'Communitarianism', pp. 828–9.

35 Amartya Sen, 'Equality of What?' in *The Tanner Lectures on Human Values*, ed. Sterling McMurrin (Salt Lake City, 1980), pp. 215–16; Galston, *Liberal Purposes*, 126; Kenneth J. Arrow, 'Some Ordinalist Notes on Rawls's "Theory of Justice",' *Journal of Philosophy* (1973), pp. 253ff.; Thomas Nagel, 'Rawls on Justice', in *Reading Rawls*, p. 9.

36 Reiman attempts to rebut this argument in 'Rawls's New Conception', but does so with an argument that has no grounding, so far as I can see, in anything Rawls ever said. I stand by my argument in this section, in part because, as becomes clear below (see my s. II B), Rawls concedes in *PL* that the 'thin theory of the good' in *TJ* is inadequate.

37 Cf. Buchanan, *Marx and Justice*, p. 116.

38 Nagel, 'Rawls on Justice,' 8; Galston, *Liberal Purposes*, pp. 125–6.

39 Reiman misses both the point and the force of the Nagel–Galson critique of Rawls on the good. The fact that the deliberators are representatives rather than *sui juris* actors makes no difference. The point of the critique, to repeat, is that the mere fact that the representative persons do not know their own conceptions of the good is no reason why they could not deliberate about conceptions of the good and select one to govern their society. If they do not know their own conceptions, then they are not acting in a self-favouring manner. (Consider

also that Reiman treats any decision that might be made in such a way as an imposition, but an argument of either a skeptical kind or one like Rawls's in *PL* is required to make that argument good. Within *TJ*, I am arguing, Rawls lacks the resources to succeed in his argument on the good, and precisely for that reason shifts ground in *PL*.

40 Galston, *Liberal Purposes*, p. 95; Schaefer, *Justice or Tyranny?*, pp. 70ff.

41 Cf. Schaefer, *Justice or Tyranny?*, p. 81.

42 Ibid., p. 124; Buchanan, *Marx and Justice*, p. 125.

43 In resting his case on the difficulty of agreement rather than on the cognitive status of comprehensive doctrines, Rawls blunts the force of one of the most recurrent criticisms of *Theory*—that it is rooted in a deep-going skepticism. E.g. Dworkin, 'Non-neutral Principles', pp. 137–9; Galston, *Liberal Purposes*, pp. 79, 82, 89–90, and cf. 125, Clifford Orwin and James Stoner, 'Neoconstitutionalism? Rawls, Dworkin, and Nozick', in *Confronting the Constitution*, ed. Allan Bloom (Washington, DC, 1990), 439.

44 Alasdair McIntyre, *After Virtue* (Notre Dame, 1981), chs. 4–6.

45 On Rorty, consider e.g. *Contingency, Irony, and Solidarity* (Cambridge, 1989); and 'The Priority of Democracy to Philosophy' in Rorty's *Objectivity, Relativism, and Truth* (Cambridge, 1991), pp. 175–96. On Strauss, see e.g., *Liberalism Ancient and Modern* (New York, 1968), vii. Reiman in his n. 9 quite mistakes my point in contrasting Rawls and Strauss as two paths from similar doubts about the enlightenment project. I meant merely to highlight how paradoxical Rawls's path was, not *ipso facto* to condemn it, as I believe my text clearly says.

46 Cf. Reiman, 'Rawls's New Conception', whose formulations come perilously close to reducing *PL* to a mere *modus vivendi*.

47 The close parallel to Rawls I's Anti-utilitarian Principle should be noted.

48 In s. II, Reiman puts forth a genuinely interesting construal of *PL*, but as they say at the assay office, 'it may glitter, but it ain't Rawls.' He has completely reconstructed Rawls's argument and turned it essentially into a prudential argument motivated by considerations Rawls rejects and lacking the elements Rawls II considers essential. Reiman's response to the Tocquevillian problem depends on accepting into the theory and giving weight to envy (the feeling of offence at having less of something than others or, in Reiman's phrase, 'the craving for equality'), a passion Rawls explicitly rejects as no part of a theory of *justice* in *TJ* and, I believe, implicitly continues to do in *PL* (see *TJ* s. 25, p. 143). Conversely, Reiman's reconstruction omits the most characteristic features of *PL*, especially the moral powers.

49 Notice the reappearance here of the line of thought (and problems) typical of *TJ*.

50 Cf. *PL*, VI.4.1, p. 223, and V.3, pp. 228–9, which suggest an even greater diminution of the Difference Principle.

51 *Pace*, Reiman, 'Rawls's New Conception, '; it is not I but Rawls who introduces the language of needs, although not the language of 'basic needs', as per Reiman. His sketch of the 'practical virtues of the difference principle' (ibid.) is an indication of the *modus vivendi* character of his reconstruction of Rawls's new theory. Perhaps Reiman is correct to argue that I have been too generous to Rawls II in my assessment of his new argument for the Difference principle.

I meant mainly to bring out the hopeful consequence of the absence of the Demand of Justice. That was merely a tentative move in my argument as my discussion below shows.

52 I thus agree (more or less) with Reiman, 'Rawls's New Conception', regarding Rawls's handling of the good in *PL*; our apparent disagreement stems from the fact that he replies to my criticism of *TJ* with an argument from *PL*.

53 Cf. e.g., Richard B. Parker, 'The Jurisprudential Uses of John Rawls,' in *Constitutionalism*, ed. J. Roland Pennock and John Chapman (New York, 1979), p. 274. Also consider Robert Lane's classic revelation of American attitudes about equality in *Political Ideology* (New York, Free Press, 1962).

54 Reiman's reply to this criticism depends on his very idiosyncratic reconstruction of Rawls's position. I have here addressed Rawls himself, and I do not believe Reiman's reply touches my point.

55 A very similar problem besets Rawls's treatment of the good within *Political Liberalism*. Here too he illicitly slides from agreement on a concept to a claimed agreement on a conception. There is no consensus regarding the propriety of severing conceptions of the good from all the myriad attributes of citizenship Rawls asserts there is. Moreover, there is no widespread agreement that the *whats* are generally irrelevant, or that the ultimate expression of human freedom is the freedom to redefine conceptions of the good. Here too he has derived a crucial part of his new system from a concealed line of thought carried over from his old system. Cf. Charles Larmore, 'Political Liberalism', *Political Theory* 18 (August 1990), p. 340.

56 Reiman raises a series of important points addressed to my questions about Rawls II's moral methodology. He raises larger questions than I can pursue in a note, so I will limit myself to a few short points: 1) I do not in fact argue that Rawls's system amounts to a *modus vivendi*. I do believe that is true for Reiman's reconstruction of it, however; 2) on the crucial issue, Reiman says, 'I agree with Zuckert that appeal to ideas in the political culture runs afoul of the logical distinction between is and ought.' That was my point, exactly; 3) he rightly insists that the desire for 'more' than an appeal to dominant ideas is not of itself sufficient to produce this 'more'. I agree, and I further agree with him that his own book represents a powerful attempt to supply a notion of the 'more'; 4) Reiman nonetheless presents a (half-hearted?) defence of Rawls's procedure on the ground that when all is said and done, such appeals to culture may be all that is possible, and that, therefore, this must count as a solution to the is-ought problem, even though he has conceded it isn't. This strikes me as roughly on a par with declaring AIDS cured when we extend patients' lives because that's all we seem able to achieve. If a genuine moral theory is unavailable or impossible, as Reiman's version of post-modernism suggests, then the more honest, courageous and philosophical response is to say just that.

4

John Rawls's New Conception of the Problem of Limited Government: Reply to Michael Zuckert

JEFFREY REIMAN

'What is crucial is always to recognize the limits of the political and the practical.'
John Rawls, *Political Liberalism*

On the question whether egalitarian liberalism is compatible with limited government, Michael Zuckert finds the situation dangerous but not hopeless. There might be a way of combining the two—but, theoretically and politically, the tendency is for the egalitarianism of egalitarian liberalism to swamp the limits of limited government. Zuckert gives two general reasons for this worry: first, Nozick's slogan that 'liberty upsets patterns' which he takes to imply that egalitarian patterns will upset liberty; and secondly, de Tocqueville's prediction that democratic states will be ever and increasingly subject to popular pressure for government intervention to reduce the differences between people's fates.

Of these two, I don't think Nozick's slogan should cause much fear, and Zuckert doesn't seem to take it very seriously. It is easily countered, as Rawls himself does, by pointing out that institutional arrangements for reducing inequality could work by infrequent and quite predictable transfers. De Tocqueville's prediction is harder to side-step, and Zuckert takes it as warrant for investigating Rawls's versions of the marriage of egalitarianism liberalism and limited government—in *A Theory of Justice* and *Political Liberalism*—as a test case to see if either has the intellectual resources to stem the supposedly ineluctable tide toward government growth. Zuckert contends that Rawls fails the test; but I shall argue that, in *Political Liberalism*, Rawls has redesigned the test in an interesting and provocative way, and that, on the new test, he scores rather well.

By now it is well known that, in *A Theory of Justice*, Rawls has defended two principles of justice, which taken together would provide the foundation for a moderately egalitarian, liberal, and limited government; these are the liberty principle (which holds that everyone should be guaranteed the maximum amount of liberty compatible with the same for everyone else), and the difference principle (which holds that economic and other social goods should be distributed equally except in so far as an unequal distribution is to everyone's advantage, in particular, that of the worst-off group in the unequal arrangement). The liberty principle limits government by declaring large areas of human activity free, and the difference principle does so by keeping the equalizing tendency within manageable confines. To shore up the principle of liberty, which Rawls takes to have priority over the difference principle, Rawls argues for the importance of liberty over further growth in social wealth (after a certain modern level is reached), and for the priority of the right over the good. The priority of the right over the good is the idea that it is in citizens' interests to limit the coercive institutions of society to the minimum necessary to protect liberty and implement the difference principle (that is, to promote justice, the right) rather than to allow the state to enforce any of the citizens' divergent conceptions of the good life.

How one sees *Political Liberalism* (hereafter *PL*) depends in large part on how well one thinks that the task of *A Theory of Justice* (hereafter *TJ*) has been accomplished. In this respect, there is a very important difference between the way Zuckert and I see the relation between *TJ* and *PL*, which needs to be stated at the outset so that the structure of my reply to Zuckert will be understandable. Zuckert thinks that the arguments in *TJ* for the two principles of justice fail for reasons that he sets forth in chapter three. Accordingly, he thinks of *PL* as replacing these arguments with new ones. He thinks these arguments are superior to the *TJ* arguments, but criticizes Rawls's attempt to defend them as based on ideas implicit in our democratic public culture.

I think that the arguments for the two principles of justice in *TJ*—particularly for the difference principle and the priority of right over good—do quite well. Thus, I see *PL* as supplementing *TJ*, rather than replacing it. On my view, then, the arguments of *TJ* are presupposed by *PL*, which in turn gives those arguments a new, and quite practical, twist. For example, I shall argue that *TJ* shows the difference principle to be a plausible principle of distributive justice. *PL* doesn't replace this argument; on the contrary, *PL* assumes its validity. What is distinctive to *PL* is that it gets us to see the justice of the difference principle as a practical virtue: its justice makes it a likely point of political agreement, and thus an element in a workable conception of limited government. A similar point will be made about the principle of liberty, in particular, its defence via the priority of the right over the good. The result is that I think the two principles of justice are sound enough to support a viable theory of limited government.

I shall proceed as follows. In section I, 'The Difference Principle, the Right and the Good', in *A Theory of Justice*,' I argue that Rawls's arguments for the difference principle and the priority of right over good in *TJ* survive Zuckert's criticisms of them. Since Zuckert's misconceptions about these doctrines are held by others, this exercise may be of independent interest. In section II, 'Limited Government in *Political Liberalism*,' I present a reading of Rawls's undertaking meant to show that it embodies a new, and quite practical, conception of the problem of limited government. I then argue that this new conception requires us to emphasize the practical implications of the *TJ* arguments for the difference principle and the priority of right over good, and that, when we do so, we see that they offer a plausible basis for limited government. In section III, 'Moral Vision or *Modus Vivendi?*,' I take up Zuckert's critique of Rawls's grounding of this theory in ideas in our democratic public culture, and I defend Rawls's view that the theory is after all a moral conception and not a mere *modus vivendi*.

Though I defend Rawls's theory here, in both its early and later statements, I must say that I do not think that Rawls has always expressed his views in the best way, or even made explicit their strengths. Thus, throughout, I take the liberty of restating Rawls's views in ways that I think make them clearest and most defensible. I believe that I say nothing that is not implicit in Rawls's own statements, nevertheless those who think that I have gone beyond Rawls's letter and spirit are welcome to regard the conception that emerges here as Rawlsian-inspired instead of as Rawlsian. Most importantly, however, I think that, when confronting the imperfections of Rawls's presentation, we should bear in mind the observation that Louis Althusser made apropos of the difficulty of Karl Marx's writings: if things look clearer to us now than they did to him, remember that we have had an advantage that he lacked, namely, his writings to read.

I. THE DIFFERENCE PRINCIPLE, THE RIGHT AND THE GOOD, IN *A THEORY OF JUSTICE*

Zuckert says early in chapter three, and I agree, that '[t]he Difference Principle is probably the signature doctrine of the Rawls of *A Theory of Justice.*' He then argues that 'the Difference Principle contradicts two of the chief grounding thoughts, or foundational principles on which Rawls constructs his theory.' Zuckert labels these foundational principles, the 'Anti-utilitarian Principle' and the 'Demand of Justice'. In this section, I shall show that the difference principle was never seriously imperiled by either the Anti-utilitarian Principle or the Demand of Justice. Then, I shall turn to Zuckert's critique of the arguments for the priority of right over good in *TJ* and show that it fails as well. This will set the stage for a much more optimistic reading of *PL*, in the sections that follow.

What Zuckert calls the Anti-utilitarian Principle is Rawls's claim that individuals are inviolable, that the greater welfare of others cannot justify the sacrifice of the individual. The Demand of Justice, says Zuckert, is that 'justice cannot be the rewarding of undeserved inequalities, more broadly, of undeserved qualities' (it is important to note that these are Zuckert's words, not Rawls's). This Demand is important because Rawls denies that people deserve their native endowments or the particular social and family circumstances into which they happen to be born. Says Zuckert, 'Rawls's point is quite radical. What one is due cannot rest of any of the natural, social, or other proscribed bases of desert.'

The difference principle is said by Zuckert to contradict these two notions for the following reasons. It collides with the Anti-utilitarian Principle by 'treating the morally arbitrary "distribution of natural talents as a common asset" according to which the less favoured derive (some of) the benefit from the natural and acquired talents, abilities, and efforts of the more favoured' (the words in double quotation marks are from *TJ*). The difference principle runs into trouble with the Demand of Justice because it allows the more talented to gain more than the less as long as the less talented are getting more from any inequality than they would have without it. Says Zuckert, '[t]o reward the greater contribution [of the more talented] is in fact to reward the "undeserved" bases of those contributions, and thus to violate the Demand of Justice.' I think that Zuckert is wrong on both counts.

The difference principle doesn't violate the Anti-utilitarian principle because it in no way assumes the strange doctrine that natural talents are a common asset. Though Rawls says some things that have invited this canard, I think it is not true of the actual working of the difference principle and in no way necessary to Rawls's theory (in the old or new testament). For example, no one is forced to train or work one way or another as would follow if talents were really thought to be a common asset. What is treated as a common asset by the difference principle are the rewards to talents, not the talents themselves. And, unlike talents, rewards do belong to the rest of society, the ones who pay for talented labour, and thus the rewards are appropriately treated as a common asset, that is, paid out subject to standards that work to everyone's benefit.[1]

Nor does the difference principle collide with the Demand of Justice. In fact, here Zuckert has made two mistakes: a simple logical error and a deeper philosophical one. The logical error is that, from the fact that a distributive system ends up rewarding the more talented more, it does not follow that it is rewarding them because they have greater talents. For instance, a system that rewards people more the more effort they exert, will probably reward people more the more they sweat. It does not follow that the system is treating the amount of perspiration as the basis of desert.

A system like Rawls's that rewards the more talented strictly as an incentive to increase the well-being of the others is taking the contribution to the others as the basis of desert. Actually the connection between rewards and contributions is looser than this suggests, because Rawls does not envisage that people will be rewarded directly for their contributions to the well-being of others. Rather, rewards will be designed to bring about a scheme of production and consumption that in its overall effect realizes the difference principle. Strictly speaking, people are rewarded for doing what this scheme promises to reward, which no doubt they are helped to do if they have greater talents. Since the scheme will work in a general way, some without greater talents will get greater rewards and some with greater talents will not, which further supports the idea that it is not the possession of greater talents as such that is the basis of desert. There will, to be sure, be a correlation between rewards and talents, as there will be between rewards and perspiration, with the same implications. Though those who qualify for greater rewards under the difference principle will generally be the more talented, they will not be rewarded because they are more talented. Since the Demand of Justice is about the basis of desert and not about the characteristics of who gets rewarded, the difference principle doesn't violate it.

Zuckert's philosophical error is his misunderstanding of the place of desert in Rawls's theory. Zuckert is mistaken in saying that for Rawls, 'What one is due cannot rest on any of the natural, social, or other proscribed bases of desert.' Rawls writes:

There is a natural inclination to object that those better situated deserve their greater advantages whether or not they are to the benefit of others. At this point *it is necessary to be clear about the notion of desert. It is perfectly true that given a just system of cooperation* . . ., those who, with the prospect of improving their situation, have done what the system announces that it will reward *are entitled to their advantages.* In this sense the more fortunate have a claim to their better situation; their claims are legitimate expectations established by social institutions, and the community is obligated to meet them. But *this sense of desert presupposes the existence of a cooperative scheme*; it is irrelevant to the question whether in the first place the scheme is to be designed in accordance with the difference principle or some other criterion. *TJ*, p. 103 (emphasis added).

Rawls is not claiming that more talented people cannot deserve greater rewards, nor is he claiming that what people are due cannot be based on natural or social facts about them. He is claiming that desert is a derivative rather than a primitive moral notion: it is derived from the terms of just co-operation. Accordingly, the terms of just co-operation must be spelled out first, and thus without assuming in advance that more talented people automatically deserve greater rewards. This is the force of the so-called Demand of Justice.[2] This is confirmed by the fact that, while the veil of ignorance rules out knowledge of people's own natural talents, it does not rule out discussion of such talents as grounds of desert. The effect of the veil is to force defenders of rules specifying natural or social bases of desert to justify them to the people who will be subject to them, when those people do not know whether or how they will in particular benefit from those rules. And this amounts to showing that the rules are just.

If a principle of distribution is to be justified in the original position behind a veil of ignorance before appeals to desert can be made, it will be a principle of mutual benefit. And that is precisely what the difference principle is, in the following important sense. Imagine that an economic system were a series of exchanges between more and less talented parties, M's and L's, who start from an equal base-line B. One such exchange leaves M's with B + 10 and L's with B + 1. Suppose, however, that M's would have settled for B + 9, with L's still ending up with B + 1. The free market would allow either exchange as just, since both sets of parties end up with more than they started with in both exchanges. But the difference principle would only allow the second exchange (if these were the only two possible), because the possibility of the second shows that the first contains an inequality that does not benefit the worse off. The increase in inequality in M's going from B + 9 to B + 10 is not productive of a benefit that was not already available to L's when M's get B + 9. (This is not even to mention the fact that if M's would be satisfied with B + 9, then the extra unit that would have brought them to B + 10 can be used to improve L's condition to B + 2.)

This (drastically oversimplified) example shows the important moral difference between the difference principle and the free market: in exchanges governed by the free market, all parties must gain something relative to their situations prior to the transaction. But this allows great gains on one side as long as there is any gain at all on the other. And this disparity may be due to arbitrary advantages, such as the possibilities for education had by the more talented or the neediness of the less talented. Furthermore, such disparities accumulate by giving better-off people even greater leverage to increase their economic advantage in the future, and that of their children, which translates into growing economic and, eventually, political inequality. By contrast, the difference principle effectively holds that every measurable increment of gain on one side should be matched by some increment on the other—not an equal increment, but something. Thus, in contrast to the free market, the difference principle insists on a symmetry (not an equality) of gains on both sides and holds that gains on one side that are no longer necessary to produce gains on the other are excessive.[3] The difference principle is chosen in the original position because, in the way just outlined, it is a more thoroughgoing principle of mutual benefit than the free market (and the other eligible candidates, which will not be considered here). This is surely a plausible way of showing that it is a just principle. Nothing in the argument assumes that the talents of the more talented are owned by the society. The more talented are free to refuse to contribute their talents. The society simply specifies how much others will pay for those talents (though it may do this after the fact by means of taxation). Likewise, nothing in the argument assumes that people cannot deserve things as a result of their greater talent, only that they cannot deserve them automatically for that reason without it first being the case that justice permits or requires it.[4]

In order to refute the difference principle, it will have to be shown that there is some true basis of desert (logically) prior to justice.[5] Since bases for desert are controversial, this is not very promising. This implies that Rawls's view that desert should be treated as derivative from a conception of justice (as mutual benefit) is worthy of more respect than its critics have given it.[6] Moreover, in the conditions of moral dissensus which constitute the setting for *PL*, the difficulty of agreeing on the bases of desert is greater and the appeal of Rawls's approach grows apace.

The liberty principle is supported by two sorts of arguments. The first sort aim at proving that, once a certain level of well-being is achieved, it is no longer rational to curtail liberty in order to achieve yet higher levels of well-being. The second sort aim at establishing the priority of the right over the good. I agree with Zuckert that Rawls's arguments for the priority of liberty over improvements in well-being fail. I think, however, that the argument for the priority of right over good works and is enough to make the case for the liberty principle.

The priority of right over good supports the liberty principle because it means that parties in the original position will favour rules of interaction that allow each to pursue his own good as far as compatible with the same for everyone else, over rules that impose a particular conception of the good on all. Zuckert has two objections to this. First, he objects that it is based on the arbitrary exclusion from the original position of the parties' own conceptions of the good (they know that they have conceptions of good, but they don't know what they are). Since the parties have an interest in pursuing their conception of the good (the details of which they don't know), they will naturally refuse to agree to rules embodying some conception of the good, since these may rule out their own. At the same time, the parties must have some conception of the good so that they can agree on anything. Here Zuckert objects to Rawls's stipulation of a 'thin theory' of goods, primarily material goods (mainly money in a market economy). Zuckert claims that it is biased against people who have spiritual conceptions of the good, 'Locke over Thoreau or Mother Teresa,' and, it 'fails to take account of the fact that the same amount of some primary goods goes much further toward satisfying some conceptions of a good life (Thoreau's) than others (Donald Trump's).'

In holding that it is arbitrary to exclude from the original position the

parties' knowledge of their conceptions of the good, Zuckert follows
William Galston who claims that impartiality in the original position
doesn't require ignorance. Since 'unanimity is required, each individual
can block an outcome that is adverse to his or her convictions'. But Zuckert
fails to understand Rawls's method. He overlooks the fact that the parties
are not choosing for themselves as real people. They are imagined beings
choosing in a representative capacity, that is, for real people, none of
whom are in the original position, and some of whom aren't yet born. Any
spectrum of actual conceptions of the good presented in the original position will likely leave out others held by the real people who will be subject
to the rules that emerge from the original position. Allowing the imagi-
nary parties in the original position to put forth 'their' conceptions of the
good jeopardizes the interest of real people in living according to their
(with no quotation marks) conceptions of the good. The same consideration works with equal force against Zuckert's related objection that 'there
is no reason the parties in the original position should be debarred from
deliberating about the good just because they are ignorant of their own
conception'. And, of course, it rules out of the original position Zuckert's
imagined Calvin or Luther who are both willing to insist on orthodoxy
even at the risk of being subject to the wrong one.

Zuckert similarly objects to Rawls's claim that the parties' conceptions
of the good are excluded because they are 'morally irrelevant from the
standpoint of justice'. Here Zuckert follows Nagel who remarks on the
seeming oddness of viewing the parties' conceptions of the good as
morally irrelevant. But this is another version of the same mistake that I
pointed out in the previous paragraph. It would be odd to say that the
good is irrelevant to justice, but Rawls doesn't say that. He says that the
parties' conceptions are irrelevant, and they are. That these parties hold
these conceptions is irrelevant precisely because they are not the real people who will be ruled by them, when the original position exercise is completed. Thus again, excluding knowledge of conceptions of the good from
the original position serves the aim of justice because it protects real people from being forced to conform to other people's (Zuckert's?, Galston's?,
Nagel's?, Calvin's?, Luther's?) conceptions of the good at the expense of
their own actual conceptions. Thus, it is far from an arbitrary exclusion in
the original position.

As for the alleged bias in Rawls's thin theory of the good, I think that
Zuckert makes a mistake here that is akin to the one that leads him (and
others) to think that the difference principle treats talents as a common
asset. It is the failure to see that goods must be produced, and thus that the
parties the original position do not only consider the goods they might
get, but the effort they might be required to put into producing goods for
others. In this light, it is reasonable for the parties to think of goods as

satisfying normal needs since those are the needs they are likely to have, and doing so protects them from having to devote extra work for people with exotic needs. Likewise, it is reasonable that the parties not take into account the special needs of the spiritual life, since such a life will either need very little (Thoreau's or Mother Teresa's), or more than people should be required as a matter of justice to provide (the Pope's).

In short, on the basis of *TJ* (although not always with the help of Rawls's explicit presentation), I think that the difference principle is a plausible principle of justice in that it is thoroughgoingly mutually beneficial, and the priority of right over good is a plausible principle of justice in that it protects people from being subjected to other people's conceptions of the good against their will. Rawls's arguments for the difference principle and the priority of right over good withstand Zuckert's objections, and survive into *PL*, where they receive a new practical twist and to which we now turn.

II. LIMITED GOVERNMENT IN *POLITICAL LIBERALISM*

In *Political Liberalism*, Rawls aims to put forth, as the title suggests, a version of liberalism that is, we might say, merely political. It is designed not to persuade everyone of the truth of a liberal moral vision, but to specify the terms of political interaction among people who differ in their overall—what Rawls calls 'comprehensive'—moral theories or world-views. This is, then, a conception of limited government twice over: first, it is limited in that, like any liberalism, it carves out large areas of human activity that are to be free of coercive, and thus government, intervention; secondly, it is limited in that the conception itself is urged only to apply to a realm of political activity in a way that leaves people largely free to follow their comprehensive outlooks in other realms of life.

To see the force and novelty of this 'political' conception of liberalism, and thus limited government, I think it helps to consider an implication of de Tocqueville's prediction. Not only is de Tocqueville correct about the democratic trend toward greater government intervention to promote equality, but the development of industrialism—which de Tocqueville could only dimly see looming—has made the trend even stronger. However, this trend doesn't just threaten limited governments that aim to be egalitarian—it threatens all limited governments generally, though not equally. It is downright malignant to Lockean-type limited governments. If you set up a purely Lockean government today, with the state limited to little more than the standard police functions and the economy set largely free, you will have to build into it a significant democratic component, since no modern populace consisting of a large number of industrial workers and professionals will stand for less.[7] And then you will get de Tocqueville's predicted democratic trend, insisting that the limits be crossed. If you try to block the trend by building Lockean limits on government action into the constitution, the people will change the constitution. They will either amend it or tear it up.

If the union of limited government and egalitarian liberalism is rendered fragile because of de Tocqueville's prediction, old-fashioned Lockean-style limited government—that makes little or no effort to bring equality into the economy—is rendered obsolete. Dead on arrival. The implication of de Tocqueville's prediction, in short, is that the only sort of limited government that has a chance is one that is doing enough for equality to satisfy the popular craving.

This means that it is fruitless to read Rawls's attempt at joining egalitarianism and limited government as an alternative to Locke's, to be measured against the Lockean version as if one could finally choose one or the other. Rawls has, I believed, tried in effect to find the only recipe for limited government that can work in the modern, post-Tocquevillean, period. To fail to see this is to underestimate the historical specificity of Rawls's project in *PL*, and the sheer, almost unphilosophical, practicality of it. It is to fail to see how very modern—even post-modern—Rawls's new conception of the task of establishing limited government is. To see that, let us go a bit further in contrasting it with the Lockean conception of the task.

We may think of Lockean limited government as functionally limited and constitutionally fixed. The government is limited to the performance of a specific number of well-known functions, among which are not included such things as guaranteeing fair opportunity, education, health care, and rough equality of political influence. And, this limitation is fixed by a constitution which (as ours once hoped to do) lists the areas in which government can act, holding the rest implicitly or explicitly out of bounds. Now democracy per de Tocqueville renders both functional limitation and constitutional fixation inherently impermanent. The functions will be extended and the constitution will be fixed if necessary.

What then can replace functional limitation and constitutional fixation if government is to be limited? In place of functional limitation, there is what I shall call 'value limitation': government is limited in the range of values it can enforce. And in place of constitutional fixation, there is what I shall call 'conversational fixation': the range of values is fixed by an ongoing, widely shared public discussion about the terms of co-operation. Of course, value limitation may make use of functional limits, and conversational fixation will surely use a constitution to make as permanent as possible its deepest shared principles.

Value limitation and conversational fixation occur in a historically specific context marked by two factors, which for the present and foreseeable

future constrain the possibilities for limited government: first, people disagree on their conceptions of the good and this is for the foreseeable future
an unchangeable feature of the political landscape. Rawls lists a number of
'burdens of judgement' (*PL*, pp. 54–8) which point to the normalcy of such
disagreement ('the normal result of exercise of human reason within the
framework of . . . free institutions', (*PL*, p. xvi)), as well as to the bleak
prospect for overcoming it. There is not going to be agreement on conceptions of the good, visions of the world, moral codes, or metaphysical systems generally, in fact, and because of this, it is unrealistic, tendentious,
and plainly dangerous to insist on the definitive, universally-binding
nature of one's own vision. I will call this the 'post-modern dissensus'.

Secondly, there is the fact—not necessary or essential or universal, but
very widely the case—that people generally hate to have other people's
values imposed on them and they will generally refrain from doing that to
others in return for not having it done to them. I will call this the 'liberal
fact'. This fact underlies Rawls's notion of 'reasonableness'—understood
as including the desire to live with others on terms that all can accept (*PL*,
p. 50, *inter alia*).[8]

Three facts, then, frame (my reading of) Rawls's attempt in *Political
Liberalism* to formulate the liberal project as that of finding the workable
terms for a morally limited government: (1) the post-modern dissensus,
(2) the liberal fact, and (3) the apparent correctness of de Tocqueville's prediction. In face of the recognition that popular forces will press governments to decrease inequality and enforce controversial conceptions of the
good, and of the recognition that no conception of the good will be universally agreed upon, the task is to find the (more limited) set of (political)
values that all people could agree on having imposed in order to protect
themselves against having the values of others imposed on them.

But note, once this is taken on in the context of the post-modern dissensus, it cannot be viewed as a philosophical problem with a philosophical solution. Rawls's proposals—the priority of right over good, the
priority of the guarantee of equal liberty, the difference principle—are not
put forth as such a solution. They are put forth as a practically achievable
basis for political accord. Thus, much as Rawls's political liberalism is a
theory of limited government twice over, it is also doubly political: it is a
theory for the political realm as a limited realm of human life, and the
argument for it is political as well. It aims to provide grounds that we and
our fellows citizens can actually agree upon, and continue to agree upon,
in the face of the tendency to enlarge government and encroach on liberty.

The doubly political nature of Rawls's project implies that the difference
principle and the liberty principle are now practical proposals that must
be evaluated by their ability to attract agreement in an ongoing political
conversation, across dissensus, in the light of the liberal fact. But, this

practical political orientation does not replace the arguments in *TJ*, it carries forth those arguments recast in a way that emphasizes their practical force. Let us then look at the arguments for the difference principle and for the liberty principle (namely, the argument for the priority of right over good) in this light.

When Zuckert takes up *Political Liberalism*, he quotes Rawls saying 'I presuppose . . . the same egalitarian conception of justice as before' (*PL*, pp. 6–7) and 'the structure and content of *A Theory of Justice* . . . remains substantially the same' (*PL*, p. xvi). Zuckert then claims that the difference principle is 'on much more solid ground' in *PL* than it was in *TJ*. What is interesting here is that all that Zuckert says of this more solid ground is that the difference principle is now justified (in *PL*) as supplying people's needs as citizens: 'below a certain level of material and social well-being . . ., people simply cannot take part in society as citizens' (*PL*, p. 166). But it should be evident that the difference principle goes beyond providing 'a certain level of material and social well-being'. It is an equalizing principle, not merely a principle of satisfying basic needs. Thus, what Zuckert calls more solid ground isn't solid enough to support the difference principle, and if Rawls is really presupposing the same egalitarian conception of justice in *PL* as he did in *TJ*, then there must be more going for it than meets Zuckert's eye. This 'more' lies in virtues of the difference principle in *TJ*, which Zuckert has underestimated.

Think of these virtues now in the framework of a public discussion in which the only hope of limiting government is to establish value limitations by conversational fixation. Here the thoroughgoing way in which the difference principle is a principle of mutual benefit is also a practical virtue in getting people to see that equality in terms of the difference principle is enough, especially in light of the legitimate fears that inspire the liberal fact. Moreover, that the difference principle is based on mutual benefit without appeal to controversial claims about the natural or social bases of desert makes it a natural candidate for agreement under conditions of post-modern dissensus.

The difference principle answers the craving for equality while allowing for liberty in choice of profession, differential rewards to different levels of ability, and a host of efficiencies with which economists are familiar. It balances the more talented ones' wish for more with the less talented ones' wish for as much. And it limits equality at the point at which the worst-off would lose if they insisted on greater equality. These facts make the difference principle capable of satisfying the craving for equality within the limits of limited government.

Zuckert thinks that the argument for the priority of right over good in *PL*, where it is based on citizens' nature as individuals who can change and thus revise their conceptions of the good, is stronger than that in *TJ*, where it is based on peoples' interest in protecting there ability to pursue their own conception of the good. He thinks this, in part, because he thinks that the latter argument did not provide a basis for excluding conceptions of the good from the original position, and thus for principles giving priority to right over good. Thus, Zuckert welcomes a new basis for this priority in Rawls's political conception of the parties as citizens with certain moral powers, including that of changing and revising their conceptions of the good.

However, once it is seen that the *TJ* argument did give good grounds for excluding the parties' knowledge of their conceptions of the good from the original position, then it is also clear that the *TJ* and *PL* arguments for the priority of right over good, are, practically speaking, the same. Citizens' interest in their ability to revise their conceptions of the good is a rough political equivalent of the earlier interest in being able to live according to their own conception of the good. Why care about citizens' ability to revise their conceptions of the good if not to protect their ability to live according to their actual conceptions? For this, we establish everyone's right to follow his or her conception to the greatest extent compatible with the same for everyone else—which is to say, the liberty principle.

Zuckert says (in a note) that he agrees with this argument but that it is a *PL* answer to his criticism of a *TJ* argument. But that is just where we differ. I think that the *TJ* argument was that it is an injustice to impose some people's conception of the good on others against their will, and all that *PL* does is to force us to see the practical implication of this argument, not replace it whole cloth. The priority of right over good is a practical accommodation to the dissensus over conceptions of the good coupled with the liberal fact that people hate to be forced to do things against their will and rarely benefit from a war of all against all compared to what they could have had by compromise. Nonetheless, the practical accommodation is likely to work precisely because it is unjust for some to impose their conceptions on others, and thus it is just to live subject to conditions under which each can pursue his or her own conception of the good freely to the greatest extent compatible with the same for the others.

The rights thus established find no foundation in natural rights, and they are in fact a batch of rights whose mix and boundaries are not eternally fixed. Zuckert thinks this invites encroachment of fundamental rights that is barred in a Lockean system. But, after de Tocqueville, the Lockean system is a paper tiger. No paper barrier will protect rights from the people if they decide to encroach them. The only thing that can do this is a society-wide conversation in which citizens can see that existing rights protect everyone from having other people's conceptions of the good forced on them, and that everyone's common interest—as people who don't want to have other people's values forced on them—lies in keeping strong legal barriers against this, and, thus in keeping the government limited in its reach.

Earlier I wrote that I agreed with Zuckert that Rawls's *TJ* arguments for the priority of liberty over all improvements in welfare were unsuccessful, and I suggested that the priority of the right over the good would be enough to shore up the liberty principle against encroachments in the name of further growth in social wealth. The argument for this claim partakes of the emphasis on practicality highlighted in *PL*. Allowing limitations on liberty when needed to increase overall productivity effectively turns the protective boundaries around liberty into temporary and movable barricades. If the state were to be governed by perfectly wise and just philosopher kings, it might be all right to allow them continually to relocate these barricades. However, given that the state will be governed by normal humans with all their standard foibles, citizens' interest in being able freely to pursue their own conception of the good gives them an interest as well in a system of liberty with fixed and known limits. Moreover, while Rawls was over-optimistic in thinking that gains in welfare will never be worth enough to justify restrictions on liberty, there is reason to believe generally that there is more risk to people's ability to pursue their own good from restrictions on their liberty than from limits on their wealth (after a certain level is achieved). These considerations taken together show that, practically speaking, it will be reasonable (at some level of productivity) to protect liberty with fixed boundaries that cannot be moved or crossed in order further to increase wealth.

In sum, when we look at their role in a public conversation about the terms of co-operation, the justification of basic liberties by the fact that they protect people from being forced to live according to other people's vision of the good, and the moderately egalitarian mutually-beneficial symmetry provided by the difference principle (without appeal to disputed bases of desert), are good candidates for convincing a substantial number of citizens that the government is doing enough for equality, and that the benefits of liberty make limiting the government here a wise and mutually beneficial choice.

I think that this shows the combined product of *TJ* and *PL* to be a more promising basis for limited government than Zuckert believes. Before concluding this, however, it is necessary to respond to a number of criticisms that Zuckert raises against the whole project of *PL*.

III. MORAL VISION OR *MODUS VIVENDI*?

Zuckert criticizes the results of *PL* in two basic and interrelated ways. First, he contends that what Rawls calls 'the burdens of judgement'—in effect, the post-modern dissensus—will undermine agreement on terms of political interaction as much as they undermine agreement on comprehensive world views. Secondly, he contends that Rawls's only resource for blocking this undermining is that his political liberalism is based on ideas already implicitly part of 'the public political culture of a democratic society' like our own (*PL*, p. 13; see also, pp. 100–1). Against this, Zuckert says that Rawls's vision of equality manifested in the difference principle is far from implicit in our democratic culture, and further, that by grounding his theory in ideas actually shared in our culture Rawls stumbles on the is-ought boundary. This has the implication that Rawls cannot make good his claim (*PL*, pp. 147–9) that his theory is a moral conception after all, rather than a mere *modus vivendi*. I shall respond to these criticisms in order.

Against the idea that post-modern dissensus will disrupt even agreement on terms of political interaction, I offer the whole practical, political tenor of Rawls's undertaking. As a philosophical exercise, post-modern dissensus is limitless (in its most virulent Derridean strain, it renders unintelligible its own expression). In these terms, there is no reason to think it will stop at the boundary of the political and leave agreement there unscathed. But these are not Rawls's terms. His view is, I think, based on the liberal fact, on the prediction that actual people will give up their claim to impose their comprehensive world views on others in return for security against having those of others imposed on them. (This does seem largely true of modern Western nations, and is arguably true of all nations as they modernize.) If people can understand and see the virtues of such an agreement beyond their other disagreements, then the burdens of judgement will not make it impossible for them to find shareable terms in which to express their agreement. Naturally, there will be continual disagreement about the specific meaning of these terms, as there is about the terms of our Constitution. But, in fact, if not in philosophy, that does not necessarily imply the impossibility of finding workable agreements.

Zuckert takes Rawls's answer to this criticism to be that his theory is built on ideas present in the culture of contemporary liberal democratic societies. And against this answer, Zuckert has two main objections. First, Zuckert claims that the conception of equality embodied in the argument for the difference principle—the effective denial that greater natural endowment, etc., is itself a basis for greater desert—is not part of our political culture's conception of equality. But, of course, if Rawls thought he was just reproducing the ideas already in our political culture, he wouldn't have introduced *Political Liberalism* as a solution to 'the impasse in the democratic tradition' or 'in our recent political history' (*PL*, pp. 338 and 368; also cited by Zuckert). Dispute over bases of desert is surely part of the impasse. What Rawls has tried to do is take other, less disputed, parts of our political culture and show that they support the difference principle as a way out of the impasse over desert. I think that the arguments which I have presented in the previous sections show that Rawls has made quite a strong case for this approach.

Secondly, Zuckert claims that appeal to the ideas in our culture bumps into the is-ought problem. Why should the fact that a view is based on ideas that people actually happen to hold be reason to believe that that view is a true moral vision, a real 'ought'? And if there is no way of claiming a real ought, doesn't Rawls's theory boil down to a mere *modus vivendi*, a non-moral agreement to disagree in order to avoid strife?

In one sense, I agree with Zuckert that appeals to ideas in the culture run afoul of the logical distinction between is and ought. I do so because I share with him the belief that more is possible, that a theory of justice can be defended on surer footing than appeal to ideas in our culture.[9] But it must also be said that both Zuckert and I are here banging our heads against a very resilient feature of the contemporary intellectual scene, namely, the view that any moral argument we make invariably appeals to the values and to the criteria for valid argumentation that happen to be endorsed in our culture. Any attempt to show that these values and criteria have validity beyond the culture will only refute itself, since it too will appeal to our actually shared moral and epistemological understandings. If one holds this prevailing view, Rawls's appeal to ideas in the culture looks different than it does to dissenters like Zuckert and me. For those who hold the prevailing view, however, appeal to ideas in the culture is all we ever had—it's the best we were ever able to do, and it has given us whatever leverage we ever had to pass over the is-ought frontier. If it can do that, it can do as much as Rawls needs.

What this means is that Zuckert's 'is-ought' objection to Rawls here is really an objection to the entire philosophical world view which denies that we can ever get beyond our own culture, at least on moral issues. This is the world view within which Rawls is operating. But to deny this world view, given the power and pervasiveness of the arguments for it, one must show that more is possible. Just wishing or stomping one's feet won't do. Until someone shows that a genuinely transcultural moral theory is possible, Rawls is entitled to appeal to the ideas in the culture as the best appeal available—both to show that political agreement is possible and that such agreement is, after all, a moral agreement and not just a *modus vivendi*.

Be that as it may, I think that there is a better way of defending the claim that Rawls's conception of limited government is a moral conception and not just a *modus vivendi*. To see this, note that the suspicion of being only a *modus vivendi* can apply both to the content of Rawls's conception and to the ground of its appeal. One might think that the conception itself is nothing more than a pragmatic compromise, a non-moral agreement to disagree peacefully rather than risk conflict. Or, one might accept that the conception itself is a moral one, but think that its appeal to people is simply as a pragmatic compromise to avoid conflict, rather than an appeal to their moral judgement.

Against the first suspicion, it seems clear to me that Rawls's theory is still a theory of justice, and a powerful one at that. I can say this, where Zuckert cannot, precisely because I have maintained throughout that the arguments from *TJ* are largely successful and must be understood to be carried forth into *PL*. The difference principle is a principle of justice because it is a thoroughgoing principle of mutual benefit, all the more attractive if one accepts the idea that desert is derivative from justice. The liberty principle is a principle of justice because it protects everyone alike from being forced to conform to other people's conception of the good life at the expense of their own. Like the difference principle, this principle has a kind of reciprocal, mutually beneficial structure, in which each gives up the claim to impose his view on others in return for a like guarantee from them in return. Thus, irrespective of the ground of its appeal, the liberal theory of *PL* is still a vision of justice—a moral conception.

As to the suspicion that this theory's appeal is no more than as a non-moral compromise to avoid strife, I will say two things. First, I think that the justice—the reciprocal, mutually beneficial nature—of the theory is part of what might make it a successful compromise. Only if we think that people will see the even handedness of the theory, will we think that it might work as a *modus vivendi*. This amounts to saying that the theory's very success as a *modus vivendi* depends on its being more than a *modus vivendi*, but a moral conception. And this applies to its appeal as well. People will only agree to disagree on Rawls's terms if they see the fairness of those terms. And I believe that they can see that, even if those terms are less than what they believe to be the best arrangement possible.

Secondly, Rawls imagines that a liberal system like his might start off as a *modus vivendi* and eventually change into more, as people came to see the intrinsic virtues of democratic institutions, individual freedom, mutually beneficial exchanges, and so on. People, though starting out merely putting up with such liberalism as a compromise to avoid strife might, after seeing its positive qualities, develop rational moral allegiance to it. I think that this hope is valid, and it implies that, even if allegiance is pragmatic at first, it might become moral in time. A limited liberal government that obtains agreement under the conditions of post-modern dissensus in light of the liberal fact might, as people lived in it and learned its virtues, come to win their rational moral allegiance. People just might learn that there is something they share with one another beyond the post-modern dissensus, a dignity worth respecting in others even when they disagree with one another about the good life. Perhaps post-modern liberal limited government will give us the historical schooling we need to graduate beyond post-modernism.

NOTES

1 That Rawls's treatment of rewards as a common asset is so often mistaken as treatment of talents as a common asset is very revealing. Aside from Rawls's own contributions to this misunderstanding, I think it results from a tendency among certain defenders of capitalism (not only, but surely including, Robert Nozick) to think that (a) free markets are a natural arrangement while everything else is unnatural, and thus (b) whatever people earn on the free market is a kind of natural fruit of their talent. But free markets are as much a product of government policy as any other kind of economic system. And what people earn for their talents will depend on many things, like how much education they have had and how needy their customers are, which are hardly natural outcomes of talents. It is just this sort of thing that the difference principle means to moderate in the direction of justice.

2 Actually, to interpret the Demand of Justice in the way Zuckert does is to saddle Rawls with a truly impossible doctrine. To say, in effect, that nothing can be deserved except on the basis of something itself deserved is to run quickly into vicious regress. Rawls has earned from us at least the presumption that he would not hold a view quite this preposterous.

3 I have developed this contrast between the difference principle and the free market in detail, in *Justice and Modern Moral Philosophy* (New Haven, Yale University Press, 1990), pp. 272–90; and earlier, in 'The Labor Theory of the Difference Principle', *Philosophy and Public Affairs* 12, no. 2 (Spring, 1983), pp. 133–59.

4 In a note, Zuckert says: 'Reiman's reconstruction of the moral demand behind the Difference Principle ('Rawls's New Conception') is much weaker than Rawls's own formulation in his Demand of Justice, and so weak that regimes of justice like Rawls's rejected "liberal equality" would be allowable under it.' I have said enough about the Demand of Justice to show that Zuckert misconstrues its contribution to the difference principle. 'Liberal equality' is essentially the free market with provisions for fair opportunity so that people can earn as much as their talents can bring them. My reconstruction is not compatible with liberal equality, because I take the difference principle to be based on the fact that it is a more thoroughgoing principle of mutual benefit than other distributive principles, including the free market. Since Zuckert has thought that the difference principle is based on the Demand of Justice, he has failed to see its other important virtues. I should add here that (a) he is not alone in this, and (b) Rawls's own presentation falls far short of a clear exhibition of those virtues.

5 Or, operating within the Rawlsian system, that there is a more perfect principle of mutual benefit. Since Zuckert doesn't want to operate within the Rawlsian framework, I can safely leave this possibility aside.

6 Note also that, though the difference principle would, as Zuckert correctly says, require considerable redistribution of current holdings, it would in fact require

much less redistribution than Nozick's entitlement principles, as long as one includes that pesky requirement of rectification of historically faulty titles, which Nozick mentions only to forget, and other libertarians just forget. Putting into people's hands the property they would likely have had had we not robbed the native Americans, enslaved black Africans, exploited immigrants, discriminated against women, and ripped off third-world countries would require massive and long-term intervention in people's lives and redistribution of their property. Liberty may upset patterns, but entitlements upset liberty far more extensively. Compared to this, engineering the economy to optimize the prospects of the worst-off group is merest tinkering at the edges.

7 Recent examples happily suggest that industrial and professional workers won't stand for less in a Stalinist system either.

8 Zuckert seems to think that Leo Strauss is more consistent than Rawls in facing the implications of post-modern dissensus. Says Zuckert, approvingly, 'Strauss reasons that if the open, free society can never produce the rational society, then political life cannot proceed on the basis of the enlightenment commitments to an open and free society.' This is unpersuasive on several grounds. First, nothing in Rawls's view implies that the open and free society can never produce the rational society; post-modern dissensus only implies that we are not likely to agree when and if it does (what else is new?). Secondly, open and free society might have other advantages, such as being less likely to produce the irrational society. Open and free society might be the worst kind of society except for all the rest. Both Strauss and Zuckert are considering the implications of the post-modern dissensus without considering the implications of the liberal fact.

9 I have made my case for this 'more' in *Justice and Modern Moral Philosophy* (New Haven, Yale University Press, 1990), without, thus far, making much of a dent in the post-modern dissensus.

5

Judgemental Toleration

MICHAEL J. SANDEL

In this chapter, I will try to argue against a familiar and influential conception of liberal toleration, with particular reference to the cases of abortion and slavery. And I will try to defend an alternative approach that might be called 'judgemental toleration'.

By liberal toleration, I mean 'non-judgemental' toleration—permitting some practice on grounds that take no account of the moral worth of the practice in question. Liberal toleration is non-judgemental in the sense that it seeks to bracket substantive moral and religious controversies; it seeks to avoid passing moral judgement on the practices it permits.

'Judgemental' toleration, by contrast, does not bracket. It assesses the moral worth or permissibility of the practice at issue, and permits or restricts it according to the weight of those moral considerations in relation to competing moral and practical considerations.

Rawls' theory offers an example of liberal, or 'non-judgemental' toleration. The principles of justice that govern a pluralist society, he argues, should not depend for their justification on any particular moral or religious conception. 'Which moral judgments are true, all things considered, is not a matter for political liberalism,' he writes. 'To maintain impartiality between comprehensive [moral and religious] doctrines,' political liberalism 'does not specifically address the moral topics on which those doctrines divide.'[1]

Aquinas, by contrast, offers an example of 'judgemental' toleration, as illustrated by his case for tolerating the rites of Jews. Aquinas concedes that 'unbelief is the greatest of sins,' and that this is *prima facie* grounds for punishing it. But just as God 'allows certain evils to take place in the universe which He might prevent, lest without them greater goods might be forfeited or greater evils ensue,' so in human government, 'those who are in authority rightly tolerate certain evils, lest certain goods be lost or certain greater evils incurred; thus Augustine says, "If you do away with harlots, the world will be convulsed with lust."'

In the case of Jewish rites, 'which of old foreshadowed the truth of the faith which we hold, there follows this good—that our very enemies bear witness to our faith, and that our faith is represented in a figure, so to speak. For this reason, they are tolerated in observance of their rites.' On the other hand, Aquinas reasons, 'the rites of other unbelievers, which are neither truthful nor profitable, are by no means to be tolerated, except perchance in order to avoid an evil, e.g., the scandal or disturbance that might ensue or some hindrance to the salvation of those who, if they were unmolested, might gradually be converted to the faith.'[2]

Although he was wrong about the Jews, Aquinas was right, it seems to me, about toleration. The structure of his argument for judgement toleration is worth detaching from the particular judgements he made. I shall try to bring out the plausibility of judgemental toleration by considering some difficulties in liberal (or 'bracketing') arguments for permitting abortion and permitting slavery. By juxtaposing these cases, I do not suggest that the cases for tolerating abortion and slavery must stand or fall together. My point is that in neither case can the decision whether to tolerate the practice reasonably be detached from the question whether the practice itself is morally permissible; contrary to the attempts of some,[3] whether abortion and slavery should be tolerated cannot be decided without reference to the moral status of the foetus in the one case, and the slave in the other.

To begin, consider two arguments for liberal toleration—one voluntarist, the other minimalist. The voluntarist argument maintains, following Kant, that law should bracket, or be neutral toward substantive moral and religious conceptions in order to respect persons as free and independent selves, capable of choosing their ends for themselves. The minimalist argument holds that, whether or not the voluntarist picture of the self is true, law should be neutral for the sake of securing social co-operation under conditions of disagreement about ultimate ends.[4] Having argued elsewhere against the voluntarist version of liberal toleration, I focus here on the minimalist version.

Minimalist liberals argue that the case for liberalism is political, not philosophical or metaphysical, and so does not depend on controversial claims about the nature of the self. The priority of the right over the good is not the application to politics of Kantian moral philosophy, but a practical response to the familiar fact that people in modern democratic societies typically disagree about the good. Since people's religious and moral convictions are unlikely to converge, it is more reasonable to seek agreement on a framework of rights that is neutral with respect to those controversies.

Minimalist liberalism sets aside the philosophical question whether some conceptions of the good are better than others, and focuses on the practical question of how to secure social co-operation under conditions of disagreement about morality and religion. The minimalist case for liberalism thus depends on the plausibility of separating politics from philosophy, of bracketing moral and religious questions where politics is

concerned. But this raises the question why the practical interest in securing social co-operation is always so compelling as to defeat any competing
moral interest that could arise from within a comprehensive moral or religious view.

One way of assuring the priority of the practical is to deny that any of
the moral or religious conceptions it brackets could be true. But this is precisely the sort of controversial metaphysical claim the minimalist liberal
wants to avoid. If the liberal must therefore allow that some such conceptions might be true, then what is to assure that none can generate interests
sufficiently compelling to burst the brackets, so to speak, and morally outweigh the practical interest in social co-operation?

We might clarify the sense in which minimalist liberalism offers a political conception of justice by distinguishing three arguments for the toleration—one theological, another metaphysical, the third political. Consider,
for example, three arguments against burning witches at the stake. The
theological argument accepts that demonic souls deserve punishment, but
says it is a presumption against God for man to mete it out. The metaphysical argument is that there is no such thing as witches; witch-hunts
are unjust because their victims are guaranteed to be innocent of the
charge. The political argument brackets the question whether there is such
a thing as witches, and if so, whether it is for man or God to punish them.
Whether burning alleged witches is just would depend on how best to
secure the practical interest in social co-operation. Under most conditions,
this aim would likely be served by banning burnings at the stake, although
it is conceivable that in some cases, possibly including seventeenth century Salem, witch-hunts could help rather than harm the prospect of social
co-operation.

This example brings out the sense in which the minimalist liberal's case
for bracketing depends for its plausibility on an implicit answer to the
question it purports to bracket. Or at least, the priority of the practical
interest in social co-operation becomes far more reasonable if the brack-
eted questions turn out a certain way.

If, for example, there really *were* such a thing as witches, then it would
surely be less reasonable to bracket theology and metaphysics in the first
place. The more we are convinced that those who believe in witches are
deluded, the greater our confidence in the case for bracketing the controversy about the existence of witches. To this extent, the political argument
against witch-hunts is parasitic on (some degree of confidence about) the
theological and metaphysical arguments.

If the example of witchcraft seems far-fetched, consider the case of abortion. Given the intense disagreement over the moral permissibility of abortion, the case for a political solution that brackets the moral and religious
issues—that is neutral with respect to them—would seem especially

strong. But with abortion as with witchcraft, the plausibility of the case for ascending (or retreating) to neutral ground partly depends on which moral or religious conviction is true. If human life in the relevant moral sense really *does* begin at conception, then bracketing the moral-theological question of when human life begins is far less reasonable than it would be on rival moral and religious assumptions. The more confident we are that foetuses are, in the relevant moral sense, *different* from babies, the more confident we can be in affirming a political conception of justice that sets aside the controversy about the moral status of foetuses.

As the contemporary debate over abortion reflects, even a political conception of justice is parasitic on a certain view of the controversies it would bracket. For the debate about abortion is not only a debate about when human life begins, but also a debate about how reasonable it is to abstract from that question for political purposes. Opponents of abortion resist the translation from moral to political terms, because they know that more of their view will be lost in the translation; the neutral territory offered by minimalist liberalism is likely to be less hospitable to their religious convictions than to those of the defenders of abortion. For defenders of abortion, little comparable is at stake; there is little difference between believing that abortion is morally permissible, and agreeing that, as a political matter, women should be free to decide the moral question for themselves. The moral price of political agreement is far higher if abortion is wrong than if it is permissible. How reasonable it is to bracket the contending moral and religious views partly depends on which of those views is more plausible.

Perhaps the most famous case for bracketing a controversial moral question for the sake of political agreement was made by Stephen Douglas in his debates with Abraham Lincoln. Since people were bound to disagree about the morality of slavery, Douglas argued national policy should be neutral on that question. The doctrine of popular sovereignty he defended did not judge slavery right or wrong, but left the people of the territories free to make their own judgements. 'To throw the weight of federal power in to the scale, either in favor of the free or the slave states,' would violate the fundamental principles of the Constitution and run the risk of civil war. The only hope of holding the country together, he argued, was to agree to disagree, to bracket the moral controversy over slavery, and respect 'the right of each state and each territory to decide these questions for themselves.'[5]

Lincoln argued against Douglas' case for a political conception of justice. Policy should express rather than avoid a substantive moral judgement about slavery. Though Lincoln was not an abolitionist, he believed government should treat slavery as the moral wrong it was, and prohibit its extension to the territories.[6]

Whatever his personal moral views, Douglas claimed that, for political purposes at least, he was agnostic on the question of slavery; he did not care whether slavery was 'voted up or down'. Lincoln replied that it was reasonable to bracket the question of the morality of slavery only on the assumption that it was not the moral evil he regarded it to be. Any man can advocate political neutrality 'who does not see anything wrong in slavery, but no man can logically say it who does see a wrong in it; because no man can logically say he don't care whether a wrong is voted up or voted down.'[7]

The debate between Lincoln and Douglas was not primarily about the morality of slavery, but about whether to bracket a moral controversy for the sake of political agreement. Lincoln argued that the political conception of justice defended by Douglas depended for its plausibility on a particular answer to the substantive moral question it sought to bracket. Even in the face of so dire a threat to social co-operation as the prospect of civil war, it made neither moral nor political sense to aspire to political neutrality. As Lincoln concluded in his final debate with Douglas, '[i]s it not a false statesmanship that undertakes to build up a system of policy upon the basis of caring nothing about the very thing that every body does care the most about?'[8]

As the Lincoln example suggests, a judgemental stance toward questions of toleration may sometimes lead to intolerance. But in such cases, provided the judgements are right, and provided the competing moral and practical considerations are properly weighed, intolerance will be justified, as it was in the instance of slavery.

NOTES

1 John Rawls, *Political Liberalism* (NY, Columbia University Press, 1993), pp. xx, xxviii.
2 Saint Thomas Aquinas, *Summa Theologiae*, II–II, reprinted in William P. Baumgarth and Richard J. Regan, eds., *Aquinas on Law, Morality, and Politics* (Indianapolis, Hackett Publishing Co., 1988), pp. 254–5.
3 In the case of abortion, such attempts include, *Roe* v. *Wade*, 410 US 113, 159–62 (1973), and more recently, Laurence H. Tribe, *Abortion: The Clash of Absolutes* (NY, W. W. Norton, 1990), pp. 113–38, and Cass R. Sunstein, *The Partial Constitution* (Cambridge: Harvard University Press, 1993), pp. 270–85. In the case of slavery, the most famous such attempt if that of Stephen Douglas, discussed below.
4 The leading examples of minimalist liberalism are Rawls, *Political Liberalism*, and Richard Rorty, 'The Priority of Democracy to Philosophy', in Robert Vaughan, ed., *The Virginia Statute of Religious Freedom* (Charlottesville, University of Virginia Press, 1986).

5 Paul M. Angle, ed., *Created Equal? The Complete Lincoln–Douglas Debates of 1858* (Chicago: The University of Chicago Press, 1958), pp. 369, 374.

6 Ibid., p. 390.

7 Ibid., p. 392.

8 Ibid., p. 389.

6

Liberty and Trust

JOSEPH RAZ[1]

I

The main purpose of government, I will take for granted, is to assist people, primarily its subjects,[2] to lead successful and fulfilling lives, or, to put the same point in other terms, to protect and promote the well-being of people. The acceptance of this claim makes my views an instance of what is sometimes called 'perfectionism'.

People's lives are successful and fulfilling to the extent that they are spent in whole-hearted and successful engagement in valuable activities and relationships. In today's conditions for most of the inhabitants of the industrialized world the good life is a successful autonomous life, that is life consisting in the successful pursuit of valuable activities and relationships largely chosen by the person involved. Here we find the freedom which is part—though no more than part—of the reason for our concern for liberty. A perfectionist government, i.e., a government aware of its duty to promote the well-being of people is bound, in today's conditions, to be sensitive to the need for people to be free in the sense of being capable of leading successful autonomous lives.

Promoting autonomy, meaning here as throughout the rest of this essay the capacity for valuable autonomous life, is a double-sided duty. On the one hand it requires the government to stand back and let people have the choice as to how to conduct their own lives. On the other hand, the government must take active steps, where needed, to ensure that people enjoy the basic capacities (physical and mental) and have the resources to avail themselves of an adequate range of options available in their society. Health, the absence of pain and physical suffering and the enjoyment of a decent standard of living, meaning the reasonable availability of the means needed to engage in valuable activities and relationships, are among the preconditions of well-being. The primary duty of government is to see to it that conditions prevail in which all its citizens enjoy physical and mental health, avoid severe physical pain and suffering and enjoy a level of education making them capable of availing themselves of the options available in their society, and that they enjoy a decent standard of living, i.e., are provided with the resources necessary to pursue options of sufficient range and variety to enable them to develop all aspects of their personality if they so choose.[3]

While all the governments that I know of fail in adequately discharging this, their primary duty, and while some may argue that all other failures pale into insignificance while this failure persists, I will say nothing more of this primary duty of governments in this essay. I will be concerned not with the question of people's access to the options available in their society, but with the role of governments in moulding those options and influencing their character. There is no doubt that governments affect the character of the opportunities available to people in their countries. The existence of governments creates careers in politics and determines their character; the involvement of governments in education, health care, social work, social services, and the general role of governments in regulating economic activities etc., deeply affects career opportunities and has a major influence in shaping the type of social relationships which are recognized and sustained by the social practices of the society.

The relations that can obtain among people in the work place, to mention but one example, will be deeply affected by whether workers have the right to participate in the management of the companies they are employed by, or not, or whether people are employed by giant corporations, or by small companies or whether they are self-employed. Whatever laws the state has regarding economic activities and relations of employment will have considerable influence on all these matters. Given that state, i.e., government, action inevitably affects the opportunities and options available in the state it is only sensible that governments when deciding on their actions should be aware of their consequences for the shaping of options in the society, and that their decisions will be affected— in part—by those consequences. This raises the question of how should governments strive to influence the options available in their countries?

Some people will think this a rather roundabout way of raising the issue. Why does it matter that governmental actions inevitably affect the nature of options in a society? Is not the fact that governments can take action in order to affect such options reason enough for them to do so? Given their duty to promote the well-being of people should they not take action to make sure that attractive options are available and that meaningless and worthless options are eliminated? This is indeed so, but there are many arguments, good and bad, which have been advanced to show that governments should avoid taking any action on the ground that it promotes the availability of good options or reduces the availability of worthless ones.[4] Whatever their merit they come up against the fact that governmental action inevitably affects the availability of good or bad options. Given the importance of the matter it would be irrational of governments to take action affecting the availability of options without taking that effect of their action into account when deciding what to do. Of course, if the results of governments' actions would be better if the actions were undertaken in ignorance of their consequences that would be the preferred policy. But even though circumstances may exist in which such exclusion of relevant considerations may be best they are unlikely to prevail in all the cases in which governments face decisions having significant differential effects on the availability of options.

II

Some people fear that a conception of government which includes these elements justifies a much greater infringement of individual liberty than is warranted, and therefore they favour other, non-perfectionist doctrines of the functions of the state. The fear betrays a misunderstanding of the implications for the doctrine of liberty of governmental pursuit of the good, and of government's duty to protect and promote the autonomy of people. Liberty, as here understood, is political freedom, the freedom that we enjoy in virtue of the structure and working of the political institutions of the society in which we live. The doctrine of liberty typically includes a doctrine of limited government, of a constitutional protection for basic rights, of judicial review and other mechanisms for the protection of liberty and the enforcement of the doctrine of limited government. The doctrine of liberty articulates and justifies a set of legal and political institutions and the principles of their conduct. It is natural to assume that their justification lies in the value of individual autonomy. What other than the value of individual freedom can justify the legal and political institutions constituting the legal protection of individual liberty?

But natural and widespread as this assumption is it is mistaken on two counts. First, the promotion of personal autonomy requires much more than the implementation of the doctrine of liberty. The educational system and the welfare and social legislation are perhaps the main ways in which the state promotes individual autonomy by securing people's ability to engage in valuable activities and their access to the opportunities available in their society. But of no less importance to the protection of autonomy are the non-discrimination doctrines which ought to be embodied in the law. They help to assure individuals that their opportunities will not be restricted by prejudiced denial of access to them.

In emphasizing the role of many aspects of state action in the promotion of individual autonomy I do not wish of course to deny that the doctrine of liberty, with its protection of freedom of speech, of association and of movement, and so on, contributes its share to the protection of personal autonomy. My sole purpose is to deny that in implementing the doctrine of liberty the government does all that it should do for the promotion of autonomy—far from it. The doctrine of liberty is not even the most important part of that task.

The second error involved in assuming too exclusive a connection between individual autonomy and political liberty is no less important. It is not the case that the doctrine of liberty is justified exclusively, or principally, by its service to individual autonomy. I am tempted to say—though I would not know how to verify such a claim—that, had personal autonomy not been valuable or had its protection not been part of the government's duty, the doctrine of liberty which is in fact justified today would still have been justified as it is by the non-autonomy-related considerations which contribute to its justification.

The fact that the doctrine of liberty rests on a multitude of considerations, of which the protection of autonomy is but one, is one reason for its great importance in contemporary industrialized societies. It is also a source of both strength and weakness in people's commitment to the cause of liberty. The different arguments for liberty need not conflict. Many of them are complementary. The doctrine of liberty rests on a range of partly overlapping arguments. Hence no single argument can support all its implications. In the war of theories this fact is often overlooked. Many of the battles are inexplicable except on the assumption—rarely, if ever, explicitly made—that if my argument is right yours must be wrong (and the other way round). But the search for a single master argument on which the proper doctrine of liberty in its entirety rests is illusory. It rests on a criss-cross of diverse and sound[5] arguments. This in itself is a reason for the precariousness of the doctrine in real life. Since to convince people of the doctrine of liberty one needs to convince them of a considerable number of different arguments the likelihood of partial failure is considerable. But by the same token the very same fact accounts for the robustness of liberty, for a complete failure is much more likely with doctrines which rest on a single master argument (unless one can rely, as Rawls does, on the doctrine deriving support from a host of misguided arguments).

My earlier remarks have already made plain the need to distinguish between the freedom an individual enjoys and his freedom from legal constraint. Normally freedom from legal constraint contributes to one's personal freedom. But sometimes it may detract from it. One's personal freedom depends on ability and opportunity to take advantage of valuable options. Without legal interference, and the constraints on the legal freedom of individuals it inevitably involves, people's autonomy may be much reduced. The obvious examples of people with disabilities, or people in remote country areas whose life is severely limited without substantial public assistance are but the extreme end of a variety of ways in which personal autonomy depends on limiting one's freedom from legal constraint. But it is equally important to distinguish between freedom from legal constraint and political liberty. Liberty includes the power to enforce one's legal freedoms, and to receive adequate compensation for their violations. It includes legally set limits on the power of the legislature and the executive, as well as access to courts to ensure that the limits are adhered to.

Put in different terms, the doctrine of liberty limits the power of legislatures and executives and increases the power of the courts. It is as much about the balance of powers between the different arms of the government as about anything else. Therefore its justification has much to do with reasons for allocating public powers between the different organs of government. Typically such reasons depend, on the one hand, on the nature of bureaucracies and bureaucratic processes, and on the other hand, on the political culture and traditions of the country concerned. Given the difference in social background, educational training, and previous careers between judges in the United States, Britain, and France it would be sheer folly to think that the same institutional arrangements which work satisfactorily in one of these countries could succeed in any of the others. Contrary to much public rhetoric, in as much as the doctrine of liberty is an aspect of doctrines of balance of power among different organs of government, far from being universally valid, it is a parochial doctrine valid for its time and place.

There is, of course, another aspect to the institutional side of the doctrine of liberty, which helps explain how it can provide a bridge between institutional considerations of the kind studied by theories of bureaucracies and the value of personal autonomy. Within certain institutional frameworks, such as those in place in the United States, Canada and the European Union, the doctrine of liberty provides for an alternative political process which bypasses normal politics. In the United States we saw in 1993 a clear example of how the same political goals can be pursued in parallel when the discrimination practised in the armed forces against gay men was coming under attack both in the courts and from the then new Clinton Administration. The case illustrates several important points. First, that often (though not always) the same objectives can be reached by normal politics or by the politics of constitutional rights (to which the doctrine of liberty belongs).[6] Secondly, the mechanism and the prospects of success in each political channel depend on very different factors. The mobilization of public opinion in the streets and through the media with the aim of influencing decisions of the United States Supreme Court in the recent abortion cases, and the way the confirmation hearings for judicial appointments have developed in recent years show that the difference should not be exaggerated. The failure of the United States Supreme Court to stand in the way of the wave of bigoted persecutions we know as

McCarthyism shows that the politics of constitutional rights was never immune from the influences which shape ordinary politics. Nevertheless, even in the United States, and certainly in other countries, the politics of constitutional rights is marked by special features.

Three of them, all familiar, can be mentioned briefly. First, individuals whose rights were allegedly violated have the initiative in starting the legal process. In ordinary politics political processes are, of course, often initiated and controlled by interested organizations. But even so they, unlike the initiators of action in the politics of constitutional rights, need to mobilize support in the country at large, or among the major political organizations or the main political pressure groups of the country. The politics of constitutional rights allows easier access to the centres of power to small groups, including those which are not part of the mainstream in society. Secondly, while the process is not free from unexplained decisions, characteristically it is conducted by the clash of arguments rather than through coalition-forming among powerful groups, and the outcome of litigation is meant to be justified by reference to the supposedly generally accepted principles of the constitution. Thirdly, legal changes once introduced by the courts are normally less likely to alter with shifts in the climate of political opinion. All the points are a matter of degree. One particular misunderstanding of the nature of the politics of constitutional rights is to see its campaigns as aiming exclusively at winning a judicial decision supporting the propositions upheld by the campaigners. In many cases winning the support of the court is only a step in the hard road of securing one's political goals, as the court's decisions are often opposed by forces who do not shrink from subverting their implementation in any way they can, fair or foul. On the other hand, sometimes the campaigners can regard their action as successful even if they fail to obtain a decision supporting their cause. The publicity gained, the public sympathy aroused, the implications of the decision which rejected their claim, may all play into the hands of the campaigners.

The social and political significance of the institutional arrangements, some of the contours of which I have reviewed, varies. There is no tight match between institutional arrangements and political processes, on the one hand, and social, political, and moral functions, on the other. Much depends on the political culture and the local conditions of different countries. In some, the main function of the politics of constitutional rights is to insulate to a degree the basic structure of a political society and its fundamental political conventions from normal politics, and subject it to different dynamics. But in the twentieth century the process has also come to have the function of protecting individuals from encroachments or neglect by the state or by others where normal politics is unlikely to offer them effective redress. More recently, and especially in the United States, the politics of constitutional rights has become an important stage for the conduct of the politics of identity, exemplifying once again the flexibility and diverse uses of institutional arrangements.

III

In my preceding remarks I tried to show how the doctrine of liberty and the moral concern for individual autonomy, while congruent and feeding into each other, have a relatively independent existence. I concentrated on the institutional aspects of the doctrine of liberty and pointed to the various social and political functions they have which are independent of concern for autonomy. I have not so far said anything directly about the principles which should govern the activities of these institutions, though my remarks about the proper functions of the institutions are highly relevant to determining these principles. I will return to this question below by drawing perfectionist conclusions strengthening the doctrine of liberty, though, interestingly enough, conclusions which do not derive from concern for autonomy. But let me get there by starting at a distance from my destination, by commenting on two common starting points for reflection on political liberty.

The first is a preference for minimum government. This preference is, in the main, correct. Governments are legitimate only if following their directives would make people do what they have reason to do or achieve what they have reason to achieve better than if they did not follow those directives, and only to the extent that it is more important that people should perform the 'optimific' actions than that they should decide for themselves what to do without authoritative guidance.[7] We can call this condition, borrowing the terminology of the law of the European Union, the condition of subsidiarity. Put crudely it says: governments have only as much legitimate power as it is necessary for them to have. Whenever adequate results can be achieved without governmental interference governments do not have the authority to interfere. If that is the import of the preference for minimum government then it is sound. But does it provide the foundation for the doctrine of liberty? I do not believe that it does. It imposes two limits on the power of governments. First, that they should not try to achieve what can be better achieved without them, or what can be achieved just as well without them. This condition of efficiency, while it affects legal doctrines generally, has little to do with the doctrine of liberty specifically.

The second condition states that governments should not intervene in those matters (say, the choice of one's friends) where it is at least as important that people should choose for themselves as that they should choose wisely. This condition contributes to the doctrine of liberty, but is only one element in its justification. It does little to explain the way governments should promote and protect people's autonomy as that requires governments actively to create the conditions for autonomy by securing people's abilities and opportunities to live autonomously.

Perhaps the most popular foundation for a doctrine of liberty is the preference for minimizing reliance on coercion. This preference is common to theorists as varied in other respects as Nozick, Rawls, and Nagel, to name but a few. While they differ greatly about the conditions which, they believe, justify the use of coercion they are at one in thinking that the need to minimize the use of coercion and to justify its use to the people at whom it is or may be directed are the basis of a doctrine of liberty.[8]

There are two typical misjudgements of the moral relevance of coercion. One derives from concentrating exclusively on the way in which coercion reduces one's options or makes them worse.[9] Seen from this perspective not all the constraints imposed by coercion are a restriction of the autonomy of the coerced. An autonomous life is valuable only to the extent that it is engaged in *valuable* activities and relationships. The loss of an opportunity to murder does nothing to reduce one's chances of having the sort of autonomous life which is of value, hence there is nothing lost in not having the opportunity to murder, and one's autonomy, in the sense of a capacity for valuable autonomous life, is not constrained by the absence of that option.[10] Since coercion, wisely used, can enhance people's autonomy all round by providing them with more opportunities there is little wonder that those who consider only the impact of coercion on people's opportunities tend to protest against the importance assigned to it by much political theory. They often say that unemployment, poverty, lack of education, or market forces are also coercive, since they too restrict, or can restrict, people's opportunities and limit their autonomy.

Whatever truth there is in such analogies regarding the way coercion restricts choice, they are totally out of place given that coercion is problematic for other reasons which do not apply to most non-coercive restrictions of options. Coercion violates a person's independence by subjecting him to the will of another. Of course in all our actions our options are shaped by the activities of others, but only when manipulated or coerced[11] are we tools in the hands of others. Only then are we affected not only by the actions of others but by actions intended to dictate ours, and to do so not by persuasion but by overriding our will. People enjoy personal autonomy only to the extent that they are the authors of their own actions. When subjected, either by coercion or by manipulation, to the will of another that condition is flouted.

The importance of independence transcends its role as a component or precondition of personal autonomy. Personal autonomy is the contemporary Western condition for personal well-being. In other societies and other cultures (as well as in various subcultures which persist in the post-industrialized world) people can have a successful and flourishing life not only by leading an autonomous life, and in some cultures well-being cannot be achieved through autonomy at all. But under all conditions a good and successful life is one of willing and whole-hearted engagement in worthwhile relationships and pursuits, and such whole-hearted commitment to one's life is incompatible with that life being coerced or manipulated by others.

Many, apprehending the importance of this consideration, were moved to think that coercion can never be justified except in self-defence or if applied to a consenting subject. This is one source of the persisting popularity of belief that governmental decrees are legitimate only if they are self-imposed, i.e., only if endorsed by the general will of all their subjects. Duly modulated this precept can lend support to the view that governmental decrees are legitimate only if they merely interpret and make concrete general principles which command universal consent. For on this understanding, even if not all consent to each of the decrees, all are committed to consent to them by their consent to the principles they make concrete.

This solution to the problem of the justification of coercion is chimerical not only because the ideal of universal consent, however attenuated, is unrealizable. To think that consent solves the dilemma over coercion is to misunderstand the challenge posed by the problem of justifying coercion. To consent to coercion is to consent to a (partial) loss of independence. If complete loss of independence is loss of autonomy and makes a valuable life impossible, and if partial loss of independence diminishes one's autonomy and makes one's life less successful and worthwhile, how can consent to the loss of independence avert these consequences? Had the value of independence been conditional on the person concerned desiring it the question would have had an easy answer. But the value of independence is absolute. Those who lack the desire for independence lack self-respect, and diminish their own life by this fact alone. So what is the relevance of consent?

The story of Ulysses and the Sirens is only one of the many examples showing that there is nothing wrong in loss of autonomy when it occurs in the right circumstances. What made Ulysses' temporary loss of autonomy justified was not that he did it to himself, but that it was done for good reasons. Had he been tied to the mast by his best friend that would have been a friendly and justified act. Various reasons may justify coercion. It may be necessary to protect another, or to protect the coerced person's own long-term autonomy, or another of his interests, or to make him do his duty, etc. Independence, we should recognize, is not all or nothing. While significant loss of independence may be hard to justify, trivial loss of independence hardly calls for justification. My best friend is about to walk into the room where a surprise party is being prepared for him, and I bodily block his way and force him to go to another room to look at a book. Does innocent coercion of this kind pose a moral problem?

A significant feature of such examples is that in cases other than forcing a person to give others their due or preventing him from violating other people's rights, in cases which are—in other words—purely paternalistic, coercion is normally justified only if used by friends or others whose good intentions are beyond doubt (e.g., the person's doctor). It is not merely a matter of the chances that the coercion is really justified by paternalistic considerations, that the coerced person is not merely used or abused by others. Even where the cogency of the paternalistic reasons for coercion is not in doubt one may well object if a stranger, let alone a potentially hostile stranger, takes it upon himself to coerce one for one's own good. The point reflects the nature of trust—a central element in all those relationships in which it is appropriate to speak of people as being loyal or disloyal to each other or to the relationship. Trust involves relaxation of the normal standards of vigilance and independence (though, of course, not their complete abandonment).

I have put the point very crudely. There is much to explore here, and many qualifications to add. The bare bones are that paternalistic coercion is justified when it meets two cumulative conditions: first, it is undertaken for a good reason, one sufficient to make reasonable a partial loss of independence. Secondly, barring emergencies, it comes from the hands of someone reasonably[12] trusted by the coerced. It is this condition of trust which explains the way consent can be relevant to the justification of coercion. It can express or establish a relationship of trust. For the rest of this essay I will explore the implications for the doctrine of liberty of the condition of trust in the justification of coercion.

IV

It is common ground among many of those concerned with individual freedom that the fact that a form of conduct is immoral and worthless, that engaging in it detracts from the agent's moral worth, or from the worth of his life, is not a consideration which governments can rely upon to justify criminalizing that conduct.[13] It is sometimes thought that perfectionists cannot subscribe to this consensus. Since, broadly speaking,[14] engaging in valueless and worthless activities does not contribute to the well-being of the agent it is perhaps understandable that some would think that it follows that supporters of a perfectionist view of the role of government must support governmental coercion to stop people from acting immorally, and to force them to act morally. As the general considerations I reviewed earlier in the essay make clear, such a conclusion misconceives the nature and rationale of the doctrine of liberty. But I want to conclude by adverting to an argument for immunity from moral paternalism which turns on the issue of trust, which as I said is a precondition for justified paternalistic coercion.

Some conceptions of legitimate authority make trust a condition of legitimacy. This seems to me unjustified. The main justifying aim of authority is that it improves conformity with good reasons. It relies on its ability to achieve better consequences than any alternative for its justification. Many social problems requiring authoritative interventions are cases of securing social co-ordination in achieving desirable goals which it is the duty of everyone to seek. Sometimes an institution in which the population has no confidence will fail to secure the required co-ordination. But if it does secure it the absence of trust is a fault with the people and not necessarily with the institution. It has earned their trust, and if popular myths about the unreliability of politicians stop people from trusting it this is regrettable but does not undermine the legitimacy of the institution. Naturally, trust is not a condition of the legitimacy of an authority in stopping people from violating the rights of others or unjustifiably harming them. One need not seek the trust of violent offenders as a precondition of having jurisdiction over them.

Success in improving compliance with reason is not, however, enough to establish the legitimacy of a government. It also depends on meeting a negative condition: that its jurisdiction does not run to matters regarding which it is better that people decide for themselves, unguided by authority than that they improve their compliance with reason. Coercive paternalism, I claimed, is a case in point. Only those trusted by the coerced can have the authority to use paternalistic coercion.

The relation between trust and coercive paternalism is but one of a number of ways in which trust in the government matters. I will say nothing of its importance in securing stability, and efficiency in law enforcement. But it is worth mentioning two other respects in which it matters. Trust is a condition of respect for government. I have in mind practical respect, respecting its actions, and its decrees. It is practical for it manifests itself in action. Respect, for example, for someone's painting in this practical sense manifests itself in taking care not to damage his work. Elsewhere[15] I have argued that respect is a reasonable, though not obligatory attitude towards a government which has earned the trust of its subjects; i.e., they are reasonably confident that their government will reach reasonable conclusions and take reasonable actions in the vast majority of cases. Such respect, I suggested, expresses itself in people holding themselves to be under a duty to obey the law. When the respect arises out of justified trust this attitude of holding oneself under a duty to obey is a reasonable and even attractive attitude to the government. It amounts to saying: because I rightly trust the government I will take it for granted that there are adequate reasons to obey its laws, and so long as the government's actions are not flagrantly outside its (morally justified) authority I will not examine the arguments for obedience on a case by case basis.

Citizenship is the second matter to be mentioned here to which trust is highly relevant. I mean, of course, not legal citizenship but the status of citizenship which makes it rationally possible for people to regard themselves as fully belonging to the political community, and similarly to regard its law as their law, and its government as their government. It contrasts with the all too familiar situation in which the government and the law are regarded as sectarian, as belonging to them rather than to us, whether the 'them' are the rich, the whites, the Jews, the Communists, or some other group.

Those enjoy full citizenship who either feel, where their feeling is not unreasonable, or who would be unreasonable to deny, that the state or the government recognizes them as people who matter in their own right, that their fate is a matter of intrinsic value in the eyes of the state and its government. This does not mean of course that every state action will serve their interests. But it does mean that they reasonably believe that their interests are given due consideration in decisions about state action. Notice that the condition is semi-objective. It turns not simply on how people actually feel, but also on how it is reasonable for them to feel. Some people are deluded into believing that the government takes their interests fully into consideration, when in fact the government and the law are systematically biased against them. On the other hand, some people feel discriminated against or oppressed when in fact they are not. People can be wrong about their own citizenship. Sometimes the problem is not to make people full citizens but to make them see that they are citizens.

At the same time the condition of citizenship has a subjective component. It turns not on how governments really treat people but on what they feel about their treatment, so long as their feeling is not unreasonable. This subjective element gives *citizenship* an independent status as a constraint on governmental actions. Had the condition of citizenship been simply that one is treated by the government as one ought to be treated it would have had no independent role in guiding governmental action. So long as governments successfully act for the considerations which should guide them, independently of any concern for citizenship, they make sure that everyone would enjoy full citizenship. However, given that the condition is partly subjective it has an independent normative force: governments should not only act justly, they should also be seen to act so, at least by all those whose beliefs on the matter are not unreasonable.

In saying this, I have assumed that it is good that all residents within the jurisdiction of a political community should be full citizens of the community. There are several important reasons for thinking that only a society in which all the inhabitants enjoy full citizenship is a good society. Some have to do with the health of the society,[16] others directly with the well-being of people. In any well-ordered political community, that is, one which is stable and which has a fair prospect of continued existence, citizenship is enjoyed by all members of that community. The existence within a political society of estranged groups, who do not identify with the state, or the nation, and regard the government as an alien, potentially hostile, government, is destabilizing. Beyond that is the fact that human beings are political animals. That means more than that they can only thrive in political societies which provide the opportunities for the activities which make their lives. It also means that feeling part of a larger community, and being able to identify oneself as a member of such communities is an essential ingredient in people's well-being. Those who are second class citizens are marked by this experience which forces a flawed life on them.

There is another aspect to the importance of citizenship, and it helps explain the significance of the objective character of the condition for the status. Sometimes, people believe themselves to be full citizens, and sometimes they do as a result trust the government, even though they have no reasonable grounds to do so. Lack of self-respect or self-esteem leads them to think that they deserve the second class status to which they are consigned, or they may be gullible and accept the propaganda which a hypocritical and deceitful government puts out, etc. Because in such cases identification with one's state is purchased at a cost of low self-esteem, and often also by absence of self-respect that kind of trust is morally unacceptable. One should identify with one's state only if it recognizes one's value, otherwise one would compromise one's own self-esteem and self-respect. That is why citizenship is not and should not be premised on a subjective feeling of belonging and identification. Only when premised on a reasonable sense of belonging and identification does it play its normative role.

Given all these points, one of the most important ways in which governments can discharge their duty to protect and promote the well-being of their subjects is to make sure that they all enjoy full citizenship, and that they all identify with their country, their nation, and their government.

Some writers on politics believe that reasonable grounds for believing that one's worth is recognized by one's political society and its organs of government can only be generated by the universal acceptance in the society of a certain framework of political principles recognizing the worth of all its inhabitants and of common methods of reasoning. There is no denying that where such common principles do exist they contribute to the generation of a sense of identification with one's political society and of trust in its organs of government. But such common principles are neither necessary nor sufficient to securing full citizenship. Indeed the matter cannot be analysed in terms of either necessary or sufficient conditions, and only vague generalizations are possible. The existence of a common culture, and of its common symbols are of vital importance, but of equal importance is mutual respect between groups within the society who have diverse cultures and ways of life. To feel part of a society, to be a full citizen of it one must be able to profess one's basic beliefs, and conduct one's life in accordance with them and with one's deepest feelings without fear of criminal sanctions, legal or social discrimination, or social ridicule or persecution.

Let us take but one example to illustrate the point. Gay men and lesbians do not enjoy full citizenship in a country where their conduct, or some aspects of it, are criminalized, where open avowal of their sexual preferences leads to discrimination in public or private employment, where portrayal of gay conduct and its culture in the public media is legally or voluntarily censored, or where they are not free to display affection in public in the same way that heterosexual people do. Such manifestations of bigotry, where officially sanctioned or socially widespread, condemn gay men and lesbians to second class status in their own society. In considering this case it is important to remember that the case I am making does not depend on the fact that homophobia is an unfounded prejudice. Groups whose own beliefs and ways of life are misguided and worthless have the same claim to be admitted as full citizens as do gay men and lesbians. Our fundamental duty is to people, a duty to protect and promote their well-being. The most elemental and fundamental way in which political societies can do that is by extending full citizenship to all their members. It does not follow, of course, that there may not be circumstances in which other considerations will override the duty to grant all members of the society full citizenship. But it is difficult to envisage situations in which someone capable of enjoying full citizenship (i.e., excluding cases of severe mental illness, serious retardation or the like) should be denied it for his own good.

v

I have considered briefly the condition of citizenship for it bears a complicated relationship to trust in the government, which is a precondition for its authority to resort to coercive paternalism. Trust in the government is a condition of its right to apply coercion to people for their own good, a condition for the legitimacy of paternalistic coercion. Citizenship is normally a precondition of trust.[17] Those who find it impossible to regard the government as their government, and to regard themselves as full citizens alongside everyone else, are unable to trust the government. Unwarranted trust, by people denied full citizenship, should be discounted and should not be allowed to extend the government's authority to cases of coercive paternalism.

There remain those who enjoy full citizenship and nevertheless have no trust in the government. My own belief is that coercive paternalism cannot be applied to them until their trust is won. But I will not discuss this case further here. For our purposes we can allow that full citizenship allows the government to take measures of coercive paternalism. This does not mean, of course, that any measure of coercive paternalism would be justified. Only those which are adequately supported by reason should be taken, but where full citizenship exists the condition of trust is normally satisfied and the principled objection to coercive paternalism is overcome.

The crux of my argument lies in the catch-22 situation which applies to coercive *moral* paternalism. If I enjoy full citizenship the government can use coercive paternalism against me where this is justified by right reason. However, if it pursues coercive *moral* paternalism against me it will, by definition, be preventing me from following my way of life, and it denies, in a purported exercise of its authority, the validity of propositions I hold true and which underpin my way of life. If it does so, however, it denies me full citizenship. It undercuts my trust that I and my interests are seriously being taken into account in deciding public action., A person who finds some of the essential aspects of his way of life, or some of his fundamental values or moral beliefs, rejected as base and worthless by the government cannot trust its ability to take his interests into account. Notice that here the subjective feelings of people, the fact that they do not in fact trust their government, are reasonable, for it is reasonable not to trust someone who condemns the fundamentals of one's life as base and worthless. This lack of trust does not imply doubting the good intentions of the government. One may allow that it is acting out of the best intentions, out of concern for the people it paternalistically coerces. Yet it is bound to seem to them as failing through moral blindness to take them and their well-being seriously, lacking the ability to give their interests the weight they deserve. The people who feel like that may be wrong. Their beliefs and way of life may indeed be worthless. But it is reasonable for them to deny that and to feel that the government has forfeited their trust.

In short, the eschewing of moral paternalism is required to secure people full citizenship. Quite apart from the fact that it is the duty of governments to grant their subjects full citizenship, a duty which—as I have claimed earlier—can be overridden, there is a further factor: the dependence of the authority for paternalistic coercion on trust. That factor means that governments cannot resort to moral paternalism for by doing so they undercut their right to do so because they lose the trust of those against whom the coercion is used. This is but one of several reasons for which perfectionists should be at one with those who reject coercive moral paternalism.

NOTES

1 Professor of the Philosophy of Law, Oxford University and Fellow of Balliol College, Oxford.

2 Primarily of its subjects for while governments—like other agents—have general moral responsibilities which are not confined to their responsibilities to their subjects, it is their subjects over whom they have authority, if they have authority at all. Their relations to their subjects is therefore special and their duties to the rest of the world are a reflection of the fact that their subjects have those duties to the rest of the world.

3 This formulation is meant to make clear that I am not assuming that all people should develop all aspects of their personality. There is nothing wrong in people choosing to concentrate on philosophy or on some other aspect of life to the detriment of others. Nor am I assuming that all must have real access to all the options available in their society. The basic moral requirement is that they should have access to sufficient opportunities to enable them to develop the different aspects of their personality, if they so choose.

4 For a fuller discussion of these issues see my 'Facing Diversity: The Case of Epistemic Abstinence' in *Ethics in the Public Domain* (Oxford, OUP 1994) (originally published in Philosophy and Public Affairs 1990), and *The Morality of Freedom* (Oxford, OUP 1986), chs. 5 and 6. For other views see Rawls, *Political Liberalism*; Kymlicka, Nagel, and Hampton.

5 This point is not to be confused with Rawls}s use of what he calls an overlapping consensus, which regards the doctrine of liberty (which is part of his theory of justice) as resting on a diversity of mutually incompatible, and therefore competing, arguments, most if not all of which are misguided and mistaken.

6 That is why for present purposes it does not matter whether all or any anti-discrimination rights belong to the doctrine of liberty or whether they should be thought of as constituting a separate constitutional doctrine.

7 This is a simplified statement of the condition of legitimacy. It does, however, touch on the two most important components of that condition.

8 See Rawls, Nagel, and Waldron.

9 Nozick's important article on Coercion has bred much subtle and sophisticated writing on whether coercion reduces choice or alters it. For my view see *The Morality of Freedom* (Oxford, OUP 1986) pp. 148–57.

10 This is not to deny that there is a considerable loss of autonomy to those who commit murder and are jailed for doing so.

11 Manipulation has special features which I will not comment on.

12 To justify paternalistic coercion the trust must be justified or reasonable. Justified trust should not be taken to refer to those whose actions will justify the trust. Rather it means that the trust is reasonable given either that there is a trusting relationship between the people concerned, or that trusting the person concerned is reasonable in the circumstances given one's hope of further developing one's relations with the other (this formulation is intended to recognize the fact that trusting someone is a way of advancing towards a relationship of trust). I will say a little about the justification of this condition later in this essay.

13 Sometimes it is said that people have a right not to be criminalized just because their fellow citizens, or the government, consider their conduct immoral. This, however, while true is a quite separate point. Even if conduct is truly immoral, let alone when it is not, the fact that it is thought by some to be immoral is no reason to criminalize it and use coercive threats to force people to avoid it.

14 This statement greatly oversimplifies. While worthless conduct as such does not contribute to the agent's well-being it may have consequences, or other aspects which do. A more accurate statement will have to be much more complex and qualified.

15 *The Authority of Law*, ch. 13.

16 And thus indirectly with the well-being of its members.

17 Though there may be exceptions to this rule where people have trust in governments whose citizens they are not, e.g., if they are tourists. These exceptions will not apply to people who should enjoy full citizenship which is denied them.

7

Being Worthy of Trust: a Response to Joseph Raz

CHRISTOPHER WOLFE

Joseph Raz is an unrepentant perfectionist. 'The main purpose of government . . . is to assist people, primarily its subjects, to lead successful and fulfilling lives, or, to put the same point in other terms, to protect and promote the well-being of people'.[1]

For most people in the developed world 'the good life is a successful autonomous life, that is life consisting in the successful pursuit of valuable activities and relationships largely chosen by the person involved'. Thus, a perfectionist government must 'be sensitive to the need for people to be free in the sense of being capable of leading a successful autonomous life'.

The focus on a 'successful' autonomous life, which means the capacity for *valuable* autonomous life, makes Raz a distinctly atypical liberal.

Professor Raz is equally unrepentant, however, in his adherence to the 'harm' principle: he is opposed to coercive moral paternalism. His chapter 'Liberty and Trust' is another part of his effort to defend this combination of perfectionism and (qualified) liberalism.[2] There is much in this chapter that I find well-reasoned and appealing, but in its most important objective—the attempt to show why coercive moral paternalism is wrong—it is, in my opinion, unsuccessful.

In this chapter, after making brief comments on some of Raz's observations on the 'doctrine of liberty' and the 'preference for minimum government', I will focus on his analysis of coercion, trust, and citizenship. While some of his arguments suggest useful *prudential* limits to moral paternalism, they do not exclude moral paternalism as a matter of *principle*.

THE DOCTRINE OF LIBERTY

In the first substantive part of his chapter, Raz argues that some people favor non-perfectionist forms of government out of a misunderstanding of the implications of perfectionism for liberty. By 'liberty', he means 'political freedom, the freedom that we enjoy in virtue of the structure and working of the political institutions of the society in which we live'.[3] The 'doctrine of liberty' normally consists of 'a doctrine of limited government, of a constitutional protection for basic rights, of judicial review and other mechanisms for the protection of liberty and the enforcement of the doctrine of limited government'.[4]

It is a mistake, Raz says, to think that this doctrine of liberty 'lies in the value of individual autonomy', meaning by this (I think) not that individual autonomy does not contribute to the doctrine of liberty, but rather that it is not a necessary and sufficient foundation for it.[5] Promotion of personal autonomy requires much more than the implementation of the doctrine of liberty, and the doctrine of liberty rests on much more than simply its service to individual autonomy.[6]

Raz rightly notes that, while '[n]ormally freedom from legal constraint contributes to one's personal freedom . . . sometimes it may detract from it.'[7] Law and its constraints can enhance autonomy. For example, laws limiting some people's freedom by requiring certain accommodations of people with disabilities enhances the personal autonomy of the disabled substantially.[8]

In the discussion that follows, Raz makes many interesting points, but I would like to focus on one omission, an omission characteristic of contemporary liberalism. The doctrine of liberty, he says,

> includes legally set limits on the power of the legislature and the executive, as well as access to courts to ensure that the limits are adhered to.
>
> Put in different terms, the doctrine of liberty limits the power of legislatures and executives and increases the power of courts. It is as much about the balance of powers between the different arms of the government as about anything else.[9]

It is true, certainly, that the doctrine of liberty to some degree shifts power from the legislature and executive branches to the courts. But the phrase 'to some degree' indicates that there is a problem. Mustn't we say that the doctrine of liberty sets limits on the power of the legislature and the executive *and the courts*? Perhaps in an earlier era—when a famed writer could confidently say that 'the judiciary, from the nature of its functions, will always be the least dangerous [department of government] to the political rights of the constitution; because it will be least in a capacity to annoy or injure them'[10]—this point would not need emphasis. But that observation of an earlier era presumed 'a government in which [the different departments of power] are separated from each other'.[11] In contrast, to deny nowadays that judges *necessarily* exercise essentially legislative power, as early American jurists routinely did, is—since the victory of the views expressed in Holmes' *The Common Law*—to invite dismissal as being naïve or tendentious. In this new world the judiciary cannot be so easily dismissed as being the least dangerous branch, as American liberals learned from pre-1937 conservative judicial activism and American conservatives learned from post-1937 liberal activism.

I have no doubt that Professor Raz would recognize that the doctrine of liberty requires limits on courts, as well as the other departments of government, but I do not think it is unfair to say that his omission of this point reflects a certain habit of mind of contemporary liberals.[12] The contrary habit of being sensitive to the need to limits courts, it seems to me, is one that merits renewed cultivation.[13] In the last part of this chapter, I will suggest that Professor Raz's chapter provides the foundations for a tyrannical use of judicial power.

THE PREFERENCE FOR MINIMUM GOVERNMENT

In the next section of his chapter Raz shifts from the institutional aspects of the doctrine of liberty to the principles which should govern the activities of these institutions. As a prelude to his discussion, he comments on 'two common starting points for reflection on political liberty', namely, the preference for minimum government and the preference for minimizing reliance on coercion.[14]

The preference for minimum government is described in this way:

> Governments are legitimate only if following their directives would make people do what they have reason to do or achieve what they have reason to achieve better than if they did not follow those directives, and only to the extent that it is more important that people should perform the 'right' actions than that they should decide for themselves what to do without authoritative guidance.[15]

Borrowing the legal terminology of the European Community, Raz says, this can be called the condition of subsidiarity.

But, while this is sound, Raz says that it does not provide a foundation for the doctrine of liberty. It imposes two limits on governments. First, governments should not try to achieve what can be better (or as well) achieved without them. This is a condition of efficiency, and it has little to do with the doctrine of liberty specifically. Secondly, governments should not intervene in those matters (e.g., the choice of one's friends) 'where it is at least as important that people should choose for themselves as that they should choose wisely'.[16] This contributes to the doctrine of liberty, but it is only one element in its justification.

It seems to me that Raz dismisses too quickly real contributions to the doctrine of liberty that subsidiarity provides by way of the first limit. Subsidiarity is not simply a principle of efficiency. That would not explain the kind of *presumption* in favour of lower levels of community that it contains: power should not devolve to higher levels unless they can perform a function *better*. Now why does a 'tie' go to the lower level? Why must a function stay at the lower level if it is performed only 'as well' and not better than the higher level of community could perform it? I think that three points can be made here, all of which show how subsidiarity contributes somewhat more to the doctrine of liberty than Raz's comments suggest. First, the underlying rationale for subsidiarity, as I understand it,[17] is that, other things being equal, functions should be performed at lower levels because doing things for oneself develops a person's capacities better than having things done for oneself. Subsidiarity is rooted most fundamentally in perfectionism, then, not in mere efficiency. Secondly, a political system with various levels of community, each performing functions which they can do as well as any higher levels could do them, provides for the more direct participation of a larger number of individuals in the process of self-government. Such participation is an education in politics that equips citizens to defend their liberty against the potential danger of tyrannical rule. Thirdly, the diffusion of power throughout various levels of community that subsidiarity encourages minimizes the centralization of power in one level of government and contributes to a sort of balance of power among various levels of government.

I make no claim that subsidiarity is a *guarantee* of liberty. As Raz wisely says about the balance of power among different parts of government, these are matters that are contingent. The balance of power 'far from being universally valid . . . is a parochial doctrine valid for its time and place.'[18] In so far as it encourages devolution of power to lower levels of community, subsidiarity may become (incidentally) the occasion for tyrannical action by those lower levels. As Madison suggested in *Federalist* No. 10, smaller and more homogeneous communities may be more likely sources of threats to freedom than larger, more heterogeneous communities.[19] But, of course, James Madison himself came to appreciate much more than he did in 1787 the importance of federalism, and state checks on federal power, as factors contributing to the maintenance of liberty.[20] I think he was right to do so.

Subsidiarity, then, as part of the preference for minimum government (at each given level of government), does make some useful contributions to the doctrine of liberty, which can be appreciated without attributing more to them than is their due.

COERCION, TRUST, AND CITIZENSHIP

The second common starting point for reflecting on political liberty that Raz examines is the preference to minimize reliance on coercion. Raz starts here by noting 'two typical misjudgments of the moral relevance of coercion'.[21] The first is to focus only on the way in which coercion *reduces* one's options or makes them *worse*. Raz correctly observes that 'not all the constraints imposed by coercion are a restriction of the autonomy of the coerced. An autonomous life is valuable only to the extent that it is engaged in *valuable* activities and relationships.'[22] The loss of the opportunity to murder, therefore, is no loss of valuable autonomy.

Some people protest what they consider the exaggerated emphasis on coercion, on the ground that other factors, such as unemployment, poverty, lack of education, or market forces, are also coercive since they can restrict opportunities and limit autonomy. Whatever truth there is in such analogies, Raz says, they are out of place because they ignore the way in which coercion is problematic for reasons that do not apply to the other restrictions.

Coercion, says Raz, 'violates a person's independence by subjecting him to the will of another'. And while in all our actions our options are shaped by others,

> only when manipulated or coerced are we tools in the hands of others. Only then are we affected not only by the actions of others but by actions intended to dictate ours, and to do so not by persuasion but by overriding our will. People enjoy personal autonomy only to the extent that they are authors of their own actions. When subjected, either by coercion or by manipulation, to the will of another that condition is flouted.[23]

This statement is puzzling, given the previous definitions Raz has laid down, and unsatisfying for other reasons as well.

Personal autonomy may require that people be the authors of their own actions, but being the authors of their own actions does not mean that people have *valuable* personal autonomy. Raz has explicitly said that 'not all the constraints imposed by coercion are a restriction of the autonomy of the coerced', since '[a]n autonomous life is valuable only to the extent that it is engaged in *valuable* activities and relationships.'[24] A person deprived of the opportunity to murder has not lost 'autonomy, in the sense of a capacity for valuable autonomous life.'[25] So the conditions for genuine autonomy are flouted, not merely when a person's actions are coerced or his will overridden, but when they are done so in cases that would have involved autonomy in the valuable sense, i.e., autonomy for valuable activities and relationships. Coercion that inhibits or prevents activities and relationships that are not valuable (because, for example, they are morally bad) does not deprive anyone of valuable autonomy.

Nor is it correct for Raz to say that when we are manipulated or coerced we are 'tools in the hands of others'.[26] The key feature of a tool is that it is simply a means to an end. The person using the tool does not aim at the good of the tool, but simply at the good to which the tool is a means. But coercion exercised in the cause of moral paternalism (or, for that matter, other forms of paternalism) aims precisely at the good of the coerced person.[27] In the case of the moral paternalist, however, the good aimed at is,

among others, the good of the coerced person himself. Of course, pater-
nalists—at least thoughtful ones—make no claim that they can 'make' the
coerced people 'good' by coercing them (preventing bad actions or commanding good ones), since virtue requires an act of the will. But they do
argue that coercion can foster the *conditions* of virtue by preventing the formation of vicious habits.[28] The argument that coercion necessarily reduces
one person to being the tool of another is, therefore, clearly unwarranted.

Raz considers the argument that coercion is never justified except in
cases of self-defence or its application to a consenting subject. Associated
with this view is the position that government decrees are legitimate only
if they merely interpret and make concrete general principles that command universal consent. Raz rightly rejects this doctrine as 'chimerical'.[29]

Raz responds in this way:

[i]f complete loss of independence is loss of autonomy and makes a valuable life
impossible, and if partial loss of independence diminishes one's autonomy and
makes one's life less successful, how can consent to the loss of independence avert
these consequences? Had the value of independence been conditional on the person concerned desiring it the question would have had an easy answer. But the
value of independence is absolute. Those who lack the desire for independence
lacks self-respect, and diminish their own life by this fact alone.[30]

The argument emphasizing consent treats autonomy as if it were valuable
in so far as it is simple independence, not autonomy (or independence) as
valuable when exercised in morally good ways. Partial loss of independence doesn't necessarily make one's life less successful—it may contribute to it—and so the value of independence is not 'absolute'. Those
who lack the desire for independence lack self-respect, it is said, but at
least a partial loss of independence is perfectly compatible with self-
respect, and may be grounds for enhancing it.

Raz points out that 'there is nothing wrong in loss of autonomy when it
occurs in the right circumstances,'[31] as the story of Ulysses and the Sirens
shows. Ulysses' temporary loss of autonomy was justified not by the fact
'that he did it to himself, but that it was done for good reasons'.[32] Had he
been tied to the mast by his best friend that would have been a friendly
and justified act, Raz points out.

Raz notes that various reasons may justify coercion: 'to protect another,
or to protect the coerced person's own long-term autonomy, or another of
his interests, or to make him do his duty, etc.'[33] He goes on to argue that
independence 'is not all or nothing. While significant loss of independence
may be hard to justify, trivial loss of independence hardly calls for justification.'[34]

An example of 'innocent coercion' is when '[m]y best friend is about to
walk into the room where a surprise party is being prepared for him, and

I bodily block his way and force him to go to another room to look at a book.'[35] Raz says that the significant feature of cases such as this (paternalistic ones, not involving duties of justice or rights of others) is that 'coercion is normally justified only if used by friends or others whose good intentions are beyond doubt (e.g., the person's doctor)'. It's not just that there are greater chances that the real motive for coercion is benevolent. Even if that were not in doubt, 'one may well object if a stranger, let alone a potentially hostile stranger, takes it upon himself to coerce one for one's own good'.[36] The point, Raz says, reflects the nature of trust, which involves the relaxation (though not complete abandonment) of the 'normal standard of vigilance and independence'.[37]

Raz summarizes:

> paternalistic coercion is justified when it meets two cumulative conditions: first, it is undertaken for a good reason, one sufficient to make reasonable a partial loss of independence. Secondly, barring emergencies, it comes from the hands of someone reasonably trusted by the coerced.[38]

WHY TRUST?

Let me begin my questions here by looking at three of Raz's examples in this section. With respect to the example of Ulysses and the Sirens, one might ask 'what if a benevolent stranger had tied Ulysses to the mast?' (imagine, perhaps, that as Ulysses stands in the back of the boat, his men facing the other way as they row, a stowaway—not a personal friend of Ulysses—who knows about the danger of the Sirens, comes out of hiding and overpowers Ulysses and ties him to the mast.) Wouldn't that too have been 'a friendly and justified act', even in the absence of 'trust'? Indeed, isn't it the absence of trust that makes the direct reliance on coercion especially plausible—since a relationship of trust might make persuasion, *instead of* coercion, a preferable tactic?

With respect to the surprise party, one must ask whether we're really dealing with coercion here. Put yourself in the position of the person who is unknowingly about to spoil his own surprise party. As you head to the door of the room, a friend bodily blocks your way and suggests that you go to another room to look at a book. It is conceivable, I suppose, that you say 'no', engage in a physical fight with your friend about whether you can go into the room you want to enter, and be physically compelled to go to the other room. But that's not a very likely scenario. Precisely if there is a relationship of trust, you would *defer* to your friend, *obviating* the need for 'coercion'.

The third example is Raz's reference to the fact that coercion is 'normally justified only if used by friends *or others whose good intentions are beyond doubt (e.g., the person's doctor)'*.[39] Again, one must ask: in what sense is the doctor using 'coercion'? On the one hand, people aren't coerced by doctors—they trust them and therefore choose to follow their advice willingly (although, as a matter of fact, in many cases, they choose to ignore the advice). On the other hand, they trust doctors though they are *not* friends. Doctors (just as such) seem to be somewhere in between 'friends' and paternalistic public officials. They are more like the former, in that they are freely chosen by the patient, who can walk away from them. They are more like the latter in being 'impersonal doers of good', trusted more for their technical than their personal qualities.

On the other hand, it may be an exaggeration to say that the intentions of doctors are 'beyond doubt'. Raz puts it well later, when he says that trust occasions a relaxation of vigilance though not a complete abandonment of it. Part of the problem with the doctor analogy—the way it skews the question somewhat—is that it ordinarily involves the relatively uncontroversial character of health as an end, and trust in the technical competence of doctors in the means to achieve that end. But what if the end of doctoring were less clear, for example, if the practice of involuntary euthanasia spreads, as it seems to be in the Netherlands—that is, if doctors aim, at least in some cases, at something other than health?[40] What might happen to the doctor–patient relationship in those circumstances?

The trust in technical competence that contributes to trust of non-friends like doctors may also be a factor in public acceptance of certain other kinds of paternalism, e.g., seatbelt laws, anti-smoking regulations, and food and drug restrictions on alleged carcinogens. Raz, as far as I know, has not indicated whether the implications of his argument against moral paternalism would apply to these cases as well. His stand on such cases would certainly be of significant interest to those who are following his ideas regarding paternalism.

Raz also says that even if reasons for paternalistic coercion are good, one might object if a stranger took it upon himself to coerce one for one's own good. But, if the reasons for the coercion were good and were serious enough, would one indeed object? Raz is correct when he says, later, that it depends on whether it is as important that the person do something himself as it is that he do the right thing. But Raz's chapter does not seem to me to give us any clear criteria for that.

I do not mean to say that trust is not a factor in evaluating paternalistic coercion. Most obviously, a paternalist would have to take into consideration the likelihood of the benevolent coercion being successful if it were employed by someone the coerced person does not trust. That would certainly be an important prudential consideration, since distrust would magnify the difficulties of achieving successful paternalistic coercion.

What I don't see in Raz's argument is any *principled* argument as to the need for trust, over and above good reasons, as a ground for moral paternalism (at least, barring emergencies—another important qualification).

TRUST AND CITIZENSHIP

In the beginning of the last section of his chapter, Raz makes some trenchant observations about the limits of arguments based on trust. First, he argues that trust is not a condition of legitimate authority. Legitimate authority rests, rather, on the fact that 'it improves conformity with good reasons'.[41] Secondly, there are cases where authorities should intervene to seek social co-ordination which it is the duty of all to seek. If it does secure the require co-ordination, then 'the absence of trust is a fault with the people and not necessarily with the institution'.[42] Thirdly, '[n]aturally, trust is not a condition of the legitimacy of an authority in stopping people from violating the rights of others or unjustifiably harming them.'[43] For example, one need not seek the trust of violent offenders as a precondition of having jurisdiction over them.

Raz also rightly notes that success in improving compliance with reason is not sufficient to establish a government's legitimacy. The government's jurisdiction must also not 'run to matters regarding which it is better that people decide for themselves, unguided by authority, than that they improve their compliance with reason'.[44] Coercive paternalism is one of these cases, he says (though, as I have argued above, I do not believe he gives us adequate reasons for thinking so).

Raz notes in passing that trust is important in securing stability and efficiency in law enforcement (the kinds of 'prudential considerations' I acknowledged above), but he emphasizes two other aspects of trust. First, trust is a condition of *practical* respect for government, for respecting its action and decrees. Respect based on reasonable trust means that 'holding oneself under a duty to obey is a reasonable and even attractive attitude to the government'.[45] Justified trust of a government makes it reasonable to assume that there are adequate reasons to obey its laws, without examining arguments for obedience on a case by case basis (as long as the government's actions are not flagrantly outside its authority).

The second aspect of trust is related to citizenship. The citizenship that Raz is concerned with is not legal citizenship but 'the status of citizenship which makes it rationally possible for people to regard themselves as fully belonging to the political community, and similarly to regard its law as their law, and its government as their government'.[46] Full citizenship he defines—and this is a very key point for my analysis of Raz's argument below—as belonging to those who either feel, where their feeling is not unreasonable, or who would be unreasonable to deny, that the state or the government recognizes them as people who matter in their own right, that their fate is a matter of intrinsic value in the eyes of the state and its government.[47]

Raz describes this as a 'semi-objective' condition. Its objectivity lies in the fact that '[i]t turns not on how people actually feel, but on how it is reasonable for them to feel.'[48] People may be deluded that government considers their interests, when it doesn't, or they may feel discriminated against, when they aren't. But there is a subjective component as well—it turns not on how governments actually treat people, but on how the people feel about it, as long as the feeling is not unreasonable. This partial subjectivity means that '[g]overnments should not only act justly, they should also be seen to act so, at least by all those whose beliefs on the matter are not unreasonable.'[49]

I think that there is substance to Raz's contention on this point, although I am unsure as to how much we agree on the reasons. I would put it this way: government's obligation to pursue the common good requires not only that government actually do so, but that, at least ordinarily, it take reasonable steps to make it clear to its citizens that it is doing so.[50] Several reasons for the latter can be given: first, the failure of government to offer its citizens reasonable grounds to believe that it is pursuing the common good will likely obstruct its ability to pursue the common good; secondly, 'civic friendship' is part of the common good, and would seem to entail, at least ordinarily, a communication of respect—in the sense of a commitment to pursue their good—to one's fellow citizens. I presume that this latter reason is similar to the principle of citizenship that Raz invokes.

PROBLEMS OF CITIZENSHIP

Raz indicates that he assumes 'that it is good that all residents within the jurisdiction of a political community should be full citizens of the community'.[51] It is unclear how he would regard the status of two classes for whom this might be problematic; and these examples also suggest problems with some of Raz's definitions. First, what about resident aliens—especially those who remain aliens of their own volition, as opposed to those who are precluded from a citizenship they desire? Presumably they are not 'full citizens', in the ordinary sense of the term. They don't 'regard themselves as fully belonging to the political community'.[52] On the other hand, they should be able to have the feeling that 'the state or government recognizes them as people who matter in their own right, that their fate is a matter of intrinsic value in the eyes of the state and its government.'[53] Not only citizens, but every human being can demand that every other human being (not just the state or government) view them in that way. Among other conclusions one might draw from this is that even if 'full citizenship' requires government to treat a person as someone with intrinsic value, treating someone as a person with intrinsic value does not require granting them full citizenship, if the latter is understood to include rights as elementary as voting.

Secondly, what is the status of imprisoned felons in a political community? They do belong to the political community and should be able to feel that government recognizes them as people in their own right, whose fate is of intrinsic value, and in that sense they have 'full citizenship'. But their participation in the political community is problematic and is frequently—and reasonably, I think—curtailed. For example, it seems reasonable to deny voting rights to imprisoned murderers and rapists and embezzlers, on the grounds that their actions have demonstrated a will sharply and substantially opposed to the common good and a willingness to act on it. If this is so, do they lack 'full citizenship'? One could probably answer that question in different ways, depending on one's definition of 'full' citizenship.

My own preference would be to say that they are full citizens, but that full citizens may sometimes legitimately be deprived of certain rights, if there are reasonable grounds for so doing.[54] Others might prefer to say that governments may sometimes reasonably deny certain citizens full citizenship. Either way, an important point is that 'full citizenship for all' is more complicated that Raz's discussion of it in his chapter suggests.

CITIZENSHIP, SELF-RESPECT, AND MUTUAL RESPECT

Raz goes on to give good reasons for the importance of citizenship. Denial of full citizenship to a group can be destabilizing to the community, if it creates estranged people or groups who regard the government as alien and potentially hostile. Moreover, since human beings are political animals, an essential ingredient of their well-being is feeling part of a larger community. Being second class citizens forces a flawed life on people.

Of course there are people who might be considered 'second class citizens' by some (it is not clear whether this would include Raz) who have a flawed life in this respect not because of the action of the government, but because their own actions have called down upon them legitimate restrictions on their status and participation in society, e.g., imprisoned felons.

Another problem of citizenship that Raz raises flows from the objective character of the condition for full citizenship, i.e., that the belief that one is a full citizen be reasonable. One can imagine circumstances in which lack of self-respect or self-esteem (perhaps fostered by hypocritical government propaganda) leads people to think that they deserve second class status. To identify with one's own state on such terms is to compromise one's own self-esteem and self-respect, says Raz.

How would Raz apply this to the case of the imprisoned felon? Presumably he *deserves* his second class status. His sense of 'belonging' to the political community should be qualified in some sense, i.e., the sense that he has set himself apart from the community by his own actions attacking it. It might even be argued, paradoxically, that government would promote his self-respect best by punishing him. Self-respect—like the sense of belonging that constitutes citizenship—must have (at least in part) an 'objective' character. One's self-respect and self-esteem ought not to rest, unreasonably, on the belief that one ought to have self-respect and self-esteem *with respect to* acts that are the proper object of censure, by oneself and by others. The self-respect that derives from being a person *capable* of a rational and morally upright life is, of course, compatible with recognizing the guilt that flows from failure to live up to this capacity— indeed 'appropriate guilt' is a testimony to our freedom, which is so intimately tied up with the foundations of our self-respect.[55] To the extent that punishment helps a person to *see* himself more clearly and to evaluate his acts properly, it conduces, in the long run, to a *legitimate* self-respect and self-esteem.

Raz argues that one important factor in citizenship (which requires having reasonable grounds to believe that one's worth is recognized by one's political society and its government) is

mutual respect between groups within the society who have diverse cultures and ways of life. To feel part of a society, to be a full citizen of it one must be able to profess one's basic beliefs, and conduct one's life in accordance with them and with one's deepest feelings without fear of criminal sanctions, legal or social discrimination, or social ridicule or persecution.[56]

The example he chooses to illustrate this point is gay men and lesbians. They do not enjoy full citizenship when aspects of their conduct are criminalized, when they face public and private employment discrimination, where portrayal of the culture is censored (legally or voluntarily), and when they are not free to display affection in public as heterosexuals do. 'Such manifestations of bigotry, where officially sanctioned or socially widespread, condemn gay men and lesbians to second class status in their own society.'[57]

Raz then 'ups the ante' when he goes on to argue that '[i]n considering this case it is important to remember that the case I am making does not depend on the fact that homophobia is an unfounded prejudice' since groups with misguided and worthless beliefs and ways of life have the same claim to be admitted as full citizens as do gay men and lesbians.[58] The most fundamental way that political societies protect and promote people's well-being is to extend full citizenship to all their members. Raz notes that some circumstances might override this duty, 'but it is difficult to envisage situations in which someone capable of enjoying full citizenship (i.e. excluding cases of severe mental illness, serious retardation or the like) should be denied it for his own good.'[59]

It is not clear to me exactly how broad a claim Raz is making when he says that his case does *not* depend on the view that 'homophobia is an unfounded prejudice'. Does this mean that any and every case against the unrepentant homosexual lifestyle is irrelevant to the case based on citizenship that Raz makes on its behalf? If so, then his claim will not bear analysis, in my opinion.[60]

First, I should make it clear that I think that a policy of discrimination that is based simply on the existence of a 'homosexual orientation'—what might be called the habitual tendency or inclination to engage in homosexual acts—would generally be unfair and thus wrong. Not only is the simple existence of such an orientation (however disordered) not wrong in itself, but homosexuals who strive to resist this temptation, recognizing it as a disordered tendency, merit our admiration and praise. It is the way of life that is based on the view of the moral licitness of homosexual acts that should be the object of our disapprobation and paternalistic intervention (where that is possible).

A somewhat useful analogy here would be the problem of alcoholism. Simply 'being an alcoholic' is not the key question, since there are many admirable alcoholics, who struggle and often master their tendency to drink excessively. On the other hand, the life of an active and unrepentant alcoholic is certainly a fit subject for social disapprobation and—in appropriate circumstances—legal prohibition. Whether, and if so, how, private drunkenness should be prohibited is a complex question, since it involves important considerations of privacy and the extent of the impact of such drunkenness on the common good. But, since the effect of even private alcoholism on the common good is clear, there is no *principled* objection to its prohibition, though there are significant prudential arguments against it. On the other hand, there are few grounds, in principle, to object to legal prohibitions of public drunkenness and none to object to public education and exhortations against it.[61]

The case against the unrepentant homosexual lifestyle can take various forms (which may overlap to some extent). One form would focus more on the well-being of individuals: the position that homosexual acts are seriously, morally wrong and therefore that society ought to prohibit them as a way of promoting, directly and indirectly, the good of those who might be tempted to engage in them.[62] Another form would focus more on the well-being of society: the position that society depends on certain institutions, such as the family, that in turn depend on certain moral dispositions in the citizenry, which are incompatible with the acceptance of the case for the unrepentant homosexual lifestyle.[63] Raz accepts the perfectionistic principle that society ought to promote the well-being of its members. The unrepentant homosexual lifestyle is alleged by some to be incompatible with that well-being. If those allegations are true, then society has reasonable grounds to discourage that lifestyle. The validity of this argument turns, then, on the truth *vel non* of the allegations about the unrepentant homosexual lifestyle, i.e., on whether 'homophobia' (in the sense of moral objections to homosexual conduct) 'is an unfounded prejudice'.

Now Raz has asserted that the demand for 'full citizenship' somehow makes the argument about the character of the unrepentant homosexual lifestyle irrelevant, but I do not see where the assertion is proven. It is true that the argument used above, with respect to imprisoned felons (murders, rapists, and embezzlers), differs from the argument about the unrepentant homosexual lifestyle, in that the former involves a direct assault on the rights of others, while the latter does not. But where has Raz shown that such a distinction is relevant, much less crucial, to the point at issue, i.e., the legitimacy of government intervention? The argument respecting imprisoned felons, to the extent that it is valid, demonstrates, I think, one of two things: either that full citizenship is perfectly compatible with criminal punishment, or that the granting of full citizenship is not always a good. It is open, of course, to Raz, to show why it is appropriate for government to deny full citizenship (or to subject those who are fully citizens to some punishment or civil disability) in cases involving direct assault on the rights of others and not appropriate to do the same in cases 'merely' involving the well-being of citizens themselves (and society less directly). But I do not see that he has made any such argument in his chapter.

For the record, I would concede that prudent public policy demands that a government that restricts homosexual acts (through a prohibition of homosexual sodomy) and educates its citizenry as to the disorder implicit in the homosexual orientation ought to make it clear to its citizens that this involves no depreciation of the intrinsic value of those who have a homosexual orientation or, for that matter, those who actively practice an unrepentant homosexual lifestyle. In fact, the basis for the government's action is an intense concern for the well-being, moral and otherwise, of *all* its citizens. Such a government should give no reasonable ground for any citizens, including active homosexuals, to believe that it depreciates them. Of course, active homosexuals, disagreeing with the government's assessment of the moral character of their actions, are unlikely to believe in the benevolence of the government, but then neither do many people who break the law and are punished for it. What counts is whether there are *reasonable grounds* for their 'lack of trust'.[64]

LIBERAL TYRANNY

But I would go further and argue that Raz's argument itself involves a denial of very important freedoms.[65] It is an invitation to liberal tyranny. According to him, 'socially widespread . . . manifestations of bigotry' such as a) denial of private as well as public employment to active homosexuals, b) voluntary censorship of media portrayal of gay conduct, and c) social hostility to public displays of homosexual affection would seem to constitute denials of full citizenship and are therefore wrong.

Parents, it appears, must tolerate active homosexuals teaching their children in public schools and even (apparently) in private schools. Their opposition to this—not only with respect to possible seduction, but much more importantly with respect to the formation of their childrens' moral ideas[66]—is itself intolerable to the liberal state. Spreading very negative views about the active homosexual lifestyle (via free speech)—if it is successful enough to lead to voluntary censorship of media portrayal of gay conduct—is intolerable. Even demonstrating *social* hostility to conduct that one considers immoral—such as public displays of homosexual affection similar to those employed by chaste heterosexuals (kissing, holding hands, etc.)[67]—is intolerable. Now Raz might legitimately argue that there is nothing wrong with perfectionistic liberals like himself refusing to tolerate certain kinds of intolerant actions. But what he cannot validly argue, it seems to me, is that 'the case I am making does not depend on the fact that homophobia is an unfounded prejudice.'[68] In fact, that is precisely the allegation on which his argument does turn.

Raz concludes by posing a catch-22 situation for moral coercion:

> If I enjoy full citizenship the government can use coercive paternalism against me where this is justified by right reason. However, if it pursues *moral* paternalism against me it will, by definition, be preventing me from following my way of life, and it denies, in a purported exercise of its authority, the validity of propositions I hold true and which underpin my way of life. If it does so, however, it denies me full citizenship . . . In short, the eschewing of moral paternalism is required to secure people full citizenship. Quite apart from the fact that it is the duty of governments to grant their subjects full citizenship, . . . there is a further factor: the dependence of the authority for paternalistic coercion on trust. That factor means that governments cannot resort to moral paternalism for by doing so they undercut their right to do so because they lose the trust of those against whom the coercion is used.[69]

But a) Raz has never given a sound reason why moral paternalism ought to be treated differently from other kinds of paternalism; b) the acceptance of non-moral coercive paternalism shows that there is nothing *intrinsically* wrong with preventing people from following their ways of life or with denying the validity of propositions they hold true and which underpin their way of life; c) Raz has not been clear as to what constitutes full citizenship, and the example of non-moral coercive paternalism shows either that full citizenship is compatible with punishment and restrictions or that granting full citizenship to all is not a necessary moral requirement of government; d) Raz never proves that resort to moral paternalism undercuts the relevant form of trust, since a refusal to trust that is unreasonable does not undercut government's legitimacy; and he has not shown that those coerced by moral paternalism have reasonable grounds for considering that the government does not consider them as people who matter in their own right, whose fate is of intrinsic value. The opposition of a government to a group's beliefs and way of life, as the example of non-moral coercive paternalism again shows, is perfectly compatible with, and indeed, may be the very way of expressing its deep concern for the value and fate of that group, as well as the rest of society.

NOTES

1 Joseph Raz, 'Liberty and Trust', ch. 6, p. 113.
2 For a discussion of earlier efforts by Raz to defend this combination of principles, see Robert George 'The Unorthodox Liberalism of Joseph Raz', *Liberalism at the Crossroads* (Rowman and Littlefield, 1994), ch. 9.
3 Ch. 6, p. 115.
4 Ibid.
5 Ibid.
6 Raz places some considerable stress on the variety of reasons undergirding the doctrine of liberty—a source both of its strength and its weakness, he says—but he does not discuss these reasons.
7 Ch. 6, p. 116.
8 Raz's initial argument—that '[n]ormally freedom from legal constraint contributes to one's personal freedom[, b]ut sometimes it may detract from it— seems to suggest that Raz has in mind that the constraint on the person contributes to his *own* freedom. But the subsequent examples given—'people with disabilities, or people in remote country areas whose life is severely limited without substantial public assistance'—seems to indicate that Raz is making a somewhat different point: constraints on some people contribute to *other* people's freedom. As the discussion of Ulysses and the Sirens below indicates, Raz and I agree that the first-impression view of the statement is also true.
9 Ch. 6, p. 117.
10 Hamilton et al. *The Federalist*, No. 78 G. Wills (ed.) (New York, Bantam, 1982), p. 393.
11 Ibid.
12 Another example may be found in Raz's statement that 'in many cases winning

the support of the court is only a step in the hard road of securing one's political goals, as the court's decisions are often opposed by forces who do not shrink from subverting their implementation in any way they can, fair or foul.' (Raz, p. 113) Some Americans, upset at judges going beyond their legitimate powers, might argue that it could just as easily be said that 'in many cases winning the support of the court, by arguments fair or foul, is the major step in the road of securing one's political goals, though the court's decisions are sometimes opposed by forces who occasionally can dredge up enough fortitude to oppose judicial pretensions.'

I do not know to what extent Professor Raz's views on this matter reflect the fact that he lives in a country in which the courts are significantly less likely to exercise the kind of power that American courts employ almost routinely.

13 For reasons discussed in my *The Rise of Modern Judicial Review* (New York, Basic Books, 1986) and *Judicial Activism* (Pacific Grove, Calif., Brooks/Cole Publishing Co., 1991).

14 Ch. 6, p. 119.

15 Ibid.

16 Ch. 6, pp. 119–20.

17 I am presuming here that the European community has inherited the notion of subsidiarity from Catholic social thought, which originated the use of that word earlier in the twentieth century, although I think the basic point of the doctrine is implicit in Catholic social thought much earlier. For a brief treatment, see Wolfe 'The Other Ground of Limited Government' in *Catholicism, Liberalism, and Communitarianism: Essays on the Catholic Intellectual Tradition and the Moral Foundations of Democracy* Grasso et al. (eds.) (Rowman and Littlefield, 1995). At any rate, this is the notion of subsidiarity that I contend contributes something to the doctrine of liberty.

   For another discussion of subsidiarity, see John Finnis *Natural Law and Natural Rights* (Oxford, Clarendon Press, 1980), especially chs. 6 and 7.

18 Ch. 6, p. 117.

19 *Federalist* No. 10, pp. 42–9.

20 One instance among many is the 'Virginia Resolutions' of 1798, authored by Madison when he served in the Virginia legislature, during the controversy over the Alien and Sedition Acts.

21 Ch. 6, p.120.

22 Ibid. (emphasis in the original).

23 Ibid.

24 Ibid. (emphasis in the original).

25 Ibid.

26 Ibid.

27 Ironically, it seems somewhat more plausible, at first glance, to make that charge about coercion directed against those who violate others' rights, which liberals and non-liberals alike consider legitimate. For example, someone might argue that murder laws aim at the good, not of the person coerced, but at the good of others—those whose rights will be protected. In fact, however, the 'defensive' quality of these laws that prevent peoples' rights from being violated make the tool image inappropriate here too.

28 See Robert P. George, *Making Men Moral: Civil Liberties and Public Morality* (Oxford, Clarendon Press, 1993).

29 Ch. 6, p. 121.

30 Ibid. It is the content of the next paragraph that leads me to construe the argument of this paragraph not as Raz's own, but those of a hypothetical defender of the notion that consent is the answer to the problem of coercion. I would find it strange for Raz to argue in this paragraph that 'the value of independence is absolute', while in the next paragraph he says that 'there is nothing wrong in loss of autonomy when it occurs in the right circumstances' and '[i]ndependence, we should recognize, is not an all or nothing.'

31 Ibid.

32 Ibid.

33 Ibid.

34 Ch. 6, pp. 121–22. It is unclear to me whether by 'trivial' in this sentence Raz means only the magnitude of the limitation on a person's independence (the extent of the constraint), or includes consideration of how *valuable* the autonomy limited is (so that substantial constraint might be a trivial loss of independence if what is lost is an opportunity to do things of little or no value). From the perspective of the latter, for example, anti-polygamy laws might involve substantial constraint—men are limited to marriage with one wife, out of all the women in the world, or even in their world'—but the loss is trivial, given the good of monogamy and lack of worth of polygamy.

35 Ch. 6, p. 122.

36 Ibid.

37 Ibid.

38 Ibid. This is the way consent can be relevant to the justification of coercion, Raz says—it can express or establish a relationship of trust.

39 Ch. 6, p. 122 (emphasis added).

40 Nor is it simply a question of substituting 'the control of pain' for 'health' in the scenario I'm invoking. Pain control is so effective today as to eliminate it as a ground for euthanasia in almost all cases. Euthanasia is based on a much more fundamental question about the 'meaningfulness' of a given human life.

41 Ch. 6, p. 123.

42 Ibid.

43 Ibid.

44 Ibid.

45 Ch. 6, p. 124.

46 Ibid.

47 Ibid.

48 Ibid.

49 Ch. 6, pp. 124–5.

50 I say 'at least ordinarily' because I can imagine unusual circumstances in which short-term failure to do so might be justified. I think an example might be constructed which is analogous to a military tactic that seems like a blunder (to fool the enemy) and which is justified even if it also fools one's own troops (assuming that the latter will obey anyway, as a matter of discipline).

51 Ch. 6, p. 125.

52 Ch. 6, p. 124.

53 Ibid.

54 This would have to be elaborated more fully, by distinguishing between rights that are so fundamental that they can never be taken away and others that are not so fundamental that they cannot be conditioned in some way. The right not to be tortured, for example, would fall in the first category, the right to vote in the second.

55 I resist any temptation to say that freedom is *the* foundation for our self-respect. It is precisely the Achilles' heel of modern philosophy that it has been able to find a foundation for human dignity only in human freedom—the will—and not in the capacity of human beings to know the truth—intellect, which is the proper guide to the will.

56 Ch. 6, p. 126.

57 Ibid.

58 Ibid.

59 Ibid.

60 The following discussion of homosexuality is more extensive than it normally would need to be for purposes of the topic of this chapter, but the position that I favour is so often misunderstood and misstated that it seemed prudent to explain myself more fully.

61 For my present purposes, I put to the side the prudential question of whether the mores of a given society permit such laws. Of course, many laws that would be desirable in an ideal society will not be possible a given society.

To avoid misunderstanding, moreover, I should say that I am not arguing that Prohibition is necessarily desirable. There is a fundamental distinction between alcohol and homosexual acts: the former may be indulged in moderately, while the latter are, I believe, intrinsically wrong.

62 'Directly', in the sense that prohibition of some immoral acts may prevent the formation of vicious habits on the part of those who can be deterred by such laws; 'indirectly', in the sense that legal moral prohibitions help to form the moral ideals of many citizens and thereby support moral views contrary to immoral acts. But in neither case is there any claim that law can itself command 'virtuous' acts, strictly speaking. The service of the law is to promote *conditions* in which virtue is more easily formed or preserved. See George *Making Men Moral*.

63 As Raz notes, the good of social well-being is also indirectly related to the well-being of its members.

64 To give a somewhat simplified practical example: I think that a government that opposed the active homosexual lifestyle should go out of its way not to give reasonable grounds for understanding itself in the way that much of the press (whether reasonably or unreasonably—an issue I put to the side for now) has interpreted Patrick Buchanan's remarks on the political agenda of active homosexuals.

This issue is clouded by the fact that it is not always easy or appropriate to make the point of one's concern for *all* people when one is making an argument that some people are engaged in conduct contrary to the morality and the common good. For example, feminist spokesmen concerned with sexual harassment have not been criticized for a lack of compassionate concern for the people who are the aim of *their* criticism. Perhaps they—like Buchanan, according to one view—should be.

It is one of the measures of Lincoln's greatness that the Second Inaugural says the truth about slavery, while manifesting an extraordinarily strong sense of a common good (and violations of it) that includes all Americans, North and South. (And yet it was probably easier to say that with victory in the war on the horizon than it would have been several years earlier.)

65 This is what I meant earlier in the chapter when I commented on Professor Raz's omission of a concern for limits on courts in his discussion of the doctrine of liberty. Some American judges would like to use the arguments of Professor Raz for non-discrimination in ways that deny traditional individuals and groups important aspects of liberty.

66 The mention of seduction usually brings howls of 'bigotry' (see the letters in the *Wall Street Journal* of 3 March 1994), but the danger of seduction, given the presence of groups like the North American Man–Boy Love Association who *call for* such seduction, is not negligible. Of course, heterosexual predators should just as strictly be excluded from schools.

But the stronger argument against private school employment of active homosexuals, in my opinion, is the likelihood that many active homosexuals, far from being predators, will be 'nice guys'. And parents with traditional moral views reasonably oppose the hiring of such people in a school for precisely the same reason they would oppose hiring racists or Nazis who were 'nice guys': childrens' views of morality are affected by the superficially attractive qualities of people they meet and like, and therefore moral education can be seriously deformed if children develop personal relations of affection with people who engage in immoral conduct without shame or regret.

67 Traditionalists might distinguish between their attitudes toward mild but public, physical displays of affection on the part of heterosexuals and homosexuals, on the grounds that the former represent steps toward fuller sexual displays that are immoral or moral depending on their circumstances, while the latter represent steps toward fuller sexual displays always and everywhere immoral.

68 Ch. 6, p. 126.

69 Ch. 6, pp. 127–8.

8

Getting Normative: The Role of Natural Rights in Constitutional Adjudication

RANDY E. BARNETT[1]

Our next question must be whether we can reconcile our natural law past with our textualist present—and whether we even want to.

Suzanna Sherry[2]

INTRODUCTION: THE NATURAL LAW REVIVAL

We are in the midst of a natural law revival. Not since the Hart–Fuller debate[3] in the wake of Nuremberg has legal academia witnessed such interest in the topics of natural law and natural rights.[4] While this development may be only the most recent aspect of the now several decades old revival of normative legal philosophy that I chronicled some ten years ago,[5] the immediate cause of this interest was, of course, the nomination of Clarence Thomas to the Supreme Court of the United States. The influence of this event on the academic imagination grew out of what were actually a series of events.

First came the criticism of Supreme Court nominee and former Judge Robert Bork—most forcefully pressed by Senate Judiciary Chairman Joseph Biden—for failing to take seriously the background rights of citizens. Exhibit number one for Biden was Bork's now famous comparison of the Ninth Amendment to an 'ink blot' which appears on the Constitution.[6] Subsequent Supreme Court nominees were required to pledge their fealty to the constitutional principle that '[t]he enumeration in the Constitution of certain rights shall not be construed to deny or disparage others retained by the people.'[7] These events unleashed a scholarly excursion into the meaning of this neglected provision that was unprecedented in American legal history.[8] As a result, we can no longer ignore this unrepealed constitutional injunction on the grounds that it is a complete mystery.[9]

Before the dust from this interest in the 'rights retained by the people' had settled, President Bush nominated for the Supreme Court Judge Clarence Thomas—a man who, in his speeches and writings, seemingly favoured using natural law when interpreting the Constitution.[10] As a result three rather startling events occurred in rapid succession. First, in complete contrast to the arguments used in opposition to Robert Bork, critics of Judge Thomas immediately reacted by characterizing his interest in natural law as kooky and outside the mainstream.[11] Secondly, this fledgling campaign was then completely undercut by Chairman Biden's ringing endorsement of natural law in his opening statement during the hearings. Remaining true to his stance during prior hearings, Senator Biden endorsed the priority of natural law but said, for him, the important question to be answered by the hearings was *which* version of natural law the nominee adopted.[12] By taking this stance, the other Democratic senators were effectively disabled from ridiculing the natural law position. Then, with the stage so dramatically set, Judge Thomas emphatically rejected the position he had seemingly endorsed and maintained that natural law had no role to play in constitutional adjudication,[13] thereby depriving Senator Biden of his debate over the proper version of natural law. Thus, in a matter of weeks the natural law issue was forcefully laid upon the table for national consideration, and scholars then proceeded to continue the debate in the law reviews.[14]

In my view, this discussion has now reached a critical juncture. It has been established beyond any reasonable doubt that adjudication based on natural rights (as distinct from natural law[15]) is excluded neither by 'textualist' nor by 'originalist' approaches to interpretating the constitution. The laboured textual and historical arguments that have been presented to the contrary[16] can be persuasive only to those who have not been exposed to the competing interpretations based, in part, on evidence omitted by the skeptics.[17]

Still, the fact that adjudication based on natural rights is not refuted by text or history does not mean that it is therefore constitutionally justified. The time has come to lay these important historical and textual debates to one side and face squarely the two questions posed by Suzanna Sherry at the conclusion of her most recent contribution and with which I began this chapter:[18] is it possible today to include natural rights in the process of constitutional adjudication and is it desirable? In short, it's time to get normative.

Professor Sherry's questions can be viewed as posing two distinct challenges. The first—'can we take natural rights into account today?'—might be considered *pragmatic* or practical; the second—'do we want to?'—might be viewed as more purely *normative*. I think this possible distinction is overdrawn. If we could not take rights into account, we surely would not want to. And the alleged reasons why we cannot are largely normative, not really practical in nature. Moreover, many would concede that we would naturally want to take natural rights into account if we could. At any rate, I intend to address both questions here. In this chapter, I shall maintain that the correct answers to Suzanna Sherry's questions are 'yes' and 'yes'. Constitutional adjudication both can and should take natural rights into account.

My argument can be summarized as follows:

(1) Those who enact laws to govern the conduct of citizens[19] claim that (a) their laws are not unjust and (b) citizens have at least a *prima facia* moral duty to obey these laws.

(2) To assess whether these claims of lawmakers are warranted, it is appropriate to ask whether their enactments have the qualities that are requisite to being both just and binding.

(3) One of these qualities is that laws not infringe the background or natural rights retained by the people.

(4) Because citizens cannot assess every law to see if it has this rights-respecting quality, there must be some procedural assurance that someone sufficiently impartial has attempted such an assessment.

(5) To be legitimate, law-making processes established by a constitution must (among other things) provide such an assurance.

(6) In our constitutional scheme, the responsibility for providing this sort of scrutiny of enacted legislation falls to the judiciary.

(7) Therefore, background or natural rights should figure in judicial review of legislation.

(8) However, there are methods for performing this task that do not require judges to specify all the background or natural rights retained by the people.

Each step of this argument is contestable, and I shall not be able to establish all of them in this chapter. My main purpose is to introduce the argument and defend its cogency.

I. THE PROBLEM OF LEGITIMACY

Getting normative requires a point of entry. We need to expose the largely hidden problem that normative analysis is intended to address. In the case of a normative analysis of the Constitution, a document that has achieved near mystical status in the United States, this question is almost taboo. It is a question based on an undisputed fact: the Constitution is simply a piece of 'parchment under glass'. The question is: why should we or anyone else care about what it says? The need to answer this question is what I shall call here the *problem of legitimacy*.

By 'legitimacy', I do not mean the question of whether a particular law is 'valid' because it was enacted according to the accepted legal process—

e.g., the Constitution specifies that to be valid a law must be enacted by majorities of both houses of Congress and signed by the President—though some may use the term in this way. Nor do I equate the legitimacy of a law with its 'justice', though these two concepts are closely related, or with the mere *perception* that a law is just. Rather, the concept of legitimacy that I am employing refers to *whether the process by which a law is determined to be valid is such as to warrant that the law is just.* That is, was a particular law made in such a manner as to provide some assurance that it is just? A law produced by such justice-assuring procedures is legitimate.

Thus, according to my usage, a *valid* law could be *illegitimate;*[20] and a *legitimate* law could be *unjust.*[21] Nonetheless, the problem of legitimacy that I raise here *links* the process that determines legal validity in a particular legal system to the issue of justice. Although a constitutional process by which legal validity is determined need not (as a conceptual matter) take justice into account, legitimacy suggests that (as a normative matter) it ought to do so.[22] For, as I shall explain in the balance of this chapter, the problem of legitimacy is to establish why anyone should care what a constitutionally valid law may command. The answer I shall give is that we should care and, consequently, may owe a *prima facie* duty to obey a law, only if the processes used to enact provide good reasons to think that it is just.

II. THE FUNCTION OF THE CONSTITUTIONAL ENTERPRISE

So why should anyone care about what is written on one particular document that lies under glass in Washington D.C.? One reason—and the reason I shall focus on in this chapter—is that the terms of this document are used to regulate an enterprise that will have a direct effect on those who live in the territory known as the United States of America.[23] In particular, this document is used to regulate an enterprise which produces commands that others act or refrain from acting in a particular way. Certain human beings referring to themselves as members of a 'duly constituted government' are going to be telling you and me what to do. Drive on the right side of the road. Don't kill or rape anyone. Pay a percentage of your income in 'taxes'. Don't smoke marijuana or inhale cocaine.

Most importantly, these persons not only threaten to sanction us in some way for disobedience, but they also claim that (a) they are justified in imposing sanctions coercively upon us and (b) we have a moral duty to obey their 'lawful' commands—that we would be acting wrongly by breaking the commands they call 'laws'. In summary, they claim *right* as well as *might* and rest this claim in important part on the fact that they are authorized to issue commands by a piece of parchment they call the

'Constitution'. So we are entitled to ask, what (if anything) it is about this paper that gives their commands the binding authority they claim?

Look at the matter another way. The Constitution is supposed to be the guiding blueprint for just another human enterprise that is producing a good or service for human consumption. In this case the product is law. But unlike other enterprises, this one purports to have the rightful or justified power to force those within its jurisdiction to consume its services, to obey its laws. What (if anything) exactly gives this enterprise this justified power? Normativity has now entered the picture, not because I have introduced it, but because those who claim the Constitution as their 'authority' for their actions also claim the *justified* power to coerce others to accept their commands. It is then perfectly appropriate to ask whether this normative claim is warranted or not. And this is, of course, a normative inquiry.

For example, when the Bureau of Alcohol, Tobacco and Firearms (hereinafter, the BATF) agents in military-style uniforms and armed with genuine automatic assault weapons[24] invaded the property of the Branch Davidians in Waco they implicitly made a normative claim that they were acting in a justified manner. It was their claim to be exercising a justified power, as opposed to my decision to write an article about this claim, that gave rise to the need to address the normative question of legitimacy. That their acts may have been authorized by the Constitution does not settle the problem of legitimacy, it raises it. For the problem of legitimacy that I am discussing here applies to the Constitution itself.[25]

But the normative inquiry does not end there. For those who claim to be empowered by the Constitution make a further claim as well. They claim that you and I are morally obliged (at least *prima facie*) to obey their commands. It is claimed (and commonly thought) that David Koresh and his followers were not only legally obliged to lay down their weapons in the face of these 'agents' of the 'duly constituted authority' acting 'under colour of law'. They were *morally* obliged as well. Their failure to obey is claimed to have been wrongful as well as illegal. Had these invaders been anyone other than the 'public officials' they called themselves, the residents of the compound would surely have been justified in defending themselves against such heavily armed marauders. But solely by virtue of the BATF agents' claim of legal authority, the normative conclusion is said to be completely reversed. Now those who might otherwise have been viewed as defending themselves from aggression are considered murderers rather than innocent victims of a potentially deadly assault (or would be if they had survived the final conflagration).

So the existence of the parchment under glass we call the Constitution raises a two-fold normative problem: what (if anything) gives the persons who claim the authority of its organizational scheme the justified power to issue commands to the rest of us? And what (if anything) creates in the rest of us a moral duty to obey these commands? Perhaps these are two aspects of the same question. It does not matter. The fact is that these questions are not ordinarily addressed because most people simply assume that both the command-issuing power and the moral duty of obedience exists, so they are not much interested in why. Why struggle with a question to which one already knows the answer?[26]

Still, the normative question is not so easily avoided. As Steve Macedo observed, '[a]t the most basic level, moral principles play an inescapable role in constitutional interpretation, and that is because the choice of an interpretive strategy, indeed the very question of how we ought to construe the meaning of "law", are themselves moral questions.'[27] In other words, whether one is an 'originalist', a 'textualist', or an adherent to the 'living constitution' school of constitutional interpretation depends on at least an implicit answer to the problem of legitimacy. Originalists, textualists, et al., are implicitly making some sort of claim about the origin of constitutional legitimacy and the individual's duty of obedience. Normativity cannot be avoided because it is omnipresent. You cannot engage in discourse about the Constitution and its proper interpretation without making implicit claims about legitimacy.

In my view, the first step to addressing the question of legitimacy of the Constitution is to ask what is the point or function of the enterprise it regulates.[28] Of course, the enterprise may very well have many more than one point but I shall focus on one particular function that I think even the most minimal of statists would concede to be central and which directly grows out of the previous discussion: it is an enterprise that is supposed to produce commands that create in the citizenry a moral duty of obedience.[29]

Some philosophers of law might rightly deny that the commands issued by the duly constituted authority *necessarily* create a duty of obedience. Robin West, for example, has argued that, 'if we wish to make our laws just, we must first see that many of our laws are unjust, and if we are to understand that simple truth, we must understand that the *legality* of those norms implies nothing about their justice.'[30] Taken as a conceptual claim, I entirely agree with this statement, although I think it is highly misleading. True, many of our laws are unjust. And it is also true that the legality *simpliciter* of those norms tells us nothing about their justice. If both of these claims are true, then it is also true that the mere fact that an edict is legal tells us nothing about whether there is moral duty to obey its dictates.[31]

But despite its validity, this syllogism is deeply problematic. For it elides the fact that people almost uniformly *believe* that because a norm is legal, it creates at least a *prima facie* duty of obedience. So, to return to the example of Waco, most people (outside of Texas) condemned the Branch

Davidians without ever asking exactly which legal 'norm' it was that they had allegedly violated. Nor was there any interest in asking whether the Branch Davidians were actually guilty of violating whatever rule was being enforced. These questions were not asked because for most people the mere fact that a *legal* norm was being enforced by the duly constituted authorities was enough for them to conclude that the Branch Davidians had a *moral* duty to comply with the orders of the BATF.

Professor West might respond that this is the very problem she is addressing. People should be far more skeptical about the legitimacy of legal norms, she might well argue, and only by insisting on the strict separation of law and morals are we likely to induce this sort of skepticism. While I agree that people should be far more skeptical than they are, I reject a radical schism between law and morals as the most efficacious path to this mind set. And I am not sure that complete skepticism is what Professor West desires. Do we want every citizen to *evaluate* entirely independently every law to assess its justice? Maybe we do. Do we want every citizen to *obey* only those laws which he or she concludes is just? Probably not. Perhaps this is why most people go with the legal flow and condemn the law breaker without themselves scrutinizing the law that was violated.

If, however, we want people to feel obliged to adhere even to some laws the justice of which they may doubt, then it cannot be the case that 'the *legality* of these norms implies nothing about their justice'. Or perhaps more accurately, although in some legal systems this statement may be completely accurate, we cannot be satisfied with such a value-neutral system of legality in a society in which 'law' is such a value-laden term. For unless we demand a system in which the legality of a norm *does* imply something about its justice we will have failed to achieve the objective of having a system of norm creation, dissemination, and enforcement that *does* create a *prima facie* moral duty of obedience in the citizenry—where, in short, the widespread perception of legitimacy is *warranted*. And lawmakers will get a powerful 'benefit of the doubt' or 'halo-effect' to which they are not entitled.

To avoid confusion, it is important to stress that, while the term law is so value laden because people generally believe that validly enacted laws bind in conscience, the conception of legitimacy I am employing is not to be equated with the public's *belief* or *perception* that enactments claimed to be laws are likely to be just. Instead, I am taking this belief as given and asking whether this perception is *warranted* given the constitutional processes that produced the enactment, just as we might ask whether the public's belief or perception that a particular law is *valid* is warranted or not. Is the law-making process such as to warrant a belief that it is likely to be delivering what it is promising to deliver: laws that bind in conscience? Thus, the concept of legitimacy is not to be confused with the *perception* of legitimacy. The public's perception of legitimacy may very well be wrong. Ensuring that it is correct is the problem of legitimacy at issue here.

We can reach this same conclusion from a somewhat different direction by distinguishing between 'producers' and 'consumers' of legal commands. In our (and I would contend every) legal culture, those who produce laws implicitly claim that citizens have a duty to obey lawful commands. And in most cultures, the consumers of the product of the legal system accept this claim of the producers. To the extent that this claim is both made and accepted, there is then an *implied warranty of merchantability* that accompanies every lawful command. Just as the grocer selling sausages implicitly warrants that the sausages are wholesome and fit for human consumption,[32] the purveyors of lawful commands implicitly warrant that their commands are just (or, at a minimum, are not unjust[33]), and these commands, by virtue of their justice, create in the citizen a duty of obedience.

This implied warranty of merchantability could be disclaimed by, for example, explicitly stating that there is no moral obligation to obey a particular enactment. The fact that this disclaimer is never issued, however, conveys to the public the intent to warrant the merchantability of lawful commands. It may be true, as Otto von Bismarck is reputed to have said, that it is better not to know how either sausages or laws are made. If, however, we are to eat the one and obey the other then *someone* better inquire as to the adequacy of the respective production processes. If each consumer has a moral duty to obey lawful commands without questioning each and every one (as people generally believe and as law-makers want them to believe), then those who produce the laws and who implicitly warrant their merchantability have a corresponding duty to put in place adequate quality-control mechanisms to ensure the wholesomeness of the commands they purvey.[34]

This part of my analysis can be summarized as follows: if law-makers claim that people have a *prima facie* moral duty to obey legal norms, and if it is desirable that people accord laws a presumption of legitimacy (albeit within limits), then the system which produces these legal norms must have the requisite institutional quality to justify this presumption. To promulgate enactments without taking steps to ensure their justice and calling these enactments 'laws' knowing that orders so labelled benefit from the presumption of legitimacy, is to promise one thing while delivering another. It is, in short, constitutional bait-and-switch. If the term 'lawful' or 'law' is to carry the normative implication that there is a moral duty to obey, then the requisite binding *quality must go in before the name 'law' goes on.*

III. NATURAL RIGHTS AND CONSTITUTIONAL INTERPRETATION

My principle objective in this chapter is to advance the argument of the preceding section—that for constitutional processes to be legitimate, they must include procedures to assure that lawful commands are justified and of such a nature as to bind in conscience. In this section, I suggest what quality enactments must have to bind in conscience and how this quality should influence our interpretation of the Constitution. Here I share the framers' belief that enactments should not violate the inherent or natural rights of those to whom it is directed. That this was their belief—and that this belief is reflected in the words of the ninth Amendment—is conceded even by those who would contest the appropriateness of judicial intervention to ensure that laws have this rights-respecting quality.[35] In addition, I contend that an assurance that a law has not infringed the enumerated and unenumerated rights retained by the people is a necessary (though perhaps not a sufficient) condition of the legitimacy of the law-making process.

What are these natural rights and why does legitimacy require that they be respected? Elsewhere, speaking not for the framers but for myself, I have offered the following definition: natural rights are the set of concepts that

define the moral space within which persons must be free to make their own choices and live their own lives. They are *rights* insofar as they entail enforceable claims on other persons (including those who call themselves 'government officials'). And they are *natural* insofar as their necessity depends upon the (contingent) nature of persons and the social and physical world in which persons reside.[36]

In sum, 'the pre-existent rights of nature', in Madison's words, are those rights that 'are *essential* to secure the liberty of the people'.[37] A respect for these rights is as essential to enabling diverse persons to pursue happiness while living in society with others as a respect for fundamental principles of engineering is essential to building a bridge to span a chasm.[38]

Natural rights must be distinguished from 'natural law' (or what some refer to as natural *right*[39]). Each of these concepts addresses different problems. Natural law or right is a method of assessing the legitimacy of individual conduct. This method is used to stipulate, for example, that persons should live their lives in certain ways and not in others.[40] The concept of natural rights, in contrast, while sharing a common intellectual ancestry and methodology with natural law, addresses a quite different problem. It asks, not what the good life is for each person and how each person should act, but what moral 'space' or 'jurisdiction' each person requires in order to pursue the good life in society with others.

In sum, whereas natural law assesses the property or *ethics* of individual conduct, natural rights assesses the propriety of *justice* of restrictions imposed on individual conduct.[41] Of course, the same conduct—murder, for example—might be thought to violate natural law because it is 'bad' (persons should not kill others except in self-defence), and because it is unjust (persons have a right not to be killed except in self-defence). But the reasons why actions are bad are not always the same as why they are unjust, and it has long been recognized that many actions that are bad are not unjust, in the sense that they violate the rights of others.[42]

Contrary to the claims of critics of liberalism, then, natural rights are not conceived of as 'presocial';[43] nor do they assume 'atomistic' individuals. Rather, the term natural rights refers to those rights that are inescapably needed precisely to protect individuals and associations from the power of others—including the power of groups and of the state—when and only when persons are deeply enmeshed in a social context. Such rights would be entirely unnecessary if individuals were not in society with each other, or if the actions of some persons did not adversely affect the welfare of others. Moreover, a constitutional commitment to protecting natural rights (as opposed to enacting natural law) does not entail any general mandate to legislate morality. Rather than imposing moral duties on persons to live their lives in certain ways, natural rights protect persons from the state and from each other.[44]

Both the claim that such background rights are necessary and the exact character of their contours are, of course, contestable and contested[45] and I shall not argue the matter here.[46] That the founding generation believed in their necessity is without question, however, and that they viewed their protection as the highest end of the Constitution is also generally conceded. Nonetheless, the relevance of this belief is open to question. Perhaps, as some have argued, the framers of the Constitution did not believe that such rights merited judicial protection unless they were expressly included in the constitutional text. I have attempted to answer this question elsewhere[47] and this is not the place to rehearse my arguments and those of others who take the same position,[48] or the arguments of our worthy opponents.[49] To date this has been one of the most hotly debated issues surrounding the ninth Amendment.

Instead, I wish to use the preceding analysis of legitimacy to address a question that has long surrounded any discussion of the framers' intent: assuming that the founding generation did believe that legislation that violated natural rights was beyond the powers of government and therefore void, why are we who are alive today bound by their beliefs, particularly if we now reject the concept of natural rights as outmoded and even incomprehensible?

According to the approach presented here we, as citizens, are not bound by the framers' intentions. Rather, I am claiming (a) that the framers wrote a constitution, the test of which some persons *alive today* purport to be governed by when they issue supposedly binding commands to us; (b) that we are bound in conscience to obey these commands only if the law-making processes established and regulated by this text provides assurance that our rights have not been violated; (c) that *if* the Constitution provides effective protection of rights, then the lawful commands of constitutional authorities may be justified and binding and, if not, then we obey solely to avoid punishment.

For these reasons, the fact that the text of the Constitution includes the words, '[t]he enumeration in this Constitution, of certain rights, shall not be construed to deny or disparage others retained by the people,'[50] is significant. For the ninth Amendment, along with the Privileges or Immunities Clause of the fourteenth Amendment,[51] supports the view that, as a descriptive matter, the assessment of constitutional validity—by the judiciary or anyone else—established by the text of the Constitution *did* (and until it is amended still does) include a constitutional solicitude for natural rights. And if this interpretation or description of the text is accepted as correct, then the Constitution may, as a normative matter, be legitimate. If it is incorrect, then the legitimacy of the Constitution is called into question.

It is, then, necessary to take a stand one way or the other as to the best interpretation of the ninth Amendment and the Privileges or Immunities Clause, just as it is necessary to take a stand on the best interpretation of the first Amendment, the Necessary and Proper Clause, and all other relevant portions of the Constitution. It is simply inadequate to point to the disagreements that exist and then blithely ignore the Constitution on the grounds that competing interpretations have been offered. A proper interpretation of the Constitution as a whole requires a proper interpretation of these passages as well as all the others. There is no escape, therefore, for anyone interpreting the Constitution—whether the interpreter be a judge or a law professor—to confront the conflicting arguments and evidence and decide which is the most convincing interpretation of the rights 'retained by the people' and the Constitution's injunction that they be neither denied nor disparaged.

To put the matter starkly, those who argue, first, that the framers' intentions matter when interpreting the Constitution and, secondly, that the framers did not intend that all branches of government strive to protect the unenumerated rights retained by the people, should hope that they are wrong on at least one count. For, if they are correct both that courts are bound by the original meaning of the constitutional text and that this text does not provide any protection of unenumerated rights, then they may have won the constitutional battle, yet lost the legitimacy war. They would

have succeeded only in proving that the constitution now in effect does
not provide what it must provide to make laws that are justified and bind
in conscience. For if those who produce and inspect legislation are not
bound to respect the rights retained by the people, then the people are not
bound to respect their laws.

Fortunately, they are wrong. The argument that the Constitution as
amended established a regime of democratic majoritarianism fettered
only by those rights which were enumerated is belied by both its text and
history—not to mention a significant part of our constitutional jurisprudence. That we should resolve our historical and textual doubts in
favour of protecting unenumerated rights is bolstered by the moral argument that even democratic majorities must justify their forcible impositions on minorities. As Jeffrey Reiman has argued,

> there is nothing inherently legitimating about the electoral process. If anything, the
> electoral process is the problem, not the solution . . . [T]he policies that emerge
> from the electoral process will be imposed on the dissenting minority against its
> wishes. And then, rather than answering the question of legitimacy, this will raise
> the question with respect to those dissenters. Why are the exercises of power
> approved by the majority against the wishes of (and potentially prohibiting the
> desired actions of) the minority obligatory with respect to the minority? Why are
> such exercises of power not simply a matter of majority tyrannizing the minor-
> ity?[52]

Our choice of among interpretations as well as interpretative methods
is, then, a normative one. The 'best' interpretation of the Constitution is
one that takes the natural or background rights of persons into account
when evaluating the legitimacy of any governmental regulation of a person's rightful exercise of his or her liberty. For unless we do, the enterprise
which the Constitution establishes and regulates will have failed in its
essential function of providing justified laws that bind in conscience.

One question remains. If we generally believe in a core of liberty or
'retained' rights that is to be protected from government intrusion (as I
think we do), if this belief is well founded (as I think it is), and if the constitutional text can fairly be read as justifying scrutiny of legislation to see
if it has infringed these retained rights (as I think it can), then: do laws that
regulate a person's conduct within this protected domain bind in conscience on those whose liberty is being regulated? There are two
approaches one can take to this question.

First, one could take the strong libertarian position that such rights may
never be regulated by anyone, including the government and that any
enactment that does so is unjust and void. Although this view may very
well be correct as a matter of moral and political theory, it is not the view
embodied in the text of the Constitution. For if natural rights are to be
absolutely protected from any regulation, then no governmental action

would withstand scrutiny. If such rights merit absolute protection (as well they may), *this* constitution neither promises or provides such protection. If that fact deprives the Constitution of all legitimacy then so be it. On the other hand, it may be that legitimacy is a relative concept, so that the Constitution's less than absolute protection of natural rights means that it is superior to many alternative political arrangements, but inferior to others.

Secondly, one may take the view that (for better or worse) the Constitution provides less than absolute protection of the background natural rights retained by the people. So, for example, the exercise of such rights may be regulated by the general government if it is exercising a delegated power and if the exercise of this power is both necessary and proper.[53] Although according to this view, the Constitution does contemplate the regulation of these background rights under these conditions,[54] the existence of these rights even when properly regulated remains significant in two respects: first, the fact that governmental actions restrict the exercise of a person's rights places the *burden of justification* on that branch of government which seeks to act in this way. Secondly, the fact that the rights retained by the people are inalienable (as I contend[55]) means that, even when their regulation is shown to be authorized, necessary, and proper, persons still retain their rights and may insist that a particular type of regulation cease when it ceases to be necessary. In sum, rights do not evaporate just because they have once been regulated. Only this second conception of natural rights permits us to reconcile the protection of the background rights retained by the people, with the government powers, albeit limited, that the Constitution acknowledges.[56]

IV. TAKING NATURAL RIGHTS INTO ACCOUNT: THE PRESUMPTION OF LIBERTY

So my answer to the second of Suzanna Sherry's questions is that we most certainly want to reconcile our natural rights past with our textualist present. But how? To some extent, I have suggested my answer to this question as well. I have suggested that the existence of inalienable natural rights that exist independently of governmental fiat means that those persons who act 'under colour of law' have a duty to respect these rights, and to show that any regulation of them is both necessary and proper. Having made this showing with respect to a particular enactment does not cause the right that has been regulated to be lost. The inalienability of rights means that when an enactment ceases to be necessary and proper, it no longer binds the conscience of the citizenry.

This approach is what I have elsewhere referred to as the 'presumptive method'[57] of protecting constitutional rights and it is based on what I have called the 'presumption of liberty'.[58] This presumptive method enables courts to protect natural rights without them ever having to use the term or compile a comprehensive list of these rights. The presumption of liberty can only be operational, however, if it is enforceable. It is woefully inadequate to insist that legislatures or executive branch officials may be the judge in their own cases when their actions are alleged to infringe upon the rightful liberty of a citizen. The whole purpose of natural rights in this context is to protect persons from legislative or executive abuses. Unless these rights are protected by relatively 'independent tribunals of justice',[59] they are virtually worthless.[60] Of course, if legislatures do take pains to regulate the rights of citizens only when it is necessary and proper to do so, we can expect them to be able to justify their actions. Regrettably, our experience with legislatures has not been so utopian. For this reason, meaningful 'scrutiny' by an impartial magistrate of legislative and executive branch actions that impinge upon the liberty of individuals and associations is required.

According to current thinking, there can be different degrees of scrutiny—so-called rational basis scrutiny, strict scrutiny, and intermediate scrutiny—and there exists a multitude of formulations of each. To the extent that *every* statute can withstand rational basis scrutiny and *no* statute can pass strict scrutiny, this distinction is disingenuous. To adopt one type of scrutiny is to eliminate all review; to adopt the other is to eliminate all legislation affecting any exercise of liberty. I have therefore deliberately chosen the phrase *meaningful* scrutiny to denote a real examination of legislation (or executive actions) to determine whether it is really necessary to restrict liberty in order to accomplish a legitimate governmental end, and whether the type of means chosen to effectuate this end is proper—that is, within the appropriate powers of government. The former question is instrumental; the latter may entail an examination of the background rights of the people.

So, for example, the power to conscript citizens into the military is not listed among the enumerated powers of Congress. If valid, conscription must be justified under the necessary and proper clause as both necessary and proper to facilitate Congress' power to raise and support an army. Is it really necessary to conscript citizens into the military to provide a national defence? Is conscription a proper exercise of governmental power? Similarly, the enumerated congressional power to establish a post office does not include the power to confer a monopoly on the post office so established.[61] Is such a monopoly really necessary for mail service to be provided? Is the grant of monopoly—which coercively puts competitors out of business—a proper exercise of governmental power?[62] Meaningful scrutiny does not presuppose any particular answer to such questions. It simply means that when a person's rightful liberty is restricted by government, that person may challenge the restriction and, if challenged, the burden is placed upon the government to justify the restriction as a necessary and proper regulation of liberty. This is not to exalt the judiciary, but the citizen. In Charles Black's words, '[i]f we are committed to anything, it is the ideal of "liberty". If that commitment doesn't really refer to anything except a good inner feeling, we ought to shut up about it.'[63]

According to this approach and contrary to the view prevailing today, the power to regulate—i.e., make regular—the exercise of liberty is not the same as the power to prohibit.[69] If the presumption of liberty did nothing other than prevent the complete prohibition of rightful conduct, it would be an important departure from the current constitutional approach.[65] Still, no classical liberal natural rights theorist—even the most libertarian—has ever identified the liberty protected by natural rights with the freedom to anything one wills.[66] There has always existed at least implicitly a distinction between liberty and licence.[67] So it is no infringement upon a person's natural rights to prevent him from violating the rights of another and the presumption of liberty would be inapt, except in so far as it is necessary to place the onus of proof on those who would argue that a particular type of action is violative of another's rights.

How is the base-line distinction between a rightful exercise of liberty (that is presumptively immune from governmental restriction) and a wrongful exercise of liberty (licence) to be established, and by whom? Traditionally, this distinction between rightful and wrongful conduct was provided by the common law which determined a person's legal rights. Consider the following explication of the 'common law' by Chancellor George Wythe, a distinguished judge and holder of the first Law Chair in the United States, in the case of *Page* v. *Pendleton*:

The portion in the sixth article of our bill of rights, namely that men are not bound by laws to which they have not, by themselves, or by representatives of their election, assented, is not true of unwritten or common law, that is, of the law of nature, called common law, because it is common to all mankind . . . they are laws which men, who did not ordain them, have not power to abrogate.[68]

That is, in contrast with constitutional law which provides rules for the conduct of government agents, the common law of property, tort, contract, restitution, agency, etc. provides principles of right conduct to regulate the conduct of persons toward each other. For example, when one injures another and this injury is considered to be 'tortious', then it is deemed to be wrongful and a duty to compensate is held to exist. A major portion of the first year of most law schools is devoted to studying the issue of rightful conduct. This body of rules and principles was judge-made at the time of the framing of the Constitution and largely remains so today. Moreover, in the United States federal system it was and still is primarily made by state court judges. Even federal judges today acting pursuant to their powers in diversity cases attempt to discern state law and consider themselves bound by it. When federal judges must decide these state law questions in the absence of state court precedent, they may be 'reversed' by subsequent state court rulings.

Thus there has evolved a division of labour. The judiciary in the several states are primarily responsible for determining rightful from wrongful conduct; while judges in the federal courts, beginning most famously with the case of *McCulloch* v. *Maryland*[69] are responsible for assessing the necessity and propriety of federal restrictions on otherwise rightful conduct. With the passage of the fourteenth Amendment, the federal government's jurisdiction was expounded to include protecting citizens from rights infringements by their own state governments.[70] This division of labour was not, of course, ever quite this neat. It was also thought appropriate for legislatures, especially on the state level, to intervene in the common law process, especially when the doctrine of precedent was thought to prevent a particular judicial reform.

Still, though this complicates the story a bit, it is important to bear in mind that such legislative interventions were supposed to be and in fact were comparatively rare. Determination of private rights were traditionally and are still overwhelmingly the province of state court judges. And, even with sweeping statutory innovation such as the Uniform Commercial Code, legislative alterations of private law rights are relatively rare.[71] Far more frequently has the common law been affected by the opinions of the non-profit American Law Institute through its highly authoritative series of 'restatements' of the law.

So emerges the great outlines of an institutional allocation of responsibility in discerning and protecting the background natural rights of all persons: *state common law processes determine the rights that each citizen enjoys against others; while state and federal judges are authorized to protect citizens from having these rights infringed by state and federal governments*. Both components of this institutional division of labour have long existed.[72] The legitimacy of the statute-making processes governed by the Constitution would be enhanced, however, if they are linked.

But does not this constitutional scheme place altogether too much power in state and federal judges? As I have already argued above, such reliance is unavoidable in a constitutional system in which courts are the only relatively 'independent tribunals of justice' available to protect citizens from majority and minority factions operating through representative government.[73] Moreover, the problem is typically grossly overrated.[74] When Congress disagrees with an assessment by the Supreme Court of the United States that its enactments have violated the background natural rights of the people, it has the power to propose a constitutional amendment. The President may take any disagreement (or agreement) with past Supreme Court rulings into account in selecting judicial nominees, and the Senate may express views during the confirmation process. A majority of the Supreme Court may well protect rights at variance from the opinion of the overwhelming majority of the people for a time, but life is, alas, all too short. This fact together with our method of judicial selection assures that, for better or worse, in the not-so-long run any opinion about the rights of the people which is opposed by an overwhelming majority of the people will be reversed.

These various mechanisms by which Supreme Court rulings protective of liberty can be challenged may take some time and effort to be effective, but this delay is in most instances salutary and, in any event, absolutely essential if legislatures are not to be judges in their own cases when their acts restrict the liberty of citizens. The more likely deficiency of this proposal in practice is that government judges are not sufficiently independent of government or of a majority faction to provide 'an impenetrable bulwark against every assumption of power in the legislative or executive . . .'[75] For this reason prior rulings *upholding* the exercise of such powers should always be subject to reconsideration when circumstances have changed.

CONCLUSION: THE LEGITIMACY OF LAW

Let me summarize the analysis I have presented here. First, I contended that it is impossible to avoid 'getting normative' about whether the unenumerated rights retained by the people merit judicial protection. For the legitimacy of the enterprise established by the Constitution depends on its ability to reliably produce enactments that bind the citizenry in conscience. And we cannot be sure that any enactment restricting the rightful liberty of a citizen has this binding quality unless we are certain that it has been scrutinized by an independent tribunal of justice to see if it is necessary and proper. Thus, the background natural rights of all persons require that a burden should be placed on those who seek to restrict liberty to justify their actions, rather than on the citizen to justify his freedom. In our constitutional scheme, this can be accomplished by linking state law determinations of rightful conduct with state and federal scrutiny of legislative and executive restrictions of such conduct.

Although we may not wish to know how either laws or sausages are made, we had better be sure that the processes of both law-making and sausage-making include a quality-control mechanism that ensures that the produce being purveyed is safe and wholesome. That such quality-control processes are imperfect in no way undermines their importance. This is particularly true when—as was tragically demonstrated once again in Waco—whether dealing with food or force, life and death may hang in the balance.

NOTES

1 Austin B. Fletcher, Professor, Boston University School of Law. This chapter was first presented at the Conference on Liberalism, Modernity, and Natural Law, sponsored by the American Public Philosophy Institute, the Symposium on Rights sponsored by the philosophy department of the University of North Carolina at Greensboro, and to faculty workshops at Georgia State University, Loyola Law School, Loyola Marymount University, Rutgers-Camden School of Law, and Boston University School of Law. Participants in these gatherings made many valuable suggestions for improvement. I also wish especially to thank Jules Coleman, Bob Bone and Richard Hyland for commenting on an earlier draft and Saba Khairi for her research assistance.

2 Suzanna Sherry, 'Natural Law in the States', 61 *Cinc. L. Rev.* 171, 222 (1992).

3 See H. L. A. Hart, 'Positivism and the Separation of Law and Morals', 71 *Harv. L. Rev.* 593 (1958); Lon L. Fuller, 'Positivism and Fidelity to Law—A Reply to Professor Hart', *Harv. L. Rev.* 630 (1958).

4 Three recent issues of law reviews have been largely devoted to the topic. See 'Natural Law Symposium', 38 *Cleve. St. L. Rev.* 1 (1990); 'Symposium: Perspectives on Natural Law', 61 *Cinc. L. Rev.* 1–222 (1992); Commentary on 'Constitutional Positivism', 25 *Conn. L. Rev.* 831–946 (1993). The latter consists of papers responding to Frederick Schauer's article, 'Constitutional Positivism', 25 *Conn. L. Rev.* 797 (1993).

5 See Randy E. Barnett, 'The Remergence of Normative Legal Philosophy' (Book Review), 97 *Harv. L. Rev.* 1223 (1984).

6 See Nomination of Robert H. Bork to be Associate Justice of the Supreme Court of the United States: Hearings before the Senate Comm. On the Judiciary 117 (1989) (Testimony of Robert Bork):

I do not think you can use the Ninth Amendment unless you know something of what it means. For example, if you had an amendment that says 'Congress shall make no' and then there is an ink blot and you cannot read the rest of it and that is the only copy you have, I do not think you can make up what might be under the ink blot if you cannot read it.

7 U.S. Const. amend IX. For an appendix reproducing the testimony of Robert Bork, Anthony Kennedy, David Souter, and Clarence Thomas concerning the Ninth Amendment, unenumerated rights and natural law, see 2 *The Rights Retained by the People: The History and Meaning of the Ninth Amendment* 427–508 (Randy E. Barnett, ed. 1993) [hereinafter cited as 2 *Rights Retained by the People*].

8 For a representative sample of this post-Borkian scholarly debate (and a bibliography of other Ninth Amendment scholarship), see Ibid.

9 Not that this scholarship has prevented Bork himself from doing so. See Robert

Bork, *The Tempting of America: The Political Seduction of the Law* 183 (1990). ('There is almost no history that would indicate what the ninth amendment was intended to accomplish.')

10 See E. G. Clarence Thomas, *The Higher Law Background of the Privileges or Immunities Clause of the Fourteenth Amendment*, 12 *Harv. J. L. & Pub. Pol'y* 63, 63–4 (1989):

[N]atural rights and higher law arguments are the best defense of liberty and of limited government. Moreover, without recourse to higher law, we abandon our best defense of judicial review—a judiciary active in defending the Constitution, but judicious in its restraint and moderation. Rather than being a justification of the worst type of judicial activism, higher law is the only alternative to the willfulness of run-amok majorities and run-amok judges.

11 The most noteworthy of these critics was Professor Lawrence Tribe who characterized Judge Thomas as 'the first Supreme Court nominee in 50 years to maintain that natural law should be readily consulted in constitutional interpretation.' Lawrence Tribe, 'Natural Law and the Nominee', *NY Times*, 15 July 1991, at A15. For a list of others who criticized Thomas's reliance on natural law, see Ken Masugi, 'Natural Right and Oversight: The Use and Abuse of "Natural Law" in the Clarence Thomas Hearings', 9 *Pol. Communication* 231, pp. 235–7 (1992).

12 See Appendix B: 'Testimony of Recent Supreme Court Nominees Concerning the Ninth Amendment, Unenumerated Rights, and Natural Law, in 2 *Rights Retained by the People*, above at n. 7, at 489 (statement of Senator Biden):

And there's a third type of natural law, Judge. It's the one that mirrors how the Supreme Court has understood our constitution for the bulk of this century. And it's the one that I believe most Americans subscribe to. It is this view of natural law that I believe—I personally, to be up front about it—think is appropriate. It is this view of natural law, the Constitution should protect personal rights falling within the zone of privacy, speech and religion the most zealously. Those rights that fall within that zone should not be restricted by a moral code imposed on us by the Supreme Court or by unjust laws passed in legislative bodies.

13 Although construing Thomas's writing as endorsing the use of natural law in constitutional adjudication is not unreasonable, his former aid and speech writer denies that he ever advocated such a practice. See Masugi, above at n. 11, at 248, n. 45 ('To my knowledge, Thomas in his pre-judicial writings never used the term *Constitutional Adjudication*'). For a defence of the coherence of this position, see Russell Hittenger, 'Natural Law in the Positive Laws: a Legislative or Adjudicative Issue?', 55 *Rev. of Politics*, Winter 1993, 5 at p. 22. ('[T]here is nothing contradictory in arguing, on the other hand, for a natural law basis of government, and indeed of positive law itself, while at the same time holding that judges ought, whenever possible, to be bound by written law.')

14 See sources cited above at n. 11. The debate has even inspired a satire. See Mark Hamilton Levinson & Charles Sherman Kramer, 'The Bill of Rights as Adjunct to Natural Law',. 4 *Det. C. L. Rev.* 1267 (1991) (neither Hamilton nor Sherman are their middle names).

15 More on this distinction anon.

16 See E. G. Raoul Berger, 'Natural Law and Judicial Review: Reflections of an Earthbound Lawyer', *Cinc. L. Rev.* 5 (1992); Philip A. Hamburger, 'Natural Rights, Natural Law, and American Constitutions', 102 *Yale L. J.* 907 (1993); Thomas B. McAffee, 'The Original Meaning of the Ninth Amendment', 90 *Colum. L. Rev.* 1215 (1990); Thomas B. McAffee, 'The Bill of Rights, Social Contract Theory, and the Rights "Retained" by the People', 16 *S. Ill. U. L.J.* 267 (1992); Thomas B. McAffee, 'Prolegomena to a Meaningful Debate of the "Unwritten Constitution Thesis" ', 61 *Cin. L. Rev.* 107 (1992) (hereinafter 'Prolegomena'); Helen K. Michael, 'The Role of Natural Law in Early American Constitutional Thought: Did the Founders Contemplate Judicial Enforcement of "Unwritten" Individual Rights?', 69 *N.C. L. Rev.* 421 (1991).

17 See E. G. Randy E. Barnett, 'Introduction: Implementing the Ninth Amendment', in 2 *The Rights Retained by the People*, above at n. 7, at 1; Steven J. Heyman, 'Natural Rights, Positivism and the Ninth Amendment: A Response to McAffee', 16 *S. Ill. U. L. J.* 327 (1992): Calvin R. Massey, 'The Natural Law Component of the Ninth Amendment', 61 *Cinc. L. Rev.* 49 (1992); David N. Mayer, 'The Natural Rights Basis of the Ninth Amendment: A Reply to Professor McAffee', 16 *S. Ill. U. L.J.* 313; Suzanna Sherry, above at n. 2; Bruce N. Norton, 'John Locke, Robert Bork, Natural Rights and the Interpretation of the Constitution', 22 *Seton hall L. Rev.* 709 (1992).

18 See text accompanying above at n. 2.

19 I include in the term 'citizens' all persons who are subject to the jurisdiction of constitutional authorities.

20 A law may be 'valid' because produced in accordance with all procedures required by a particular law-making system, but may be 'illegitimate' because these procedures are inadequate to provide assurances that a law is just.

21 A law might be 'legitimate' because produced according to procedures that assure that it is just, and yet be 'unjust' because in this case the procedures (which can never be perfect) have failed.

22 To the extent the issue is thought to be conceptual as opposed to normative, the traditional natural law-positivist debate is sterile. Even Aquinas was quite capable of distinguishing as a conceptual matter between those human laws that were just and those that were unjust when he declared that '. . . [l]aws framed by man are either just or unjust.' Thomas Aquinas, *Summa Theologica*, in *Twenty Great Books of the Western World*, p. 233a (1952)). Rather, for Aquinas and other natural law thinkers, the issue of lawfulness is not conceptual as it is for modern positivists, but normative. Only just laws 'have the power of binding in conscience . . .'. It is this issue of 'binding in conscience' that informs his endorsement of Augustine's statement that 'that which is not just seems to be no law at all; therefore the *force* of a law depends on the extent of its justice.' Ibid., p. 227b (emphasis added).

23 That, at least, is the theory. The normative argument presented here rests on the assumption that the enterprise of law-making is really governed by the provisions of the Constitution. To the extent that significant provisions of the Constitution have been either ignored or interpreted out of existence, this assumption and the normative argument that rests upon it is undermined.

24 As distinct from the semi-automatic so-called 'assault weapons' recently prohibited by the Congress.

25 To see why *authority* by itself is not enough, suppose that you are my agent and I authorize you to take someone's car by force if needed. When the car owner resists, you tell her that I have authorized you to take the car, which is true. She may then appropriately ask what gives me the right or power to authorize such a thing. Why should she care what I have or have not authorized? In addition to showing that your acts were authorized, you must also show that either you or I had the justified power to take the car by force and that she had a duty to refrain from interfering. The BATF agents' attempt to justify their conduct solely by appealing to the authority of the Constitution is like appealing to the authority that I granted my agent. It leaves out the normative dimension of the claim being made. Of course, had their actions been *unauthorized*, then the problem of legitimacy raised by the Constitution would not be implicated. They would have been acting illegally as well as, perhaps, unjustly.

26 Although most constitutional scholars ignore this question, at least one philosopher has both considered the problem and addressed it in much the same way as I advocate here. See Jeffrey Reiman, 'The Constitution, Rights, and Conditions of Legitimacy', in *Constitutionalism: the Philosophical Dimension* (Alan S. Rosenbaum ed., 1988), at p. 127.

27 Stephen Macedo, 'Morality and the Constitution: Towards a Synthesis for "Earthbound" Interpreters', 61 *Cinc. L. Rev.* 29, 30 (1992).

28 Cf. Reiman above n. 26, at p. 132. ('[I]t is not possible to choose . . . [the appropriate method of constitutional interpretation] without having some theory of what the Constitution *is*, what its point is, what its source of obligatoriness is, and so on.')

29 Ibid. at p. 133. ('Legitimate power means (at least) power with which we are morally obliged to comply.')

30 Robin West, 'Natural Law Ambiguities', 61 *Cinc. L. Rev.* 831, 831 (1992).

31 It is possible to argue that people also have a moral duty to obey unjust laws for reasons of, say, the need to maintain social order. Indeed, Aquinas himself so argued in the passage immediately following that quoted, above at n. 22. Although I do not reject such a claim, it is, needless to say, in need of substantial elaboration and defence.

32 See U.C.C. §2–314(1) (1990):

> Unless excluded or modified . . ., a warranty that the goods shall be merchantable is implied in a contract for their sale if the seller is a merchant with respect to goods of that kind. Under this section the serving for value of food or drink to be consumed either on the premises or elsewhere is a sale.

33 I have in mind the many laws that are entirely conventional in nature, such as traffic regulations, and not in themselves requirements of justice. Such laws are conventional in the sense that, although there may be many different ways to accomplish a particular end, some way must authoritatively be settled upon. Still, it is appropriate to ask of any particular convention whether it is unjust.

34 Cf. Reiman, above at n. 26, at 131:

> [L]egitimate government is not simply one that keeps to a pre-established

recipe for legitimacy but one that has built into it an institutional mechanism for continually reflecting on the conditions of its legitimacy and for effectively translating the results of that reflection into law.

35 For example, Thomas McAffee, Philip Hamburger, and Michael McConnell all agree that the framers were very much concerned with natural rights. See E. G. McAffee, 'Prolegomena', about at n. 16, at p. 119, n. 41 ('[T]here is reason to think that the founders sought to establish a fairly particular vision of natural law and natural rights rather then an open-ended methodology in which subsequent decision-makers would feel free to reject their decisions as to the basic content of natural rights.'); Hamburger, above at n. 16, at p. 915 ('[L]arge numbers of Americans spoke about government, liberty and constitutional law on the basis of some shared assumptions about natural rights and the state of nature.'); Michael W. McConnell, 'A Moral Realist Defense of Constitutional Democracy', 64 *Chi-Kent L. Rev.* 89, 99 (1989) ('The founders of the United States were believers in natural right . . . The Constitution was framed in accordance with the people's understanding of natural right; we know this from the preamble's statement of intentions.'). Rather, these writers question whether the founders contemplated or intended the *legal enforceability* or *judicial protection* of these rights.

36 Randy E. Barnett, 'The Intersection of Natural Rights and Positive Constitutional Law', 25 *Conn. L. Rev.* 853, 862 (1993).

37 1 *The Debates and Proceedings in the Congress of the United States* 454 (J. Gales and W. Seaton ed. 1834) (Speech of Rep. J. Madison) (emphasis added). In the passage from which these phrases are taken, Madison is arguing that the right of trial by jury enumerated in the proposed amendments, though a 'positive right', is as essential to secure the liberty of the people as any natural right.

38 Although I do not claim that all Americans in the founding generation shared this (or any) conception of natural rights, it is clear that some did. For example, Pastor Elizur Goodrich (1734–97), made a functional argument of this sort in an 'election sermon' he delivered to the governor and general assembly of Connecticut on the eve of the Constitutional Convention:

The principles of society are the laws, which Almighty God has established in the moral world, and made necessary to be observed by mankind; in order to promote their true happiness, in their transactions and intercourse. These laws may be considered as principles, in respect of their fixedness and operation, and as maxims, since by the knowledge of them, we discover the rules of conduct, which direct mankind to the highest perfection, and supreme happiness of their nature. *They are as fixed and unchangeable as the laws which operate in the natural world.*

Human art *in order to produce certain effects*, must conform to the principles and laws, which the Almighty Creator has established in the natural world. He who neglects the cultivation of his field, and the proper time of sowing, may not expect a harvest. He, who would assist mankind in raising weights, and overcoming obstacles, depends on certain rules, derived from the knowledge of mechanical principles applied to the construction of machines, in order to give the most useful effect to the smallest force: And every builder should well understand the best position of firmness and

strength, when he is about to erect an edifice. *For he, who attempts these things, on other principles than those of nature, attempts to make a new world; and his aim will prove absurd and his labour lost.* No more can mankind be conducted to happiness; or civil societies united, and enjoy peace and prosperity, without observing the moral principles and connections, which the Almighty Creator has established for the government of the moral world.
Elizur Goodrich, 'The Principles of Civil Union and Happiness Considered and Recommended', in *Political Sermons of the American Founding: 1730–1805* (Ellis Sandoz ed. 1991), at pp. 914–15 (emphasis added).

Lest this quote reinforce a modern misconception about traditional natural rights theory, note that although Goodrich identifies God as the original source of the laws that govern in the moral world, so too does he identify God as the source of the laws that govern agriculture and engineering. With both types of principles and laws, once established by a divine power they become part of the world in which we find ourselves and are discovered by human reason. Thus, today one can no more disparage natural rights because eighteenth century thinkers attributed their origin to a divine power than one can disparage the laws of physics because eighteenth century scientists believed that such laws were also established by God. Whatever the source of these moral laws, Goodrich's argument is that they must be respected if we are to achieve the end of happiness, peace, and prosperity. This view of moral laws assumes, of course, that happiness, peace, and prosperity are appropriate ends. Should anyone question this assumption, additional arguments will need to be presented.

39 See E. G. McConnell, above at n. 35 (consistently referring to natural right as opposed to natural rights). But cf. Masugi, above at n. 11, at p. 245, n. 5. ('In accordance with the rough practice of the American Founders, I use natural rights and natural law interchangeably. *Natural rights* is the more comprehensive term.') Although I agree that the founders were far from uniform in their usage, the political writings I have read seem almost invariably to use the language of natural rights as opposed either to natural law or natural right. See E. G. Roger Sherman's draft of the Bill of Rights, in 1 *The Rights by the People: The History and Meaning of the Ninth Amendment* 1 (Randy E. Barnett, ed. 1989) [hereinafter 1 *The Rights Retained by the People*] ('The people have certain natural rights which are retained by them when they enter into Society. . . .'); *Madison's notes for Amendments Speech*, 1789, ibid., at 64 ('Contents of Bill of Rights . . . 3. natural rights retained as speach [sic].'). Indeed, use by the founders of the term natural right would have been quite aberrational.

More importantly, Masugi's use of natural right as the more comprehensive term elides the appropriate distinction between the two modes of thought. It also seems to be at odds with the usage of contemporary writers who systematically prefer the term natural right to natural rights and in contexts that suggest that they really mean natural law. Russell Hittenger, for example, uses the term in the context of natural law, as opposed to natural rights, and attributes it to Aquinas. See Hittinger, above at n. 13, at 5 (referring to 'the only article of the *Summa* exclusively devoted to the issue of natural right (*Ius Naturale*)'). In sum, the recent tendency to supplant the term natural rights with that of natural right has only compounded the normal academic confusion of the concept of natural law with that of natural rights. This terminological development seems to be associated with scholars who have been influenced by the writings of Leo Strauss.

40 See E. G. Henry B. Veatch, for *An Ontology of Morals* (1971).

41 I do not claim that everyone, or even most people, use all these terms in precisely this way. I claim only that natural law thinking is distinguishable from natural rights thinking and that this terminology best describes the difference between them. Moreover, running these two modes of thought together leads to serious confusion.

42 For example, natural law theorist Thomas Aquinas, writing centuries before natural rights developed as a separate methodology, argued:

> Now human law is framed for a number of human beings, the majority of which are not perfect in virtue. Therefore human laws do not forbid all vices, from which the virtuous abstain, but only the more grievous vices, from which it is possible for the majority to abstain, and chiefly those that are to the *hurt of others, without the prohibition of which human society could not be maintained*; thus human law prohibits *murder, theft and the like*.

Aquinas, above at n. 22, at p. 232a (emphasis added).

43 These rights are, however, conceived of analytically as pre-governmental. Perhaps the charge that liberals conceive of rights as pre-social is persistent because some critics of liberalism are so committed to statism that they equate government with society.

44 For this reason, the constitutional protection of these rights may include *both* a 'negative' duty of government to refrain from infringing these rights and a 'positive' duty upon government to protect the rights of its citizens from infringement by others. See Steven J. Heyman, 'The First Duty of Government: Protection, Liberty and the Fourteenth Amendment', 41 *Duke L. J.* 507, 510 (1991). ('[T]he classical conception of liberty was not merely negative, but had a crucial positive dimension—the protection of individual rights under law.') Of course, to claim that a constitution imposes positive duties on *government* is not to concede that it imposes positive duties on the *citizenry*. In the main, the Constitution 'constitutes' the government of the United States and regulates its powers; it does not purport to regulate the rights of the people.

45 Some eschew the term natural rights because of metaphysical claims they associate with it; they prefer instead the term 'moral right' or 'human right'. Adopting this terminology does not affect the analysis presented here, provided that (1) a moral right is considered to be an enforceable claim, or what the classical natural rights theories called a 'perfect' right as opposed to 'imperfect' moral rights which are unenforceable; and (2) a moral right is not the equivalent of a legal right, but is a concept used to evaluate the justice of legal rights.

46 I have provided a functional account of the core rights traditionally recognized by liberalism—several property and freedom of contract—in Randy E. Barnett, 'The Function of Several Property and Freedom of Contract', 9 *Soc. Phil. & Pol'y* 62 (1992). There I argue that these concepts are essential because they address the pervasive social problems of knowledge, interest, and power.

47 See Barnett, above at n. 17; and Randy E. Barnett, 'Reconceiving the Ninth

Amendment', 74 *Corn. L. Rev.* 1 (1989). A revised version of this article appears
as 'Introduction: James Madison's Ninth Amendment', in 1 *The Rights Retained
by the People,* above at n. 39, at 1.

48 See E. G. Heyman, above at n. 17; Massey, above at n. 17; Mayer, above at n. 17;
   Norton, above at n. 17; Sherry, above at n. 2; Sherry, above at n. 17.

49 See the authors cited above at n. 16.

50 U.S. Const. amend IX.

51 See U.S. Const. amend XIV. ('No State shall make or enforce any law which
   shall abridge the privileges or immunities of citizens of the United States . . .')
   Obviously the framers of this amendment were able, along with Aquinas, to
   distinguish conceptually between a validly-enacted and a binding and enforceable 'law'.

52 Reiman, above at 26, at p. 134. As he elaborates:

   These questions not only point up the error of taking electoral accountability as an independent source of legitimacy, they also suggest that it is mistaken to think of electoral accountability and constitutional provisions as
   alternative sources of legitimacy. Rather, the Constitution *with its provisions
   limiting the majority's ability to exercise power* is the answer to the question of
   why decisions voted by a majority are binding on the minority who disagree.

53 For a discussion of the distinct meanings originally attached by the founding
   generation to the terms 'necessary' and 'proper', see Gary Lawson and Patricia
   B. Granger, 'The "Proper" Scope of Federal Power: a Jurisdictional
   Interpretation of the Sweeping Clause', 43 *Duke L.J.* 267 (1993).

54 As explained below, according to their conception of the Constitution, the regulation of natural rights is to be distinguished from their infringement. A
   purely libertarian conception of natural rights might well find that the
   Constitution also sanctions the latter. For example, the Sixteenth Amendment
   permits the taxation of income, and the Fifth Amendment permits takings of
   private property for public use when 'just compensation' is made.

55 For several reasons why some rights are inalienable, see Randy E. Barnett,
   'Contract Remedies and Inalienable Rights', 4 *Soc. Phil. & Pol'y* 179 (1986).

56 See Henry B. Veatch, *Human Rights: Fact or Fancy?* pp. 202–8 (1985) (defending
   from a natural law perspective a conception of inalienable—rather than
   absolute—natural rights that are justified because they afford the necessary
   conditions for the living of a good life, and that must be protected by an independent judiciary lest either the public authorities or the private individual be
   made a judge in his own cause.)

57 See Barnett, above at n. 17, at pp. 10–46 (describing and defending the adoption
   of a 'presumption of liberty'). Elsewhere, I have identified two other methods
   of protecting unenumerated rights. See Barnett, above at n. 47, at pp. 30–8 (distinguishing between the originalist, constructivist, and presumptive methods
   of interpreting unenumerated rights). The 'originalist method' seeks to identify
   the founding generation's conception of natural rights by surveying the same
   historical materials in which originalists seek evidence of the original meaning
   of other Constitutional provisions. See e.g., Jeff Rosen, 'Was the Flag Burning
   Amendment Unconstitutional?', 100 *Yale L. J.* 1073, pp. 1072–81 (1991)

(enumerating the framer's conception of natural rights); Donald S. Lutz, 'The States and the Bill of Rights', 16 *So. Ill. L. J.* 251 (1992) (comparing state ratification convention proposals and state bills of rights with Madison's proposal to Congress and the enacted Bill or Rights). The 'constructivist method' attempts to construct a theory of the rights retained by the people and then uses this theory to ground particular rights. The Supreme Court's construction of the 'right of privacy' from various textual passages of the Constitution is one way of employing the constructive method. See e.g., *Griswold* v. *Connecticut*, 381 U.S. 479 (1965).

58 This and the next three paragraphs summarize the analysis I have presented at greater length elsewhere, after which I describe some additional features of this approach.

59 The phrase is taken from Madison's speech to the first House of Representatives in defence of his proposed amendments to the Constitution: 'If they are incorporated into the constitution, independent tribunals of justice will consider themselves in a peculiar manner the guardians of these rights . . .' 1 *The Debates and Proceedings in the Congress of the United States*, above at n. 37, at p. 457 (statement of James Madison), reprinted in 1 *The Rights Retained by the People*, above at n. 38, at p. 51.

60 Cf. Reiman, above at n. 26, at p. 144:

On my view, the Court's decisions must be legally binding precisely because they are decisions about the conditions of legitimate governance by the other branches, conditions whose determinations cannot be left up to those branches. Unless the Court's decisions are legally binding, a necessary condition of legitimacy, namely, a built-in mechanism for not only monitoring but effectively correcting the conditions of legitimacy, is lacking.

61 The Articles of Confederation *did* expressly confer such a power upon Congress. See *Art. of Confederation*, art. IX.

62 The ratification conventions of four states—Massachusetts, New Hampshire, New York, and North Carolina—formally requested that prohibitions on granting monopolies be included in the Bill of Rights. See Appendix B: Amendments to the United States Constitution proposed by State Ratification Convention, in 1 *Rights Retained by the People*, above at n. 39, at pp. 354–4, 360, and 369. New York's proposal read: 'That the Congress do not grant monopolies, or erect any company with exclusive advantages of commerce.' Ibid. at p. 360. In his speech to the House concerning the *constitutionality* of the first national bank, Madison condemned the proposal, in part, on the ground that '[i]t involves a monopoly, which affects the equal rights of every citizen.' Appendix A: Madison's speech on the constitutionality of the bank of the United States, in 2 *Rights Retained by the People*, above at n. 7, at p. 423.

63 Charles Black, 'On Reading and Using the Ninth Amendment', in 1 *Rights Retained by the People*, above at n. 39, at p. 345.

64 The distinction between regulation and prohibition is not always easy to maintain in practice. Any regulation of liberty necessarily prohibits its exercise in ways that are contrary to the regulation. So, for example, time, place, and manner regulations of speech in public spaces necessarily prohibit speech that

conflicts with these regulations. Still, a regulation of speech should not be intended to effectuate a prohibition, and at the extremes this distinction may be quite clear. Thus, it is not difficult to distinguish the regulation of the liberty to use intoxicating drugs from a prohibition of such use. For a discussion of how the existence of 'hard cases' of constitutional interpretation does not preclude the existence of 'easy cases', see Frederick Schauer, 'Easy Cases', 58 *S. Cal. L. Rev.* 399 (1985).

65 The prevailing orthodoxy is that a presumption of constitutionality applies unless a particular enactment violates an enumerated fundamental right, affects a discrete and insular minority group, or affects the electorial process. See *United States* v. *Carolene Products Co.*, U.S. 144, 152 n. 4 (1938). Recently, however, Justice Stevens argued that the refusal of government to regulate a particular action could be justified, if challenged, by a presumption of freedom: 'Freedom is a blessing. Regulation is sometimes necessary, but it is always burdensome. A decision not to regulate the way in which an owner chooses to enjoy the benefits of an improvement to his own property is adequately justified by a presumption in favor of freedom.' *Federal Communications Commission* v. *Beach Communications, Inc.*, ??U.S.??, 113 S. Ct. 2096, 2105 (1993) (Stevens, J., concurring). Whatever encouragement is provided by Justice Stevens' concurrence, is undercut by the opinion of Justice Thomas, which rests heavily on 'a strong presumption of validity'. Ibid. at 2102. Ironically, given the fear that he would use natural law to strike down offending legislation, Justice Thomas enthusiastically embraced the prevailing view that:

> those attacking the rationality of the legislative classification have the burden 'to negative every conceivable basis which might support it,' . . . Moreover, because we never require a legislature to articulate its reasons for enacting a statute, it is entirely irrelevant for constitutional purposes whether the conceived reason for the challenged distinction actually motivated the legislature . . . In other words, a legislative choice is not subject to courtroom fact-finding and may be based on rational speculation unsupported by evidence or empirical data.

Justice Stevens took issue with this standard: 'In my view, this formulation sweeps too broadly, for it is difficult to imagine a legislative classification that could not be supported by a "reasonably conceivable state of facts'. Judicial review under the 'conceivable set of facts' test is tantamount to no review at all.' Ibid. at 2106 (Stevens J., concurring).

66 Compare Robert Nozick, *Anarchy, State, and Utopia* 171 (1974) ('My property rights in my knife allow me to leave it where I will, but not in your chest.') with *Republica* v. *Oswald*, 1 U.S. (1 Dall.) 319, 330 n.* (Pa 1788) ('[T]hough the law allows a man the free use of his arm, or the possession of a weapon, yet it does not authorize him to plunge a dagger in the breast of an inoffensive neighbor.' [statement of representative William Lewis to the Pennsylvania General Assembly]).

67 See e.g. John Locke, *Two Treatises of Government*, pp. 288–9 (Peter Laslett ed. 1967) (2d ed. 1970):

> But though this be a *state of liberty*, yet it is *not a state of license* . . . The *State of Nature* has a Law of Nature to govern it, which obliges everyone: and

Reason, which is that Law, teaches all Mankind, who will but consult it, that being all equal and independent, no one ought to harm another in his Life, Health, Liberty, or Possessions.

Although I disagree with the implications he draws concerning the role of judicial review, a recent insightful discussion of how natural rights theorists treated this issue is provided by Philip Hamburger. See Hamburger, above at n. 16, at pp. 922–53.

68 *Page* v. *Pendleton* (1793), in *George Wythe, Decisions of Cases in Virginia by the High Court of Chancery* 216 n. (e) (B. B. Minor ed. 1852) as it appears in Sherry, above at n. 2, at p. 186. Cf. John S. Baker, Jr., 'The Natural and the Positive in American Law', in *Saints, Sovereigns and Scholars: Studies in Honor of Frederick D. Wilhelmsen* 157, 163 (R. A. Herrera, James Lehreberger and M. E. Bradford eds., 1993). ('Originally common law was viewed as the embodiment of natural law. Then it became understood in historicist terms as simply custom and eventually in purely positivist terms as judge-made law.')

69 17 U.S. (Wheat. 316 (1819).

70 Thus the fact that the entire Bill of Rights, including the Ninth Amendment, was originally intended to apply only to the federal government—as the Supreme Court decided in *Barron* v. *Baltimore* (7 Pet. [32 U.S.] 243 (1833])—does not mean that the Ninth Amendment is irrelevant to actions of state governments. Of necessity, the people retained their *inalienable* rights against the states as well as the federal government. This is evidenced by the swift incorporation of provisions similar to the Ninth Amendments into many state constitutions after Madison devised this express restraint. However, it was the Fourteenth Amendment that extended *jurisdiction* to the federal government to protect these rights from state government infringement, thereby altering the pre-existing jurisdictional arrangement. This is not to claim that the Fourteenth Amendment somehow 'incorporated' the Ninth, but that the Privileges or Immunities Clause extended the federal jurisdiction to protect the enumerated and unenumerated rights retained by the people against infringements by state governments.

71 It is a tricky, but necessary, business to distinguish those legislative actions that are a proper codification, regulation, systemization, or correction of common law rights from those that constitute state governmental interference with these rights. While this problem merits further discussion, it does not affect the efficacy of federal scrutiny of *federal* legislation that interferes with otherwise rightful exercises of liberty. Nor does it affect scrutiny of the clear majority of state actions that do not and cannot purport to be determining the private rights that citizens have against each other. This leaves only the important question of determining when state legislation *purporting* to improve upon the scheme of common law rights is actually infringing the relatively abstract background natural rights of its citizens. I do not think, however, that this question can be shirked solely because it may be difficult to identify a general theory that distinguishes genuine regulation from improper infringements of liberty. Without such a theory, citizens and their freedoms are left to the tender mercies of legislative majorities who may represent either majority or minority factions.

72 Professor Hamburger has recently offered an insightful interpretation of the

relationship that the founding generation saw between natural and civil law. He notes that while Americans unquestionably conceived of freedom of speech as a natural right, they 'frequently discussed the extent of freedom of speech in terms of common law constraints upon it. Even when Americans talked about the freedom of speech and press as a broader principle or generality, they often distinguished between liberty and license, without clearly alluding to natural rights or natural law.' Hamburger, above at n. 16, at p. 953. The distinction between liberty and licence needs to be defined conventionally because the concept of natural rights is too abstract to permit all but the most extreme of cases to be decided deductively from first principles. As Hamburger correctly observes, 'being only a very abstract manner of reasoning, natural law was typically not understood to require the adoption of a particular set of civil laws. Moreover, though considered immutable, natural law was understood to permit variations in civil laws to accommodate the different circumstances in which such laws would operate.' Ibid. at p. 937. However, because *more than one* set of legal rules is consistent with the abstract injunctions of natural rights, this does not mean that *every* set of legal rules is consistent. Particular common law formulations can be criticized for being inconsistent with abstract natural rights and consequently unjust. The issue being discussed here, however, is who makes this decision, and traditionally this was primarily the province of state court judges, with occasional correction by state legislatures.

Where I part company with Professor Hamburger is over his claim that '[a] failure of the constitution to reflect natural law was a ground for altering or abandoning the constitution rather than for making a claim in court.' Hamburger, above at n. 16, at p. 940. He has missed a crucial third possibility that was unlikely to have been missed by the framers who had practised civil disobedience long before they became revolutionaries: that the failure of a constitution to *respect* natural *rights* was a ground for disregarding laws that are promulgated pursuant to its authority.

73 Although this proposal makes the most out of the constitutional scheme that we currently have, it is not the only constitutional arrangement imaginable. I have speculated on more radical possibilities in Randy E. Barnett, 'Pursuing Justice in a Free Society: Part Two—Crime Prevention and the Legal Order', *Crim. Just. Ethics*, Winter/Spring 1986, at 30, pp. 37–49 (describing a polycentric legal order).

74 See Barry Friedman, 'Dialogue and Judicial Review', 91 *Mich. L. Rev.* 577 (1993) (arguing that courts are not systematically less majoritarian than the political branches of government).

75 The phrase is, once again, Madison's. See 1 *The Debates and Proceedings in the Congress of the United States*, above at n. 37, at p. 457 (speech of Rep. J. Madison), reprinted in 1 *The Rights Retained by the People*, above at n. 39, at p. 51. See e.g. *Korematsu v. United States*, 323 U.S. 214 (1944) (upholding the constitutionality of confining citizens of Japanese ancestry in detention camps).

9

The Illegitimacy of Appeals to Natural Law in Constitutional Interpretation

WALTER BERNS

I

I begin by stating the obvious: federal judges are not in the habit of invoking natural law to support their constitutional decisions. Rather, they invoke one or another—and sometimes a handful—of specific constitutional provisions. This is not an accident. Their authority is limited to deciding cases and controversies—for my purposes here, cases arising 'under the Constitution' or 'the laws of the United States'—which they weigh in the balance with the relevant constitutional provision. And most of these provisions, or at least the provisions most frequently cited, have to do with rights which, again, is not by accident since, as we are taught by the Declaration of Independence, the purpose of government is the securing of rights.

True, there once were occasions when Supreme Court justices appealed to something at least formally akin to natural law. For example, in the very early *Calder* v. *Bull*, Justice Samuel Chase would have grounded his decision on 'the first principles of the social compact' (which led the dissenting James Iredell to protest that a court was not entitled to hold a legislative act void on the ground that it was contrary to 'natural justice'),[1] and a few years later Justice William Johnson, in a concurring opinion, joined in the invalidation of a state law by invoking 'the reason and nature of things: a principle which will impose laws even on the Deity'.[2]

But these extra-constitutional excursions have long since fallen into disrepute, at least nominally. The modern Chase or Johnson eschews reliance on 'natural justice' or the 'reason and nature of things' in favour of some constitutional text that, as he reads it, makes such excursions unnecessary. As sometimes read, these texts prove to be more capacious or commodious than earlier justices could have imagined. Thus, in the Connecticut birth control case, Justice William O. Douglas referred to various guarantees in the Bill of Rights and found in them 'penumbras, formed by emanations', which, in turn, contained 'a right of marital privacy'. Three of his concurring colleagues found that right in the ninth Amendment.[3]

This sort of jurisprudence found no favour with Justice Hugo L. Black. He denounced it as the 'natural law due process [or "whatever"] philosophy', and, in case after case, denied that the Court had any such jurisdiction. 'If these formulas based on "natural justice", or others which mean the same thing, are to prevail, they require judges to determine what is or is not constitutional on the basis of their own appraisal of what laws are unwise or unnecessary.'[4] Although Black may be right about the purpose for which they are employed, these 'formulas'—natural law or justice and reserved rights—do not in fact mean the same thing. In fact, they mean different things.

But Black was not alone in failing to distinguish them; so, too, did the venerable Roscoe Pound. Hoping to breathe some life into the 'forgotten' ninth Amendment, Pound seized upon the possibility that, with their reference to the '[rights] retained by the people', the framers of the Constitution had in mind natural rights or—like Black, he tended to confuse them—natural law. But he was not willing to accept the understanding of these rights, or this law, current at the time of the founding. In the fashion of those jurists and scholars who promote the cause of a 'living constitution', he came up instead with the idea of mutable law and rights mutable but—*mirabile dictu*—still natural. 'Unlike the law of nature of the eighteenth century,' he said, 'the revived natural law is not a fixed system of precisely formulated rules to stand fast forever.' The same is true of natural rights: '[f]rom this standpoint,' he said, 'the Ninth Amendment is a solemn declaration that natural rights are not a fixed category of reasonable human expectations in civilized society laid down once for all in the several sections of the Constitution.'[5]

Except as a term used to lend dignity or authority to a judge's idiosyncratic policy preferences, the idea of nature simply disappears from Pound's jurisprudential musings. What is *natural* about a right or a law that has no fixed definition? How can *nature* provide the standard by which we measure our laws and policies if, like them, the idea of nature changes with the times? Yet, clearly, although they may have defined it differently, those who first employed the term 'nature', whether in connection with law (Cicero and Thomas Aquinas) *or* right (Thomas Hobbes and Thomas Jefferson), intended that it provide such a standard and understood its meaning as fixed.[6] It is, of course, the idea of a fixed meaning, not the idea or need of a standard, that is unacceptable to so many modern judges and constitutional lawyers. But, as I have argued elsewhere, you cannot have the one without the other.[7]

II

I have made the point that natural law and natural rights are not interchangeable terms. This is readily illustrated, if not demonstrated, in the work of the United States Supreme Court. Black may denounce his colleagues for employing what he calls the 'natural law due process [or "whatever"] philosophy', or, as he put it in another case, the 'natural-law-due-process formula',[8] but the natural law, strictly speaking, played no role whatever in these cases, particularly in the most notorious among them, *Griswold* v. *Connecticut, Roe* v. *Wade,* and *Bowers* v. *Hardwick.*[9] There the justices (in *Bowers,* the four of them in the minority) relied not on the natural law but on a right, specifically a right of privacy: for contraception, abortion, and homosexual sodomy, all practices specifically condemned by natural law properly, or at least traditionally, understood.[10]

What, then, do we mean by moral philosophy and what is its role in constitutional interpretation? These, I presume, are the questions that inspired this book, and their investigation ought to begin at our beginning. As to that beginning, and the moral philosophy by which it was guided, here is John Quincy Adams writing in 1839 on the occasion of the Constitution's 50th anniversary:

[The Constitution's] VIRTUES, its republican character, consisted in its conformity to the principles proclaimed in the Declaration of Independence, and its administration must necessarily be always pliable to the fluctuating varieties of public opinion, its stability and duration by a like overruling and irresistible necessity, was to depend on the stability and duration in the hearts and minds of the people of that *virtue,* or in other words, of those principles proclaimed in the Declaration of Independence and embodied in the Constitution of the United States of America.[11]

The Declaration begins by invoking both 'the Laws of Nature and of Nature's God' and, in the following paragraph, the self-evident truth that government is instituted to secure the 'unalienable rights' with which all men are equally endowed by their 'Creator'. It identifies the most important of those rights—the rights to life, liberty, and the pursuit of happiness—but it says nothing further about those laws, nothing to aid us to identify them or their relation to the unalienable rights. Both the laws and the rights derive from, or are the gift of, the Creator, Nature's God. but who is He?

According to John Courtney Murray the well-known Catholic theologian, He is the God who revealed himself in the Bible. The Declaration of Independence, he says, recognizes the sovereignty of this biblical God; the rights of which it speaks are the rights of Englishmen and the product of 'Christian history'; these rights, even in the form they take in the Bill of

Rights, are 'tributary to the tradition of natural law, to the idea that man has certain original responsibilities precisely as man'; which is to say, the rights of man are derived from his responsibilities (or duties), or responsibilities are primary, rights secondary or derivative.[12] Here Murray might have quoted Matthew 22:37–40: 'You shall love the Lord your God with all your heart, and with all your soul, and with all your mind. This is the great and first commandment. And the second is like unto it, you shall love your neighbour as yourself.' Whatever rights we have are, presumably, dependent on our obedience to this law. John Locke, of course, had it otherwise. He said the state of nature has a law of nature to govern it, which law obliges everyone 'as much as he can, to preserve the rest of mankind,' but to do this only 'when his own preservation comes not in competition'.[13]

Now it is obvious that the Declaration does not speak of the rights of Englishmen; it speaks of 'certain unalienable rights' which, on the face of it, would seem to suggest that rights are primary, as Locke said they were. One of these rights is the right to pursue happiness, presumably (although this will require argument) a happiness that each of us defines for himself. Was this a right enjoyed by Englishmen? The basis of this right would seem to be freedom of conscience. Did English law, modelled, as Murray says, on the natural law, recognize freedom of conscience? Freedom of conscience would find expression in a separation of church and state. Did England separate church and state? Be that as it may, does Roman Catholicism recognize freedom of conscience? Murray's answer to this is emphatic: Catholicism, he says, rejects 'the absolute primacy of conscience', and his account of the provenance of the Bill of Rights requires him to say that freedom of conscience is not embodied in the first Amendment.[14] This amounts to saying that the principles of the first Amendment are not those of John Locke who, in his *Letter on Toleration*, said that 'the care of . . . everyman's soul belongs unto himself, and is to be left unto himself,' or of Thomas Jefferson who said that 'the operations of the mind [unlike] the acts of the body, are [not] subject to the coercion of the laws [and that] our rulers can have no authority over such natural rights, only as we have submitted to them [but the] rights of conscience we never submitted, we could not submit.'[15]

Murray's question, and ours, come to this: to understand the 'Laws of Nature and of Nature's God' do we turn to Thomas Aquinas or John Locke?

Murray acknowledges the difference between Thomas' 'natural law' (or, as Thomas sometimes writes, 'law of nature'), and Locke's law of nature; the last chapter of his book is devoted to explaining it. Locke's law of nature, he says, was the creature of the Enlightenment, and it was 'as fragile, time-conditioned, and transitory a phenomenon as the Enlightenment itself.'[16] So, too, with the 'theory of natural rights', whose philosophical scaffolding he dismisses as 'philosophical nonsense'.[17] Locke's ideas of the law of nature, the rights of man, and the origins of society, he says, 'are not derived from what is "real", from the concrete totality of man's nature as it really is'.[18] Apparently, Locke did not see that, as a rational being, man can know the good toward which he is by nature inclined (which is the foundation or, better, the condition of the natural law as Thomas expounded it); indeed, although Murray does not point this out, Locke expressly denied that 'the Law of Nature [is] inscribed in the minds of men' and that 'the Law of Nature [can] be known from the natural inclination of mankind'.[19]

According to Murray, quoting Thomas, men can know the natural law that forbids killing, or more precisely, murder. But according to Locke's law of nature, men may 'destroy noxious things', which means, as Locke subsequently makes clear, the law of nature allows men to kill other human beings. His position here is similar to that of Hobbes who baldly states that a justly condemned murderer has a right to murder his jailers in order to save his own life.[20] I could go on to make a list of the ways in which Locke's law of nature differs from the traditional natural law—contrasting their views on the basis of human sociality, legitimate government, the conscience, happiness, the care of children, the honour due parents by children, and so on—but this work has been done elsewhere. The question is, what does this have to do with the United States?

Murray's answer is nothing, or nothing much. Locke's ideas were picked up by 'the French enthusiasts', he says, but not by the common-sensible British or, as he would have it, by the Americans. Whatever its vitality today, the United States was conceived in 'the tradition of natural law', not, he argues, Locke's law of nature.[22]

But if Murray is mistaken about this, if we have a constitutional right to worship as we please or not to worship at all, and if this constitutional right derives from our natural right of conscience, or, in Jefferson's words, from our natural right to worship twenty gods or no god, or from our unalienable right to define happiness as we see fit because, as Locke puts it, there can be no definitive understanding of happiness,[23] and if that natural right of conscience derives from the providential fact that the care of each man's soul belongs to himself alone, which means that, contrary to the Bible as read by Catholic, Protestant, and Jew alike, as well as to the Koran, God has not provided for the care of souls; if, in a word, the provenance of the Declaration of Independence and the Constitution is in the thought of John Locke, 'America's philosopher', as he used to be called, then what follows for John Courtney Murray and, to bring this home to us, the proponents of a natural law based judicial review?

But the great body of evidence shows that Murray was wrong. It is undeniable that the Declaration adopts the language of Locke ('pursuit of happiness', 'long train of abuses', mankind 'are most disposed to suffer.')[24] It is undeniable that Jefferson, who drafted the Declaration, spoke of Locke as one of the three greatest men ever to live (the others being, interestingly, Bacon and Newton). It is also undeniable that James Wilson, one of its principal framers, spoke of the Constitution as founded on 'the revolutionary principle [of] Mr Locke'; this new Constitution, he said, will establish the first government in history grounded unambiguously on the true principles of natural right, and 'the great and penetrating mind of Locke seems to be the only one that pointed towards even the theory of this great truth.'[25] It is also undeniable that the founders spoke repeatedly of natural right and the state of nature—which has no place in Thomas's classic natural law—and, further, that this was, as Jefferson said, the common language spoken by Americans at the time, federalists and antifederalists alike, including the simple citizens of Lenox, in the Massachusetts Berkshires.[26] It is also undeniable that, in his explication of the Constitution, Publius (James Madison in this case) spoke of 'the Social Compact' and, like Jefferson in the Declaration, of 'the transcendent law of nature and of nature's God'.[27] It is also undeniable, I think, that it was Locke's and Montesquieu's view of man's nature that lies behind Madison's famous statement in *Federalist* 10 that the 'latent causes of faction are . . . sown in the nature of man'. Finally, it is also undeniable that Madison, having said that justice is 'the end of government [and] civil society', proceeds to define justice by referring to 'a state of nature' and in terms made familiar by Hobbes and Locke.[28]

Again, I could go on, but I think enough has been said to prove that what Murray calls the American proposition is, contrary to what he says, Lockean in origin, not Thomistic. For Thomas, as well as his English counterpart, Richard Hooker, the natural law is grounded on the eternal law—which is to say, on God himself, or on his providence or governance—and derives its strength ultimately from the threat of divine punishment but immediately (and necessarily) from the more evident threat of civil punishment. The reason for this derives from the fact that while the first principles of the natural law are (or are said to be) promulgated and known to all men, in so far as they are rational, those principles alone are not sufficient guides for human action. This means that the natural law has to be supplemented by civil law; this law, modelled on the natural law, provides a surer guide to virtuous action. The existence of such a natural law rests on certain presuppositions, generally an understanding of human nature bound up with a teleological view of the universe.[29]

I shall not—indeed, I am not qualified to—enter into a discussion of whether natural law is possible without those presuppositions. Nor shall I enter into a discussion of the political consequences—most importantly, the possibility of constitutionalism—if, as is widely assumed, modern science has made it impossible to believe in a teleological universe or, stated otherwise, if Nietzsche was right about the death of God, 'Nature's God' as well as the God of Revelation. Those consequences have, I think, been definitively described by Professor Levinson.[30]

My purpose is to consider whether judges are justified in declaring laws unconstitutional because they conflict with the natural law. I took this to mean the pre-modern natural law which, I implied, was rejected by the framers of the Constitution in favour of the laws of nature as defined by Thomas Hobbes and John Locke. The natural law they rejected directs men's action, by means of commands and prohibitions, toward a variety of ends which possess a natural order, 'ascend[ing] from self-preservation and procreation via life in society toward knowledge of God'.[31] According to this pre-modern natural law, self-preservation is a duty (which means suicide is forbidden), but according to Hobbes and Locke, self-preservation is a right (which, as I indicated above, means one may murder his executioner). These new laws of nature (mere deductions from the fundamental right of nature to preserve ourselves) simply direct us to seek peace by entering into a contract with others according to which we enter into civil society and agree to surrender our natural rights or powers in exchange for the civil rights or liberties which are to be secured or protected by government.[32] Thus, our natural rights to life and liberty are exchanged for the civil rights—or, in our case, the constitutional rights— not to be deprived of them without due process of law.

But, as Jefferson said, and the religious provisions of the first Amendment imply, our natural right of conscience is not surrendered, we cannot surrender. This, more than any other principle or provision of the Constitution, characterizes the American system of self-government: the laws may deprive us of life and liberty but not of the right to pursue the happiness we define for ourselves. In this respect, which can rightly be said to be the decisive respect, we are governed by ourselves, not by the law. In a word, rather than taking its bearings from a natural law that prescribes the means to the various ends given by nature—a law that tells us how to live our lives—the government of the United States is obliged to leave us alone.

But if, under the Constitution, the Congress is forbidden to take cognizance of the natural law when it legislates, does it not follow that the judiciary is forbidden to take such cognizance when it adjudicates? And given the fact that the traditional natural law rests on presuppositions that no contemporary judge—or at least none known to me—would accept, is it not likely that any judicial reference to such a law is, as Justice Black said it was, simply a cloak for what the judge thinks governmental policy ought to be?

Professor Barnett, in chapter 8, addresses that question in the context of the ninth Amendment which, of course, speaks not of natural law but, instead, of the '[rights] retained by the people'. In line with this, nowhere in his 49 page introduction to the volume he edited on the ninth Amendment is there any reference to natural law.[33] Instead, and quite properly in my judgement, he addresses the two questions that arise from the ninth Amendment: what are these unenumerated rights and are they justiciable?

We all agree that the Bill of Rights was intended to impose restrictions only on the federal government; this means that it was only the federal government that was forbidden 'to deny or disparage [the other rights] retained by the people'.

We also agree that the Supreme Court, beginning in 1925, has incorporated most of the provisions of the Bill of Rights, including, presumably, the ninth Amendment, into the due process clause of the fourteenth Amendment, thereby making them applicable as restrictions on the states as well as on the federal government.

I note that, to the extent that the ninth Amendment has been invoked by the Supreme Court, this has been done only in state cases, never, to my knowledge, in a case involving federal legislation. I am impelled to ask, why not?

Is it that Congress has never enacted a law that can be said to have deprived a person of an unenumerated right? That, to coin John Marshall's phrase, 'is too extravagant to be maintained'. Is it, then, that the justices do not dare to invoke an unenumerated right to strike down a provision adopted by both houses of Congress and signed into law by the President of the United States, in short, a law enacted by a national constitutional majority?

Writing in the 78th *Federalist*, Alexander Hamilton, said that 'it would require an uncommon portion of fortitude in the judges to do their duty as faithful guardians of the [written] Constitution, where legislative invasions of it had been instigated by the major voice of the community.' I suggest that more than fortitude would be required of the judges to invalidate such legislation by invoking a right nowhere specified in the Constitution.

It seems to me that any worthy ninth Amendment argument must address the question of whether the framers intended the judiciary to exercise such an extraordinary power. Such consideration might begin by noting what the framers did *not* do—for example, they did not *expressly* authorize any kind of judicial review, and they repeatedly rejected Madison's call for a Council of Revision with the authority to 'examine every act of the National Legislature before it shall operate'—and what they *did* do. For example, they contrived to have the country governed by carefully structured constitutional majorities, and authorized these majorities to 'make all Laws which shall be necessary and proper for carrying into Execution the [previously delineated] Powers, and all other Powers vested by this Constitution in the Government of the United States, or in any Department or Officer thereof.' Did they also authorize the judiciary to override these laws by substituting a definition of necessity and propriety found in a right 'retained by the people' or, as Professor Barnett's critics would have it, in the 'bottomless well' or the 'Pandora's box' of the ninth Amendment?

If, to quote Marshall again, this 'is too extravagant to be maintained', what was the purpose of the ninth Amendment? I am obliged to address this question, if only briefly.

In the course of shepherding the Bill of Rights through the House of Representatives in the First Congress, Madison asked whether it could not fairly be said that the amendments proposed by the House committee (on which he served) were not, with exceptions he noted, the amendments demanded by the various state ratifying conventions.[34] What he neglected to mention was an amendment proposed by New York, Massachusetts, North Carolina, Rhode Island, and especially his own state of Virginia. This was an amendment acknowledging a right that without question everybody at the time understood to be fundamental: the right to reserve rights, or, stated differently, the right of the people to decide *whether, how,* and *where* or *by whom* they shall be governed; in short, the right exercised by the people in 1776.

During the Virginia ratification debates, Patrick Henry, the most prominent of the anti-federalists, said 'there are certain political maxims, which no free people ought ever to abandon . . . *That all men are by nature free and independent, and have certain inherent rights, of which, when they enter into society, they cannot by any compact deprive or divest their posterity.*'[35] His colleague, Edmund Randolph, made the same point: what was needed in a bill or rights was a 'perpetual standard . . . around which the people might rally' if or when the legislature should violate the limits of its powers. In other words, the constitution should remind the people of their ultimate sovereignty, or their right 'to alter or abolish' a government that, in their judgement, had violated the trust bestowed on it, or, as still another Virginian put it, to renew or give it a 'fresh spring at stated periods'. A statement of this sort was put at the head of the Virginian constitution, so why not, he asked, at the head of this constitution of the 'general confederation'?

Madison, and the federalists generally, did not disagree with the principle, but, as Herbert Storing has demonstrated in his definitive study of the origins of the Bill of Rights, Madison especially was determined that a statement of that principle not be given a prominent place in the Constitution:

Recurrence to first principles does not substitute for well-constituted and effective government. In some cases, it may interfere. Does a constant emphasis on unalienable natural rights foster good government or a sense of community? Does a constant emphasis on popular sovereignty foster responsible government? Does a constant emphasis on a right to abolish government foster the kind of popular support that any government needs? The Federalists did not doubt that these first principles are true, that they may be resorted to, that they provide the ultimate source and justification of government. The problem is that these principles, while true, can also endanger government. Even rational and well-constituted governments need and deserve a presumption of legitimacy and permanence. A bill of rights that presses these first principles to the fore tends to deprive government of that presumption.[36]

If my reading is correct, that 'perpetual standard', or that statement of first principles, was not pressed 'to the fore', not, as it was in the case of Virginia, placed at the head of the Constitution; rather, it was consigned to the ninth Amendment. There, but in a much less conspicuous place, and in language much more sober than Patrick Henry's, it serves as a reminder to the people that they are the source of the powers exercised by government.

It is of some interest to note that the people of Virginia claimed to be exercising this right in 1861 when they adopted an ordinance repealing the ordinance of 25 June, 1788, ratifying the Constitution—in a word, when Virginia pretended to secede from the Union. The right to consent to government, they said, implies the right to withhold that consent and to withdraw that consent. Such a right, they said, was expressly recognized in the ninth Amendment.[37]

The fact that the ninth Amendment was cited in the secession debates, and that the debates in all the seceding states are filled with statements to the effect that the right to withdraw consent is *the* fundamental right retained by the people,[38] does not *prove* that my reading of the Amendment is correct; but what was said in those debates does bear an uncanny resemblance to what was said in 1788 by Patrick Henry, Samuel Adams, and the other anti-federalists in their call for a bill of rights. If this, then, is what they meant by a right 'retained by the people', it is a right that was adjudicated not in any court, state or federal; it was adjudicated (so to speak) on the battlefield.

NOTES

1 *Calder* v. *Bull*, 3 Dallas 386, pp. 387–8 and 398–9 (1798).
2 *Fletcher* v. *Peck*, 6 Cranch 87, 143 (1810).
3 *Griswold* v. *Connecticut*, 381 U.S. 479, pp. 484 and 487ff. (1965).
4 Ibid., at pp. 511–12. Dissenting opinion.
5 Roscoe Pound, 'Introduction', Russell B. Patterson, *The Forgotten Ninth Amendment* (Indianapolis, The Bobbs-Merrill Co., Inc., 1955), at pp. iii, iv.
6 Nature as guide or measure is, perhaps, best illustrated in this soliloquy spoken by the bastard son of the Earl of Gloster (Shakespeare, *King Lear*, Act I, scene 2):

> Thou, Nature art my goddess; to thy law
> My services are bound. Wherefore should I
> Stand in the plague of custom, and permit
> The curiosity of nations to deprive me,
> For that I am some twelve or fourteen moonshines
> Lag of a brother? Why bastard? Wherefore base?
> When my dimensions are as well compact,
> My mind as generous, and my shape as true,
> As honest madam's issue? Why brand they us
> With base? with baseness? bastardy? base, base?
> Who, in the lusty stealth of nature, take
> More composition and fierce quality
> Than doth, within a dull, stale, tired bed,
> Go to th' creating a whole tribe of fops,
> Got 'tween asleep and wake?—Well, then,
> Legitimate Edgar, I must have your land:
> Our father's love is to the bastard Edmund
> As to th' legitimate: fine word,—*legitimate*!
> Well, my legitimate, if this letter speed,
> And my invention thrive, Edmund the base
> Shall top th' legitimate. I grow; I prosper:—
> Now, gods, stand up for bastards!

7 Walter Berns, 'Preserving a Living Constitution', in Robert A. Licht (ed.), *Is the Supreme Court the Guardian of the Constitution* (Washington, The American Enterprise Institute, 1993), at pp. 34–45.
8 *Griswold* v. *Connecticut*, at p. 515. Dissenting opinion.
9 *Roe* v. *Wade*, 410 U.S. 113 (1973); *Bowers* v. *Hardwick*, 478 U.S. 186, 199ff. (1986).
10 Russell Hittinger, *A Critique of the New Natural Law Theory* (Notre Dame, Ind., University of Notre Dame Press, 1987), p. 63.
11 John Quincy Adams, *Jubilee of the Constitution—a discourse delivered at the request of the New York Historical Society . . . on the 30th of April 1839* (Samuel Colson, 1839), p. 54.
12 John Courtney Murray, *We Hold These Truths: Catholic Reflections on the American Proposition* (New York, Sheed and Ward, 1960), at pp. 37–9.
13 John Locke, *Two Treatises of Government*, II, s. 6.

14 Murray, above at n. 12 at pp. 53–4.
15 Locke, *A Letter Concerning Toleration*, para. 36; Thomas Jefferson, *Notes on the State of Virginia*, query XVII.
16 Murray, at p. 299.
17 Ibid., at p. 316.
18 Ibid., at p. 305.
19 Locke, *Questions Concerning the Law of Nature* (Ithaca, N.Y. and London, Cornell University Press, 1990). Introduction, Text, and Translation by Robert Horwitz, Jenny Strauss Clay, and Diskin Clay. Questions IV, VI.
20 Locke, above at n. 13, II, sec. 8–12, 87.
21 Thomas L. Pangle, *The Spirit of Modern Republicanism: The Moral Vision of the American Founders and the Philosophy of Locke* (Chicago and London: The University of Chicago Press, 1988), chs. 13–21.
22 Murray, at pp. 37–9, 291, and 307.
23 Locke, *Essay Concerning Human Understanding*, II, xxi, 55; I, iii, 6; II, xxi, 42, 55, 65.
24 Ibid., II, xxi, 43, 68, *Reasonableness of Christianity*, para. 245 ('pursuit of happiness'); *Two Treatises*, II, s. 225 ('long train of abuses'); *Two Treatises*, II, s. 230 (mankind 'are more disposed to suffer').
25 James Wilson, in Jonathan Elliot (ed.), *The Debates in the Several State Conventions . . .* (New York: Burt Franklin, n.d.), vol. II, p. 456. John Quincy Adams made the same point. The principles of the Declaration of Independence and the Constitution, he said, had been 'especially expounded in the writings of Locke'. Adams, above at n. 11, p. 40. And, contrary to Murray, Adams says (p. 9) that 'English liberties had failed them . . . the colonists appealed to the rights of man.'
26 'The Essex Result', in Philip B. Kurland and Ralph Lerner (eds.), *The Founders' Constitution* (Chicago and London, The Un. of Chicago P., 1987), vol. I, at pp. 112–18.
27 *Federalist*, nos. 49, 43.
28 *Federalist*, no. 51, Pangle, above at n. 21 at pp. 118–19.
29 Ernest L. Fortin, 'The New Rights Theory and the Natural Law,' *The Review of Politics*, vol. 44 (1982), pp. 590–612. For the presuppositions, see Heinrich A. Rommen, *The State in Catholic Thought: A Treatise in Political Philosophy* (St Louis and London, B. Herder Book Co., 1945), at pp. 169–70.
30 A participant in the conference in which this chapter was first presented.
31 See Leo Strauss, 'Natural Law', in David L. Sills (ed.), *International Encyclopedia of the Social Sciences* (New York, Crowell Collier and Macmillan, Inc., 1938), vol. 2, at pp. 80–90.
32 Hobbes, *Leviathan*, ch. 14; Locke, *Two Treatises*, II, ss. 87, 128–31.
33 Randy E. Barnett (ed.), *The Rights Retained by the People: The History and Meaning of the Ninth Amendment* (Fairfax, Va., George Mason University Press, 1989).
34 *Annals of Congress*, vol. 1, p. 775.
35 Patrick Henry, speech in the Virginia state ratifying convention, 16 June 1788, in Herbert J. Storing (ed., with the assistance of Murray Dry), *The Complete Anti-Federalist* (Chicago and London, The University of Chicago Press, 1981), vol. 5, at pp. 246–7.

36 Herbert J. Storing, 'The Constitution and the Bill of Rights', in Gary L. McDowell (ed.), *Taking the Constitution Seriously: Essays on the Constitution and Constitutional Law* (Dubuque, Iowa, Kendall-Hunt Publishing Co., 1981), p. 277.

37 George H. Reese (ed.), *Proceedings of the Virginia State Convention of 1861* (Richmond, Virginia State Library, 1965), vol. 3, at pp. 24–5; vol. 1, at p. 709.

38 The following statement from Mississippi is typical: 'There is, however, a great principle underlying all constitutions and government . . . the right of the people to alter, to change, to amend, aye, to abolish the form of government whenever to them it shall seem proper. That, gentlemen of the Convention, is the great principle which underlies not only your federal constitution, but which lies at the basis of your State constitutions—the right of the people, the power of the people, aye, and the duty of the people, to resume the powers of government with which they have entrusted their agents whenever those agents have proven and manifested themselves to be unfaithful in the discharge of the trust.' E. Barksdale, State Printer, *Journal of the Convention and Ordinances and Resolutions adopted in January, 1861* (Jackson, Miss., 1861), at p. 166.

10

The Moral Point of View

The philosophy of Thomas Aquinas has been called the *philosophia peren-nis*—the perennial philosophy. If that is applied specifically to natural law, the philosophy most closely identified with Aquinas, one may be driven to conclude that it is like the perennials that are pictured heavy with blossoms in seed catalogues but, planted in one's garden, come back year after year with never a bloom at all. For, although natural law has its adherents and periodically prompts a fierce attack from its detractors, the blunt truth is that philosophically it is a curiosity outside the mainstream, regarded mostly as a side-show and not to be taken very seriously. Defending natural law as philosophy, one becomes accustomed to seeing a wry smile on the faces of listeners, as if one were describing a private and somewhat peculiar hobby.

In moments of crisis, it is true, natural law flowers briefly. John Locke summoned natural law in defence of Whig interests against the claims of monarchy. So also did the American revolutionaries in their struggle against the crown. After World War II natural law emerged as a response to the encounter with appalling human evil, carried out with the matter-of-fact directness of the commonplace. Nowhere in those efflorescences, however, is there anything that can be regarded as a philosophy of natural law. The crises to which Locke and the eighteenth century Americans responded were political; and so were their responses, at least so far as natural law is concerned. Although Locke believed that there is a natural law and was deeply interested in it, he did not trouble to defend or even to explain it; in the *Second Treatise*, in which the normative aspect of natural law (as the source of natural rights) is most evident, he simply threw in a reference to natural law wherever his argument came unstuck.[2] The Americans wrote manifestos, not treatises. The post-war development is more complicated; there was an effort to frame a theory. But its starting point was not so much intellectual as it was a passionate need to frame an alternative to brute force. What theory there was turned out toe little more than revulsion against accepting the phenomenon of Nazism as itself within the natural order.

In the past two decades, there has been a revival of serious discussion about natural law along two rather distinct tracks. The first is largely jurisprudential and includes theories about the nature and process of law, among which the work of Ronald Dworkin is prominent, and also more specific theories of constitutional interpretation and some constitutional history. The second is moral theory in the first instance, which includes law as an important but subsidiary topic. This has been prompted in large measure by the work of Germaine Grisez, Joseph Boyle, and John Finnis, the philosophic grounds of which are set forth most clearly in Finnis's book *Natural Law and Natural Rights*.[3] It is striking, however, that the considerable impact of the former theories on legal philosophy has not in the main led to adoption of the approach or even the label of natural law along with them. And the moral theory, although comfortably wearing the mantle of natural law, has not extended its influence on moral philosophy much beyond the narrow range of natural law itself.

It is easy to pass by this marginalized situation of natural law, just because there is so little sustained engagement between those who defend it and those who dismiss it out of hand. We ought to take notice, however. For there is something odd about a philosophy that is perennially with us and yet is so much a shape-shifter and, withal, so peripheral. We ought to find out the source of the oddity, which may help us to decide whether there is anything worth preserving in the natural law tradition after all.

I

Not the least of our difficulties is that there is so little agreement about what counts as natural law. If there is any common element in all the current diversity, it is simply the assertion of some moral principle (or set of principles) as certain and dispositive of the matter at hand. If the topic being discussed is natural law itself, rather than its application to some more particular controversy, there will probably be a reference to the truth or validity of the principle rather than its certainty. But the label of natural law is so often attached simply to the assertion of principle without any consideration of the standard of truth or validity, that certainty seems the more inclusive criterion. I do not myself think that that is adequate to define a philosophic position. Certainty, after all, has many forms, which may range from proof to pigheadedness.[4] Nor do I think that it accurately reflects the natural law tradition. But just about every kind of certainty has paraded under the banner of natural law. Before we exclude any of them, we need to consider their claim to do so.

If moral certainty is indeed all that natural law now signifies, both its variety and its philosophical inconsequence are easily explained. For, on one hand, people are certain about a great many moral matters; and on the other, none of their certainties can be shown to be beyond challenge.

Within jurisprudence, for example, Dworkin's theory of interpretation is an effort to import into the law moral principles that are not dependent on being posited as law nor merely conventional but are not quite objective moral truths either.[5] Most commentators have found value in his description of how the legal and especially the judicial process of reasoning works. For the most part, however, they have located his enlarged conception of the materials that compose a judicial decision within the framework of legal positivism; for, as Dworkin reluctantly acknowledges, a judge must finally remain true to the law or strike out on his own, in the name of overriding but unverifiable moral conviction.[6] So also, David Richards's theory of 'methodological natural law' relies on the constitutional tradition to lend objectivity to what are otherwise contestable normative principles.[7] It is the method of natural law only in so far as it takes (his preferred reading of) the Constitution as the indisputable starting point for the legal issues under consideration.

I do not depreciate the contribution of these theories to our understanding of law. Since they are so plainly theories about law and comfortable to positivist premises, however, it is an interesting, if collateral, question why they should have been associated, by their authors or by others, with natural law.[8] The answer, I think, is that these theories are the culmination of the debate between legal positivism and natural law in the aftermath of World War II. That debate was prompted by the moral certitude that Nazism provoked, which made it imperative to find a basis for rejecting its appropriation of ordinary social institutions.[9] Now, scarcely fifty years later, the Nazi experience is reduced to history and use of it as an example seems itself to have become little more than a rhetorical trope.

Less needs to be said about references to natural law in support of a position on some public issue, among which statements of Martin Luther King and, more recently, Clarence Thomas are notable. It will perhaps offend some and please others that the two are named together; and in fact the principles that each of them referred to as natural law are quite different. The use that they made of natural law, however, is well within the tradition of political debate, in which such use serves mainly to place one's first principles beyond challenge. But, also comfortable to the tradition, they do not offer much other than their own certitude to support the principles.

All of these jurisprudential theories and political arguments stumble over the familiar rule that normative propositions are not matters of fact and cannot be demonstrated as matters of fact. Their validation requires another normative proposition, which is in turn dependent on a further normative proposition. The certainty that we reach about many matters of fact is, therefore, unavailable for normative propositions, however general or specific. According to that rule, therefore, if certainty is to be achieved, one must either slip some *assumed* normative premise into the argument, as Dworkin and Richards do, or refuse to debate. Either way, whatever the merits of the argument in other respects, so far as it parades as natural law, it is not of much interest as a distinct philosophical position.

We reach a different level of discussion in Finnis's deservedly much discussed book. Because Finnis writes from within the natural law tradition and with a deep appreciation of it, his theory exposes most clearly the modern dilemma of natural law. Most importantly, his theory of practical reasonableness, as he calls it, does not depend explicitly or implicitly on any assumed normative premises. Instead, Finnis describes in considerable detail seven 'basic forms of human good'—life, knowledge, play, and so forth—which, he says, are known to be such simply by reflection.[10] They are 'self-evidently a form of good', and together they contain 'the outlines of everything one could reasonably want to do, to have, and to be'.[11] Finnis also states nine methodological requirements of practical reasonableness: 'a coherent plan of life', no 'arbitrary preferences' among values or among persons, and so forth.[12] Although he notes that for these we have the aid, and perhaps need, of 'two millennia' of philosophical inquiry, they also are not derived from other normative premises; they are 'fundamental, underived, [and] irreducible'.[13] By application of the requirements of practical reasonableness to the basic goods, one arrives, he says at morality.[14] The detail with which the basic goods and methodological requirements are discussed conveys the impression that the morality at which one arrives is also specific, including a considerable body of concrete moral prescription, also asserted as true. And indeed, Finnis says that 'diversity of moral opinion' arises because persons are not 'simply reasonable'.[15]

Some time ago, I wrote that Finnis regarded these moral prescriptions as self-evident, for which Robert George has taken me to task.[16] He insisted, correctly, that Finnis does not assert that concrete moral prescriptions are self-evident but describes them, rather, as the outcome of a process of thought. In view of the apparent certainty of their demonstration from principles that are themselves self-evident and the objective truth that Finnis ascribes to them, George's point seems like a quibble. It is perhaps unclear on the face of the argument whether Finnis believes that there are objectively true moral prescriptions for the conduct of one's life but that we cannot be certain what they are or that there are such prescriptions and we can, when we put our minds carefully to it, attain them and know that we have attained them. If it is the former, however, we are in the same situation whether there are such truths or not. Finnis's theory would then very much resemble the opaque normative order against which Thomas Aquinas set his theory of natural law. And in fact, the whole edifice of Finnis's argument seems to be constructed in order to show that by relying on our reason alone—being 'simply reasonable'—we can recognize objective moral truths. It is just that which makes his theory, proceeding without explicit normative premises, distinctive. But it does not succeed.

Life, Finnis says, is a basic human good.[17] Among the requirements of practical reasonableness is a rejection of consequentialism: '. . . [O]ne should not choose to do any act which *of itself does nothing but* damage or impede a realization or participation of any one or more of the basic forms of human good.'[18] Those two propositions seem to me to lead unequivocally to the conclusions that abortion for no reason other than to terminate an unwanted pregnancy is morally wrong and likewise that suicide in order to terminate a life that has become unbearably and unalterably burdensome is morally wrong. I do not want to debate either proposition. Many people in this country, perhaps most, would subscribe to one or both. All the same, to assert, in the face of all the contrary opinion of thoughtful, concerned people, that they are objective truths and that careful reflection must lead to recognition of their truth seems merely willful. One's confidence in the capacity of the basic goods and requirements of practical reasonableness to yield certain conclusions is undermined further by Finnis's conclusion that, notwithstanding the basic good of human life and the rejection of consequentialism, capital punishment is not always wrong. This is so, he says, because 'the defining and essential . . . point of punishment is to restore an order of fairness which was disrupted by the criminal's criminal act'; it is not, therefore, 'a direct attack on the good of human life'.[19] Again, I do not want to debate Finnis's conclusion. But to suggest that all that is involved is being 'simply reasonable' (rather than what will appear to many people as an exercise in casuistry to support a conclusion reached on other, undisclosed grounds) will convince only the already committed. Unless the basic goods and methodological requirements are kept at a suitable level of abstraction, from which conflicting concrete propositions can be derived, they are themselves not self-evident. They amount to wise but quite general moral counsel, which is neither absolute nor, applied concretely, certain. To suppose that conclusions so grounded are themselves certain or that anyone who believes otherwise is simply mistaken, despite the disagreement of so many morally serious people, betrays a staggering confidence in one's own moral judgement and, at the deepest level, confusion about the nature of moral reasoning itself.

I have made much of Finnis's account of practical reasonableness because it exemplifies the most considered recent defence of natural law. It is not unfair to characterize the typical argument for natural law as a combination of large claims about the objectivity of morality in general and singular reticence about the truth of any concrete moral propositions in particular, or at least ones that anyone would be inclined to dispute.[20] That is why Nazism has loomed so large in the defence of natural law. Its immorality was both overwhelming and appallingly concrete. If a philosophy of natural law requires the establishment of certain moral truths, there is no more to be said, because significant moral truths cannot be established with certainty as a matter of fact and are neither self-evident nor demonstrable. Natural law must then be regarded not as a philosophy but as a type of argument, in which one asserts the truth of one's moral premises on the basis of some authoritative source or simply because one is certain.

This whole approach to natural law, however, rests on a mistake.

II

Few will disagree that the defining moment for the philosophy of natural law was its formulation by Thomas Aquinas toward the end of the thirteenth century. But just as the name he gave it can be traced to Cicero, the philosophy itself has deep roots in the classical Greek conception of the universe as normatively ordered. God's Providence is the Christian equivalent of Greek concepts—*moira, physis*, later on the Stoic *Logos*—that express a fundamental belief that there is a purposive force in the natural order that directs the course of events. However, this conception of normative natural order was elaborated, it gave meaning to the human experience, which was lifted out of the impersonal, implacable succession of events and justified, even when, from a human point of view, it seemed arbitrary. The association of the Greek abstract idea with the Judaic conception of an individual God, concerned about and involved in human affairs, greatly transformed it; but the problem of meaning, more definitely circumscribed, remained. In the Judaic–Christian context, the meaning that was at stake was not some unknown destiny, but specifically human significance; it required concretely that what befalls individual human beings be according to their desert, comprehensible in human terms.[21]

The specific intellectual problem that Aquinas confronted was how to reconcile the Providence of an all encompassing God with individual human freedom and responsibility. That problem had confronted Christianity from the beginning; but the Aristotelian revival that began at the end of the twelfth century gave it a new dimension and urgency. Natural law was his solution. In place of the multiple, often contradictory, and remote accounts of natural law that had accumulated over the centuries in between, he restored to it a meaning not so unlike the Stoic notion of *Logos*, immanent Reason, with a Christian face. As he wrote:

Now among all others the rational creature is subject to Divine providence in the most excellent way, in so far as it partakes of a share of providence, by being provident both for itself and for others. Wherefore it has a share of the Eternal Reason, whereby it has a natural inclination to its proper act and end: and this participation of the eternal law in the rational create is called the natural law.[22]

In the world of the thirteenth century, that statement, which to us may sound merely formulaic, had great importance. It meant generally that faith and reason—Augustine and Aristotle—are not irreconcilably opposed but are complementary. At the individual level, the personal, human dimension of the search for meaning was validated. Human beings are responsible, and their perception of their own responsibility is not altogether irrelevant to the universal order but has a place within it. Individual desert, comprehensible in human terms, is a reflection of the divine purpose.

All the same, natural law as posited by Aquinas was an affirmation, not, in our terms at any rate, an explanation. He did not say how the reconciliation between God's Providence and human responsibility was accomplished. For that, one relied not on reason but faith. Nor did he say much about the specific content of the providential order concerning human beings, which, seen through the lens of human responsibility, would constitute a moral code. One was remitted to the teachings of God's holy Church. There are in Aquinas's writings some actual prescriptions; but except for general, indeterminate abstractions like 'good is to be done and pursued, and evil is to be avoided,'[23] they express the conventional morality of his time. There is nothing surprising in that, although modern readers are sometimes startled by the absence of more substantial moral content. For although it required that morality be accessible, his argument was not built on a demonstration of the truth of moral principles. Rather, it was the other way around. The argument established that people could rely on the moral principles in which they believed. The fact that completion of the argument depended on faith in God's Providence and acceptance of the authority of the Church was not in Aquinas's view a weakness. Those were unquestioned premises from which he started.

Aquinas spoke from within and for the Church, and the Church (eventually) adopted his view as formal doctrine. As a matter of doctrine, unequivocally incorporating his premises and integrated with other doctrine, natural law does elaborate the reconciliation of universal order and individual responsibility, and in many respects it prescribes how the latter is to be exercised concretely. From the perspective of the long philosophical tradition that preceded it, however, those doctrinal matters were no more essential to his formulation of natural law than they had been to the Greek sources. First and foremost, the philosophy of natural law is not a pronouncement of moral truths; it is, rather, an affirmation of the truth or, more precisely, the reality of morality.

It is hardly surprising that moral reality should now be rendered as moral truths.[24] No one doubts that morality is 'real' in the sense that it motivates us as individuals, affects social policy, and so forth. It anything more than that is meant, well, we just do not speak that way. Moral principles do not describe what is the case. Rather, they are valid or invalid; according to some people they may be true or false, although even that is stretching a bit. Pursuing natural law in that direction, however, leads, as I have suggested, to a philosophic dead end. The task of natural law is to identify, in a form acceptable to the modern mind, some aspect of human existence that validates moral principles themselves as part of the description of reality. It is that distinctive ontological claim that sets natural law apart; without it, natural law is not a philosophy but at best one moral theory among others, and, like the others, dependent for its validity on debatable normative premises.[25]

As it was for Aquinas, human responsibility is the starting point, not the conclusion. No process of reason, no intellection, is needed to support the proposition that human beings are responsible; nor is there any process of reason that could lead us to it. Our awareness of human responsibility is immediate and direct, arising out of the experience of our own agency and the agency of others. At the same time, it is not among the ordinary, empirically verified phenomena of our experience. Although particular attributions of responsibility may be uncertain and controversial, the fact of human responsibility as such is structural; it cannot be contradicted without altering our experience, not merely in some concrete particular(s) but fundamentally, making it a different experience entirely and altogether beyond our grasp. In a general way, with some difficult cases around the edges, responsibility marks the difference between persons and things, according to which all human beings are persons and all persons are human beings.

Responsibility implies desert. That a person acting responsibly incurs desert, good or bad, is part of what responsibility means. Although it may be a question in a particular case *what* a person, acting responsibly, deserves, *that* she deserves is not. Desert, furthermore, has the direct normative implication that a person ought to get whatever it is that she deserves. Desert is too portentous and too demanding for most ordinary conduct, which even though it be responsible, does not call strongly for approval or disapproval. Even if it does, we may doubt our own authority to administer desert in the form of praise or blame or especially reward or punishment; we may think it correct, as we say, to 'leave her to heaven'. In special circumstances—*pace* Kant—other human concerns may outweigh the normative force of desert, and we may conclude that a person ought not to get what she deserves. But the general normative implication is not in doubt. It is contained within the idea of desert; and it is contained within the idea of responsibility as well.

The problem of human meaning that natural law addresses has its focus there. The experience of agency was no less immediate and direct for a Greek in the fifth century or a Christian in the thirteenth century than it is for us. When a Greek is told by the oracle that he will kill his father and marry his mother, he does not murmur, 'Too bad,' and wait for it to happen; he kisses his parents goodbye and leaves town. Nor did the Christian just wait for God's Providence to unfold. Responsibility was, then as now, incontestable. Although our metaphysical world view is radically different, the experience of responsibility is the same and makes the same demand on our reason. The supposition of a purposive natural order—*moira* or Providence—has been displaced by causal order, no less determinative or encompassing. So, instead of the challenge that Jocasta threw at Oedipus,

> Why should man fear since chance is all in all
> for him, and he can clearly foreknow nothing?
> Best to live lightly, as one can, unthinkingly.[26]

We confront the determinist's challenge: all human behaviour, no less than other occurrences, is fully determined by prior events. Even when a person acts, as we think, responsibly, his action is the effect of causes that immediately or mediately are altogether beyond his control, the experience of agency to the contrary notwithstanding.

I shall not review here the vast literature about the debate between free will and determinism, although it is worth noting how vast and ultimately how inconclusive it is. Neither side of the issue, responsibility or causal order, considered separately, is seriously questioned. A strict behaviourist may ruminate that no one is 'really' responsible for anything; but he does not conduct his life that way. Nor, on the other hand, is there much doubt that nature and nurture and mere circumstance have a great deal to do not only with what happens to a person but also with whom and what that person is and what he does. In a sense, what he is—his natural aptitudes or lack thereof, his pleasant or disagreeable disposition, his good and bad habits—just happens to him. The demand on reason is not that one or the other, responsibility or causal order, be eliminated but that they be reconciled.

The currently favoured way to meet this demand is to deny that any reconciliation is necessary. An attribution of responsibility and a causal explanation for the same occurrence, it is said, are not opposed; they simply view the occurrence from different perspectives. So long as one distinguishes the perspectives, no conflict or confusion results.[27] That, however, is philosophical whistling in the dark, the sound of which is reassuring only if the melody is very faint. Suppose, for example, after sentencing an offender to a long term in prison, a judge were to conclude her remarks: 'It is true that from another, no less valid perspective, you have a complete excuse and are not at all responsible for what you did. But I have to choose somehow. In order to be completely fair, I tossed a coin. You lost.' Or suppose the judge in a civil suit were to find for the defendant and observe after announcing the verdict: 'There was convincing evidence in this case that when the defendant wrecked the plaintiff's car, he knew exactly what he was doing and could easily have avoided doing it, without injury. However, although I do not know what made him so careless, something must have done or else he would have behaved differently. I can hardly regard him as responsible for the plaintiff's loss if, from another perspective, its true cause was something I cannot even identify.'[28]

If responsibility and causal order are not thus pinned down concretely, it is easy to regard them as different 'perspectives' on an occurrence, because most of the time there is no controversy about which is appropriate and the alternative perspective is not even considered. When there is controversy, furthermore, we have no firm way to resolve it; considered separately from each other, both perspectives may be persuasive. So we may be convinced that a criminal is responsible *and* equally convinced that an explanation for his conduct can be found in a combination of his natural capacities and the circumstances of his history, for neither of which is he individually responsible. Having no way to resolve the conflict, we may regard its resolution as a matter of choice, or perspective. Often, which we finally adopt is a matter about which we can agree to disagree, without concrete consequences, because as a practical matter the person's desert is not in issue. Nevertheless, an attribution of responsibility or, alternatively, an explanation of the causes of an occurrence, however contestable, is part of the description of what happened and, as such, a matter of fact. It is not something that the observer brings to it, a point of view that he can adopt or reject as he likes. (It is true, however, that an attribution of responsibility is a distinctly *human* perspective; whether any other terrestrial creature has anything like a conception of responsibility is problematic at best, as is the question whether we ought to suppose that extraterrestrial creatures, if there are any, have such a conception.)

Some philosophers have an additional reason for their conclusion that responsibility and causation are a matter of perspective. There is in principle, they say, no resolution of the conflict, no unified perspective that integrates responsibility and causal explanation, because they are strictly inconsistent. There being no resolution, they conclude that there is no conflict.[29] But it is, to say the least, not obvious that human intellectual capacity sets the bounds of what is the case. The conflict does not originate in reason but in our experience. If we cannot bring it within the bounds of reason, we must perforce get past it in another way.

An attribution of responsibility requires that we regard a person as *duly* constituted, that is, as having with respect to the conduct in question the attributes that the *rightfully* his and not merely the effect of circumstances beyond his control. If, and only if, that is so can we conclude that his action, traceable to those attributes, is attributable to himself, or his self, and not to external causes. It is out of the question, however, so to regard a person simply as he is, although we may like to think otherwise when we contemplate our more attractive features. No one naturally is due his good looks, broad intellect, fleet foot, or even his sunny disposition; and if those are not his due, neither are the other attributes or the achievements that are their fruits. No more is anyone due his bad complexion, narrow interests, lack of co-ordination, gloominess, or the other attributes and the (lack of) achievements that stem from them. Whatever the cause—nature, nurture, or some combination of both—cause and effect have no room for consideration of what is due. That is, however, precisely how we regard a person who has his rights. Rights *rectify* the causal natural distribution of favourable and unfavourable attributes and assign a person what is rightfully his, more than he has in some respects and less in others. Constituted descriptively as a bundle of attributes the causes of which he may not even know, a person is reconstituted normatively as a bundle of rights, which are his due. And, exercising his rights, he is responsible for what he does.

Although we usually think of rights 'at large', as something that one simply has, the significance of a right is attached to its actual or potential exercise as the action of a responsible person. Having a right (and the right being honoured), a person is responsible so far as it extends. Having no right, a person is not responsible, and to that extent responsibility for the outcome (or its explanation) lies elsewhere. Similarly, if a person is responsible in some respect, it must be the case that he has a commensurate right, for otherwise the outcome is not, as we say, up to him. Unexceptional most of the time, this connection between responsibility and rights may seem to fail in some familiar situations. A person may be held responsible and blamed just because he had no right to act as he did; so, for example, a thief is responsible for taking his victim's wallet and is condemned because he had no right to take it. Or one may be regarded as responsible and praised for an act of civil disobedience, despite having no legal right to act as he did or even especially because he had no such right. In the former case, however, the thief's responsibility depends on his having had the rights, so familiar that we scarcely notice them, that are comprised by our ordinary liberty, including specifically in this instance the right *not* to take the wallet; he would not be responsible if, for example, someone had coerced him to take it or if he were under a proper duty to do so. (Nor would not stealing a wallet have anything to do with a person's responsibility if he had not the liberty to be on the street and to act independently if, for example, he were locked up or under heavy guard.) Conduct counts as civil disobedience and merits praise only if the actor is regarded as having a (non-legal) right superior to the law's prohibition; otherwise, it is simply breaking the law. Although one might still admire his courage, absent the right, one could not approve his action, all things considered.

Looking in the other direction, the rights that we assign, or fail to assign, demarcate the range of a person's responsibility. They specify not only what he can do with as he wants (whether as a matter only of permission or, more amply, of protection or provision) but also what he must make do with as he can. Since one is not obliged to exercise a capacity even if it is his right, there is no occasion to assert for oneself a right to have less. But one is responsible for the attributes of his rightfully constituted self, those that he wishes were otherwise as well as those that he enjoys. Having no right to something different, such attributes and their effects are all, as we say, his own responsibility. The responsibility of the more intelligent or industrious disabled student who is given extra time to take an examination and the responsibility of the less intelligent or industrious student without such a disability who is not given extra time are both measured according to their respective rights: what we believe is rightfully their due.

Closely examined in this way, precisely and in detail, responsibility and rights are not simply connected; they are one and the same. Although matters of responsibility are cast retributively and matters of rights cast distributively, both alike specify what is a person's due, that is to say, what he deserves. *Rectifying* the causal order, substituting rights for the causally determinate circumstances of our individual beings, the concept of rights and its concrete embodiments occupy the place that was formerly occupied by the ideas of normative natural order and Providence. Possessed of rights, human beings are responsible. Being responsible, human beings have rights.[30]

There is a further step in the argument. In a normatively ordered universe, constituted wholly according to the right, persons would have only the physical, intellectual, and emotional attributes, character traits, and capacities that are rightfully theirs. So constituted, a person could not but do what, according to his nature, it was right for him to do. Such a being, lacking freedom, would not be personally responsible. Responsibility, furthermore, is individual. It requires that an act be *self*-determined, in the strong sense that it is the act of a fully constituted, unique individual, differentiated from all the others not only descriptively as cows, trees, and rocks are but also normatively as well. The contingency of right is concretely the (incomplete) dependence of individual rights on the determinate circumstances of one's being. It is that uniquely human condition, part of nature and apart from it, that alone makes possible individual responsibility, or moral freedom, which may well be described as the essential human characteristic.[31]

One of the strongest indications of the correspondence between rights and responsibility has special relevance here. Both concepts bridge the separation between descriptive and normative discourse. Although an attribution of responsibility is not like other attributes that describe a person or his conduct, it is nevertheless a matter of fact, contained within the description of the occurrence in question. 'George jumped out of the window,' and 'George fell out of the window,' describe different occurrences; although we may not know which description is correct, we can be certain that if one is correct, then the other is not. It makes no sense to say that someone *ought* to be responsible in some respect or that he *ought not*. What could such a statement mean? It is like saying that chipmunks ought to be responsible, a comment on the Creation. (One can say that a person ought, or ought not, to be *held* responsible, or that a person ought to behave more responsibly. But those assertions are different from the ascription of responsibility itself, on which, at least in the first instance, they depend.) All the same, an attribution of responsibility has direct normative significance, because it is a declaration about a person's desert.

We are likely to place rights on the other side of the divide. We assert rights most often to call attention to a duty somewhere else; so their normative aspect is prominent. Yet rights present themselves as a matter of fact as firmly as does responsibility; one has a right or she does not. The ubiquity of legal rights makes it easy to suppose otherwise; it is altogether familiar to say that one has a legal right but ought not, or that one ought to have a legal right but does not. However, unless one is referring to a right within a system of rules and asserting that there ought to be a rule conferring some right, it is unintelligible to say that a person *ought to have* a right, because being normative, the validity of such a statement is dependent on the validity of some other, more general normative proposition. But it is precisely the point abut rights that they are not so dependent; rather, many normative propositions depend on them. The direction of thought is not, 'Since I ought to have a vacation, I have a right to a vacation,' but 'Since I have a right to a vacation, I ought to have a vacation.'

Professionally embarrassed by the facticity of rights, philosophers have adopted various stratagems to evade it. Rights are said to be logically primary or fundamental to moral discourse—meaning only that they do not depend on further normative premise;s.[32] Judith Thomson, who has written extensively and persuasively about the concept of a right, calls rights 'moral facts'.[33] She is, I think, correct. But (aside from the fact that there are not supposed to be any moral facts) that characterization of rights makes all the more urgent the questions of how rights are verified and how we come by knowledge of them.[34]

Therein, I believe, lies the present (and, so far as one can tell, the future) of natural law. No abstract deduction of reason or induction from ordinary empirical data leads us to an awareness of rights or to the identification of specific rights. Rather, they arise directly in our experience—that is to say, within reality itself—concurrently with our awareness of human beings as responsible, morally situated individuals. Except for a small number of rights, imprecisely defined, that all human beings possess, because without them there is no responsibility and no personhood at all, rights depend not on metaphysics but on the deep conventions of a community—what the Greeks called *nomos*—that establish when a human being is responsible and when not. Yet rights are not 'merely conventional'; giving specific content to the structure of our experience, they describe what is the case—the range of individual responsibility and desert. Ascribing responsibility or not ascribing it in concrete situations, we learn what rights a person has, those that one has so incontestably that they go unnoticed as well as those that are controversial. Although in an ongoing, well-ordered community, many rights will be in the former category, none is in principle incontestable; they are written not in the stars but in a human hand. The specific programme of natural law at the end of the twentieth century is to sustain the reality of our moral experience by working out a coherent conception of rights along these lines.[35]

III

The role of natural law is not now any more than it was in the past to provide us with moral certainties. The experience of freedom and responsibility within a determinate natural order and the moral uncertainty that it provokes are not a qualified, less perfect, version of an absolute, transcendent reality; they are the human condition and the source of the human meaning of our existence. A philosophy of natural law affirms the moral sufficiency of our uncertainty not merely as an attitude but as a practical reflection on our actual situation. That will sound like a strange description of the natural law of Thomas Aquinas to those who are more familiar with its doctrinal certainties; but even as applied to him, from the perspective of the larger tradition it is not inaccurate.

Is that enough to sustain our interest? If all that natural law holds for us is an account of what we know to be true without reflection, had we not better direct our effort elsewhere? Perhaps. It all depends on what one's interests are. If one's concern is moral truths or the elaboration of moral principles and their applications, I doubt that natural law has much to offer. Although I think that the theory of rights that I have outlined has important practical consequences, they can be pursued without reference to natural law. The proper place of natural law is not within moral debate but in defence of the moral point of view against skepticism or its modern counterpart, existentialism. That, also, justifiably engages our attention.

NOTES

1 Dane Professor of Law, Harvard Law School.

2 In the *Second Treatise*, Locke declares that it is 'certain' that there is a 'Law of Nature', which is 'as intelligible and plain to a rational Creature, and a Studier of that Law, as the positive Laws of Common-wealths, nay possibly plainer.' John Locke, *Second Treatise of Government*, s. 12, in idem. *Two Treatises of Government* (Peter Laslett ed.) 2nd ed. (Cambridge, Cambridge University Press, 1967), at p. 293. Elsewhere, referring to the Law of Nature, he says, 'Reason . . . is that Law.' Ibid., s. 6, p. 289. There is no further explanation., He says that 'it would be beside my present purpose, to enter here into the particulars of the Law of Nature.' Ibid., s. 12, p. 293. He is not more forthcoming in the *Essay concerning Human Understanding*.

Locke did write extensively about the law of nature, but the writings were not published in his lifetime or, indeed, until 250 years later. See John Locke, *Essays on the Law of Nature* (W. von Leyden ed.) (Oxford; Clarendon Press, 1954). Von Leydon provides a thorough discussion of the subject in his Introduction. Ibid., at pp. 1–92.

3 John Finnis, *Natural Law and Natural Rights* (Oxford, Clarendon Press, 1980). Many writings of Grisez, Boyle, and Finnis alone or in collaboration are cited in Finnis's book. Other more recent works are cited in notes to his essay, John Finnis, 'Natural Law and Legal Reasoning', in Robert P. George, ed., *Natural Law Theory* (Oxford, Clarendon Press, 1992), at pp. 152–5.

4 'Certitude is not the test of certainty. We have been cock-sure of many things that were not so.' Oliver Wendell Holmes, 'Natural Law', *Collected Legal Papers* (New York, Harcourt, Brace, 1920), at p. 311.

5 See Ronald Dworkin, *Law's Empire* (Cambridge, Mass., Harvard University Press, 1986), at pp. 225–75. 'According to law as integrity, propositions of law are true if they figure in or follow from the principles of justice, fairness, and procedural due process that provide the best constructive interpretation of the community's legal practice.' Ibid., at p. 255.

6 'Perhaps the law of the United States, properly interpreted in deference to integrity, did include the Fugitive Slave Act enacted by Congress before the Civil War. If a judge's own sense of justice condemned that act as deeply immoral because it required citizens to help send escaped slaves back to their masters, he would have to consider whether he should actually enforce it on the demand of a slave owner, or whether he should lie and say that this was not the law after all, or whether he should resign.' Ibid., at p. 219. Dworkin believes that such situations are extremely rare.

7 David A. J. Richards, *The Moral Criticism of Law* (Encino, Calif., Dickenson, 1977).

8 Dworkin had a brief, on-again off-again flirtation with natural law. See Ronald

Dworkin, ' "Natural" Law Revisited', *University of Florida Law Review* 34 (1982) at pp. 165–88. As so often happens in relationships when one party tries to remake the other to conform to his own desires, the flirtation came to nought. For some earlier doubts, see *Taking Rights Seriously* (Cambridge, Mass., Harvard University Press, 1977), at pp. 160–8.

9 See, for example, the debate between Hart and Fuller in H. L. A. Hart, 'Positivism and the Separation of Law and Morals', *Harvard Law Review* 71 (1958) at pp. 593–629; Lon L. Fuller, 'Positivism and Fidelity to Law—A Reply to Professor Hart,' *Harvard Law Review* 71 (1958) at pp. 630–72.

10 Finnis, *Natural Law and Natural Rights*, at pp. 59–99 ('basic forms of human good,' p. 85). Finnis uses a number of other, equivalent expressions to describe the seven goods. See also 'Natural Law and Legal Reasoning,' ('basic human goods').

11 Finnis, *Natural Law and Natural Rights*, at pp. 92, 97.

12 Ibid., at pp. 100–33.

13 Ibid., at p. 102.

14 Ibid., at p. 126.

15 Ibid., at p. 127. The diversity of moral opinion has its source, Finnis says, 'in too exclusive attention to some of the basic value(s) and/or some basic require-ment(s), and inattention to others,' 'an uncritical, unintelligent spontaneity,' 'the bias and oversight induced by conventions of language, social structure, and social practice,' and 'the bias of self-love or of other emotions and inclina-tions.'

16 Lloyd L. Weinreb, *Natural Law and Justice* (Cambridge, Mass., Harvard University Press, 1987), at p. 111. George's objection is in Robert P. George, 'Natural Law and Human Nature', in George, *Natural Law Theory*, at p. 36.

17 Finnis, *Natural Law and Natural Rights*, at p. 86. 'To regard human life as a basic reason for action is to understand it as a good in which indefinitely many beings can participate in indefinitely many ways, going far beyond any goal or purpose which anyone could envisage and pursue, but making sense of indef-initely many purposes, and giving rational support to indefinitely many goals.' Finnis, 'Natural Law and Legal Reasoning', at p. 135.

18 Finnis, *Natural Law and Natural Rights*, at p. 118.

19 John Finnis, *Fundamentals of Ethics* (Washington, D.C., Georgetown University Press, 1983), at pp. 128, 130. A 'paradigm case' of 'what can loosely be called justifiable killing' is 'the act of the public officer deliberately killing as a lawful and justified act of upholding punitively or quasi-punitively the order of jus-tice in his community.' Ibid., at p. 132.

20 In writings not concerned especially with the theory of natural law, Finnis in particular has taken a strong stand on moral issues of great current interest. See, for example, John Finnis, 'The Rights and Wrongs of Abortion: A Reply to Judith Thomson', *Philosophy and Public Affairs* 2 (1973) at pp. 117–45, and the extract from his legal deposition on the subject of homosexuality, in *The New Republic*, 13 Nov. 1993, at pp. 12–13.

21 For an account of this development, see Weinreb, *Natural Law and Justice*, at pp. 15–66.

22 Thomas Aquinas, *Summa Theologica*, I–2, qu. 91, art. 2 (trans. Fathers of the

English Dominican Province), 3 vols. (New York, Benziger, 1947), vol. I, at p. 997.

23 Ibid., I–2, qu. 94, art. 2, at p. 1009.

24 The principal exception is Michael Moore, who has insisted on moral reality as the correct issue. Michael S. Moore, 'Moral Reality Revisited,' *Michigan Law Review* 90 (1992) at pp. 2424–533. See also the earlier article, Michael S. Moore, 'Moral Reality,' *Wisconsin Law Review* 1982 (1982): 1061–1156. While he and I agree in that respect, his rendering of 'reality' seems to me too thin. His ontological thesis is that 'there are objective moral truths', 'Moral Reality Revisited', at p. 2425, by which he means that there are in the real world objective correlates for true moral propositions. Ibid., at p. 2433. So far as I can tell, however, the objective correlates that he has in mind are not at bottom distinguishable from the symptoms and effects of firm moral judgement. Although I welcome his commitment to moral realism, therefore, it seems to me open to the objection that it is irrelevant. See generally Jeremy Waldron, 'The Irrelevance of Moral Objectivity' in George, *Natural Law Theory* at pp. 158–87, and Moore's response, Michael S. Moore, 'Law as a Functional Kind', ibid., at pp. 188–242.

25 See n. 35 below.

26 Sophocles, *Oedipus the King* at pp. 977–9 (trans. David Grene, David Grene and Richmond Lattimore, eds.) *The Complete Greek Tragedies*, 2nd ed. (Chicago, University of Chicago Press, 1992), vol. II. *Sophocles*, at p. 52.

27 See, for example, P. F. Strawson, *Skepticism and Naturalism: Some Varieties* (New York, Columbia University Press, 1985), at pp. 31–50. Compare Thomas Nagel, *The View from Nowhere* (New York, OUP, 1986) pp. 110–37.

28 A judge would not, of course, say anything like that in either of the scenarios and would justify her actual choice of perspective by her institutional role. Whether the perspective that is adopted is a matter of individual decision or institutional role, however, the problem of justification, or explanation, remains.

29 '[T]he appearance of contradiction arises only if we assume the existence of some metaphysically absolute standpoint from which we can judge between the two standpoints I have been contrasting. But there is no such superior standpoint—or none that we know of; it is the idea of such a standpoint that is the illusion. Once that illusion is abandoned, the appearance of contradiction is dispelled. We can recognize, in our conception of the real, a reasonable relativity to standpoints that we do know and can occupy. Relative to the standpoint which we normally occupy as social beings, prone to moral and personal reactive attitudes, human actions, or some of them, are morally toned and propertied in the diverse ways signified in our rich vocabulary of moral appraisal. Relative to the detached naturalistic standpoint which we can sometimes occupy, they have no properties but those which can be described in the vocabularies of naturalistic analysis and explanation (including, of course, psychological analysis and explanation).' Strawson, *Skepticism and Naturalism: Some Varieties*, at p. 38.

30 The argument that is very briefly outlined here is developed much more completely in Lloyd L. Weinreb, *Oedipus at Fenway Park: What Rights Are and Why There Are Any* (Cambridge, Mass., Harvard University Press, 1994).

31 For further elaboration of this point in particular, see ibid., at pp. 94–5.
32 E.g., H. J. McCloskey, 'Rights—Some Conceptual Issues', *Australasian Journal of Philosophy* 54 (1976) at pp. 100, 104; Joel Feinberg, 'The Nature and Value of Rights', *Journal of Value Inquiry* 4 (1970) at p. 252. Dworkin's famous rubric that 'rights are trumps' is similar. E.g., Dworkin, *Taking Rights Seriously*, at p. xi ('political trumps').
33 Judith Jarvis Thomson, *The Realm of Rights* (Cambridge, Mass., Harvard U.P., 1990), p. 373.
34 Thomson believes that those questions are not answerable. See Judith Jarvis Thomson, *Rights, Restitution, and Risk* (Cambridge, Mass., Harvard U.P., 1986), at p. 253.
35 Constructivist ethical or political theories, which derive normative principles from the ongoing, established conventions and institutions (usually of a political nature) of a community, may follow a similar direction, without coming within the ambit of natural law. Rawls's effort to derive the principles of a just society from the traditions and understandings of western liberalism may be so regarded. See John Rawls, *Political Liberalism* (New York, Columbia University Press, 1993). Rawls is explicit that the constructivist political conception of justice that he expounds is 'political and not metaphysical'. Ibid., at pp. 10, 97. Dworkin's theory of constructive interpretation is another example. See Dworkin, *Law's Empire*, at pp. 225–75. Although the specific outcomes of the two approaches need not differ markedly, their conceptual underpinnings are quite different. Constructivist theories are distinctly normative. Taking the phenomenon of moral awareness as such for granted, they eschew the metaphysical or, as I have referred to it, ontological issue that is at the heart of natural law. So doing, however, they are exposed to the objection that they are only one moral theory among others, all of them at bottom equally unfounded.

In a discussion of Rawls's theory, Dworkin has contrasted a 'natural model' and a 'constructive model' of moral theory. The former, which is evidently a model generally of natural law theories, depends, he says, on the assumption that there is an objective 'moral reality' that is discovered by a special faculty of moral intuition; one's moral intuitions are a clue to moral principles, as physical observations are clues to fundamental physical laws. In contrast, he says, the constructive model makes no assumption about an objective moral reality, which the model 'does not deny, any more than . . . affirms'; 'the moral ontology that the natural model presupposes' is simply irrelevant to the constructive method. Dworkin, *Taking Rights Seriously*, at pp. 160–2. Dworkin's portrayal of natural law theories as regarding one's individual moral intuitions as unassailable data—'discrete observations of m oral reality,' ibid., at p. 163—from which moral principles are constructed is a caricature, which resembles no natural law theory of which I am aware. On the other hand, his assertion that the constructive model has no need of moral reality leaves that model—as he declares—with no foundation except 'independent reasons of political morality,' ibid., at p. 163. What the foundation of the latter is Dworkin fails to mention. He thus leaves the whole enterprise up in the air.

11

Lloyd Weinreb's Problems with Natural Law

DANIEL N. ROBINSON

Lloyd Weinreb begins his characteristically thoughtful and instructive chapter with something of a jeremiad owing to the failure of Natural Law to be taken seriously by philosophers. Something of a 'side-show', as he says, it has been invoked only sporadically by the likes of John Locke and the founders of the American Republic, together marking out those metes and bounds over which even great monarchs must not trespass; or again, by those Nuremberg jurists of the post-war period seeking to make clear the principles by which belligerency and unpardonable wickedness are to be distinguished.

But to say that Locke 'threw in a reference to natural law wherever his argument came unstuck' is, I should think, to say much more than Professor Weinreb means to say. It is akin to saying that Kant 'threw in' the concept of the pure intuitions of time and space 'whenever empirical accounts of these failed'; or that the founding fathers included Natural Law in their manifestos because, unlike treatises, these documents were not held to very high standards of analytical rigour. (One wonders what theory Jefferson might have espoused in a *treatise*.) And one wonders further whether the Nuremberg jurists somehow could exercise their passions more easily with the aid of Natural Law reasoning than with, say, Rule-Utilitarianism. I think Sir Frederick Pollock got it right when he insisted that any fair appraisal of Locke's political writings begins with the recognition that Natural Law assumptions still prevailed, challenged if at all only by those who took Scripture to be dispositive.[1]

All in all, then, I find Professor Weinreb's introductory *apologia* ironic. But his question is not: just why has Natural Law theory remained in the margins of both jurisprudence and moral philosophy? To answer this question, Professor Weinreb raises and answers several others, and it is to his framing of these pivotal questions that I shall devote my own critical comments. But even before this, I should offer without elaboration here my own answer to Professor Weinreb's question. Natural Law theory has suffered its apparent lack of influence in jurisprudence and in moral philosophy in much the same way that number theory is seldom discussed by geometers. Considered under a certain light, then, Professor Weinreb's insistent question is akin to asking why, if the alphabet is so integral to prose and poetry, writers tend to say next to nothing about it. Let me now begin to argue for this conclusion by examining more closely what it is that would have Professor Weinreb resist it.

His resistance is based first on the failure of Natural Law theorists to give univocal or unequivocal meaning to the term. He finds one school advocating 'moral certainty' as the defining stamp of the theory; a position he easily defeats by noting that all sorts of 'certainties' are held by persons, each of them readily challenged. Even Ronald Dworkin, he notes, under pressure from legal positivists, must acknowledge that judges otherwise moved by moral principles are either faithful to the statutes or are in the thrall of what Professor Weinreb refers to revealingly as 'unverifiable moral conviction'. Each of these concerns, the concern about the diversity of convictions and about their 'unverifiability', warrants comment.

I assume that Professor Weinreb means 'unverifiable' to be understood in the suspect sense of an earlier logical empiricism; some parent-positivism minted by the Vienna Circle and designed to honour the spirit of Ernst Mach and his war on metaphysics. But of course verificationism itself is 'unverifiable' empirically. Before long, vintage-positivism was to lose the allegiance of the one community is so faithfully courted; the community of theoretical physicists. Alas, had the strictures of positivism been adopted by this community, the first casualty would have been modern physics itself, a loss too great to endure for the mixed pleasures of a reassuring theory.

Let me not stray. The so-called unverifiability of moral convictions is problematic only to the extent that verificationism is the right model of explanation. To assume that it is the right model in the domain of law and morals is to beg the question, not to settle it. But of course it isn't the right model to begin with even in the physical sciences so some of Professor Weinreb's fears can be abated. In his choice of terms, however, he makes matters still more difficult for himself by choosing the word 'convictions'; our 'moral convictions', he says, are unverifiable. Well, if there is one thing we *can* verify it is just such convictions. Nonetheless, even if these were identical throughout the world, there is no version of Natural Law theory that would be sustained or in some sense validated. It is precisely *because* the realm of conviction is cluttered and unstable that it cannot be foundational for Natural Law theory. What the theory would reach are not convictions per se but *principles of a certain kind* invoked to justify one's convictions.

Having said this much, however, I would not want to be counted among those who acknowledge the absence of so-called objective moral criteria and then go on to apologize or compensate for it. Rather, I would suggest that the very concept of objectivity is normative, and that the objectivity routinely claimed in scientific contexts cannot be fully understood in non-moral terms. To refer to the 'objective facts' of, say, physics or chemistry is to refer to findings or observations we record while holding our hopes or beliefs at bay, so to speak. A fact becomes 'objective' when stripped of the percipient's ownership-claims and served up in utterly depersonalized form. But all this is available only within that irreducibly moral context in which we are ever mindful of the influences our biases and interests otherwise have on the manner in which we record and report the events of the world; mindful of the manner in which interpretation can diffract or diffuse the bare light of experience and convey a picture quite different from the original. All of the 'objective' standards of objectivity arise within a culture of thought in which nothing less than a *moral* necessity requires distinctions between personalized and depersonalized knowledge. This is a large subject calling for far greater attention. I address it briefly here because of the tendency of legal philosophers such as Lloyd Weinreb to regard the moral and the objective realms as mutually exclusive.

Of comparable power in forming Professor Weinreb's skepticism about Natural Law theory is that old Humean chestnut which, as Professor Weinreb phrases it, precludes the establishment of any normative proposition as a matter of fact (the alleged fact/value divide). Perhaps it is time to suppress the customary awe inspired by this expanse, if only to test the possibility that the wrong instruments are being used.

As Kant was at pains to make clear, the moral realm is the domain of 'intelligible' events, distinguished from purely natural events in having a rational point or in calling for justifications. Let us recognize that the laws of physical determination make no more sense than their negations, and never call for justifications. 'F = ma' makes no more sense that does 'F = m/a' or 'F = ma^2'; nor *ought* 'F = ma', for the laws of science are dispositive, but not obligatory.

Events brought about by agentic beings, however, those capable of giving and understanding *reasons for action*, occur within an entirely different realm, the potentially *moral* realm of praise and blame, right and wrong, good and evil. The only standard or modulus available for assessing the quality of events filling this realm is the standard of rationality itself. If any event is judged herein as one that *ought* to occur, the judgement arises from a premise or principle ordained by reason. Applied to the instant case, the principle then compels a course of action not as a matter of *fact* but syllogistically. If the act or event in question were compulsory *as a matter of fact*, it would be entirely natural and beyond the range of moral concern. The issue Professor Weinreb raises, therefore, is a popular one in philosophy, but I submit a counterfeit, no more authentic because those who should know better have agreed to trade in it. Moral duties are created by moral principles. If the principles are valid, they are able to generate certain moral outcomes otherwise known as duties, rights, and obligations. What is at issue, then, is not specious claims for and against the is/ought barrier, but the nature of the validity that might be claimed for moral principles. I should think that John Finnis's explicit rejection of inferences that would proceed from fact to value is best understood in these terms.

The standard of validity here must have some direct relation to the very point of life itself beyond the biological and other determinative factors by which it is brought about and materially sustained. At the level of physiology, life has no 'point' for the same reason that no fact qua fact has a point. Nothing about life in the merely physiological sense is obligatory even if there are laws of physiology that are dispositive. To return to the sources of Professor Weinreb's consternation one might say that what all theories warranting the label 'Natural Law' have in common is the assumption that there is a point to life apart from the physical fact of it, and that this point is bound up with non-physical, indeterminate possibilities immanent in it. To be the potential beneficiary of these possibilities is thus to be regarded as having an *interest*, the official rejection of which constitutes the denial that there is a point to life.

But to deny this is to invoke or assert or affirm a theory; it is to *justify* a course of action or inaction; it is to make a claim and thus to acknowledge some place or part for dialogue. In a word, it is to refute the theory that grounded the claim. It is only the complete skeptic, and not merely the moral skeptic, who can avoid contradiction at this point; the complete skeptic here being one who rejects even the prospect of valid scientific or factual knowledge. For the limited skeptic, who accepts that there are facts to be discerned and that such facts permit inferences to more general and valid conclusions, the very act of contesting moral claims offers evidence of the desire of the disputants to gain understanding; the willingness to regard each other as possessing sufficient rationality and autonomy as to be won over by successful arguments, and to attach oneself to them. All of this already tacitly assumes or presupposes at least one of the very points of life; namely, self-improvement through rational discourse. This, then, is the right rational foundation for any version of Natural Law theory, whatever other and distinctive arguments might then be built on it.

How much of Professor Weinreb's challenge have we attended to? We've moved this far, at least: Natural Law theory is not put on notice by the fact that persons differ in their convictions. Such convictions are *not* unverifiable, but verifiability is the wrong standard in any case. A uniformity of conviction would neither support nor refute Natural Law theory, for it is not a theory about convictions, but about principles for living. That there are such principles is true just in case life has a point and purpose beyond the constitutive physical facts and physiological laws of life. A theory of law or of duties and obligations enjoys a measure of validity, then, to the extent that it supplies or is grounded in just those principles that express the point of life, defined tentatively as the potentiality for realizing possibilities of an otherwise and physically undetermined or underdetermined nature. Space does not permit needed refinements of this definition. Certain possibilities such as the potential for murderous, destructive, anti-social behaviour can be shown to be ruled out, for they serve not only to limit the realization of possibilities in other lives, but also violate the very canons of rationality necessary for the establishment of justifications.

This would be the place to consider Professor Weinreb's criticisms of Professor Finnis's theory of seven basic forms of human good, but space is too limited. Let me say only that I can readily envisage Natural Law theories that are far less specific in their conclusions; still others that might well be even more granular in their delineations. I do not think that Professor Finnis or Professor Grisez regards himself as having concluded that part of the long debate concerned with law and morals. As best as I have been able to discover in their influential and unavoidably difficult and truncated arguments, they have attempted to show that such finality in the moral domain must be at the price of that very practical reasoning that would be informed by moral science. A deductive argument that disposes of every moral problem by ruling out choice is an argument that eliminates moral life itself.

To enlarge this important point (on which Professor Finnis and I might well disagree), I should say that I take *moral life* to be one marked out by struggles and strivings; by that *Protrepticus* apparently bequeathed by Aristotle in which the claims of contemplation and purification are challenged by those of the needs of the world. The problem for one who would seek to live a moral life is not that there are competing goods, such that any significant choice must be at the cost of a recognized good. The problem is that the grounds of choice itself tend to be shifting, uncertain, and inextricably bound up with larger cultural traditions and perspectives not easily disregarded. Were there a device or calculus or word of God to be applied at every such choice-point, the price we would pay for moral incorrigibility would be just the *moral life*. The only basis upon which it would still be a *struggle* to avoid what is now established as the morally incorrect choice is the struggle against *immorality*. This, however, I take to be the struggle that must be overcome for a moral life to begin at all. But this is a matter being considered by Professor Finnis, as it does raise something of a question about his own understanding of the choices faced by rational beings already committed to morally approved courses of action.

A few additional words are in order here, however, on one source of much confusion in this general area; namely, the concepts of the self-evident (*per se nota*), the indemonstrable (*indemonstrabilia*) and the requirements of practical reasonableness. Let us be clear that nothing in Thomistic philosophy requires that the self-evident is evident to every 'self'. The Euclide;an definition of parallel lines includes that they are non-intersecting, and thus it is self-evident that an acute angle cannot be formed by any pair of them. Whole graduating classes these days may be oblivious to this self-evident axiom. Thus, the demography of assent is irrelevant to the question of whether a proposition, if true, is true *per se nota*. I suspect, in reading Professor Weinreb on this matter, that he conflates two of Locke's three principal modes of knowing. Locke carefully distinguished between and among what he called the *intuitive*, the *demonstrative*, and the *perceptive* means by which knowledge is possessed. What is known intuitively is known with certainty, is known instantly, and is known without deliberation. Thus, up is not down, black is not white, and a thing cannot simultaneously be, and not be. Demonstrative knowledge, however though certain is not instant. Rather, a formal argument is needed which depends on the rational and judgemental powers of the knower. Accordingly, there is a definite connection, and surely not some sort of dialectical opposition between judgement and demonstrative knowledge. Furthermore, and as Aristotle was perhaps the first to make explicit, all understanding cannot be *demonstrative*, for demonstrative knowledge is based upon principles and, were all understanding demonstrative, there would be an infinite regression at the level of principle (*Post. Anal.* 72^{b}20–25). There must be a starting point of common notions or 'posits', as he calls them, which are not themselves demonstrable. They are instead originating axioms.

Returning now to that feature of Natural Law theory of which Professor Weinreb seems especially wary that is, where human life is taken to be a reason for action it is sufficient to note that all evaluative discourse is predicated on the fact of life, and that to be neutral on the good of life is to be left with no coherent answer to the question, 'Good for what?' That life is a basic good is *indemonstrabilia* in just the sense that any and all demonstrative knowledge in ethics must have a starting point, and *the good of life* just is the starting point.

But are there not conflicts arising when abstractions give way to concrete conditions, as when the prolongation of life must be at the cost of intractable pain and relentless suffering? Might not basic goods collide and generate Hobson's choices? The answer is, of course, yes. But, as Natural Law theory is not a machine for cranking out infallibly correct answers to all problems, it is not at all clear why room for debate and moral confusion should tell against it. The problem here is not, as Professor Weinreb would have it, that Natural Law theory '. . . requires the establishment of objective moral truths'; less is it because these allegedly needed truths '. . . cannot be established as a matter of fact and are neither self-evident nor demonstrable'. It should be obvious by now that the foundational principles of Natural Law theory must be indemonstrable, for that is what makes them foundational. And, to be sure, there is a difference between a 'truth' and a 'fact', in that the former refers to the logical standing of premises and conclusions, whereas the latter is a property of experience. The problem is that the rough and tumble of actual life will inevitably lead to quandaries as regards the extent to which actions and prevailing conditions match up with what are otherwise accepted as dispositive moral maxims. We are, as it were, participants in a game of chess, but with multiple sets of vexingly indistinct pieces already distributed randomly among the faded patches on an old board with uncertain boundaries. If, indeed, this piece *is* a bishop, we know we cannot move it laterally; but *is it* the bishop, and, given the conditions of the board, would the move actually be a *lateral* one?

In criticizing Natural Law theory, Professor Weinreb takes evidence of the uncertainty of results to establish an uncertainty of the principles from which results would derive their justifications. But he is far more lenient when developing his own theory of rights as the means by which we go about rectifying the consequences of bad moral or constitutive luck. He knows very well that there is no perfect compensation in such matters, nor is there even the hope of an 'objective' scale of compensation. What is called for is judgement. Professor Weinreb is not skeptical about rights and deserts, even if he can't render them in a quantitatively precise and, however he means this term, 'objective' fashion. He is not skeptical about them because, on the assumption that we are responsible only for what is in our power, these rights, duties, etc. are what? Why, they are, dare I say it, *per se nota*. And when, nearly as an aside, Professor Weinreb refers to that 'small number of rights, imprecisely defined' that must be granted if there is to be a human form of life at all, he has again come face to face with the *per se nota*. His credentials as a Natural Law theorist at this point are nearly in order.

As for narrower claims defended by Professor Weinreb, some conceptual, some historical, I shall say only a few words. I am not as confident as he that 'rights and responsibility are one and the same'. I do not think that persons accept their rights *so that* they will have responsibilities, though it does make sense to say that they will take on certain responsibilities in order to preserve or protect one or another right. I, too, accept that no right is incontestable, but I would shy away from the notion that, because something is not written in the stars it is written by the human hand. The rights that men and women have died for and still die for rise above mere convention and have an ontological standing that is more than literary.

I would also urge upon Professor Weinreb an awareness of the thoroughness with which Natural Law reasoning has permeated the history of law, and the progressive influence this reasoning has had. The tradition is not to be dismissed as a medieval curiosity, but as one of the sturdier pillars on which even such competing theories as Hobbes's or later versions of utilitarianism firmly rest. Nor would I be as comfortable as Professor Weinreb with a definition of the ancient Greek *Nomos* as '. . . the deep conventions of a community'. Here I think he refers to *ethos*. For *nomos* I would take Aristotle's understanding: law, then, is reason without passion. *Dioper aneu orexios nous o nomos estin.*

In the end, therefore, I remain less than reassured by Professor Weinreb's abject resignation before that great canvas he calls 'the human condition', at least if this 'condition' is meant to discourage the search for right answers to morally difficult problems. The 'human condition' is broad and various enough to nurture more than one theory of justice. It certainly does not rule out *a priori* the one Professor Weinreb finds so unconvincing.

NOTE

1 Sir Frederick Pollock, *Essays in the Law* (London, MacMillan, 1922) ch. 3.

12

Good Without God

MICHAEL S. MOORE[1]

I. INTRODUCTION

The pun in the title is intentional. Read one way, the title gives us the question that I wish to examine: can there be objective moral properties like goodness in a world without God? Read another way, the title states my answer: it is good to be without God as we seek to vindicate any belief in the objectivity of morals, for we don't need him in this task.

The question is a familiar one to both theists and atheists. Certainly atheists like the late John Mackie have every reason to ask 'what we can make of morality without recourse to God, and hence of what we can say about morality if, in the end, we dispense with religious belief[2]—for given the absence of any religious faith by atheists, this is simply to ask how things stand with morality. But even theists have long asked this question.[3] What validity would morality have, Grotius asked, 'if we should concede that which cannot be conceded without the utmost wickedness, that there is no God . . .'?[4] Such suspension of religious belief has long helped theists separate out their ethics from their theology.

The most familiar answer to this familiar question I take to be the opposite of mine. My sense is that most people, theists and atheists alike, share the sentiment that Dostoevsky put in the mouth of Ivan Karamazov: 'without God, everything is permitted.'[5] Karamazov's conclusion was certainly the view of post-World War II French existentialism, where God gets frequent mention in a kind of post-mortem: 'what do we do now that God is dead?' Kai Nielsen states this asserted connection between God and good succinctly: 'If there is no God . . . the classical natural law theory is absurd . . .'[6]

Even those theists who seek to separate their ethics from their theology by suspending religious belief usually end up finding some work for God to do in tending the ethical garden. Grotius, for example, could only find a 'degree of validity' to his views on natural law in the absence of God.[7] Kant, who famously sought to show how morality could be known to be objective within the limits of reason alone, nonetheless thought God necessary both to make possible human realization of the highest good and to guarantee a motivating proportion between virtue and experienced happiness.[8] John Finnis is a prominent contemporary example, for Finnis wrote his masterful *Natural Law and Natural Rights* (which defends the objectivity of morality within a general theory of practical reasonableness) while explicitly not relying on God's existence.[9] Yet, by the last chapter, God is turned to for help in (ultimately) explaining how it is that objective morality exists.

Before turning to the reasons I have for resisting this most popular answer, I shall utilize the remainder of this introduction to say more about the question. We need two clarifications at the outset in order to have a meaningful question to ask. These are: (1) what do we mean by the 'objectivity of morals', and (2) what do we mean by 'God'? For if moral objectivity is conceived of in terms of divine command, or God is given an ethical definition (as the highest good at which we should aim, say), then we will have begged our question before we shall have asked it. To have a question to ask, we need a non-religious idea about morality's objectivity and a non-ethical idea about God; then we can meaningfully inquire what relation might exist between them.

Morality's objectivity should be defined as what modern moral philosophers call moral realism.[10] Moral realism itself has two leading conceptualizations, one ontological and the other semantic. According to the ontological conceptualization, morality is objective if and only if: (a) moral qualities such as goodness, wrongness, etc., exist (the existential condition); and (b) the existence of such moral qualities does not depend on what any person or group of persons believes about them (the mind-independence condition). Quite similar is the semantic conceptualization of moral realism, according to which morality is objective if and only if: (a) moral propositions (such as 'slavery is unjust,' 'bullfighting is wrong') have a truth value, and some of such propositions are true; and (b) the truth of such moral propositions does not depend on any person or group of persons believing them to be true. Either way of conceptualizing objectivity will do here, for neither has any religious presuppositions built into the ideas of qualities, existence, truth, or independence.[11] Moreover, these are the two standard ways for defining objectivity about any number of fields beyond ethics, such as mathematics or natural science; it is the heart of what we usually mean when we talk about the possibility of objectivity of knowledge in any field. It is true that when objectivity in ethics is talked about popularly, emphasis is placed on attributes like the timelessness of morality's eternal truths, their unchanging or invariant nature, their universal applicability to all persons and all cultures, the existence of right answers to moral dilemmas, and the like. Yet these popular notions are by and large the surface corollaries of the deeper if more technical notions definitive of moral realism.

The more technical notion of objectivity nicely separates the varieties of moral anti-realists. Such anti-realists are either idealists or skeptics, depending on which of the two conditions definitive of realism they deny. Idealists admit the existence of moral properties and grant that moral propositions are sometimes true, but they deny the mind-independence condition of moral realism. They relativize moral properties or truths to the beliefs of historical persons. Such idealists are thus often called relativists, since they hold that the truth of any moral proposition is relative to the beliefs of some individuals or some societies. Moral skeptics, by contrast, deny the existential condition of moral realism, and so do not reach the mind-independence question. Some skeptics deny that moral propositions have any truth value, being mere expressions of emotions or prescriptions or orders to others. Other skeptics admit that moral propositions have a truth value, but assert that that value is always the truth value, 'false'. We shall on occasion need to return to these varieties of moral anti-realism as we ask in what ways God could help to overcome moral skepticism or moral relativism, because sometimes it matters (to what work there might be for God to do) what variety of anti-realism we are seeking to overcome.

'God' is less easy to give a non-controversial definition of, for the theists with whom I am familiar tend to get a bit mysterious here.[12] Nonetheless, it is essential that 'God' be given a non-ethical definition; for if God were defined as the objective good, say, we could not separate the question of God's existence from the question of good's existence.[13] I realize that in requiring a non-ethical definition of God I have touched on a raw nerve for many theologians. For on their view, necessarily God is good, by which they mean either a metaphysical necessity (God is identical to goodness) or an analytic necessity ('God' means 'goodness'). That is their faith, so that they cannot separate the question of God's existence from the question of good's existence. Thus Patterson Brown, for example, holds that:

'God' is ordinarily a partially moral term. In our civilization, and thus in our language, it would not be strictly proper to call a being 'God' whose actions were not perfectly good or whose commands were not the best of moral directives. That God is good is a truth of language, since one of the usual *criteria* of Godhood is that the actions and commands of such a being are perfectly good . . .[14]

Yet if one posits that God is good necessarily by supposed analytic truths or otherwise then one cannot even raise the question of this chapter. Whereas those theists who regard God's goodness to be a contingently true fact about God can imagine possible worlds in which God exists but he is not good, and in which goodness exists without God. Such theists can join me in asking whether the second is the actual world in which we live.

John Finnis gives a non-ethical definition of God,[15] and both the clarity of his proposal, and its responsiveness to a popular conception of God, will suit our purposes. According to Finnis, God is: (1) the first cause of all other causes, and thus, an uncaused cause; this, with some extension, makes God the example of free will, for his will (at least in its initial exercises) is uncaused; (2) such free causation is not merely an event, but it 'can be described as an *act* . . .'[16]; God acts, in a sense of action stronger than the metaphorical 'actions' of sulfuric acid 'dissolving' lead, for example; (3) God's acts are *chosen*, in the sense that alternative possibilities are represented and some subset of those representations are then used to guide divine action; (4) some of those divine representations are logically and semantically general, so that one can speak of the divine plans as laws and of God as a law-giver; (5) some of those laws are directed at human beings, whereby God intends to communicate them to us.

If one sums up these attributes of God, not surprisingly what is revealed is an anthropomorphic conception of God. As Finnis himself notes, 'inasmuch as the speculation suggests that D *acts* and *knows*, it suggests that D's existing is conceivable on the model of *personal life*.'[17] Put in my language: this anthropocentric conception of God plainly mirrors the essential attributes of persons, God being conceived of as a person-like entity, only with powers greater than those of ordinary persons.

Many theologians would add to this list another attribute of God, which is that he cares for us, loves us, or has the potential to be our friend.[18] They do this in order to make what such a God could will closer to things that are good for us. That is, just as friendship, love, and altruistic concern between persons are constituted at least in part by caring for the good of another as one cares for one's own good, God too is conceived in these ways so that he must be concerned with our good. This does not beg the crucial question by identifying God as what is good. Thus, this additional definition of God does not make it impossible to raise a question we do need to ask, which is whether God's will crates what is good or merely conforms to an (antecedently existing) goodness. The idea motivating those who define God as a loving God is that a loving God would never will things that were not good for us, so we never face the *real* possibility of seemingly evil willings by God. Even so, so long as the connection between loving another and always acting for the good of the love-object is contingent, we may add this definitional requirement without precluding either option about the connection between goodness and God's will.

Having said a bit about moral objectivity and about God, it remains to ask after the relationship between them that most assert and I deny. As a first attempt, one might say that the relationship is one of necessity: must God exist for morality to be objective? Yet strict necessities are notoriously hard to verify positively, so we should examine a much weaker relation: would the existence of God help at all in justifying our belief that morality is objective? Would God's existence strengthen the case for morality's objectivity?

In general, there are two ways in which we might proceed in arguing the negative on this question. One would be to show that morality is objective without making any use of the notion of God. If non-theistic grounds for the belief in moral objectivity are fully sufficient, then theistic grounds are not necessary. This way of proceeding is of course just to do meta-ethics, not theology. My own and others meta-ethical efforts should thus be seen as one possible way of establishing the non-necessity/unhelpfulness of religious belief in defending moral objectivity.[19] Yet this I have done already. In this chapter I wish to make the alternative defence. This is to assume that God does exist, then to examine each of the ways God might be thought to be helpful to morality's objectivity, and finally, to show why, despite appearances, God isn't doing any work.

Proceeding in this second manner demands that we have some idea of how God might be helpful in seeing the objectivity of ethics. Seeing these possibilities, in turn, is partly a matter of culling the literature of theological ethics for suggestions;[20] as importantly, it is also a matter of understanding the kinds of skeptical challenge that moral realists must surmount in order to defend morality's objectivity. If we grasp these principal skeptical challenges, we are in a position to see how if at all God might help the moral realist surmount them.

In a much earlier paper I surveyed what I took to be the leading skeptical challenges one must overcome in order to defend moral objectivity. With some rearrangement and deletions to fit the present purposes, the pertinent skeptical challenges that I shall examine are:

1. The challenge from ontology: that moral qualities are 'queer' in the sense that they do not fit in easily with the more ordinary things we think to exist.
2. The challenge from prescriptivity: that moral qualities must obligate in an absolute way in order to exist, and no such sort of obligation is possible absent from One to whom such obligations are owed or from whom they emanate.
3. The challenge from motivation: that moral qualities must subjectively motivate us to want to be moral in order to exist, or at least in order for us to care whether they exist.
4. The challenge from psychology: that the psychological limitations of persons are such that they cannot know the objective good, even if it exists, nor can they attain it, even if they know it.
5. The challenge from cosmology: that even if all other challenges were met, morality would still be a merely human-relative thing, absent a larger purpose in the universe.

There are doubtlessly other challenges where God has been thought to help, but on my reading of both skeptical meta-ethics and theological ethics, these are the most pertinent ones. They are in any event the ones I shall examine *seriatim* in what follows. The question to be examined with respect to each of them is whether belief in God makes it easier to answer the moral skeptic.

II. GOD AS THE CURE TO THE ALLEGED METAPHYSICAL QUEERNESS OF OBJECTIVE MORAL QUALITIES

The place to start is with what I sense to be the most popular of the beliefs that God helps in making out the objectivity of morals. This is the belief that if moral laws and the moral qualities such laws describe can be shown to originate with God, then those laws and qualities are less objectionably strange (or 'queer', in the late J. L. Mackie's lexicon[21]) than they are without God. A version of this belief surfaced recently at a conference on natural law held at the University of Texas. While I was discussing moral realism a member of the audience interrupted with what she obviously took to be a knock-down winner of an objection: 'where do these moral laws come from, according to you?'[22] Note the suppositions of such a question: laws must have a source, and this source must itself have spatial and temporal location.

To us post-Enlightenment moderns, such a question seems to lack sense because its suppositions are so obviously false.[23] Laws and qualities, being universals, do not have spatial or temporal location. Asking where a moral law is, or when goodness came into being, is like asking where the number 2 resides or when it was created. Universals, if they exist, do not exist like that, so it is senseless to demand that they 'come from' somewhere.

Despite this, I shall here explore three senses one might give to the demand that moral laws and the moral qualities to which they refer come from somewhere. First, one might argue from the essence of laws generically, thinking that laws are such that there must be a law-giver for anything properly called a law. Secondly, one might think that the requirement (that there be a law-giver for there to be laws) must at least be true for *prescriptive* laws, i.e., laws that tell us what we ought to do. Thirdly, one might think that Godless moral qualities, even without any law-like or prescriptive features, require an ontology of Platonic forms or something equally strange, whereas moral laws as commands or thoughts of God require less of our ontological imagination.

All Laws Essentially Require a Law-Giver?

Thomas Aquinas is a well known example of the first of these arguments. According to Aquinas, laws must be promulgated by someone. On Aquinas's view, one of the essential properties a thing must possess to be a law is that it be promulgated by one who has the care of the community.[24] Now the objection would be that moral laws without a God would not be promulgated by anyone, making them metaphysically impossible.

The response of a secular natural lawyer to this kind of objection should be obvious. It is to deny that an essential property of laws is that they be laid down by someone. Think of the laws of science, such as Kepler's laws of planetary motion or Snell's law on the diffusion rate of gas through a porous membrane. These are perfectly good laws and yet they are not laid down by anyone.

One might think that Kepler or Snell laid down the laws named after them. After all, prior to their respective discoveries such laws had never been formulated. Yet for a theist to admit that Kepler or Snell laid down the laws that bear their names would be to miss what is being claimed when it is claimed that all laws must promulgated. Advert to the ancient query: does the extensional equivalence between what is good and what God commands come about: (1) because God, being omniscient, only commands good things; or (2) because God being omnipotent, makes what he commands good by the fact that he has commanded it? The first possibility grants to God no ability to lay down the moral law; he like everyone else, must discover that law which exists antecedent to his will. God may be better at such discovery than the rest of us, being omniscient and all, but God in no sense creates, lays down, or makes true by assertion the moral laws.

Those who would claim that all laws must have a source, in the sense of being promulgated by someone, must eschew this anaemic sense of 'promulgation-as-first discovery-and-first-formulation'. For if the only promulgation needed is that by the discoverer of laws antecedently existing, there would be nothing metaphysically queer about laws existing without God laying them down. One might interpose an epistemic objection—that we humans couldn't adequately know the moral law if there is no God—but there would be no metaphysical objection to be made to such Godless moral laws.

Only in an equally harmless, anaemic sense do scientists 'lay down' the laws of science that they discover. The counter-example of the laws of science thus still holds. Something may be a law, the proposition such law expresses may well be true, and the qualities to which it refers may well exist, without anyone promulgating it. The planets, after all, obeyed Kepler's laws just as well before Kepler as they did after Kepler

formulated the laws that described planetary behaviour. Kepler's formulation of those laws added nothing to their existence, however much that
formulation better enabled *us* to know of their existence.

One might urge that the laws of science are not real laws, that only promulgated laws are real laws. Theorists as diverse as Aquinas[25] and John
Austin[26] have adopted this response. Yet it is wholly inadequate. Either as
a matter of the essence of the thing, law (Aquinas), or as a matter of our
concept or word, 'law' (Austin), one could easily concede the point and
still urge the analogy of (unpromulgated) moral 'laws' to (unpromulgated) scientific 'laws'. The analogy of morals to science, in other words,
holds irrespective whether enacted law has a monopoly in the correct, 'primary', 'focal', or 'dominant' usage of the word 'law'.

Prescriptive Laws Require a Law-Giver?

Theorists about natural law thus have to break the analogy of moral laws
to the unpromulgated laws of science. The obvious move is the second of
the three arguments I wish to explore. The move is to distinguish prescriptive norms from descriptive generalizations. Scientific laws describe
(unpromulgated) phenomena, whereas moral laws prescribe to us how we
ought to behave; and, the argument concludes, prescriptive laws require a
prescriber. As H. P. Owen puts this last point, 'it is impossible to think of
a command without also thinking of a commander.'[27] If one is to avoid
non-cognitivism, subjectivism, or conventionalism about morals where
the prescriber is either each person or each culture, then God is needed as
the Grand Prescriber.

To assess the force of this suggestion we need to pay more attention to
this idea of prescriptivity. It is almost always true that when we make
moral statements, we (as speakers) do so with intended prescriptive force:
we intend to tell ourselves or others what to do, what to feel, what kind of
a person to be, etc. Prescriptivity is thus, initially at least, a kind of speech-
act people do when they use words in certain ways. Moreover, such common usage patterns for certain words (like 'good', 'greedy', 'brutish', etc.)
gives those words a conventional illocutionary force—what William
Alston once called their illocutionary act potential.[28] On some suitably
extended notion of semantics, this elevates prescriptivity into part of the
'meaning' of certain words; one might say, as many ordinary language
philosophers did, that such words have a 'prescriptive meaning' as well as
a 'descriptive meaning'.[29]

Yet according to the moral realist these behavioural and linguistic con-
struals of prescriptivity are themselves the surface phenomena caused by
a deeper moral truth: moral qualities not only exist in a way that allows us
to describe them, but their very existence gives us reasons to act in certain

ways and not others. The moral realist, in other words, takes prescriptivity to be a feature of the (moral) world, and not just a feature of our talk about that world. This allows us to see the best construal of the objection here considered. This is that for moral qualities to give us objectively binding reasons for action—for such qualities to obligate us, to prescribe how we ought to behave—only a God could have created them. Qualities that prescribe behaviour to us must, in other words, have been created by a Grand Prescriber.

It is a real worry whether the existence of objective reasons for action binding on all of us demands, or at least is helped to be made intelligible by, a God. Indeed, I take this problem to be *the* most serious worry that God may be needed to make sense of objective morality. I shall accordingly reserve discussion of it for a separate, subsequent section of this chapter.

What we can do here is some metaphysical nibbling around the edges of the objection. For notice that so far nothing in our analysis of prescriptivity (in terms of objective reasons for action) in any way breaks the analogy of moral laws to scientific laws. True, scientific laws do not give reasons for action; yet they do give reasons for belief. Kepler's laws of planetary motion do not tell me how to behave with respect to the planets, nor what I should feel about them; but those laws do give me reasons to believe certain propositions, and not others, about what the planets are doing now, what they have done in the past, and what they will do in the future. Should the existence of such reason-giving qualities (as mass) in those laws require the existence of a Grand Believer or a Grand Describer? Nothing thus far has been said about prescription and reasons for action that could not equally well be said about description and reasons for belief.

There are two ways for the natural law theist to go here. One is to admit the last analogy, and to argue that, in order to make sense, both the laws of science and the laws of morality require God. This is John Finnis' ultimate move here,[30] and I shall consider it when I consider in the last section whether realism about both science and morality requires a Guarantor of order. The other is to continue to deny the analogy between moral laws and scientific laws. One might urge here that it is not the prescriptivity as such of moral qualities that requires God, the Grand Prescriber; rather, it is the fact that moral qualities *both* describe something and prescribe action that requires God.

it is true that this conjunction of features has troubled some moral theorists about objective moral qualities. How, the late John Mackie asked, can a quality, by the very fact of its existence, give us a reason to act one way rather than another? How can such a quality have 'have-to-be-doneness' built into its very nature? The ontological oddity of such a combination lead Mackie to his well known 'queerness' objection to the ontology required by moral realism.

I and others have sought to defuse this queerness objection to moral realism.[31] But the relevant point here is not to rehearse this rebuttal. Rather, conceding at least *arguendo* that the objection is a serious one, the question to be asked is whether positing a God helps in any way in answering the objection. If God were found to have decreed the laws creating such qualities, would they be any less queer in their reason-giving capacities?

John Mackie himself argued that perhaps God could help explain such metaphysical queerness and, thus, render it somewhat less queer:

[W]e might well argue . . . that objectively intrinsically prescriptive features, supervening upon natural ones, constitute so odd a cluster of qualities and relations that they are most unlikely to have arisen in the ordinary course of events, without an all-powerful God to create them . . . There would be something here in need of explanation, and a being with the power to create what lies outside the bounds of natural plausibility or even possibility might well be the explanation we require.[32]

Yet does the theistic explanation for reason-giving moral qualities in any way diminish their alleged queerness? Isn't Mackie really saying that he finds objective moral qualities so beyond ordinary explicability— 'queer'—that the only 'explanation' there could be for them is one that is so equally queer that the inference to be drawn is the one Mackie himself drew from these suppositions: neither God nor objective moral qualities exist?

There is an analogy to the positive laws of a legitimate secular authority that is to be resisted here. For one might say that when such a legitimate practical (secular) authority issues a valid decree prohibiting killing, then the quality, causing-the-death-of-another, now itself possesses the prescriptive quality of, 'is to be avoided'. It thus may seem that divine command can help make intelligible the reason-giving capacity of otherwise natural qualities. The reason this is an inapt analogy is because the secular decreer does not *create* the qualities his decrees prescribe; he describes pre-existing qualities that are then prescribed. Whereas God, remember, on the view here considered creates qualities like goodness by his decree. As Brian Davies puts this view, 'God's will creates moral standards.'[33] God gives 'good', 'right', etc., the only content they have by virtue of those decrees. That is how God can make it true that any act is good or bad, by such a 'super-performative' speech act.

God, thus, unlike a secular authority, does not diminish the queerness of reason-giving qualities. The queerness of reason-giving moral qualities remains even if we explain their existence as the causal product of divine decree. At most, all we would have done is to regress the queerness, substituting a queer object of God's intention for the queer quality that that intention is supposed to explain.

Non-natural Properties and Platonic Forms as Queerer than God?

I now come to the third of my metaphysical worries about objective moral qualities without God. Sometimes moral qualities like goodness or wrongness are taken to be metaphysically queer without regard to their reason-for-action-giving (or prescriptive) capacities. Tables, chairs, ocean liners, and other physical objects are commonly taken to be our model for what exists. Theoretical entities such as kinetic energy or force fields, plus events, states, and other spatio-temporally located particulars that are not objects, plus mental states and mental events, and perhaps also numbers, kinds, properties, classes, and relations, may also be grudgingly admitted into such a macro-level, physicalist ontology. But moral qualities are more ghostly than any of these. They are 'non-natural' and therefore *prima facie* queer. Robert Adams states this ontological worry about objective moral qualities succinctly:

If we are tempted to say . . . that there are no objective facts of right or wrong at all, it is chiefly because we have found so much obscurity in theories about objective, non-natural ethical facts. We seem not to be acquainted with the simple, non-natural ethical properties of the intuitionists, and we do not understand what a Platonic Form of the Good or the Just would be.[34]

God is supposed to help here. According to Adams, the notion that moral qualities exist as commands by God 'provides us more clearly with matter for thought than the intuitionistic and Platonic conceptions do'.[35] What I gather Adams finds less queer (than Moorean non-natural properties or Platonic Forms) is the identification of moral qualities with 'facts about the will or commands of God'.[36]

Surely this argument is a non-starter. The argument concedes an empiricist starting point on ontological questions: what exists are observable objects and whatever else is necessary to make sense of them. The argument then *seems* to lessen the non-physical queerness of moral qualities by analogizing them to the mental acts of willing or commanding with which we are familiar from our dealings with other persons; this *seems* to give moral qualities spatio-temporal location, like the utterances of a military commander. Thus Adams tells us that 'it is God's *revealed* will—not what he wants or plans to have happen, but what he has told us to do—that is thought to determine the rightness and wrongness of human actions . . . It is best, therefore, in a metaethical theory, to say that wrongness is contrary to God's *commands*, and commands must have been issued, promulgated, or somehow revealed.'[37] Yet all this seeming spatio-temporal locatability is of course ultimately taken away, for God isn't like any human commander in this regard. God's commandings are thus as much a shock to empiricist sensibilities as any Moorean non-natural property or Platonic Form could be.

From the vantage point of my own empiricism about what exists, I think we do well to dispense with all three such notions. My own metaphysics, argued for elsewhere,[38] is to refuse to countenance the existence of objective moral qualities unless they cause other (non-moral) entities, qualities, and events to occur, and such a causal role can exist for moral qualities only if they supervene upon, and in some sense are identical to, non-moral (i.e., natural) properties.[39] Since moral qualities do cause natural phenomena to exist, and since they are supervenient and 'token-identical' to natural properties, we have no need of Forms, Gods, or non-natural properties to make sense of moral realism. Nothing in this kind of ethical naturalism should shock empiricist sensibilities about what can exist.

III. GOD AS THE OBJECTIVE MOTIVATOR OF OBJECTIVE MORALITY

What is the Question: Objective, Non-Prudential Reasons for Action?

We come now to the question deferred from the last section: is God helpful in making sense of the idea that morality is in some sense normative? There are various ways of putting this question. Jeff Goldsworthy puts it as a question of morality's *authority*: 'the most fundamental claim made by morality [is that] its precepts are authoritatively binding in a sense which transcends even enlightened self-interest.'[40] John Finnis puts the question as one of obligation: 'what makes it *obligatory* to choose the right and the due and to avoid the wrong and the undue?'[41] My own preferred way of putting the question is in terms of reasons for action: is God helpful in making sense of the idea that morality gives us objective reasons for action?

The first thing to do with this question is to clarify it. Basic to understanding what the question asks is to grasp the distinction between subjective reasons and objective reasons. Subjective reasons have to do with some person's actual mental states of desire. If you want ice cream, then you have a subjective reason to act so as to get some. If you do get some ice cream, and your desire caused your action in the right way, the desire explains your action by showing what motivated you to do what you did.[42]

Objective reasons need have nothing to do with your actual mental states nor are they given to explain your behaviour.[43] If a starving person finds food in an abandoned cabin, he has reason to eat it even if he is so starved that he has lost all desire to eat. If he eats the food belonging to another, we would cite this objective reason to justify his action (even if there were no corresponding subjective reason for that action).

A strong tradition stemming from Hume denies that there are objective reasons for action. A moral realist, however, ought to be committed to the existence of such objective reasons and to the proposition that moral qualities give us such objective reasons to behave in certain ways and not others. The question relevant here is whether positing God in any way helps the moral realist to defend these commitments.

Having sharpened the question with the distinction between objective and subjective reasons allows us to see another, alternative question that could be asked if one had a somewhat different view of moral realism. Suppose that one thought that moral qualities, if they exist, must not only give each of us objective reasons to conform to their dictates, but that such qualities must also give us subjective reasons. That is, suppose one thought that the objectivity of morality requires that if an act is morally right, then the moral rightness of that act must subjectively incline us to do that act. Then a relevant question would be whether positing God wouldn't help explain how moral qualities are necessarily motivating in this subjective sense.

One Christian answer to this question is a very familiar one. God helps here in that the divine creation of human beings instils in each of them a natural inclination to do the good. That natural inclination is distorted by Man's fall from grace in the Garden but is nonetheless still present. A competing, non-theistic answer would posit a human nature that has evolved to the point that each person is inclined to do the good (which is itself then explained in terms of species-survival value).

The problem with this alternative question (and the explanatory work that it makes possible for God to do), is that the best construal of moral realism does not require that moral qualities necessarily motivate each of us subjectively. A moral realist should admit that the existence of a moral quality tends to cause a belief that it exists in each of us; but those of us who are called 'externalist moral realists' deny that a belief that some act is good necessarily motivates the believer towards that act.[44] There are, after all, amoralists, those people who freely admit that some act would be good to do and yet who truthfully deny the existence of any desire within them to do that act. There is thus no explanandum here suggesting God, man's divine origins or his fall from grace, as explanations. There is no universally present human nature inclining each of us to behave ourselves. Well socialized human beings brought up in a decent society will tend to want to behave morally; savages and Hitler Youth will not.

We return thus to the first alternative question we framed in this section: would the existence of God help to make sense of how or why moral qualities give us objective reasons to act in certain ways? Another familiar argument here will help us to further sharpen our question. This is the argument that divine sanctions are necessary for morality to obligate us. If we are good, we will live in eternal bliss in the afterlife; if we are bad, we will suffer eternal damnation in hell. Such divine sanctions, it is popularly said, create the reasons each of us have to be moral.[45]

This popular vision allows us to introduce another distinction in order to clarify the question relevant here. This is a distinction between two kinds of objective reasons we each have, reasons of morality and reasons of prudence. A reason of prudence appeals to our self-interest, whereas a reason of morality may appeal to some social good (or to no good at all, being categorical). Consider by way of illustration the reason citizens might have for obeying the laws of a reasonably just regime in which they live. One reason commonly suggested is that each citizen implicitly consents to be ruled by such laws, and consent is morally binding. Another reason is that of gratitude: each citizen has benefited by some laws of such a regime and so should obey them all, even those that in no way benefit him. These are both reasons of morality, if they exist. But now suppose one were to suggest that the best reason citizens have to obey the law is that they will be punished if they do not. Since punishments inflict harms to the real interests of persons, each citizen does have an objective reason to obey the law (or at least those laws whose violation will likely be detected and the violator apprehended). Yet this last is a reason of prudence, not of morality. As such it is out of place when we ask the familiar question of political theory, why obey the law?[46]

Such reasons of prudence are similarly out of place when we seek to explain our obligations generally (and not just our obligation to follow the law, if there is one). To explain morality's reason-giving capacity in terms of divine punishments is to explain morality away. The very phenomenon to be explained is how moral qualities can give each of us objective, non-prudential reasons for action. A punishing God cannot be the answer to that question.

There seem to me to be three sorts of arguments seeking to establish that God helps make sense of the (objective, non-prudential) reason-giving capacity of moral qualities. The first of these focuses on the source of moral norms, returning to the idea that a prescription requires a prescriber. The second argument focuses on the recipient or beneficiary of moral obligations, the person or thing to whom such duties are owed; God is posited to be the thing to which all duties are ultimately owed and the only thing to which some duties could be owed, ultimately or mediately. The third argument focuses on another aspect of those objective reasons for action we call moral duties, and that is their 'absolute' nature; the argument is that only with God could we account both for the text-like nature of moral norms and for the categorical force they exhibit versus other sorts of objective reasons. I shall consider each of these in turn.

Prescriptions and Prescribers Again

It is not easy to get a handle on the root of the intuition that God helps to make sense of the reason-giving capacities of moral qualities. I take it that behind this intuition is a general sense that the members of the subclass of objective reasons we call moral obligations are always, at bottom, created by another person's acts of will, so that a generally applicable obligation must be the product of a suitably powerful will, namely, God's. John Finnis calls this, aptly enough, the 'will theory of obligation.'[47] Finnis's prime example of the holder of such a general theory of obligation in theology is the sixteenth century Vitoria, who held that 'it is unintelligible to me how anyone can sin unless he is under some obligation, and I don't see how anyone can be obligated unless he has a superior.'[48]

The central idea of the will theory of obligation is that obligations can only be created by someone's act of will. The hard question is why anyone would think that. One (probably quite common) basis for this intuition we already ruled out. This is the idea that denies that there are objective reasons for action. Prescriptivity on this view is analyzed exclusively in terms of demands by one person on another. All that 'objective' prescriptions could be for such a view would be the demands of some Big Person on all of the rest of us. Thus, God. The reason why we have put this intuition aside is because of its denial of moral objectivity in any useful sense right from the start. Moral realism is the view that moral qualities give each of us objective, non-prudential reasons for action, and it will not do in asking how God helps in sustaining moral realism to deny the latter's truth. Moral realism is committed to the view that prescriptivity is to be taken as a feature of the world—objective reasons for action—so this direct route, from universally applicable prescriptions to Grand Prescriber, must be ruled out.

We thus must cast about for some better basis for the intuition that God helps to make sense of the reason-giving capacities of moral qualities. Consider two more genuine possibilities. The first takes commands, promises, requests, oaths, and acts of consent as the best, or perhaps our only genuine, examples of obligations. When a duly elected official in a reasonably just regime commands all cars to drive on one side of the road, when we promise a stranger to do a certain thing, when we swear allegiance or consent in some other way, or when a friend requests something of us, we often rightly think that we are now obligated to act in ways that we were not before. Such familiar examples show us in daily life how obligations can come into being. By our very familiarity with this mode of the creation of these kinds of obligations, we may then think that *all* obligations must be created in this way.

Yet this last move reverses the priority we should instead perceive here.

Requests, promises, commands, vows, and consents are special and extra-ordinary ways of creating obligations, and they make sense only against a background of obligations that we do not create in these ways. We should see these obligation-creating acts as part of our limited moral sovereignty, that is, the capacity which each person possesses to alter the moral land-scape through his exercise of will, a limited sovereignty Joseph Raz aptly dubbed our normative powers.[49] That we have some such sovereignty at all is only because other obligation-creating norms permit us to have and to exercise such powers. We do not need a request to honour requests, a promise to honour promises, a command to obey commands, in order to justify why these are obligation-creating acts (for if we did, we'd face an infinite regress). Rather, over a limited range of subjects, in a limited range of circumstances, other non-willed but binding moral norms so empower us.[50]

It is surely a familiar question, 'why should I do the act I promised yesterday,' or 'why should I honour my dead friend's request?' The answer cannot be 'because I promised to honour the promise,' or 'my friend requested me to honour his requests.' Rather, the answer must be independent of our promise, of our friend's request, or of the secular authority's command. Some other moral reason has to exist to justify why these acts create obligations.

Why should these other reasons themselves be the product of someone else's request, promise, or command, if they needn't be (and indeed, cannot be) the product of our *friend's* request, *our* promise, or the secular *law-giver's* command? Why would one posit a divine requestor, a divine promisor, or a divine commander in order to create the binding norms that themselves bind us to obey certain human requests, promises, or commands? Surely this is mostly a failure of imagination in the face of the most familiar obligations of daily life, but not much more. Certainly, that *some* obligations can be created by these human exercises of will is no basis whatsoever for thinking that *all* obligations must be created by someone's will. *Prima facie*, our moral experience with all the obligations that are not created by any human will—like the obligation not to kill another—tells us just the opposite.

Now consider a second possible reason for thinking that all obligations are created by someone's act of will. This was stated by Francisco Suarez, Vitoria's intellectual descendant in the Spanish revival of scholasticism within Catholic theology:

[N]o real prohibition or prescriptive obligation is created solely by a judgment, since such an effect cannot be conceived of apart from volition . . . the mere dictate of intelligence apart from will . . . cannot impose upon another being a particular obligation. For obligation is a certain moral impulse to action; and to impel another to act is a work of will.[51]

The central insight here is one of psychology, Suarez adopting the ancient faculty psychology distinguishing cognitive judgement and belief from motivating states of will that move us to action. Since morality moves us to act (by giving us those reasons to act we call obligations), morality must be the product of will.

There are three crucial steps to Suarez's argument here. The first is to adopt the folk psychology, as old as Aristotle and as modern as Donald Davidson, that distinguishes subjective states of desire (wish, intention, will, pro-attitude, etc.) from subjective states of belief, and to say that beliefs alone are incapable of moving us to action.[52] Although we choose our acts in light of our beliefs about the world, it requires desired ends for these beliefs to do any act-related work for us in selecting means.

All well and good. The second step requires that we recognize the distinction between objective reasons and subjective reasons, a distinction not apparent in the quotation from Suarez. If we recognize this distinction, then Suarez must be supposing that this crucial belief / desire distinction in subjective reasons is mirrored by a similar distinction in objective reasons. More specifically, Suarez must be supposing that there must be some feature of morality's objective reasons that has the capacity to cause within us subjective desires. This is what allows us to be subjectively moved by morality's objective reasons. This, too, I think is correct.[53]

The third step is the crucial one. It is that the only aspect of morality's objective reasons that could have this capacity to cause subjective desires is the aspect, having-been-created-by-another-desire. For it is this step that is crucial to Suarez's conclusion that God's desire is necessary to *our* desire (which is necessary to our action).

When openly exposed, surely this third premise does not carry conviction. Why should it be the case that our desires are only ultimately responsive to the desires of another like being? Isn't our experience just the opposite, namely, that *what* we desire and will is not the object of anyone else's desire or will but is some inanimate object or action? My desire to eat ice cream, my desire to be a more courageous person, my desire never to harm others unnecessarily, are not experienced as desires reflective of other persons' desires; rather, the objects of those desires are experienced as desirable *tout cour*, for their own sake, not as desired by someone else.

One can thus grant Suarez's intuitively plausible, Aristotelean psychology without for a moment conceding his conclusion about all obligations stemming from some act of will. *We* may indeed only move ourselves to action through our motivational states of desire, but that does not mean (or even suggest) that this capacity of moral obligations to so move us can exist only if it is responsive to some like motivational state of some like, personal being.

Once we break free of the will theory of moral obligation,[54] what can be said for the idea that a person-like entity, God, is needed to make sense of the bindingness on us of moral obligation? 'Very little' is the intended conclusion of this subsection. Yet perhaps if we focus on less general aspects of the obligatoriness of moral qualities we can find some need for God. That will be the inquiry of the following two subsections.

Duties as Requiring Person-like Entities to Whom They Are Owed

Distinct from any claims based on the essential reason-giving nature of obligation are claims based on what we might call the *relational* aspect of obligations. The basic idea here is that moral duties are not owed *tout cour*; rather, they are always owed to someone. Yet, the argument goes, in many cases there are no persons to whom our various moral duties are owed. We may plausibly be supposed to have a duty with respect to creating or not creating future persons, for example. Or we might have a duty not to contaminate a distinct planet, even though no one will ever get there or see it. If we do not think potential persons or remote planets are enough like actual persons to be owed duties, then we must think of something else that is more like a person to whom such duties can be owed. And if *these* duties are owed to such a person-like entity, we might well conclude that *all* duties are ultimately owed to God, even when mediately owed to other actual persons.

The crux of this argument lies with its initial premise, that obligations are necessarily relational, that duties are always owed to some person or person-like entity. One reason for subscribing to such a relational view of obligation we can put aside quickly in this context. This is the well known correlativity thesis, according to which, when we say, 'x owes a duty (that x do act A) to y,' we are committed to saying, 'y has a right (that x do act A) as against x.' Such correlativity does demand that duties be owed to someone because there must be a someone to hold the correlative right.

We should brush this suggestion aside for two reasons. In the first place, duties to God seem to violate the correlativity thesis, for many theologians would not want to speak of God as having moral rights against us; this makes God *too* person-like, as if he needed to have rights the way persons do. Secondly, the duty-implies-a-right half of correlativity is false.[55] Although it is very plausible to suppose that when one person has a moral right to a certain action being done another person must have the moral duty to perform that action, it is not equally plausible to suppose the converse. We plainly owe duties respecting animals, for example, without animals having the capacities needed to hold moral rights.

A more interesting basis for thinking that obligations are relational stems from a more general view of value that has come (following Derek

Parfit) to be called the 'person-regarding' view of value.[56] William James was a subscriber to such a view of value:

[I]t appears that such words [as 'good' and 'obligation'] can have no application or relevancy in a world in which no sentient life exists. I imagine an absolutely material world, containing only physical and chemical facts, and existing from eternity without a God, without even an interested spectator: would there be any sense in saying of that world that one of its states is better than another?[57]

On this person-regarding view, evaluations of states of affairs as 'good' is always elliptical for, 'good for someone', and evaluations of actions as 'right' or 'obligatory' is always elliptical for, 'right for someone' or 'obligatory to someone'.

Such a person-centred view of value does not of course have to lead one to theism, although that is where the view did lead William James. The alternative is to deny that we ever do have moral duties that are not owed to some (non-God-like) persons.[58] About duties to procreate or not to procreate, for example, one could either deny that there are such duties, or one could say that such duties are owed to unborn but otherwise quite real persons, or one could say that these are 'imperfect' duties that one owes to one's self. Likewise about duties not to despoil a permanently uninhabited planet, one could either deny that we owe such duties, or one could say that it is either ourselves or others who are owed such duties. Yet I find none of these escape routes acceptable. I do think we have duties with respect to the potential persons of future generations and with respect to the environment, and I do not think we capture the nature of those duties accurately by conceiving of them as owed to ourselves or to presently nonexistent but potentially future persons. For me, therefore, James' person-regarding view of value presents a serious challenge to my thesis that God isn't needed for moral objectivity.

Nonetheless, there are two reasons to reject James' theistic conclusions here. The first is that it is not at all clear that James' person-regarding view of value is compatible with moral objectivity. Since our question is whether God helps at all in defending moral objectivity, a view of value that requires God but presupposes that morality is not objective will not advance the discussion.

We have defined moral objectivity in terms of moral realism, and one of the two theses constitutive of moral realism is the independence thesis: to be objective, moral qualities must exist independently of anyone's beliefs that they exist. Such a condition is not violated by a view which held that there would be no moral duties if there were no persons because all that need be meant by this statement is that without persons to owe duties there would be no duties owed. This is compatible with realism. Such a view might say that Kepler's laws of planetary motion would not exist if there were no planets. While certain forms of modal realism would deny this, the realism we have defined can admit it without contradicting the independence condition.

The person-regarding view of value asserts something much more troubling, however. It is that there would be no duties, even if there were people in existence who owed them, so long as there were not other persons or person-like entities to whom such duties are owed. The question is whether this relational view of value in general, and moral obligation in particular, is compatible with the mind-independence partly constitutive of moral realism. David Heyd has argued recently that they are not incompatible:

'the person-affecting approach is fully compatible with both ethical realism and the objectivity of moral values (or judgments) . . . it is of utmost importance . . . to distinguish between the nature or content-conditions of value, that is, value as a *relational* property, and the way value judgments and attributions are grounded or validated, that is, from which perspective they are justified. The person-affecting thesis applies only to the first, and confounding it with the second . . . leads to the fallacy that objectivism requires impersonalism.'[59]

Heyd's thought here is best captured by his reliance on R. B. Perry, who held that relational facts such as value V being a value *for* person M are not necessarily 'relative to M's judgment about it, or to the judgment of any other subject. The judgments about such facts may be as universal or absolute, as true or false, as any logic or theory of knowledge can possibly require.'[60] As Heyd captures Perry's point here, 'value can exist independently of the act of valuation . . . but it must affect *someone, somehow*.'[61] Put in my language, the Heyd/Perry point is this: saying that values only exist in so far as they are values for someone is not to say that values exist relative to the beliefs of that one, or of anyone else; such values would in that sense be independent of the judgements of anyone, including the person(s) for whom they are values.

What this convinces me of is that I and others have defined the independence condition of moral realism too narrowly. I earlier have defined it as *belief*-independence, and Heyd/Perry are right: the person-affecting view of value can be belief-independent. Yet our notion of objectivity should be broader than belief-independence. To be objective, the existence of moral qualities should not depend on the wants, intentions, volitions, or other motivational or conative states of persons. Moral realism should include what Heyd describes as an *im*personal view of value, namely, the view 'which regards value as an attribute of the world existing apart from any of these human "pro-attitudes" '.[62] Moral objectivity should be the view that we owe various moral duties no matter what we (or anyone else) want.

I suspect that the person-affecting view can itself be adjusted so that it is not human *want*-relative even if it is human *need*-relative, and this would satisfy even my revised independence condition. So let me turn to my second objection, good against even this revised person-regarding view of value. My second objection is that the person-regarding view is false. States of affairs can be good or bad, better or worse, without reference to persons' wants, needs, or interests; we owe moral duties *tout cour*, that is, without owing them to some persons or person-like entity.

Consider the kind of example with which we began this discussion, James' material world without sentient life. Wouldn't that be a *better* world if it were full of beauty rather than one that is monotonously ugly? Or take our obligations with respect to animals, the dead, and the unborn: do not we owe obligations with respect to all of such things, without conceding for a moment that they are person-like things *to whom* we owe such duties? These have been much debated questions since the prototype of such debate by Henry Sidgewick and G. E. Moore at the turn of the century,[63] but my own view of morality and value is with Moore: pristine lakes have value, full stop, without regard to the question, value for whom, and we have duties, full stop, without regard to the question, duties to whom. If I am right in this substantive moral position, we don't need a person-like entity such as God to be the kind of back-stop recipient of these states of goodness or obligation that James thought necessary.

Divine Commands as the Basis for the Agent-Relative Aspect of Moral Obligation

As we have seen, God is no help in understanding or explaining the reason-giving capacity of moral qualities generally. Yet if we leave these most general considerations about obligation and objective reasons for more discrete aspects of moral obligation, perhaps we can find some work for God to do. In this section I consider two such discrete aspects of the way in which we think moral qualities obligate us. Both aspects are involved in the popular conception of objective morality as consisting of 'moral absolutes'. The first I shall call the 'textual claim': moral laws are text-like in that they have a canonical formulation whose generalizations are not subject to an indefinitely large number of unspecified exceptions. The second I shall call the deontological claim: the reasons of morality are special sorts of reasons in that they categorically demand of each of us that we not ourselves violate the moral laws (even when such violation by one of us could prevent more violations by the rest of us).

I categorize these claims about morality to be claims about the *content* of morality, not claims about morality's metaphysical or epistemological status. They are ethical claims—claims about *what* morality requires—not meta-ethical claims about the status of morality's requirements. As such, these ethical claims can be (and often are) disavowed by those who are (meta-ethically) moral realists. Thus, if one were to conclude that God helps to make out these aspects of morality, it would always be open to the moral realist to disavow this kind of morality. Nonetheless, a popular view of morality's objectivity connects it to these content claims, and since I myself have a great deal of sympathy for one of them, I shall here inquire how God might help in their defence.

The textual claim is that moral laws can be formulated in the sort of short and snappy injunctions as can be fitted onto one stone tablet. 'Do not kill another human being,' for example. The distinctive text-like quality of such injunctions resides in two features.[64] The first is their resistance to reformulation. Like statutes and unlike common law rules, if the moral text is against *killing*, then one doesn't get to paraphrase to some related description, say 'strangling', 'torture-murdering', 'harming', etc. Texts are canonically formulated rules, and the claim is that moral laws are text-like in this way.

Secondly, the textual claim excludes the possibility of unformulated exceptions. If the injunction says, 'no killing', it does not mean, 'no killing except in self-defence, when necessary to prevent serious harm to others, in a just war, etc.' The injunction is absolute in the sense that it applies to all killings no matter what their differing circumstances.

The deontological claim has to do with the force of the reasons created by moral laws. The claim is three-fold. First, moral obligations ordinarily (or perhaps always) *trump* non-moral, objective reasons for action. Whatever is intrinsically good to achieve or right to do *trumps* whatever reasons for prudence there may be against doing it. Secondly, moral laws are not justified by, nor interpreted by reference to, some other (even moral) goods that might be achieved by obeying them. Moral laws command obedience without regard to there being some good such obedience achieves. Thirdly, moral laws speak to each of us individually, enjoining each of us not to violate them even when by violating them we could minimize violations by others. There may be situations, for example, where by torturing the innocent relative of a terrorist I can induce the terrorist to release five others whom he will otherwise torture. By torturing one, I could prevent the torture of five others. The deontological claim is that the moral norm prohibiting torture does not enjoin us to minimize tortures, by ourselves or others; rather, such norm tells us not to do any torturing ourselves, full stop.[65]

It should be apparent how God might seem to help in accepting these two claims about morality's content. If morality's norms are text-like in the two dimensions just surveyed, that seems to fit handily with seeing such norms as decrees issued by God. It is after all authoritative decrees that typically give us texts to be interpreted, so if morality is a kind of text, that suggests its origin in the acts of a supreme authority.[66] Similarly, the deontological nature of moral norms may seem to suggest a communication directly to each individual by an author of moral norms.[67] One way of making sense of a morality whose norms are overridingly important, unbacked by further reasons, and personal, is to view that morality as a series of parent-like commands by God, directed to each of us individually.

Since I believe the textual claim about morality to be false while I qualifiedly accept the deontological claim, I shall separate the discussion of them. Consider the textual claim first. Kant provides a convenient example illustrating why textualism is not a plausible claim to make about morality. Kant famously proclaimed that norms such as those against lying were absolute in the sense of exceptionless. Even when the known murderer knocks on your door to inquire as to whereabouts of his next victims, you may not lie.[68]

This I take to be a preposterous view of morality's content. Why should one think of its norms in this simple way? As a mnemonic device, 'thou shalt not kill' is fine; as a description of the morality of killings, however, it is atrocious. Not only is one permitted to kill on certain occasions, one is obligated to kill on certain other occasions, such as where one's family will otherwise be killed by the one you must kill.

This is not just a point about the length of the texts that morality must contain. Rather, the point is that moral norms cannot be taken as texts at all. New exceptions will always be in principle discoverable. These will be discovered as the novel situations calling for them either actually or imaginatively occur. There is nothing text-like about norms the formulation of which are always open to further and further amendment. The non-text-like laws of science are like this; statutes and other truly authoritative tests are not.[69]

There is thus no basis for regarding morality as a kind of text whose objectivity then demands that there be an authoritative author. The most that can be said of this textualist view of morality is that such a view may be a helpful heuristic in the moral education of both children and adults. That is, it may well be that children at a certain stage of their moral development require morality to be packaged as a set of short and snappy (and thus learnable) rules. It may also be that even as adults we do well to inculcate and reinforce in ourselves dispositions to be revolted by certain acts, no matter what their circumstances, because such acts are generally wrong.[70] If either of these points of psychology is true, then we have reason to pretend sometimes that morality consists of text-like rules. Yet one should not confuse such learning devices with the thing learned: morality itself does not consist of text-like rules, howevermuch approximating the truths of morality may require us to pretend at times that it is.

What about the second of the attributes of absoluteness here considered, that of deontology? Take the third aspect of this view of morality first, its personal (or 'agent-relative') claim. Although it is highly controversial, my own substantive view of morality is that its obligations are 'agent-relative' in the manner described earlier:[71] if killings are usually wrong, we are individually enjoined not to do any (of the bad ones) even if on occasion our doing so would prevent the doing of more (equally bad) killings by others. The question then is whether positing God helps make sense of this deontological aspect of morality.

It is important not to mischaracterize what is puzzling about this aspect of morality. The puzzle is not about intrinsic rightness as such. That supposed puzzle I will discuss in a moment. The puzzle that is specific to the 'agent-relative' aspect of deontology is rather raised by the personal nature of moral norms. They seem personally addressed to each individual, making him care about his own conformity to moral norms in a way different from the way he cares about the conformity of other people's behaviour to those same norms. It is this aspect that leads many to call this the 'agent-relative' aspect of morality.

The puzzle about agent-relative moral norms is this: how can it be rational to prefer less of a good to more of it? How can it be rational to prefer the state of affairs where I don't torture one but someone else tortures five, to the state of affairs where I torture one and no one else tortures anyone? If the state of being tortured is an intrinsic bad, or if the act of torturing is intrinsically wrong, why are not less of those bads and wrongs to be preferred to more of them? Why is it rational (or moral) for me to care so much about what I do *vis-a-vis* what others do?

This is a genuine puzzle for agent-relative views of the content of morality, but I doubt that adding God helps with the puzzle in any way. For notice that if one were to explain the agent-relative aspect of morality as due to God communicating his wishes to each of us personally, that only regresses the puzzle to God: why should he wish each of us to conform to the moral laws, even when our doing so allows or causes others to break them? Indeed, is not the puzzle exacerbated by God? Hard as it may be to make sense of each of us caring infinitely more about our own moral virtue at the expense of the virtue of others, what sense can we make of one Being who, although he cares for each of us equally, doesn't care to minimize moral failure or maximize moral success? How could one Being with a God-like overview of human society care infinitely about the moral success of each individual even when that success is purchased by the moral failure of other individuals?

Max Weber once opined that to enter politics is to give up one's virtue. One interpretation of that aphorism is that to enter upon the design of social institutions—'politics'—is to give up the special concern each of us has for keeping our own moral house in order. It is to adopt a legislative overview according to which one person's moral success cannot be preferred to another's, even if the one in question is oneself. God as supreme legislator of morality seems subject to Weber's injunction. If there were a God it is thus more puzzling to think that he would create an agent-relative morality than if one conceives of such a morality as simply existing, uncreated by anyone.

Of course, it could make sense for God to create a *belief* in each of us in an agent-relative morality; such belief could be the best means to minimizing moral failures by humanity as a whole.[72] God might think that if we each keep our own moral houses in order and ignore the opportunities our doing so leaves open for others to perform badly, that will minimize moral failure. But it doesn't take a God to make sense of beliefs in agent-relative morality in this way. If this consequentialist calculation is true, we each have reason to inculcate in ourselves and our children belief that moral norms are agent-relative. In neither case, with God or without him, would we have explained why morality *is* agent-relative; only, why it is good that we pretend that it is. In either case, such an explanation again confuses means with ends, heuristics to knowing morality, with morality itself. Indeed, such a confused explanation rules out the possibility that we had sought to explain, which is why moral norms *are* agent-relative in the way that they obligate us.

About the first and second aspects of the deontological view of morality, we can be more brief. Many pretend to find puzzling both the priority of moral reasons over prudential reasons and the priority within moral reasons that is characteristic of deontology, namely, that of the right over the good. The latter priority they say is particularly puzzling; how can it be that some actions are intrinsically right or wrong to do without the rightness of those actions being a function of their contributing to some further good?

Consequentialists like Patrick Nowell-Smith argue that only commands by a Parent-like figure to his children could make sense of the unreasoning 'mustness' of a deontological morality.[73] Parents do not explain the goods served by the rules they lay down, and parents demand that their children obey such rules even when they conflict with other objective reasons for action. For morality to be like this, Nowell-Smith concludes, there must be a Big Parent whose children we are.

Yet once we concede that there are objective reasons for action—a concession we must make if we accept morality's objectivity—what is peculiar about thinking that some of those objective reasons (the moral ones) are characteristically more important than others of them (the prudential ones)? Indeed, if the notion of objective reasons for action is intelligible to us, why should reasons of *obligation* seem peculiar to us unless they are mere proxies for reasons of goodness? Any theory of goodness itself has to think that some states of affairs are intrinsically good—good, that is, by itself, and not because it contributes to some other good. Why cannot such states of intrinsic goodness be that certain actions are or are not performed? True, that obligation-conforming actions are done would be a good state of affairs not because they serve some other good, but good intrinsically, on the deontological view. Yet that is no stranger that any other kind of intrinsic goodness. Some consequentialists posit human happiness, or God's happiness, as being intrinsically good. Yet why *must* we pursue these goods, if they are intrinsically good? Only because we must—because goodness gives objective reasons to pursue it.

III. GOD AS THE SUBJECTIVE MOTIVATOR OF MORALITY? VIRTUE CANNOT BE ITS OWN REWARD?

A skepticism about morality that is at least as old as Glaucon in Plato's *Republic* proceeds by demanding that there be a prudential reason backing every moral reason and, finding the demand unsatisfied, thus becomes skeptical. This is the view, revived by modern Hobbesians, that unless morality is backed by self-interest, it cannot be objective, in some sense of that word.

I have always found this to be a peculiar form of moral skepticism. To begin with, the demand for prudential backing to moral reasons almost guarantees 'skepticism' of this variety: after all, the demand is that we produce self-interested reasons, for an exclusively self-interested person, that he act sometimes against his own self-interest, i.e., morally. Secondly, this form of 'skepticism' is not sufficiently skeptical: why should we privilege egoistic reasons over altruistic reasons? What makes it obvious that there are such objective reasons of egoism if there are no objective reasons of altruism?[74] Surely a true skeptic should be more Humean, doubting that there are *any* objective reasons binding us, whether they be moral or prudential.

I thus construe this ancient skepticism in a more Humean way. The demand is that we must have some subjective desire that would be satisfied if we behave morally, and the skepticism results from the psychological observation that some of the time some of us have no such desires. Ethics textbooks often put this as the 'question of moral motivation', namely, what *subjective* reason do any of us have to be moral?

The skepticism here considered is not the skepticism discussed in the early part of the last section. There, 'internalists' about morality objected that moral qualities, if they existed, would have to be subjectively motivating, and the idea of qualities the very existence of which are necessarily subjectively motivating each of us, is a queer idea. Now the objection is not metaphysical, but psychological: as a matter of contingent empirical fact, not everyone has desires giving them subjective reasons to behave morally.

If it is legitimate to demand of objective morality that it give each of us subjective reasons to be moral, then God may seem to be helpful in satisfying the demand and thus, in making out the objectivity of morality. Rather surprisingly (in light of his famous separation of subjective reasons or 'inclinations' from rationality), Kant is the most famous example of finding a need for God in this way. According to Kant, God is necessary for each of us to be properly rewarded for our virtuous behaviour by the happiness we each desire:

> The acting rational being in the world is not at the same time the cause of the world and of nature itself. Hence there is not the slightest ground in the moral law for a necessary connection between the morality and proportionate happiness of a being which belongs to the world as one of its parts and as thus dependent on it. Not being nature's cause, his will cannot of its own strength bring nature, as it touches on his happiness, into complete harmony with his practical principles. Nevertheless . . . in the necessary endeavour after the highest good, such a connection is postulated as necessary: we should seek to further the highest good (which therefore must at least be possible). Therefore also the existence is postulated of the cause of the whole of nature, itself distinct from nature, which contains the ground of the exact coincidence of happiness with morality . . . therefore, it is morally necessary to assume the existence of God.[75]

This well known passage from Kant's second critique is subject to diverse interpretations. The one that interests me here is the following:

(1) Objective morality ('the moral law') exists only if in content it demands that we each seek to attain the highest good through our actions.
(2) Morality does and can demand this of us only if we have the capacity to attain the highest good.
(3) We have such a capacity only if happiness is proportionate to virtue (i.e., the attainment of the highest good makes us supremely happy).
(4) Happiness will always be proportionate to virtue only if there is a guarantor of such a match.
(5) The only possible guarantor of such a match is the cause of all nature, any cause within nature being insufficiently powerful.
(6) We are not such a cause; only God is.

Therefore:

(7) Objective morality exists only if there is a God.

This is hardly the inexorable chain of inferences that Kant seems to have thought. For our purposes, the crucial premise is (3), the idea that happiness must be the reward of virtuous behaviour if we are to have the capacity to act morally. Why might one accept this? Robert Adams fleshes out Kant's argument here in terms of the need of each of us for subjective reasons to be moral if we are to act morally: 'The conviction that every good person will be very happy in the long run has often contributed, in religious believers, to a cheerfulness and single-heartedness of moral devotion that they probably would not have had without it.'[76] The reason this is so, Adams assures us, is because 'virtually everyone has a deep and strong desire for his own happiness.'[77] Adams, like Kant, takes this to provide important advantages for the theist: 'We may fairly count this as a theoretical advantage of Kantian theism, if we are intuitively inclined to believe [as Adams does] that moral judgments have a force that implies that virtually everyone has [subjective] reason to follow them.'[78]

One can of course quibble with Adams' psychology: as he himself recognizes, someone may 'seriously and reflectively want to live always as he morally ought, even if doing so really costs him his only chance at happiness.'[79] If most people are like this, then it takes no guarantee (and thus, no Guarantor) that virtue is rewarded with happiness in order to motivate people to behave morally. But the more crushing rejoinder to Kant/Adams is the more sweeping one: there is no reason to think that human psychology must be such that it matches morality's objective reasons with subjective desires all of the time, for each of us; and this is no warrant for skepticism, because there is no reason to think the objectivity of morality depends on there being some such match.

Morality is objective if but only if moral qualities exist independently of our wanting them to exist or believing that they do exist. Such objectivity does not require that we each have some desire that can be appealed to in getting us to act in conformity with the reasons given by such moral qualities. I say this, recognizing that if our nature were such that we never desired to act morally—or indeed, if we had other desires that moral action always frustrated so that to act morally was the recipe for a guaranteed miserable and unhappy life—then morality would be unfair, a kind of cruel joke on the human race.[80] This caveat then might lead one to adopt a much softened version of Kant's premises (1)–(3), namely, a version proclaiming that morality is objective only if many people's natures are such that sometimes acting morally brings a kind of happiness with it. That much takes the sting out of morality being a kind of cruel joke on the human race; but saying that much does not require a God, only a plausible enough, non-theistic explanation (in terms of the survival value of human communities constituted by such kinds of persons).

V. GOD AS THE GUARANTOR OF MORAL SUCCESS?

We should distinguish the question of whether we can justify certain moral propositions to be worthy of belief (i.e., true) from the question of whether fallible and not perfectly virtuous creatures like us can know and act on those moral truths. One form of moral skepticism denies that we have the psychological capacities to discover and act on whatever moral truths there might be.[81] While such a skepticism does not deny that moral truths exist, it denies that they can be used either to guide our actions or to blame us when our actions are not so guided. They would be truths, in other words, that would do us no good (except to remind us what a cruel hoax morality is).

There are two psychological capacities at issue in this form of moral skepticism, one cognitive and the other volitional. The cognitive capacity that we need is the capacity to know the good. The volitional capacity we need is the capacity to will ourselves to do what we know we ought to do. A skeptic of this variety denies that we have enough of either capacity to be able to use moral truths to guide our behaviour or to be blamed where our behaviour is not so guided.

As an example of the supposed lack of requisite cognitive capacity, consider Beccaria's well known reservations about our ability to know the moral truth about what someone else deserves for their misdeeds: 'What insect will dare take the place of divine justice . . .? The gravity of sin depends upon the inscrutable wickedness of the heart. No finite being can know it without revelation.'[82] If we can't know what is in another's heart (or mind?), we can't know what that person deserves. Enter, God. For Beccaria, as for many theists, God's epistemic help may allow us to grasp those moral truths that would otherwise elude us.

Such help could be given by God in a variety of ways. God could build such knowledge into our nature, either through giving us inclinations to believe only morally true propositions or by giving us desires to do actions which are in fact moral, which desires then allow us to infer what is desirable (i.e., good). Or God could speak to us through the written word, supplementing the natural law (that part of the moral truth, the eternal law, knowable through our nature) with what Aquinas called the divine law. Or God could speak to us directly, by a kind of telepathic speech, revelation. In any such cases, God could transmit to us moral knowledge we would otherwise be unable to acquire.

Yet surely this need for God is a wholly manufactured one. One first makes morality unduly mysterious and unknowable only to create a need for a communicator of morality to us, God. Why should we think morality so mysterious and unknowable? The answer to *that* question cannot be, 'because morality is what God wills or thinks, and the mind of God is not knowable by us.' Such an answer seems to be implicit in why Beccaria and Aquinas find moral truths (Aquinas's 'eternal law') to be so difficult for us humans to know, but such an answer soundly begs the question at issue here, which is whether we need God for morality to be objective. Of course, if morality *is* God's will or thoughts, we need God to know morality, that is, what is on his mind.

The plain fact of the matter is that morality is not so epistemically elusive. If we sometimes face intractable moral dilemmas, we as often face easy moral decisions: we shouldn't kill babies for fun, we shouldn't torture animals, we shouldn't deceive our friends for our own profit, etc. These truths are hard to grasp only if we already demote them to *evidence* of some deeper truths that they imperfectly express, truths about God's mind or the like.

As an example of the supposed lack of volitional capacity, consider Kant's famous argument that human beings unaided by God lack the capacity to attain the highest good at which morality enjoins them to aim.[83] Therefore, we need God in order to guarantee a moral success to ourselves that, unaided, we lack the capacity to achieve.

One response to this alleged need for God, made by Brian Davies, is to question the necessity of its being God that gives us this aid. 'Why cannot a top-ranking angel do the job?,' Davies cheerfully asks.[84] Yet the relational question that I have framed does not require that God be strictly necessary for morality's objectivity; the question was whether positing God was at all helpful, and Kant's argument would answer that question affirmatively if God guarantees our moral success.

The real problem with Kant's argument is why we need such a guarantee of moral success. Suppose that without God-like capacities greater than our own we could never achieve the highest good. On the 'ought implies can' principle, if we can't achieve the highest good then it is not the case that we ought to achieve it. But does this mean that we should not *seek* to achieve it? If we at least have the capacity to avoid some greater evils, and thus, to make choices that are better than many of their alternatives, and if we make such better-if-not-best choices most often by seeking to make the best ('highest good') choice, then there is no unfairness to a morality that enjoins us to seek the highest good even while acknowledging that we never attain it.

In addition, it shouldn't be conceded that we never attain the highest good. As long as one doesn't again beg the question by smuggling into the notion of the highest good some necessary ineffability (because knowable only by God), surely we sometimes do attain the highest good, and even know with reasonable certainty that we have done so. To take a very 'unKantian' example: if it is in fact the case that only by torturing the person who buried a school bus full of children can I save the children from suffocation, I achieve the highest good possible in this situation by torturing that person.[85] In an ideal world, I wouldn't face such awful alternatives, but in this world I do, and when I choose to torture in such a situation I do attain the highest good.

Perhaps a purer example of alleged volitional incapacity is one I have used before, weakness of will. St Paul laments in Romans 7 that he knows the good but does the opposite. St Paul goes on to claim that only God can help him (and us) do better. Yet how could God help him out of his predicament? God, the story goes, gave St Paul, as each of us, a free will mirrored on his own so that we could achieve either virtue or responsibility, depending on how we exercise it. How can God move St Paul's will to virtue without robbing St Paul of moral credit for the action? Surely an omnipotent God hurts more than he helps here,[86] as the centuries-old predestination debate evidences.

VI. GOD AS THE LARGER PURPOSE GIVING MEANING TO AN OTHERWISE MERELY HUMAN GOOD

There is a common tendency for theists to pull one last arrow from their quiver, even when conceding that none of the preceding arrows by them have found their target. The tendency is to think that the objectivity of morality as I have described it is merely 'human, all too human', without God. It is the tendency to think that even if moral qualities objectively exist, and even if we each have sufficient reason to do what they enjoin, nonetheless we would not have shown them to be 'fully objective' unless we explain their existence by God. It is only with their creation by God so as to fulfill his divine purpose that those qualities can have a value beyond the merely human.

John Finnis nicely exemplifies this tendency, for Finnis eschews most of the theology / ethics connections I have explored while yet coming back, at the end of the day, to theology in order to save ethics from a kind of relativity to the merely human.[87] Finnis rightly rejects any use for God, either in making out the objective existence of moral qualities, in justifying our moral beliefs, or in accepting that such moral qualities give each of us sufficient objective reasons to act in accordance with them. Yet despite this autonomous ethics, 'practical reasonableness', as Finnis calls it, he nonetheless brings in God to save morality from 'a certain relativity or subjectivity not so much the subjectivity of arbitrary opining, but rather the "subjectivity" of the *merely* relative to us . . .'[88] The relativity Finnis has in mind is that of the good to the good *for us* (human beings). Finnis finds this relativity to be 'a debilitating subjectivity'[89] because it doesn't allow that there is any point or value served by our acting reasonably in Finnis's sense, i.e., acting according to the objective reasons given by moral qualities. Whereas with God, Finnis urges, moral qualities can be:

more than a fortuitous agglomeration of entities and states of affairs devoid of any significance that could attract human admiration and allegiance. Practical reasonableness gains for them the significance of a partial imitation of God; the basic values grasped by practical reason gain an objectivity; and practical reason's methodological requirements of constancy and impartiality are reinforced by the worth of adopting the viewpoint of God . . .[90]

With God, there is a point or value or reason for us acting according to the dictates of practical reason, and in this sense, 'a more basic account of obligation would become possible' and 'a new and pertinent reason' for being reasonable would exist.[91] Seeing this, Finnis then ultimately concludes that 'God is the basis of obligation,'[92] despite his own clear-headed refusal to explain obligation generally in terms of conformity to superior will.[93]

I shall call this last argument connecting the objectivity of morality to God, the 'ethical cosmological argument'. The name derives from the steps of the argument as I would analyse them. The first two steps constitute what is usually called the cosmological argument proper. The cosmological argument proper is a purely explanatory argument for God's existence, having by itself no ethical implications. The argument is an ancient one. Popularly put, the causal version of the argument is that 'the universe must come from somewhere,' it must have had a beginning, and that beginning must itself be an uncaused beginning (else it would be caused by something prior to itself, and thus would not be the beginning).

Finnis fully endorses a version of the cosmological argument proper. Along with Germain Grisez,[94] whom he follows here, Finnis makes what I shall analyze as the first step of a four step argument. Finnis argues that we must explain the existence of the universe as a whole. This means that we must explain why the universe exists at all and why it exists in the form that it does.[95] The latter *explanandum* consists of the facts that the world is physically ordered, that the world has a moral order, that both such orders are at least partially accessible to human knowers. Finnis argues that these cosmological questions are genuine questions, that even when we have explained each event, state, or object that has occurred by some prior event, state or object as its cause, still left unexplained are, (1) why the whole causing sequence of all events, etc., exists; and (2) why the first natural event, etc., with which we are familiar in the natural order of things, exists.

Among the cosmological questions to which Finnis requires genuinely explanatory answers are those relating specifically to that part of the universe we call the moral order. If one is a moral realist, one believes that a variety of moral qualities like goodness and moral entities like rights exist. Even if one explains each such quality or entity in terms of some other, left unexplained is why there are any objective moral qualities at all.

The second step of Finnis' argument is to answer the cosmological questions that the first step of the argument showed to be genuine questions. Specifically, for Finnis as for a two thousand year old tradition in theism, the answer to the cosmological question is God. The best explanation for why the universe as a whole exists, and for why it has the order it has, including its moral order, is because God created it to answer to his own purposes.[96]

The third step of this reconstructed argument is parallel to the first step, except that the questions argued to be genuine are evaluative questions, not explanatory ones. That is, here the argument is that secular moral objectivity isn't objective enough because of the 'merely human' relativity of the demands of objective morality *on us*. Secular moral realism can show us that objective moral qualities exist and that they give us objective reasons for action by their existence, but the good of conforming to the dictates of those objective reasons is still a merely human good. Needed to make such objective morality non-relative (in this deeper sense) is some *non*-human good that is served by the good (for us) of conforming to the demands of reasons (for us).

The fourth step of the argument is to take the answer to the explanatory questions as the answer to the evaluative questions, as well. More precisely, it is to say that *because* God created the universe and its order, God also is the source of the non-human value needed to make the objective-good-for-humans non-relative. The universe exists as it exists because God is the first cause, a cause without a cause; in order to be a *first* cause, God's causing must be like that of human choice, i.e., it is free (where 'free' is construed as, 'uncaused'). In some sense, the universe might not have existed, or it may have existed but quite differently ordered; these were genuine alternative possibilities that God could have freely chosen. This means that God selected *this* universe, ordered as it is, in answer to some divine purpose. It is this divine purpose that gives meaning to all that exists, including the moral order. The very Being who created everything did so for a reason, and it is this non-human reason or value that eliminates any relativity to the merely human for morality.

This is the 'ethical cosmological argument' that I wish to consider. It is, I think, a fair reconstruction of John Finnis's argument. Whether it is precisely so doesn't interest me as much as whether it does capture a popular and maximally appealing way of connecting moral objectivity to God.

Now let me consider the argument critically. It is admittedly tempting to stop the argument at its first step by denying that cosmological questions are genuine questions. If there is nothing here to explain, God can't be argued for on the grounds that he is the best explanation of these things. Let me call this the Bertrand Russell response, after Russell's famous radio debate in which he said that 'the universe is just there, and that's all.'[97] (A rather 'smart-mouthed' version is Jack Smart's; to the cosmological question, why does anything exist, Smart quipped, 'why shouldn't it.'[98])

Theists such as Finnis and Grisez seek to avoid this Russellian response by analogizing cosmological questions to ordinary explanation-seeking questions. Surely, they argue, if we need to explain each effect by its preceding cause, we also need to explain the entire series of causal relations. Similarly, if we need to explain each thing presently existing, we need to explain the whole collection of things existing, namely, the universe.

It seems to me there is a kind of middle ground between theists who accept the cosmological argument and Russellian critics who deny sense to cosmological questions. This middle ground concedes that the questions are not senseless. As I have argued elsewhere,[99] it is not the case that a causal sequence of events is not itself a complex event whose existence could be explained. There thus *could be* answers to cosmological questions. But, contra Finnis and Grisez, there needn't be answers to all such questions. There is no necessity that every aggregation of causal sequences itself have a separate explanation (beyond the separate explanations for its separate parts), and thus there need be no explanatory incompleteness if there are no answers to all such questions, as Father Copleston assumed in his radio debate with Russell.[100] When we have a complete explanation cannot be settled *a priori*, in advance, and across the board. There may be a good explanation for why there are objective moral qualities, why the behaviour of matter is sufficiently regular that it can sometimes be described by knowable scientific laws, why the entire state of the universe is as it presently is, or why the Big Bang banged, or there may not. I see no notion of complete explanation that demands that for every individuatable item in the universe and for every individuatable combination of smaller items there must be an explanation. Explanations, like the things they explain, are where you find them.

Consider the example of breaking a rack in billiards.[101] On one very plausible metaphysical reading of events the movement of each ball is one event, but the intervals of movement of each ball are also events, part of the larger event, and the movement of all balls ('breaking the rack') is also an event with the separate movements of the separate balls as its parts. I see no necessity that there be a separate explanation for each level of individuation of this complex of events. If we have explained the movement of each ball, we probably have explained the breaking of the rack; and if we have explained the latter (say, by the direction and velocity of the cue ball), we probably have explained the former events too. I say 'probably', because my middle ground denies both that there *must be* separate explanations at all levels and that there *cannot be* such separate explanations.

This middle ground is enough to get the cosmological argument started. It isn't what most believers of the argument want, which is to show how God is necessary because the question to which he is the best answer is necessarily raised. Yet this middle ground is enough to allow a kind of explanatory competition that the God hypothesis could win. If the cosmological questions are sensible enough questions to ask, one can argue that God exists because God is the best explanation for the cosmos—so long as one realizes that the God answer has to compete with 'no explanation' as the best explanation, along with other explanations.

What about the second step of the cosmological argument, that God *is* the best explanation for the existence of the universe and its order? I doubt this very much, since I take brute facts (no explanation) and infinite causal series to be superior explanatory possibilities to uncaused causes. Still, for the purposes of this chapter I have been conceding that a personal God exists, so as to better frame the question of whether that God helps in making out the objectivity of morals. So we should assume that the personal God hypothesis wins out as the best explanation for why the universe and its order exists; that is, God exists and the cosmological argument shows that he does.

It is the third and fourth steps that get us to the ethical relevance of the cosmological argument. The third step denies a full objectivity to morality unless there is some non-human value served by us human beings doing what we have valid, objective reasons of morality to do. I find this denial unintelligible. If there are objective reasons given by the existence of objective moral qualities, morality is objective, full stop. There is no room for it to be 'more objective' or 'less subjective' or 'less relative'.

Finnis focuses on the relativity of the good (without God) to us human beings: objective reasons are only reasons *for us* to act in certain ways, the good of our doing so is only *our* good. Finnis wants some more objective (less human-relative) reasons and goods. Yet Finnis wants this only because he is one of those for whom objective values are *personal*. Finnis does not admit of states of affairs that are good *tout cour*; rather, Finnis, like David Heyd, William James, and Henry Sidgwick, denies that it is meaningful to 'assert both (a) "it is good for x to occur or happen" and (b) "the value of x's occurring is altogether independent of the interests or concerns of any person in the universe." '[102] It is this denial of impersonal good that leads Finnis to recognize that ' "human good" is an anthropocentric category'[103] and that therefore there would be a 'debilitating subjectivity' to objective values unless we find some further, larger than human value that is served by human good.[104]

Yet what if values are impersonal, as I, Tom Nagel, and most moral realists believe? That is, what if goods are not only not relative to the beliefs or wants of anyone (that much is required by moral realism); but also not relative to the interests, needs, or well-being of any person(s)? Then to discover that play, friendship, knowledge, etc., are good activities, relations or states for persons to do or be in, is *not* to discover a 'person-relative' or 'anthropomorphic' moral fact. When we enter into such activities, relations, or states, we are not 'participating' in the human good, as Finnis often puts it. Rather, our actions, relations, or states possess the quality of goodness, a quality existing in the universe like wetness. Even if it turned out (as I think it does not) that the only things in the universe possessing this quality of goodness were human actions, institutions, states, and relations, that would no more make goodness a kind of relative goodness-for-persons than would the fact that only dogs could get wet make wetness a kind of relative wetness-for-dogs. That would be to confuse the universal with the particulars that happen to possess it.

Values are, as I argued in an earlier section,[105] impersonal. We owe duties without necessarily owing them to some person, actions are right without necessarily satisfying a right of some person, states of affairs are good even if they are in no person's interest or enhance no one's well-being. There is thus no further value to be introduced once we satisfy ourselves that our action accords with what is intrinsically right and intrinsically good. There is thus no need and no room for a God to create some larger-than-human value by his purpose.

One can see this superfluity of God and his supposed larger-than-human values by attending to the reason-giving aspect of moral qualities like goodness and rightness. As we have seen, if an action is morally right, or a state of affairs morally good, necessarily we have an objective, non-prudential reason to pursue it. Suppose this is the case for some act or state of affairs: is there need or room for some further reason for us to pursue such acts or state of affairs? Think what that would mean. Although we have an objective reason to do some action A, not outweighed, cancelled, or in any other way defeated by any other reason for action we might have, nonetheless we need a further reason to do act A. How could this be? How can we have an undefeated reason to do an action and still need some further reason to do it? We either have sufficient reason to do the act, or we don't. Moral realism asserts the former, leaving no room for God's or any other further reasons.

Finnis could reply by saying that the existence of God gives us a new and additional reason to do what morality without God already gives us reason to do. This is the objective analogue to what Freudians call 'overdetermination' by reasons, where happy fate gives us more than one sufficient reason to do some action. But on this interpretation, no increment of objectivity is lacking in morality's reasons that God's reasons could supply. Rather, the coincidence of God's reasons with morality's reasons would be like the coincidence (often) of prudential reasons with moral reasons—a happy coincidence, no doubt, but not a coincidence that adds a whit of objectivity to morality.

Finnis thus must eschew this overdetermination interpretation. He thinks that we need some deeper reasons to act on morality's reasons. As he himself puts it, we need some reason for 'living according to the principles and requirements of practical reasonableness'.[106] Yet we no more need a reason to act reasonably (i.e., on the balance of reasons) than we need a deductive derivation of the forms of valid deductive inference. In neither case would we have added any objectivity to reasons or logic by 'supporting' them by reasons or logic.

Despite all of this, it may seem that there is room and need for some deeper reasons, some deeper goods, with which theology could supply ethics if that theology were true. Consider in this regard the relatively young Bertrand Russell's concession that without God the universe is 'purposeless' and 'void of meaning':

That man is the product of causes which had no prevision of the end they were achieving; that his origin, his growth, his hopes and fears, his loves and his beliefs, are but the outcome of accidental collocations of atoms; that no fire, no heroism, no intensity of thought and feeling, can preserve an individual life beyond the grave; that all the labor of the ages, all the devotion, all the inspirations, all the noonday brightness of human genius, are destined to extinction in the vast death of the solar system, and that the whole temple of man's achievement must inevitably be buried beneath the debris of a universe in ruins—all these things, if not quite beyond dispute, are yet so certain that no philosophy which rejects them can hope to stand. Only within the scaffolding of these truths, only on the firm foundation of unyielding despair, can the soul's habitation henceforth be safely built.[107]

Contrary to Russell's own affirmation of this tragic vision, many find this picture demoralizing.[108] They thus think that there must be room, and need, for deeper values served by morality, values to be supplied by God.

Yet this issue of whether we are or are not demoralized by a godless but nonetheless fully objective morality is surely irrelevant to morality's objectivity. It may well be that for most people, the fact that there are objective reasons for how they ought to behave is not enough to keep them from being dispirited by the prospect of the death of themselves and the whole of humanity. It may well be that they want the universe to care about them in a way that, even with objective morality, it does not. It may well be that they want to be the most important or significant part of the universe, which, without God even if with objective morality, they are not. Most religions respond to what are admittedly quite real needs of such people,

by promising them individual life after death, survival of human achievement, concern by the creator of the universe if not of the universe itself,
and an importance unmatched by any other items in the universe because
they are made in the image of the creator of it all.

Yet this kind of comfort, possible only if God exists, in no way supports
or gives value to objective values. Such values have precisely the same
objectivity in a theistic world that they have in a godless world. Many persons might well be more comfortable, more happy, even more moral in
their behaviour, in the world in which God affords them these guarantees;
but then the same could be said about conditions of economic plenty, conditions of instinctual satisfaction, conditions of universal love, etc. There
are lots of things that could make our fate more pleasing than it is, and
such things could thus make us less dispirited and more moral, but the
existence of such things, with their pleasant consequences, is completely
irrelevant to the objectivity of morality.

I have not yet said anything about the fourth step of Finnis' ethical cosmological argument. Suppose that I am wrong about the third step, so that
there is room for some larger, non-human value to make even more objective the goods that should guide our lives. Can God's existence supply us
the larger purpose, the meaning, the non-human value, that we supposedly lack? The affirmative answer given by many religions is based on
God choosing to create the universe we have for some divine purpose; it
is this purpose that suffuses the universe with meaning and which backs
up our moral reasons with the promise that by being moral we also participate in the divine plan.

I find this to be a decidedly peculiar answer. For if one is worried about
values being relative to us in the sense that goods are always goods-for-
persons, it is extraordinary to seek to overcome this relativity by inventing
a Big Person and relativizing values to his Plans and Purposes. Values will
still be person-relative, even if they are Big Person-relative, if this is the
answer we give. If we truly wish to escape this relativity, we should dispense with the need of any person's plans, willings, commands, or purposes to be the source of values; but once we see this possibility for
objective values, we will of course not need any non-human but still personal source of such value.

Aside from the failure of this answer to escape a person-relativity of values, it also doesn't work. For why should we think that participating in
someone's plans is a good thing? If you plan to murder a saint, is there
anything good-making about my participating in your plans? Of course,
we are supposing that the creator whose plans we seek to participate in is
the one who created the entire universe. Yet why should this matter? So he
is very powerful, so he gave us life: a political tyrant in a totalitarian state
who has completely remade that state and who is also our parent also is

very powerful and created both us and much that surrounds us, but neither his plans nor our participation in them gain an increment of goodness from those facts. Of course, God is *all*-powerful and created *everything* around us, but an infinite amount of morally irrelevant attributes is still morally irrelevant.[109]

Perhaps such an all powerful God is, after all, Dr Faustus's playful playwright: just when humankind reaches the zenith of its moral perfection, God destroys it so that he can have the pleasure of watching the entire spectacle again. Or perhaps God is Kurt Vonnegut's superpowerful space alien, whose plan in creating humanity is to get some help in making a spare part needed to get him home. Is there anything good about participating in plans such as these? Why should we care what God had in mind when he created us and the universe around us?

The answer of traditional theology is as follows: because God is not only the all-powerful creator, but is also 'wholly good. He must perfectly exemplify all the qualities which we know to be binding on us in our human life.'[110] Then we indeed have reason to participate in his plans, because such a being would only plan good things. But notice: we have no *more* reason to participate in his plans than we had without his plans. God's plans add nothing to the reasons we already had to be good, given by goodness itself. One might respond: but God created goodness.[111] Even so, that genesis of goodness in no way deflects its independence from God's (other) plans. If God's other plans are good, that's nice but it does not mean that goodness is whatever God plans, nor does it mean that doing acts in accordance with good plans is any better than doing identically good acts without such plans. God, in short, doesn't add anything that we don't already have with objective moral qualities like goodness.

VII. AFTERWORDS

Somewhere in the one of the *Untimely Meditations*, Nietzsche wrote that we should only argue against positions that tempt us at least enough to interest us; otherwise, we do battle without real inner adversaries and thus, without passion. Since early childhood I confess that the question of God's existence has been that kind of question for me. It was and is just too obvious to me that nothing exists answering to a personal conception of God and that the human needs to create such a fictional creature are the only explanation why so many people have come out the other way on the question.

My interest in writing this chapter thus does not stem from some doubts about God's existence and thus, some interest whether my own morally realist metaphysics could be bolstered theologically. My genuine interest in the (for me, purely academic) question of whether God would help in making out the objectivity of ethics stems from the following kind of experience. When I reveal to those who know my morally realist metaphysics (and its accompanying retributive theory of punishment and soft determinist theory of responsibility) that my father was a lay minister and my great-grandfather, a widely published theologian, I can almost hear the mental tumblers of such persons falling into place: 'of course, now it all makes sense, he is a closet Christian.' Or, as my friend and colleagues, Stephen and Jean Morse have said for years, 'you are the most religious person we know.'[112]

Well, I am not not religious, at least, in any sense of that phrase connoting belief in a person-like God. My own morally realist meta-ethics have always been motivated by the incremental, inferential arguments I have detailed elsewhere, not by some hidden or unconscious belief in God. It has seemed to me that realism about certain moral qualities and entities has been the best explanation of various facets of our common moral experience. This is a fallible, scientific inference, not an unseemly leap of faith.

Despite this mode of argument for moral realism, examining why people nonetheless attribute hidden religious aspirations to secular realists like me, is to examine a deeply and widely entrenched prejudice: that God is necessary to make sense of moral objectivity. The only way to root out this prejudice is to examine why people at least say they hold it, that is, exactly what it is they think that God does for the objectivity of morals. The best of these thoughts I have tried to work through in this chapter, concluding that God does no work at all here.

In closing let me throw a little kerosene on whatever fires this last conclusion may have started. I have argued that belief in God does not help in making out the objectivity of morals. Now let me suggest that belief in God positively hurts, when that belief is coupled with a belief in his relevance to morals, for such beliefs together betoken a fundamentally anti-objectivist stance about morality. For think again why it is theists believe that God helps in making out the objectivity of ethics: God is necessary because all laws require a person-like being who lays them down; or because only an omnipotent God could make true by assertion the moral laws; or because only an omniscient God could add prescriptive force to antecedently existing descriptive laws; or because only such a God could be the One to whom all moral duties are owed; or because only such a God could be the author of morality's texts; or because only such a God could be the communicator of those personally directed communications that are the moral laws; or because only such a God would know to guarantee human beings their due proportion of happiness if they obey the moral laws; or because only such a God could infuse an otherwise dumb, mechanical universe with a larger purpose, itself necessary for human

striving to have meaning; etc. In each case, laws, reasons for action, obligations, and even meaning and value, are conceived in *personal* terms.[113]
Laws don't exist *tout cour*; a person has to legislate them, which means
they exist as historical texts and not simply as atemporal universals.
Prescriptive laws are not primarily reasons for action; they are person-
sourced directives that then create reasons for action.[114] Obligations don't
simply exist as reasons for action of a particularly stringent kind; they are
obligations of personal fealty, communicated by someone and owed to
that someone. Objective reasons binding on all rational agents are not
enough to make sense of morality's obligatoriness; in addition, morality
must be either built into each human being (through subjective inclinations to be moral) or through a guarantor of happiness in proportion to
virtue. Meaning and value cannot simply be one of the species of things
that exists in the universe; they must be personal in the sense that they are
created by a person's purposes.

What is so striking about these suppositions is how similar they are to
the suppositions of moral non-cognitivists and other moral skeptics.[118] For
the latter too suppose that *subjective* reasons must be what obligatoriness
is about, that demands always require a personal demander as their
source, that values are always relative to someone's purposes, etc. The
only difference between such theists and such moral skeptics is that the
theist adds a Big Person to the picture to make morality objective. Yet
the same person-relative suppositions about morality remain. At bottom,
the theist who grounds his ethics in his theism shares all the basic beliefs
of the moral skeptic albeit such a theist seeks to save himself from skepticism with one last desperate manœuvre. While we may have to grant such
theists card-carrying membership in the moral realist club because of that
last desperate manœuvre, nonetheless we should regard their allegiance
with suspicion: for all save one of the suppositions leading to their morally
realist bottom line are those of the moral skeptic.

We should thus not only ask, is God necessary for morality's objectivity;
we should also question whether God is even compatible with morality's
objectivity. The same suppositions that lead most theologians to answer
affirmatively the first of these questions ought instead to lead them to
wonder whether a negative answer isn't more appropriate to the second.

NOTES

1 Leon Meltzer Professor of Law and Philosophy, University of Pennsylvania. My
 thanks to John Finnis, Ron Garet, and Robert George for their suggestions as to
 what a novice in theological ethics such as myself should read in order to write
 this chapter. Such thanks are particularly appropriate since such theistic natural

lawyers could so easily predict that they would not agree with my reading of the literature that they so kindly suggested.

2 J. L. Mackie, *Ethics: Inventing Right and Wrong* (London, Penguin, 1977), p. 48.

3 See John Finnis, *Natural Law and Natural Rights* (Oxford, OUP, 1980), p. 43, who traces the history of the suspension of belief in God in theological ethics.

4 Hugo Grotius, *De Jure ac Pacis*, Prolegomena, para. 11, trans. Kelsey (Oxford, OUP, 1925).

5 Dostoevsky, *The Brothers Karamazov* (New York, Random, 1933).

6 Kai Nielsen, 'The Myth of Natural Law', in S. Hook, ed., *Law and Philosophy* (New York, N.Y.U. Press, 1958), p. 129.

7 Grotius, above at n. 4.

8 Kant, *Critique of Practical Reason*, trans. L. W. Berk (New York, Liberal Arts Press, 1956), pp. 130, 147–51; Kant, *Religion Within the Limits of Reason Alone*, trans. T. M. Greene and H. H. Hudson (New York, Harper, 1960), pp. 5–7. See generally Allen Wood, *Kant's Moral Religion* (Ithaca, N.Y., Cornell University Press, 1970), and Bernard Reardon, *Kant as Philosophical Theologian* (London, 1988).

9 Finnis, above at n. 3, at pp. 48–9.

10 I define moral realism in greater detail in Moore, 'The Interpretive Turn in Modern Theory: A Turn for the Worse?', *Stanford Law Review*, vol. 41 (1989), pp. 871–957; Moore, 'Moral Reality Revisited', *Michigan Law Review*, vol. 90 (1992), pp. 2424–533.

11 Nor do I intend to beg any questions against the theist with these ideas. Professors Taliaferro and Garcia both worry that my notion of mind-independence precludes a moral objectivity conceived as God-created. I have no such slight-of-hand in mind. If God creates moral qualities whose existence is independent of *our* beliefs in their existence, these qualities are objective, by my notion of objectivity.

12 My present commentators are no exception. Taliaferro reaches for 'a richer notion of Divinity . . . in which God is eternal rather than temporal, simple (not containing parts) and nonphysical rather than embodied as a physical organism, . . . *sui generis*, pure act, necessarily existing.' Likewise, Garcia seeks to enrich my spare, person-like God with the more specific attributes of God in the Biblical story. A better example of the kind of retreat into mystery that I have in mind here is the God of Rheinold Neibuhr's 'As Deceivers, Yet True', in his *Beyond Tragedy* (New York, Scribner, 1937).

13 Charles Taliaferro takes issue with me here. He argues that no question I wish to ask would be begged if I allowed that 'God is necessarily good,' that 'what God does cannot but be good,' and even that ' "moral rightness" and "moral wrongness" should be analyzed in terms of Divine Judgments.' Professor Taliaferro urges that I can be more generous to my theistic opponents without begging any questions. Unfortunately, the questions Taliaferro has in mind were not questions I asked: (1) whether 'there *is* such a being,' whether 'there *probably* is such a being,' or even whether 'there is *possibly* such a being'; (2) 'whether the notion of such a being is even intelligible'; (3) 'whether the existence of value . . . is itself best accounted for by assuming such a being.'

Whether God exists, whether the idea makes any sense, whether God created values, are not the questions I raise below. Rather, I ask whether, if we have good grounds for believing that God does exist, that would aid the case for arguing that objective values exist as well. I *assume* that the notion of God is intelligible and that God exists. My question is relational: given these assumptions, are we any better off in showing that values are objective? If God *is* goodness, or if what God does or commands is goodness, or if the objectivity of values just means, 'commanded by God', then of course the God hypothesis helps. But it helps in just the same way as the assumption that there are objective values would help the argument that there are objective values.

14 Patterson Brown, 'Religious Morality', *Mind*, vol. 72 (1963), pp. 235–44, at 235.

15 Finnis, above at n. 3, at pp. 388–98.

16 Ibid. at p. 389.

17 Ibid. at p. 392.

18 See, e.g., Robert Adams, *The Virtue of Faith*, chs. 7, 9, 10 (New York, OUP, 1987).

19 For examples of secular moral realism, see, e.g., Moore, 'Moral Reality', *Wisconsin Law Review*, vol. [1982], pp. 1061–156; Moore, 'Moral Reality Revisited', above at n. 10; David Brink, *Moral Realism and the Foundations of Ethics* (Cambridge, Cambridge University Press, 1989); Boyd, 'How to be a Moral Realist,' in G. Sayre-McCord, ed., *Essays on Moral Realism* (Ithaca, Cornell Univ. Press, 1989); Lycan, 'Moral Facts and Moral Knowledge', *Southern Journal of Philosophy*, vol. 24 (supp., 1986), pp. 79–94; Railton, 'Moral Realism', *Philosophical Review*, vol. 95 (1986), pp. 163–207; Sturgeon, 'Moral Explanations', in D. Copp and D. Zimmerman, eds., *Morality, Reason, and Truth* (Totawa, NJ, Rowan and Littlefield, 1984); Werner, 'Ethical Realism', *Ethics*, vol. 93 (1983), pp. 653–79; Torbjorn Tannsjo, *Moral Realism* (Savage, Md, Rowan and Littlefield, 1990); Mark Platts, *Moral Realities* (London, Routledge, 1991).

20 As those familiar with the theological literature will notice, I freely intermingle arguments explicitly directed to my question—is God necessary or even helpful to morality's objectivity—with arguments culled from theological discussions of another question, namely, does the objectivity of morality argue for the existence of God. I do so because logically these are one and the same relation: if I say, 'morality is objective only if God exists,' or if I say 'if morality is objective, then God exists,' I have said the same thing, namely, that God's existence is a necessary condition for morality's objectivity and that morality's objectivity is a sufficient condition for God's existence. We use the first phrasing when, as in this chapter, we assume God to exist and we wish to see if morality could be objective without him; we use the second phasing when, as in 'the moral argument for God', we assume morality to be objective and we wish to see whether God exists.

21 Mackie, above at n. 2, ch. 1.

22 Well after the Texas debate I came across the same question from the theistic side of the street in the Oxford debate between Dennis Prager and Jonathan Glover: 'But where does universal law come from? The universe? Neptune? Does Neptune form the Ten Commandments? Does human reason? Give me a break.' 'Can We Be Good Without God?,' *Ultimate Issues*, vol. 9, Issue 1 (1993), pp. 3–22, at p. 6.

23 For a helpful summary of the change in our conception of laws, from laid down

commands to impersonal truths, see Jeffrey Stout, 'Truth, Natural Law, and Ethical Theory,' in R. George, ed., *Natural Law Theories* (Oxford, OUP, 1992), pp. 72–77.

24 Aquinas, *Summa Theologica*, I–II, Q. 90. More contemporary Catholic philosophers have shared Aquinas's view about laws requiring lawgivers. See, e.g., Elizabeth Anscombe, 'Modern Moral Philosophy', *Philosophy*, vol. 33 (1958), pp. 1–19, at p. 6. ('To have a *law* conception of ethics is to hold that what is needed for conformity with virtues . . . is required by divine law. Naturally it is not possible to have such a conception unless you believe in God as a law-giver, like Jews, Stoics, and Christians.')

25 Ibid.

26 John Austin, *Lectures on Jurisprudence*, vol. I (London, 5th edn. 1885), Lecture I.

27 H. P. Owen, *The Moral Argument for Christian Theism* (London, Allen and Unwin, 1965), p. 49. Non-cognitivists often share with theists this assumption. See, e.g., Garner, 'On the Genuine Queerness of Moral Properties and Facts', *Australasian Journal of Philosophy*, vol. 68 (1990), pp. 137–46, at 143. ('It is hard to believe in objective prescriptivity because it is hard to make sense of a demand without a demander . . .')

28 W. Alston, *Philosophy of Language* (Englewood Cliffs, N.J., Prentice-Hall, 1964).

29 See, e.g., R. M. Hare, *The Language of Morals* (Oxford, OUP, 1954); Hare, *Freedom and Reason* (Oxford, OUP, 1963).

30 Finnis, above at n. 3, ch. XIII. Charles Taliaferro heads in this (cosmological) direction also.

31 Moore et al., above at n. 19.

32 J. L. Mackie, *The Miracle of Theism* (Oxford: OUP, 1982), pp. 115–16.

33 Brian Davies, *An Introduction to the Philosophy of Religion*, 2d edn. (Oxford, OUP, 1993), p. 172.

34 Adams, above at n. 18, at p. 145.

35 Ibid. at p. 146.

36 Ibid. at p. 105.

37 Ibid. at p. 140.

38 Moore, 'Moral Reality Revisited', above at n. 19, at part III.

39 This is admittedly quite sketchy as here presented, and my brevity unfortunately has misled my commentators. Taliaferro correctly points out that 'the relation of supervenience is not an identity relation.' True enough, but as I point out in the article cited in n. 38, the co-variance between properties that is supervenience cries out for explanation, and the best explanation of such co-variance is in terms of what are misleadingly called 'token-identities' between such properties. Most functionalists in the philosophy of mind accompany their supervenience claims (about the relations between mental states and brain states) with such identity claims. Garcia worries that my identity claim is so reductionist that moral qualities do not exist for me. Yet even if I were an unqualified type-identity reductionist (of moral properties to natural properties), that would hardly drum me out of the moral realist club. Does anyone think that 1960's style type-identity materialism about mental states denied the reality of mental states? One would have to think it to be an analytic truth that

no mental state could be a physical state in order to answer this question affirmatively.

40 J. D. Goldsworthy, 'God or Mackie: The Dilemma of Secular Moral Philosophy', *American Journal of Jurisprudence*, vol. 30 (1985), pp. 43–78, at 77. (Goldsworthy concludes that only with God could morality have such authority.)

41 Finnis, above at n. 3, at p. 44. (Finnis, too, ultimately concludes that 'God is the basis of obligation,' at p. 407.)

42 For the form of subjective reason-giving explanations, see Moore, *Law and Psychiatry: Rethinking the Relation* (Cambridge, CUP, 1984), ch. 1.

43 For this distinction, see Moore, 'Law, Authority, and Razian Reasons,' *Southern California Law Review*, vol. 62 (1989), pp. 827–96, at 841–5.

44 Moore, 'Moral Reality', above at n. 19, at pp. 1120–2; Brink, above at n. 19.

45 Consider by way of example this bit of pop theology:

As regards 'He'll punish you' making God a 'blackmailer in the sky', well, count me, my friends, as one who votes for such a 'blackmailer in the sky'. I pray with all my heart that the people who deliberately hurt people get punished. I would sit in depression if I truly believed that the torturers and their victems have the same fate, which is, of course, what the enlightened atheists believe—we all die and become oblivion.

Prager, above at n. 22, at p. 12.

46 I argue this about this example in Moore, 'Three Concepts of Rules', *Harvard Journal of Law and Public Policy*, vol. 14 (1991), pp. 771–95, at 789.

47 Finnis, above at n. 3, at pp. 348–50. I have in general relied heavily on Finnis's 'Excursus on Will Theories of Obligation,' in the discussion that immediately follows.

48 Vitoria, *De eo ad quod tenetur homo cum primum venit ad usum rationis*, pat II, para. 9 (1535), quoted in Finnis, above at n. 3, at p. 45, n. 61.

49 Joseph Raz, *Practical Reasons and Norms* (London, Hutchinson, 1975), s. 3.2.

50 This insight goes back to Plato in the *Euthyphro*.

51 Francisco Suarez, *De Legibus*, Bk. II, ch. 6, para. 13, 22 (1612), quoted in Finnis, above at n. 3, at p. 350.

52 For this folk psychological account of practical reasoning, see Moore, *Law and Psychiatry*, above at n. 42, ch. 1. I further distinguish between motivating states of desire and conative states of willing and intending in Moore, *Act and Crime: The Implications of the Philosophy of Action for the Criminal Law* (Oxford, OUP, 1993), ch. 6, but we need make no use of this latter distinction in this context.

53 As I argue in Moore, above at n. 43, at pp. 841–5.

54 The will theory of obligation is as implausible as two similar theories of legal obligation in jurisprudence, the sanctions theory of Austin and the social rules theory of Hart. According to Austinian and Benthamite legal positivism, legal obligation is no more than liability to legal sanctions. According to H. L. A. Hart's later version of legal positivism, legal obligation is no more than a social convention towards which certain subscribers to that convention have the appropriately deferential, 'internal' attitude. Both of these notions have long been criticized in jurisprudence for leaving out the obligation in 'legal

obligation', for in no sense of the word is anyone *obligated* by threats or by social agreement. Likewise, no one is obligated by commands, willings, requestings, etc. Shouting a command at an adult over whom one has no authority obligates no more than does threatening such an adult with sanctions, or obtaining the agreement of other adults that the first is bad. These are all far too positivist to capture the critical force of, 'one is morally obligated to do act A.'

55 I argue this in Moore, *Law and Psychiatry*, above at n. 42, at p. 91.

56 Derek Parfit, *Reasons and Persons* (Oxford, OUP, 1984), at p. 363.

57 William James, *Essays on Faith and Morals* (New York, Longman's, 1949), at p. 189.

58 This is where the person-centred view of value leads David Heyd, for example. See Heyd, *Genethics: Moral Issues in the Creation of People* (Berkeley, University of California Press, 1992).

59 Ibid. at pp. 82–3.

60 R. B. Perry, *General Theory of Value* (New York, Longman's, 1926), p. 38.

61 Heyd, above at n. 58 at p. 239, n. 10.

62 Ibid.

63 G. E. Moore, *Principia Ethica* (Cambridge, CUP, 1903), s. 50. Compare Henry Sidgwick, *The Methods of Ethics* (London, Macmillan, 1907), Bk. 1, ch. 1X, s. 4.

64 I explore the nature of texts generally in Moore, 'Interpreting Interpretation', *Tel Aviv University Law Rev.*, vol. 18 (1994), pp. 359–86 (in Hebrew), reprinted (in English) in Andrei Marmor, ed., *Law and Interpretation* (Oxford, OUP, 1995). In my discussion in this section I have put aside one of the crucial points defended in the latter article, namely, that there are many authoritative texts where either there is no author or there is no authority attached to the author that does exist. Obviously, if morality were text-like, one would then have to confront these possibilities before concluding that God was necessary as the authoritative author of morality's texts.

65 For a detailed defence of the deontological claim with specific reference to torture, see Moore, 'Torture and the Balance of Evils', *Israel Law Review*, vol. 23 (1989), pp. 281–344.

66 For a defence of this connection, see P. H. Nowell-Smith, 'Morality: Religious and Secular', *Christian Ethics and Contemporary Philosophy*, Ian Ramsey, ed., (New York, MacMillan, 1966). Nowell-Smith, being neither a theist in his theology nor an absolutist in his ethics, found it particularly congenial to link the two.

67 Suggested by Bernard Williams, in J. J. C. Smart and B. Williams, *Utilitarianism: For and Against* (1973). See also the suggested connection of God to deontology in Nowell-Smith, above at n. 66; G. E. M. Anscombe, 'Modern Moral Philosophy', above at n. 24; P. T. Geach, *God and the Soul* (New York, Schucken Books, 1969), pp. 121–25.

68 Kant, 'On a Supposed Right to Lie From Altruistic Motives', in L. W. Beck, ed., *Critique of Practical Reason and Other Writings in Moral Philosophy* (Chicago: U. of Chicago P., 1949).

69 Many, I think, would grant that norms like that against lying or killing are rightfully violated when acts of lying or killing are done to a would-be murderer who seeks to continue murdering one's family. Yet some might seek to

preserve the alleged text-like quality of such moral norms by saying that killing and lying, even when done in such necessitous circumstances, is still in some sense wrong. It is at least, one might say, *prima facie* wrong to lie or to kill in such circumstances. And this leaves room to argue that morality does consist in a kind of text, a set of canonically formulated norms that at least fix for us what is *prima facie* (or defeasibly) wrong.

There are two things wrong with even this limited textual claim. One is its assumption that what is even *prima facie* wrong has been canonically formulated, as in a criminal statute setting out the *prima facie* case of criminal liability. Morality is not authoritatively fixed like that, even as a matter of *prima facie* wrongs. We might think, for example, that incest is *prima facie* wrong, and yet further experience might reveal to us that we were in error in this belief. We might come across (actually or imaginatively in literature) incestuous relationships that enhance the dignity of persons in ways we had not anticipated. In which event we might withdraw our initial judgement that incest is even *prima facie* wrong.

The second error of this limited textual claim lies in its assumption that *'prima facie* wrong' is anything more than an epistemic way station on our way to discovering what is really wrong. Epistemically, we may indeed put on our pants one leg at a time by separately and initially asking a general question: 'is an act of this type (killing, incest, etc.) generally wrong?' Yet the textualist wants to transform this reasonable-enough epistemic way station into an ontological category. He wants to say that even those particular acts of killing, incest, etc. that are not wrong given their circumstances, still retain the status of being *prima facie* wrong. One should feel guilty, it is argued, whenever one kills, even if the killing is done to save one's family, and the virtue of feeling such feelings is taken to be evidential of the residue of wrongness attached even to such justified killings.

Viewed in this way, exceptions to norms like 'thou shalt not kill' are seen as a kind of staining permissions—one is permitted to kill to save one's family, but doing so stains one with a kind of moral guilt. This is what I find objectionable about such a view. It views justified killings as still in some sense wrong to do. It thus blurs the line between justification and excuse. It also weakens the content of exceptions in an immoral way. It tells the defender of his family who kills that he in some sense did wrong, even though it is a permissible wrong. Aside from the conceptual stretch required to say such things, morally it is pernicious to so view justified killings, stealings, etc. If there is an exception permitting the behaviour, then it is in no sense morally wrong to do it. Indeed, in the case of some exceptions, such as that permitting killing to save others, the act is not merely permitted but morally required. One who would not kill or even lie to save his family is in no sense a saint, but rather, a kind of misguided moral leper.

70 See A. Boyce Gibson, 'Duty and God's Will: Discussion', in *Christian Ethics and Contemporary Philosophy*, Ian Ramsey, ed. (New York, MacMillan, 1966), at p. 115:

> [S]itting loose to the rules can be a perilous adventure for the unprepared; it often means not rising above them, but sinking below them . . . We are

constantly pricked by desire or enraged by opposition; and the best thing
we can do is to sit on ourselves till we come round. To that end [God's]
rules are a great stand-by, and they are most serviceable when most inflex-
ible: otherwise we shall make exceptions in our own favor.

71 Moore, above at n. 65.

72 This seems to be Geach's main idea. God, being infallible, has no need of moral
absolutes, but we, being quite fallible, do. So God commands us absolutely not
even to consider those (potentially justifying) good consequences of our *prima
facie* evil actions. Geach, *God and the Soul*, above at n. 67, at p. 124. As noted in
the text, this make God a consequentialist who pretends to us that morality is
deontological when he knows that it really isn't.

73 P. H. Nowell-Smith, above at n. 66. See also Geach, above at n. 67, at pp. 121–2:
In post-Kantian moral theory another sort of reply has been offered as relevant—an appeal not to an agent's Inclinations but to his Sense of Duty. Now
indeed you can so train a man that 'You *must* not,' said in a peculiar manner, strikes him as a sufficient answer to 'Why shouldn't I?'; he may feel a
peculiar awe at learning this . . . it may even be part of the training to make
him think he *must* not ask why he *must* not . . . To myself, it seems clear that
although '*You mustn't*' said in this peculiar way may psychologically work
as a final answer to 'Why shouldn't I?', it is no rational answer at all.

74 For this reason I omitted Glaucon / Hobbes from my earlier taxonomy of skep-
ticisms about morality (Moore, 'Moral Reality', above at n. 19); one could well
be a moral realist metaethically, and an egoist ethically. (e.g., Rick Fumerton,
Reason and Morality: A Defense of the Egocentric Perspective (Ithaca, NY, Cornell
University Press, 1990).

75 Kant, *Critique of Practical Reason*, pp. 129ff.

76 Adams, above at n. 18, at p. 156.

77 Ibid. at p. 158.

78 Ibid.

79 Ibid. at p. 157.

80 I suppose that one could construct a teleological argument for God's existence
even in this tragic scenario: such a situation could only have been created by a
Being with a wicked sense of humour. I sometimes think that the differing
needs between the sexes to be the best proof of God's existence on precisely this
ground.

81 Se Moore, 'Moral Reality', above at n. 19, at pp. 1103–4.

82 Beccaria, 'On Crimes and Punishments', J. Grigson, trans., *The Column of
Infamy*, A. Manzoni, ed. (Oxford, OUP, 1964), pp. 17–18.

83 This is the argument discussed in s. 4 above, with the removal of any reference
to happiness as necessarily proportional to virtue, or happiness as a needed
subjective motivator of morality. Without these references to happiness, this is
usually thought of as Kant's theoretical argument for God, not his practical
argument. See Adams, above at n. 18, at p. 150.

84 Davies, above at n. 33, at p. 177.

85 Argued at length in Moore, 'Torture and the Balance of Evils', above at n. 65.

86 As Kant for one plainly saw. See A. W. Moore, 'A Kantian View of Moral Luck',
Philosophy, vol. 65 (1990), pp. 297–321.

87 Finnis, above at n. 3.

88 Ibid. at p. 373.

89 Finnis, *Fundamentals of Ethics* (Oxford, OUP, 1983), p. 145.

90 Finnis, above at n. 3, at p. 397.

91 Ibid. at pp. 406–7.

92 Ibid. at p. 407.

93 Ibid. at p. 403.

94 Germain Grisez, *Beyond the New Theism* (Notre Dame, University of Notre Dame Press, 1975), chs. 4–5.

95 Finnis thus combines elements of the teleological argument with the cosmological argument proper. Finnis, above at n. 3, ch. XIII.

96 Ibid.

97 Reprinted in the British edn. of *Why I Am Not a Christian* (London, Watts, 1927).

98 J. J. C. Smart, 'The Existence of God', *New Essays in Philosophical Theology*, A. Flew and A. MacIntyre, eds. (London, 1955), p. 46.

99 Moore, *Act and Crime*, above at n. 52, at pp. 96–97, 376.

100 Russell: 'But when is an explanation adequate?
Suppose I am about to make a flame with a match.
You may say that the adequate explanation of that is that I rub it on the box.'
Copleston: 'Well, for practical purposes—but theoretically, that is only a partial explanation.
An adequate explanation must ultimately be a total explanation, to which nothing further can be added.'
Russell, above at n. 97, at p. 150.

101 This example is from Moore, *Act and Crime*, above at n. 52, at pp. 96–97.

102 Finnis, *Fundamentals of Ethics*, above at n. 89, at p. 62.

103 Ibid. at p. 145.

104 Ibid.

105 See s. III above.

106 Finnis, above at n. 3, at p. 405.

107 B. Russell, *Why I am not a Christian*, Paul Edwards' American edn. (New York, Simon and Schuster, 1957), p. 107.

108 E.g., Adams, above at n. 18, at pp. 151–3. See also Prager, above at n. 22, at p. 4. ('If there is no God, you and I are purely the culmination of chance, pure random chance. And whether I kick your face in, or support you charitably, the universe is as indifferent to that as whether a star in another galaxy blows up tonight.')

109 Compare Geach, *God and the Soul*, above at n. 67, at pp. 126–7:
A defiance of an Almighty God is insane: it is like trying to cheat a man to whom your whole business is mortgaged and who you know is well aware of your attempts to cheat him, or again, as the prophet said, it is as if a stick tried to beat, or an axe to cut, the very hand that was wielding it . . . I shall be told . . . that . . . my attitude is plain power-worship. So it is: but it is worship of the Supreme power, and as such is wholly different from, and does not carry with it, a cringing attitude towards earthly powers.

I should have thought the worry for Geach should not be for his character—cringing or upright—but for what such power-worship says about his meta-ethics. Fear of a punishing God hardly is a moral reason to do anything.

110 H. P. Owen, above at n. 27, at p. 38.

111 Geach again: 'We cannot balance against our obedience to God some good to be gained, or evil to be avoided, by disobedience. For such good or evil could in fact come to us only in the order of God's Providence . . .' Geach, above at n. 67, at p. 129.

112 Cf. Illtyd Trethowan, *Absolute Value* (New York, Humanities Press, 1970), pp. 208–9:

> [T]here was that incident in the Fellows' Garden at Trinity College, Cambridge, when George Eliot, after some dismissive remarks about religion, breathed out the word 'duty' in a tone of almost ecstatic awe and wonder. Such a person, I contend, is religious without realizing it.

See also Trethowan's identical conclusion about Iris Murdock's secular moral realism. Ibid. at pp. 238–41.

113 Cf. H. P. Owen, *The Moral Argument for Christian Theism*, above at n. 27, at p. 49: 'On the purely moral plane [i.e., without God] we are unable to give any further account of their [moral entities'] existence. They just "are"—enigmatic entities in an uncharted sphere. Their enigma consists in the fact that, taken in themselves, they are *impersonal*.'

114 Cf. Owen, above at n. 27, at p. 50: 'bare belief in an impersonal order of claims, while it is compatible with their absolute character, does not provide the personal basis which their imperatival quality requires.'

115 See, e.g., Owen, above at n. 27, at 82: 'Since an independently existing order of values is inexplicable . . . it would seem natural to accept a theistic explanation.' Owen is like the moral skeptic John Mackie, who also finds objective values inexplicable, but Mackie, rather than seeking to explain the inexplicable, more reasonably infers that such values do not exist. For another example of the closeness of theism to skepticism, see also Trethowan, *The Basis of Belief* (London, 1960), p. 118: 'The absoluteness of moral obligations, as I see it, is so far from being self-explanatory that if it were not made intelligible by being found in a . . . theistic . . . context, I should be greatly tempted to hand it over to the anthropologists and the psychologists.'

13

'Deus sive Natura': *Must Natural Lawyers Choose?*

J. L. A. GARCIA[1]

Spinoza thought the relationship of natural order to divine will so close that he shocks us by using the terms almost interchangeably. He sometimes makes claims about what is done by, or is true of, *'Deus sive natura,'* meaning that whichever term one chose would make no difference—one would be saying the same thing.[2] Michael Moore takes the opposite view. His 'Good without God' argues that the existence of God is of no help in making a case for the sort of moral objectivity to which he thinks proponents of natural law should give their allegiance, and he suggests it may be an impediment. His chapter critically examines a large number of arguments for morality's dependence on God and finds them all wanting.[3] Moore covers an enormous amount of ground here, with erudition and skilful philosophical argumentation. Inevitably, little is covered adequately and some remarks are so terse as to border on superficiality. I will pursue only a few points here.

I disagree with little in Moore's principal contention.[4] The bare existence of some divine Being with the attributes Moore assigns of being 'a person-like [esp., an agentive] entity only with powers greater than those of ordinary persons,' does not by itself significantly 'strengthen the case for morality's objectivity'.[5] The more interesting question is whether the sort of story about God and about God's relationship to humanity which most of the great natural law thinkers have accepted, the Biblical story, is likewise irrelevant. I think not. I will confine myself to just a few areas where the God of Jews and Christians helps us to make sense of what I take to be some important features of our moral life. I conclude with some remarks about Moore's worries that 'the theist who grounds his ethics in his theism shares all the basic beliefs of the moral skeptic' whose 'allegiance' to moral realism 'we should regard . . . with suspicion' because it is questionable 'whether God is even compatible with morality's objectivity'.[6]

First, let us think about a feature of morality to which Moore's chapter does not attend: the fact that considerations of moral duty should override other considerations. In saying this, I am not endorsing the dubious view

that it is a necessary condition of a norm's being part of my morality that
I assign it priority over other norms. I am not making a logical claim but a
moral one. it is a moral failing to treat other matters as more important
than the most serious moral considerations. We don't normally say someone is imprudent if, out of regard for some important moral consideration,
she acts contrary to her manifest best interest. Nor do we usually say that
a person is simply being rude if she subordinates concern for the demands
of etiquette to countervailing moral requirements. However, we do say
that she is being immoral in so far as she puts concern for her own interests or etiquette ahead of her moral responsibilities. It is, perhaps, excessively optimistic to suppose that what is most eligible morally and what is
most eligible with respect to self-interest will always coincide.[7] However,
we should not expect living morally to lead to personal disaster. Surely,
the very possibility of such a clash with rational prudence calls into question the claim that living in accordance with objective moral standards is
a rational enterprise.

Such seeming imprudence appears to be rational. Can the God of the
Bible help to allay this worry? It seems to me that we should answer affirmatively. If acting immorally risks eternal damnation, then there is a limit
to how far one strays from prudence in following the moral law even onto
the gallows or into the torture chamber. Schopenhauer sneered that in the
Postulates of Practical Reason even Kant's Categorical Imperative could
be seen with hand extended asking for its reward for a good life.[8] As I have
urged elsewhere, Schopenhauer's complaint is unfair.[9] Perhaps Kant
meant only to set limits to his (I think, right-headed) rejection of the reduc-
tion of moral requirements to 'hypothetical imperatives' of prudence or
skill. What concerned Kant was that, even if morality should not be seen
as a rational calculation designed to advance one's self-interest, neither is
its claim to be a rational system secure if living morally can lead to unredeemed personal calamity for the agent. To demand that morality not
blow up in one's face is not, *pace* Schopenhauer, the same thing as
demanding that it pay off. Perhaps living morally needn't advance one's
self-interest; perhaps it may even set it back. But if living morally is not to
be madness, if it is to be a sensible business, then there must be a limit to
how much living morally will set one's interests back. If I have Kant right,
he thought the only way to make sense of the paramountcy of moral
requirements, given that following the moral path into unredeemed
personal calamity cannot be sensible, is by recourse to the 'postulates' that
a just God exists who will see to it that personal suffering is not the end of
the story for the righteous agent. We needn't here bother with Kant's
device of 'postulates of pure practical reason'. What matters is that there
is a serious challenge to what we might call the reasonableness of morality and that the existence of a certain sort of divine order alleviates the

problem. Perhaps Michael Moore thinks this a mere pseudo-problem, or that there is something else that meets this challenge to morality as well as or better than does divine justice. Perhaps he is right. But Kant couldn't find it, and neither could Sidgwick. It seems perverse, in any case, to deny that God's justice strengthens the case for the stature of objective morality's norms in the face of the challenge that when virtuous, conscientious people accord them the status of overriding considerations they are being unreasonable and even mad.

Secondly, consider the way in which acting morally sometimes appears to lead to disaster not just for the agent himself but for everyone involved, even for the whole world. Decent people think that injustice may not be committed even if 'the heavens tumble', and Moore himself accepts some 'agent-relative' restrictions.[10] How can this be sensible? Moore's chapter raises the question, but offers no solution.[11] He merely says that, while '[t]his is a genuine puzzle for agent-relative views of the content of morality,' he doubts that 'adding God helps with this puzzle in any way.' To introduce God only 'regresses the puzzle to God: why should He wish each of us to conform to the moral laws, even when doing so allows or causes others to break them?' He asks, '[w]hat sense can we make of one Being who, although he cares for each of us equally, doesn't care to minimize moral failure or maximize moral success?'[12] The God of the Bible, however, is concerned primarily with the souls of His people, not with their earthly fate. Moreover, what matters about their souls is whether they are charged by love for each of their neighbours and for God, love which contain the whole of the moral law itself.[13]

This suggests what I have elsewhere called an 'input-centered' account of the moral justification of actions, as well as a relational conception of the moral life. When I do wrong I wrong someone by failing to act in an adequately loving way towards him.[14] If I do something that will harm you, then that might indicate that I don't care enough about you to find out whether my action will harm you, or it might show that I don't care enough about you to eschew the action out of virtuous concern for your welfare. However, it might be that my action does not show an insufficiency of love toward you. Perhaps there was no way for me to avoid harming someone, and I chose to perform this action from no malice or vicious disregard for your needs. If that is the case, there may be no reason to impugn the lovingness of the action, and thus no reason to think it immoral.

On such an understanding of morality, maximizing the total amount of good is of no special importance and neither is maximizing the number of people benefited. Think of a few cases. Suppose you could as easily help both A and B, who are in the same need, but you choose to help only A. To the question why you didn't help B, you seem to have no response other than that you don't care enough about him. Suppose now you could either help both B and C or help only A instead, but again you choose to help only A. This time, to the question why you didn't help B, you can properly answer that you loved A just as much as B and showed no vicious disregard for B in failing to help him. You have the same answer available to the question why you didn't help C. Moreover, these answers suffice to explain why you didn't help both B and C. You do not need a special, additional answer for that question. So, the numbers by themselves needn't matter in Christian morality. It will matter, however, how far removed from love one's alternatives are. If, for example, the only way to save B and C from being murdered is deliberately to kill A yourself, then the law of love rules out the latter option. For, in as much as love is benevolence, wishing the other well, aiming at her welfare, you would act in a way more greatly removed from love if you deliberately killed A than you would if you let B and C be murdered as a result of your refusal to kill A. If you kill A you aim to deprive him of the good of life, if you refuse to kill him, B and C will die but without your aiming at any loss to them. So, your killing A would be wrong because it is more opposed to neighbour-love in its instrumental intentions than is letting B and C die, and because killing A is no more loving in its goal.[15] In so far as loving someone consists in wishing her well, it is not hard to see why intentionally causing or allowing one person to come to harm is morally worse (further removed from the virtue of charity) than is causing or allowing harm to several people without meaning to do so.

Absolute prohibitions appear paradoxical when we assume that what makes wrong actions wrong is that their outcomes are worse than those of their alternatives. The Christian doctrine of neighbour-love, however, allows us to see that what makes wrong acts wrong is the viciousness of their inputs (i.e., their motivational history and structure). What God wants from us is to be loving. Loving is the point of our lives, even as it characterizes the social life of the Divine Persons. Outcomes matter only indirectly on such a view.[16]

The Christian view of the human story also helps us to see the place of morality in our lives and in the world. All creation is relational, a result of God's loving action of creation, and the point of human existence is to give each person opportunity to return to the Creator from Whom the sin in Eden distanced us. This sort of view of morality helps immunize us against the modernist view that morality consists merely in placing constraints on the individual's pursuit of what is taken to be the basic business of life—satisfying his desires (nowadays dressed up in Rawlsian garb as 'living according to her own conception of the good'), which some theories treat as givens. From this perspective the superior dignity of the individual over the group becomes clearer, even if it was only late in the history of Christian thought that this came to be appreciated and the classical privileging of the community over the individual overcome.[17] Surely, Caiaphas's proto-consequentialist motto that it is better for one to suffer than for the group would be an unseemly moral principle for a follower of Christ to endorse.[18]

Some philosophers have challenged moral realists such as Moore to explain 'the place of value in a world of facts'. Meeting this demand is surely an important part of making the case for the objectivity of morality.[19] The skeptic dares the realist to explain how values fit into the world and how it can be sensible to live morally. The Christian rejects the very premise of the skeptic's challenge by denying that the world is a totality of value-free facts; rather, in his view, the world of facts is already pervaded by 'value' as it results from, is ultimately structured by, always reflects, and finally returns to, the root of all facts in the reason and will of the God Who is His Love.

How well does Moore himself handle this last sort of challenge? Not very well. Moore thinks that 'values', including moral duties, are natural and 'impersonal' qualities of things in the world, 'like wetness'. To say that values are like wetness, only different (because values give 'objective reasons to act') does not mark much progress, in ninety years, over the claim in *Principia Ethica* that good is just like yellow, only different (because good is 'non-natural'). Value is not much like wetness (or like yellow), as can be seen by attending to our evaluative discourse.[20] Moore's view cuts off so-called 'intrinsic value' and rightness from ordinary value and rightness. (All my explicit references to Moore are to Michael Moore.) The latter are always related to purposes, plans, needs, functions, and so on, as in 'This isn't the book I asked you for; you didn't bring me the right book.' Moore's position also offers no explanation why only things related to person's needs, interests, plans, etc., have value. Santayana skewered Russell on this score during the period when Russell was writing under the influence of *Principia Ethica*. He accused Russell of advancing a doctrine that made it impossible to explain why only some things could be good.[21] Moore denies that only things related to human needs, etc. can have value; he thinks a beautiful but unseen mountain on a deserted planet still has value.[22] Even if he is right about that, however, isn't the reason we continue to call the mountain beautiful the same as the reason we could continue to say it was awe-inspiring or breathtaking, or thrilling? That is, isn't it because of some implicit counterfactual reference to how rational and emotional observers would respond to it? Is there anything to value in abstraction from all persons?

Moore's position also gives us no clue *how* a natural quality that is at all similar to wetness could give us reasons to act. Normally, the reasons we have for action derive from our own needs, plans, and desires or those of others. It is true, as Moore says in a related connection, that the mere fact that most familiar examples of a phenomenon have a certain feature does not entail that all examples must have it. However, if all familiar examples derive from a certain feature, then that entitles us to ask what does the work of this feature in the alleged examples from which it is missing. What makes value give people reasons to act if that value has no necessary connection to what advances any person's goals, projects, plans, needs, purposes, or function? In light of this, I think most people with a firm grip on reality, whether they are theists or not, will find Moore's metaphysical axiology simply incredible.

I close with a different point. Moore thinks that moral realists should be wary of theism because theism tempts people to see value (which, for Moore, includes moral duty) as somehow dependent on the mind of God. Moore defines moral realism as denying that moral qualities and propositions are mind-dependent. Why should realists worry that moral qualities and propositions somehow depend on God's mind? The answer is not obvious, since it seems the motivation must be quite different from that which drives them to deny that moral qualities and propositions depend on human minds. The latter denial is rooted in such facts as these: (a) one human mind differs from another; (b) a human mind even differs from itself over time; (c) human minds are imperfectly rational; (d) human minds always lack some important knowledge; (e) human minds are sometimes swayed by ignoble or excessive passions or desires. Making morality dependent on human minds (at least, on actual human minds) threatens to undermine its objectivity by tying it to what is fallible and merely subjective in the sense of being variant and manipulable over time, space, and contingencies.

However, none of these things is true of God's mind. God is like the Hypothetical Ideal Observer, which Enlightenment thinkers dreamed up and modelled on God as they wanted something to take the place of the God in Whom intellectuals had begun to lose faith. Ideal Observer theories (such as Smith's or Firth's), like hypothetical contract theories (such as Rawls's),[23] and universalist rational constructivist theories (such as Kant's) are usually thought to preserve objectivity, even without strong metaphysical realism. Indeed, when Plantinga proclaimed himself a metaphysical 'anti-realist' because of his doctrine of 'divine creative anti-realism', according to which such abstract objects as qualities and propositions were all created in the (eternal, necessarily existent, and perfectly rational) mind of God, he was predictably accused of putting forward a position that was anti-realist in name only.[24] People on both sides complained about the way that this divine anti-realism sided with virtually all of the criticisms that realists had levelled against other anti-realists, and bore almost none of the deflationary potential and anthropocentric aspects ('a human face') that anti-realists had claimed as virtues of their position. One wants to know what Moore fears he will lose in morality if it somehow depended on the mind of a God Who is by nature, even if not by Moore's preferred definition, necessarily existent, omniscient, self-sufficient, perfectly loving, and indefectibly just.

Suppose that morality depends on God's mind in this way. The moral requirements and virtues that apply to creatures of a certain possible kind are fixed by the nature of such creatures, by what they need and want and how they naturally relate to one another, and so on. God, however, chooses which kinds of creatures to create and, in creating some rather than others, determines which natural moral requirements are actualized. God also backs up these natural requirements and makes them more explicit by commanding the actions already naturally required.[25] God's commands are not irrelevant to morality on such a view. They provide additional moral ground to perform the required actions. They can provide important insight into what our nature really does require.[26] Moreover, when God's rational legislative will underwrites in this way the natural moral order inherent in Creation, then all morality takes on a special importance. This, again, helps to justify the seriousness and paramountcy of moral considerations and the integrality of morality to personal development in accordance with nature, against those who think a sensible person will sometimes set aside moral considerations (usually too narrowly construed) to attend to supposedly conflicting interests in developing friendships and cultivating personal tastes.[27] It is hard to find the link that Moore claims to see between a theistic natural law position of this sort and anything that deserves the title of 'moral skepticism'.[28]

NOTES

1 I am grateful to Laura Garcia and Russell Hittinger for discussion of these topics and helpful suggestions on an earlier draft, and to Christopher Wolfe for inviting me to participate in the American Public Philosophy Institute's deliberations. Throughout this chapter, I draw on my recent work in moral philosophy which was supported by Georgetown University's generous sabbatical assistance, and by grant from NEH and from Harvard's Programme in Ethics and the Professions.

2 This may have shocked his contemporaries a good deal less. Glenn Olsen reminds us that some medieval writers were accustomed to speak of 'Natura, id est deus,' treating the natural order as a personification, agent, and expression of God, as God's 'other book'. Glenn Olsen, 'Secularization and Sacralization', a talk to an October, 1993 Wethersfield Institute conference, in New York City, on Christopher Dawson's thought. Olsen cites Gaines Post, *Studies in Medieval Legal Thought* (Princeton, Princeton U.P., 1964).

3 Moore sees the doctrine of natural law as essentially committed to two principal theses: (a) a reality thesis, which maintains that morality is objective (in a
sense he defines), and (b) a relationality thesis, which maintains that morality
places limits on the content of positive law. His focus in 'Good without God' is
on arguing that the existence of God doesn't help establish (a). He doesn't raise
the question of whether God's existence would help proponents of natural law
to establish (b). Neither shall I.

4 For my own arguments against theological voluntarism, see 'Divine
Commands, Special Exemptions, and Moral Dilemmas', a talk to the October
1992 Midwest Regional Meeting of the Society of Christian Philosophers in St
Paul. A version of that paper will be published as 'Norms of Loving', in
Christian Theism and Moral Philosophy, edited by Michael Beaty, et al., forth-
coming.

5 Moore, s. I. Moore identifies the objectivity of morality with his preferred version of moral realism. At the end of this chapter I raise questions about this
identification. Without really arguing for it, Moore suggests, at the close of his
chapter, that the existence of God may even impede effort to defend moral realism. I will not respond to that claim here, though I think relevant to this issue
the doubts I later raise about Moore's view that moral realists should extend
the mind-independence of moral propositions and qualities to exclude even
their deriving from God's legislative and creative will.

6 Moore, s. VII.

7 One way of insuring this coincidence, of course, is to understand morality as a
means to one's independently-describable self-interest; another way is to
define self-interest as inherently predicated upon being in good shape morally.
Epicurus, Hobbes, and many others seems to have taken the first path; Plato,
Aristotle, Aquinas seem to number among those who took the latter path. For
more on these options, see Samuel Scheffler, *Human Morality* (New York, OUP,
1992), ch. 4.

8 Arthur Schopenhauer, *The World as Will and Idea*, vol. 2, trans. by Haldane and
Kemp (London, 1964), p. 146.

9 See J. Garcia, 'On "Justifying" Morality,' *Metaphilosophy* 17 (1986) at pp. 214–23.

10 Moore, s. III.

11 He does, however, say a number of things that muddy the waters. He ascribes
to those who believe in 'moral absolutes' the foolish belief that 'moral laws can
be formulated in the sort of short and snappy injunctions that can be fitted into
one stone tablet,' but objects to the claim that morality 'consist[s] of text-like
rules,' insisting instead that 'new exceptions will always in principle be discoverable.' (Moore, s. III) This is confused.

    First, people who think morality is based in the virtues, as most natural
lawyers have thought, deny that it consists in rules at all, whether or not 'text-
like'. Secondly, few people think that the whole of the morality of killing, for
example, can be given concise and canonical formulation. The question is
whether statements laying out the viciousness of killing people includes any
interesting concisely-statable moral truths about when killing is impermissible.
It seems so. If Moore really thinks that the truths 'Killing people for trivial
reasons is immoral' or 'Torturing children just for kicks is wrong' admit of

exceptions, then we should want to hear what the exceptions might be like and why he believes in them. Thirdly, one wonders whether Moore's rule that every moral rule may have unformulated exceptions admits of exceptions itself. It if does, then there may be exceptionless moral norms. If it does not, then Moore's revisability claim is not merely an application of the once-trendy general Quinean view that every truth is revisable, and we are entitled to an explanation of what the flaw is in moral rules that prevents any of them from achieving the stability and immutability of, e.g., Moore's revisability thesis.

12 Moore, s. III.

13 'He who loves his neighbour has fulfilled the law. The commandments "You shall not commit adultery, you shall not steal, you shall covet," and any other commandment there may be are all summed up in this, "You shall love your neighbour as yourself." Love never does any wrong to the neighbour, hence love is the fulfilment of the law.' (Romans 13: 8–10)

14 See J. Garcia, 'The New Critique of Anti-Consequentialist Moral Theory', *Philosophical Studies* 71 (1993) at pp. 1–32; 'The Right and the Good', *Philosophia* 21 (1992) at pp. 235–56; 'The Primacy of The Virtuous', *Philosophia* 20 (1990) at pp. 69–91.

By the way, I allow that sometimes we wrong ourselves by insufficient love as when, for example, a person subordinates a concern for her own true welfare, which is the concern she owes herself, by merely indulging some lower preference. This sort of self-abuse by self-indulgence is typical in some of the sins of carnality that Professors Finnis and Macedo discuss in this volume, but this 'self-regarding' sphere of morality is not the one that is my focus here.

15 If I don't mean to harm Persons B and C, then I don't wish them ill in the relevant sense, and if I don't wish them ill when I refuse to do what I could to save them (i.e., when I refuse to kill A), then I do not treat them in as unloving a way as I would treat A if I did intentionally kill her. This paragraph is a greatly compressed sketch of an argument against consequentialist reasoning that I present in 'The New Critique'. There I offer more careful elaboration of these points.

16 This allows the Christian a way out of the apparent paradox in the old question 'If we're here to help others, then what are the others here for?' They are help to help too. Everyone is. The point of the arrangement is simply that everyone act lovingly. It need not be the most efficient way of getting benefits to each person.

17 Some prefer to say that in such tragic circumstances, the agent cannot avoid immoral action. This sort of purported solution, however, seems to pose another challenge to the reasonableness of the moral life. It raises serious questions about the consistency of morality if its demands can conflict in such a way that an agent may sometimes be unable to fulfill all the moral demands that apply to him. Williams once argued that moral realism was inconsistent with the admission of moral dilemmas, but Foot insists that realism by itself poses no obstacle to the possibility that agents sometimes are so situated that they cannot but do wrong. (See Bernard Williams, 'Consistency and Realism', in Williams, *Moral Luck* (New York, CUP, 1981); and Philippa Foot, 'Moral Realism and Moral Dilemma', *Moral Dilemmas*, Christopher Gowans, ed. (New York, OUP, 1987). I take the suggested compatibility between moral dilemmas

and realism to be an embarrassment to the realist. If there can be dilemmas, therecognition that a course of action would be immoral all things considered is not a decisive objection to it, not even a decisive *moral* objection to it. To my mind, such a position undermines the seriousness of objective moral requirements no less than does the view, confronted above, that sometimes a sensible person will just set aside worries about morality. Again, Christian thought can provide a way to block this difficulty. Whereas secular moral philosophers, even ones with realist sympathies, have had severe troubles showing that such 'moral dilemmas' are impossible and have sometimes even endorsed them, elements of Christian doctrine make it most implausible that there could be moral dilemmas.

In 'Divine Commands', above at n. 4, I present several reasons for Christians to reject moral dilemmas. These include:

First, since morality coincides with God's will, even if theological voluntarism is false, then if someone were morally obligated to do each of two incompatible things, God must will for her to do each of two incompatible things. However, it is irrational for God (or anyone) to will each of two things when it is known that they cannot both happen.

Secondly, if God's legislative will underwrites the natural law, placing the agent under an obligation any time the natural law itself requires something of him, then, if people were sometimes in moral dilemmas, God would be placing them under conflicting moral requirements. But if God placed people under conflicting requirements, then God would be requiring them to do something that is wrong, whichever they chose. To demand that another do wrong, however, is itself wrong. So, putting people into moral dilemmas would be contrary to the divine goodness.

Thirdly, allowing dilemmas into Christian ethics runs afoul of St Paul's remark (Romans 3:8) that it is a slander to accuse Christians of claiming that people sometimes ought to do things that are evil to achieve good results.

18 Unfortunately, that has not stopped some *soi disant* 'revisionist' or 'proportionalist' moral theologians from taking this line. Bernard Hoose offers a useful, although too friendly, survey of this movement in his *Proportionalism* (Washington, Georgetown University Press, 1987). For a vigorous and authoritative criticism of this degenerate strain of Christian thought, see John Paul II's encyclical letter of 1993, *Veritatis Splendor*.

19 On the general question here, see Harman, 'Is There a Single True Morality?', *Morality, Reason, and Truth*, David Copp and David Zimmerman, eds. (Lanham, Rowman and Allenheld, 1985).

20 Attending to our discourse ('language games') was, of course, the method of the linguistic philosophers of mid-century. Moore scorns aspects of their philosophy of meaning, but it is not clear that he has learned from their method. In returning to *Principia Ethica*'s simplistic analogies, Michael Moore seems to be repeating the mistakes of a past from which he has not learned. Hegel thought intellectual progress was achieved by transcending both thesis and antithesis in a new synthesis, which incorporates elements from both. Michael Moore simply rejects the ordinary language philosophers' method, without appreciating the force of their critique of the position of *Principia Ethica*. This seems to be mere reaction.

A little reflection should make it clear that the adjective 'good' operates in a radically different way from that in which 'yellow' operates. When something is good it is good for something, or good at something, or good of its kind, or good in a certain respect. It makes no sense to talk this way of yellow or wetness. That in which one type of thing's 'goodness' consists may be diametrically opposed to that in which a different type's consists: a hammer may be good in that it is hard rather than soft while a blob of putty is good in so far as it is soft rather than hard. 'Good' is perhaps best understood as acting like a function, predicating different qualities of things in different verbal contexts, as it predicates being hard of the hammer in the phrase 'This is a good hammer' but softness of the putty in the phrase 'This is some good putty.' I could go on, and the matter becomes more complicated when we consider the wide range of things (garbage, dust, numbers, etc.) that, without special circumstances, we cannot sensibly call good (or bad) at all. For our purposes, it is enough to observe that the grammar of 'good' is so different from that of 'yellow' or 'wet' that it is implausible to suppose that it picks out a certain single quality ('Goodness') as they do. There are good people, deeds, bedknobs, and broomsticks, but it is fallacious to infer there is some one thing goodness. Aristotle pointed that out long ago in refuting the Platonists of his day. G. E. Moore and Michael Moore did not learn the lesson, but the less credulous among us, theists or not, will remain skeptical about Moorean Goodness.

(For fuller critique of simplistic naturalism and its successor meta-ethical theories see, for example, Vendler, 'Grammar of Goodness', in Zeno Vendler, *Linguistics in Philosophy* (Ithaca, Cornell University Press, 1967; Foot, 'Goodness and Choice,' in Foot, *Virtues and Vices* (Berkeley, University of California Press, 1978); and Peter Geach, 'Good and Evil', in *Theories of Ethics*, P. Foot, ed. (Oxford, OUP, 1967), and Geach, 'Aquinas,' in Elizabeth Anscombe and P. Geach, *Three Philosophers* (Ithaca, Cornell University Press, 1961. An important recent addition to this distinguished body of work is Judith Jarvis Thomson, 'Goodness and Utilitarianism', *Proceedings and Addresses of the American Philosophical Association* 67 (1993), at pp. 145–59.)

21 George Santayana, 'Hypostatic Ethics', and Bertrand Russell, 'Elements of Ethics', both in *Readings in Ethical Theory*, 2nd edn., Wilfrid Sellars and John Hospers, eds. (Englewood Cliffs, Prentice-Hall, 1970).

22 Moore, s. III.

23 I have in mind the Rawls of *Theory of Justice,* before he spurned moral theory for political theory.

24 Alvin Plantinga, 'How to Be an Anti-Realist' (Presidential Address), *Proceedings and Addresses of the American Philosophical Association* 56 (1982–3) at pp. 47–70. Also see Plantinga's dispute with David Lewis about whether Lewis's reductionist account of possible worlds deserves the title of modal realism. (Alvin Plantinga, 'Two Concepts of Modality: Modal Realism and Modal Reductionism,' *Philosophical Perspectives*, James Tomberlin, ed. (1987) at pp. 189–231.)

25 Carlton Fisher offers a view along these lines in 'Because God Says So', *Christian Theism and the Problems of Philosophy*, Michael Beaty, ed. (Notre Dame, University of Notre Dame Press, 1990). I think this sort of view shouldn't count

as a divine command theory, but the point has been disputed. See Terry Christlieb's review of Beaty's book in *Faith and Philosophy* 10 (1993) at pp. 279–82. I endorse a similar position in 'Divine Commands' above at n. 4.

Whereas we might call this natural moral order inhering in Creation the natural law or the moral law, using the term 'law' in an extended sense, most Christians also believe that God moves this natural moral order closer to law (in what Finnis calls the focal sense of that term) by making elements of it accessible to rational reflection on our nature. In doing this, God 'promulgates' the moral order to us. As a result of this, the natural law more closely approximates Aquinas's account of law as an ordinance of reason that is promulgated for the common good by one with care of the community. (I owe this point to Russ Hittinger.)

26 This has helped traditional Christian moral thinkers from following the general culture into the view that promiscuous and otherwise perverted sexual conduct is something 'natural' and therefore permissible, a view that in our country has brought such widespread social and personal devastation, especially to the young, poor, and women.

27 See Bernard Williams, *Ethics and the Limits of Philosophy* (Cambridge, Mass., Harvard U.P., 1985. Also see Susan Wolf, 'Moral Saints', *Journal of Philosophy* 69 (1982), and Robert Adams's response, 'Saints', in *Virtue of Faith* (Oxford, OUP, 1987).

28 I won't dispute Moore's right to call himself a moral realist, but others might. Moore seems to prefer a reductionist account of moral qualities in which, as he puts it, moral qualities 'supervene upon, and in some sense are identical to, non-moral (i.e., natural) qualities'. (Moore, s. II. His awkward phrasing invites the unanswerable question of how a moral quality can be identical to a non-moral quality.) Some would insist that to explain away a quality reductionistically should count as a kind of anti-realism. See *Essays on Moral Realism*, Geoffrey Sayre-McCord, ed., Editor's Introduction (Ithaca, Cornell University Press, 1988).

14

God's Natural Laws

CHARLES TALIAFERRO

Given certain conceptions of God and values, theistic arguments that objective moral truths are grounded in the will of God seem like non-starters. I first address the framework for such theistic moral arguments and then propose how a successful argument can be constructed in which the nature of God is employed to account for the existence of objective moral values. I conclude by considering two respects in which theism may contribute to moral reflection; the first bears on moral methodology and the second on how theism enlarges the domain of values. A chief aim in what follows is to take issue with Michael Moore's chapter. I employ the concept of God that has taken shape in the great monotheistic traditions of Judaism, Christianity, and Islam.

I. GETTING A THEISTIC MORAL ARGUMENT OFF THE GROUND

To get an argument going, the concepts of God and objective moral values need to be clarified. Moore introduces a curious constraint as to how the-istic moral arguments may be constructed and it will prove instructive to consider first whether this constraint is warranted.

Moore is content to allow theists to begin with the notion that God is an omnipotent, omniscient Creator, a person-like reality, but he is not willing to allow theists to assume at the outset, even for the sake of argument, that God is necessarily good. In order not to beg the question the theist needs to employ a 'non-ethical idea of God'.[1]

> If moral objectivity is conceived of in terms of divine command, or God is given an ethical definition (as the highest good at which we should aim, say), then we will have begged our question before we shall have asked it. To have a question to ask, we need a non-religious idea about morality's objectivity and a non-ethical idea about God; then we can meaningfully inquire what relation might exist between them.

Is this right? I do not think so.

Theistic moral arguments *can* be constructed to account for objective moral values on the basis of a 'non-ethical idea' of God, but why should they be? Most theistic natural law theorists believe God is necessarily good; God's existence is itself good and what God does cannot but be good. This was Aquinas's position, who followed Dionysius the Aereopagite, Augustine, Bonaventure, and others in identifying God's very nature as goodness itself. Historically, Christian Platonists and Aristotelians have diverged in their articulation of this claim, but it was a widely endorsed tenet in medieval philosophy of religion, and the 'impeccability of God' is still upheld by many contemporary philosophical theists.[2] If atheists, or opponents of whatever stripe, grant the permissibility of using this notion of God in a moral argument, have any questions been begged against them? Certainly it has not been conceded yet that there *is* such a being or that there is *probably* such a being, or even that there is *possibly* such a being. Theists who argue that the goodness in creation is derived from the goodness of God should certainly resist putting to one side their 'ethical' concept of God on the basis of appeal to fair play in debate. To do so would be as absurd as making an essential condition for a fair debate over the cosmological argument that theists not make any use of the notion that God necessarily exists or God is self-explaining or (in Aquinas's terms) God's essence includes God's existence. The whole point of most versions of the cosmological argument is to provide reasons for thinking there is such a being, and by advancing the argument along the lines of Aquinas, Clarke, Leibniz, and others; the atheist interlocutor is not at all prohibited from questioning the ultimate intelligibility of supposing that a necessarily existing being exists. Similarly, I do not see why one cannot allow the provisional admission of an ethical conception of God at the outset of a theistic moral argument—if only to be challenged later.

An analogy from another area of philosophy may be helpful in driving home this observation. Imagine that you and I dispute a conceptual analysis about knowledge claims. I think that a person knowing X, in which 'X' stands for some state of affairs, amounts to the person having a justified, true belief that X. As it happens, you think the matter is much more complicated and propose that for a person to know X involves the person having a justified true belief that X and, furthermore, that the justification does not essentially rely upon any reasoning that employs a false premise. Is it somehow unfair for you to begin an argument for your analysis with your richer depiction of knowledge as a working assumption? Perhaps doing so would miss the point if my *real* aim is not to challenge you with a competing analysis, but to take issue with the whole enterprise of conceptual analysis itself. If I think *all* conceptual analyses rest on a confused theory of meaning, debate will have to take place several steps back, if at all. But in a debate about the proper analysis of knowledge claims, a legitimate, commonplace move is to allow you to advance the richer analysis and then test your case by considering the conceptual clarity of the notions you are employing and by the familiar example and counter-example method. Can I describe plausible cases in which your definition is not satisfied and yet we still have knowledge? If so, I have grounds for sticking with my analysis and resisting your proposed extension.[3] In the same way, opponents of a theistic moral argument can provisionally allow the theist the notion that God is necessarily good, and then consider whether the existence of values in the cosmos (the rightness and wrongness of actions) is itself best accounted for by assuming that there is such a being or, more fundamentally, consider whether the notion of such a being is even intelligible.

If one may legitimately launch a theistic moral argument in which an ethical conception of God is taken under consideration, can one also start off with the proposal that 'moral rightness' and 'wrongness' should be analysed in terms of Divine judgements? Why not? The argument does not stop there; no one need *accept* the claim at the beginning. The subsequent argument can take the familiar route of the opponent presenting (perhaps very plausibly) cases in which the properties of rightness and wrongness can be entertained and ascribed quite independently of Divine judgements.

What *would* be a clear case of question begging? Presumably one begs the question against a theist if one assumes without any argument at all that God does not exist or one simply waves a linguistic arm and defines one's terms (without any argument, appeal to the phenomenology of moral and religious experience or whatever) to establish one's views true by philological fiat. When it comes to begging questions one must always consider the charge with respect to the specific issues at hand, the opportunity for rejoinders, and so on. In a debate between a Moslem and a Christian on the role of Christ it would not be question-begging for each to assume there is a God; in a debate with an atheist it would be.[4]

Adopting a richer notion of Divinity has the advantage of connecting the moral argument more closely with the extant religious traditions it is designed to have a bearing on, and it also underscores why classical theists have been reluctant to think of God as simply 'a Big Person', to use Moore's term. In debating the moral argument Moore employs what he calls 'an anthropomorphic conception of God', although he acknowledges the theologian's aim of not making God 'too (punily) person-like'. 'Put in my language: this anthropocentric conception of God plainly mirrors the essential attributes of persons, God being conceived of as a person-like entity, only with powers greater than those of ordinary persons.' This is somewhat misleading. Historically Jewish, Christian, and Islamic philosophical theologians have recognized profound differences between human persons and the Divine, in which God is believed to be eternal rather than temporal, simple (not containing parts) and nonphysical rather than embodied as a physical organism, God is *sui generis*, pure act, necessarily existing. Moreover God's essential goodness does not amount to a trivial disanalogy between Creator and creature. Notwithstanding this great divide, I think it is still fitting to think of the God of these monotheistic traditions as personal, but in doing so it is imperative not to overlook the profound disanalogies between *types* of persons, if the term 'person' is to be employed at all.[5]

Introducing a fuller notion of the Divine provides the theist a powerful resource in replying to many of Moore's worries about arbitrariness. Moore worries that grounding moral objectivity on God's will allows for too much ontological precariousness and Divine whimsy. For the theist in the classical tradition of Anselm and Aquinas, there is no metaphysical possibility that God does not exist, or that God would command or perform an evil act. God's essential goodness and existence is not a contingent affair.[6]

So, at the outset, I propose that introducing a richer notion of the Divine is not itself question-begging in any pernicious way, but rather that it links the argument much more securely with theistic philosophical and theological tradition, and gives the theist an important asset in replying to some of Moore's objections. Does the theist give up anything substantial if goodness is conceptually built into the very idea of God? If so, this is not clear. Some theists have wanted to revive a radical notion that God is self caused (*causa sui*) and thus responsible for God's very nature, including God's essential goodness. I do not find this stance plausible, and see nothing theologically amiss with thinking that God is not responsible for creating God's very being.[7] But if you do adopt this more substantial view of self-creation, nothing need impede your accepting the notion that God is essentially good, and still running the argument proposed in the next section of this paper. All one has to do is offer an additional argument that God's essential goodness need not be taken as an ultimate and not further explained but that it can be accounted for on a deeper level of Divine agency.

In outlining the structure of a theistic moral argument below, I join Moore, and Jorge Garcia in acknowledging objective moral values. This assumption would, of course, be considered question-begging against a moral skeptic, but there are recourses in arguing for objectivism. Moore himself has argued against moral scepticism in various places. What strikes me initially as a much more likely case of question-begging than the one Moore attributes to theists is Moore's own depiction of moral objectivity. I consider this briefly.

Moore begins his chapter with defining moral objectivity in ontological and semantic terms. Consider the first: 'morality is objective if and only if (a) moral qualities such as goodness, wrongness, etc., exist (the existential condition); and (b) the existence of such moral qualities does not depend on what any person or group of persons believes about them (the mind-independence condition).' If Moore's analysis amounts to asserting that an essential condition of the objectivity of a moral proposition is that it does not depend on God (God being a person), then agreeing with this at the outset would be tantamount to giving up a theistic argument from the start. In keeping with the observations made about begging the question, I do not think there is anything amiss with a theist granting Moore's position *provisionally*, subject to further debate. But surely to assume it at the beginning, and for it to be an unquestioned regulative principle of debate, would be to tip the scales from the outset against the theist. A theist should thus only accept Moore's thesis tentatively with an eye to challenging it, just as a classical theist should not endorse wholeheartedly a general depiction of objectivity of the same form in which qualities are considered objective if and only if they are mind-independent. Most theists believe in the mind-dependent character of the created cosmos and hence the mind-dependent character of moral qualities that are borne by the beings that exist. But it would surely be odd to characterize such theists either as subjectivists, or as jettisoning an objectivist view of the cosmos in general or of morality in particular.[8] For some fact to be 'objective', it does not itself have to be mind-independent; it is an objective fact that minds exist, presumably.

Moore dismisses several other depictions of moral objectivity, according to which an objectivist believes in the 'timelessness of morality's eternal truths' (are timeless and eternal different?), 'their unchanging or invariant nature', and so on as 'by and large the surface corollaries of the deeper if more technical notions definitive of moral realism'. This seems like an odd claim. If moral truths *are* eternal, invariant, necessary, could that explain why what Moore casts as the 'semantic' version of objectivism is true? (If one were to take such a route, then semantic claims could be based on ontological ones.) In any case, I think a more desirable way to cast the thesis of objectivism would be to highlight the *necessity* of moral truths (slavery is necessarily wrong) and to leave unsettled at the outset whether acknowledging such necessity is compatible with believing them to be derived from God's will.[9] Theists who want to claim that moral truths are not necessary could still *provisionally* adopt this picture of ethics and they would not fare any worse than if they accepted Moore's original proposal which explicitly rules out *both* their position and the one I go on to articulate.

While I believe the necessity claim is entirely satisfactory, I will not insist on it and propose a conciliatory stance involving a slight alteration of Moore's thesis. I suggest that one way to construe objective moral qualities is to say that they exist and that their existence is not *constituted* by anyone's beliefs. In the next section, I sketch an argument to the effect that moral rightness and wrongness depends on God's willing them to be so— God is their essential Creator—though they are not constituted by, or identical with, God's willing. Rightness does not consist in something being approved by God or any created person, though its rightness depends upon God's willing it to be the case. Some theists, R. M. Adams and H. P. Owen for example, may want a stronger Divine constitutional thesis, but I hope to show that a theistic moral argument can be fashioned even if the constitutional thesis is mistaken.

II. A COSMOLOGICAL-ETHICAL ARGUMENT

The version of the theistic moral argument I develop here is closer to Finnis's than the others Moore discusses, though I will not indicate all the points at which my formulation diverges from Finnis's. To fully vindicate the argument a lot of philosophical work needs to be done that is not possible to carry out here, so the following should be considered a bare outline of the argument.[10] The argument brings together a version of the cosmological argument and some of the new work being done in philosophical theology rekindling a Cartesian understanding of God's power. Consider first the prospects of a cosmological argument.

I join the ranks of a number of philosophers, such as Richard Taylor, William Craig, Germain Grisez, Bruce Reichenbach, Richard Swinburne, Hugo Meynell, and others, who think that a version of the cosmological argument can be vindicated.[11] I do not think theism can be *proved* with such an argument, but that it, along with other arguments (from religious experience and teleology) can provide some reason for accepting theism, sufficient reason (I believe) to make theism more reasonable than its denial or agnosticism.[12] The way natural theology is constructively carried out in the present literature is with a keen sense of the need to build a cumulative case, in which various arguments are brought to bear on each other, providing mutual support. It is worth pausing to underscore this point about the interconnection of various arguments.[13]

Few would be so naïve as to accept the version of the argument Moore attributes to R. M. Adams under the heading 'Non-natural Properties and Platonic Forms as Queerer than God?', because of its failure to address metaphysical issues consistently. Moore sets up the argument in such a way that an empiricist standpoint is conceded at the outset (which Moore appears to equate with physicalism), and then later a radical, nonempirical notion of God is introduced, with apparent ignorance of the conflict this creates. Moore writes: 'God's commandings are thus as much a shock to empiricist sensibilities as any Moorean non-natural property, or Platonic Form, could be.' Clearly, if one *does* object to Moorean and Platonic *entia* because of contemporary materialism, one is not going to be more sanguine when it comes to classical theism. But this version of the argument misrepresents Adams's own position (who endorses neither empiricism nor physicalism). The point I want to underscore here is that currently in the philosophical theology literature there is an increased sense of the importance of showing how different philosophical positions intersect and have a bearing on one another. A successful employment of the cosmological, moral, ontological and other arguments for theism must, among other things, address the challenge of contemporary materialism, for example. This is something that is rarely overlooked in the current literature.[14]

The aim of not just the cosmological argument, but the teleological (or design) argument as well, is to provide a comprehensive metaphysical scheme that can account for the existence and continuity of the contingent cosmos, locating that account in the activity of God as a necessarily existing being. On Moore's scheme, the cosmos exists, replete with moral features, and yet there is no underlying supreme, singular cause for this. Unlike some atheologians, Moore concedes that it is intelligible to seek a reason for the cosmos as a whole. Some critics try to rule out as nonsense the question of why there is a cosmos, and I join Moore in being dissatisfied with such strictures. Moore writes that 'there could be answers to cosmological questions. But . . . there need not be answers to all such questions.' Moore seems to assume that his stance is on a par with the theistic alternative explanation of the cosmos, but I believe this is misleading for Moore's alternative is not an articulately developed competing hypothesis. Instead, his view seems to be that the explanation of cosmic origin and continuity is that there is no explanation. Moore maintains 'that the God answer has to compete with "no explanation" as the best explanation'. But in what sense is the absence of an explanation an explanation? Addressing cosmic questions Moore writes that '[t]here is no explanatory incompleteness if there are no answers to such questions.' On the contrary, it seems his position amounts to the thesis that there is an essential explanatory incompleteness. Moore is content to 'take brute facts (no explanation) and infinite causal series to be superior explanatory possibilities to uncaused causes.' In my view both are unreasonable compared with the theistic alternative, though there is not space here, of course, to lay out all the pro and contra points at issue.

The cosmological and other theistic arguments are fuelled by different principles of evidence, including the appeal to *a priori* probability, principles of analogy, abduction, induction, explanatory norms made evident either in experience or through rational reflection (e.g., some claim that a principle of sufficient reason can be known *a priori*), and the like. Undergirding much of the reasoning is the advancement of theism partly on the grounds that its explanatory comprehensiveness is more simple that the alternatives. Richard Swinburne and others have launched a sustained defence of the merits of simplicity as a condition for plausible theoretical schemes, bolstering the adage that *simplex sigillum veri*, or simplicity is a mark of the truth.[15] An impressive number of cases can be presented from the history of science in which competing theories, otherwise equally matched in terms of evidence, are rightly considered more plausible depending upon the simplicity involved. Witness, for example, the dispute between Ptolemaic and Copernican astronomy which at a certain stage seemed equally matched in terms of explaining appearances, though the latter could do so more elegantly with fewer explanatory posits. The terrain in the philosophy of science and in metaphysics here is hotly contested, but I suggest that we are currently in a better position today to appreciate the resources of a theistic metaphysic in providing a singular, comprehensive explanatory account of moral truths as well as other essential truths. This has come about as part of a revival of a very much revised Cartesian treatment of God's power. If theism is able to provide an explanatory account of not just the bare existence of the cosmos, but the existence of moral facts that in part define the cosmos, perhaps supervening on its nature, then the singularity and breadth of the 'God hypothesis' has a marked simplicity and force missing from its competitors.

Descartes embraced a radical understanding of God's omnipotent creativity according to which God made it the case that certain truths are necessary, but God could have done otherwise.[16] This appears to make moral truths too precarious and subject to Divine tinkering. A range of recent philosophers, however, R. M. Adams, Michael Loux, Fred Fredosso, T. V. Morris, Christopher Menzel, Alvin Plantinga, James Ross, and others, have proposed that certain necessary truths are indeed necessary, and that their necessity can be accounted for in terms of God's necessarily willing them to be the case.[17] This would provide a comprehensive, sweeping account of numbers, along with other *abstracta*, and, I submit, the truths of objective morality, in a singular source. God's action here is no less of an action in view of the fact that God necessarily wills that they be so, or, to put it in a now fashionable idiom, God wills that they be so in every possible world. God is not constrained to will these by some outside force. As Morris and Menzel put it, 'the necessity of His creating is not imposed on Him from without, but rather is a feature and result of the nature of his own activity itself, which is a function of what He is.'[18] This theistic strategy may be applied in the ethical case, and not just with respect to *abstracta* like numbers and propositions.

This line of argument does not rest upon a *disanalogy* between moral laws and the laws of nature but upon their analogy. Moore keeps stressing that there is a serious problem with the theist treating moral laws in a way that makes them like laws of nature. 'Theists about natural law thus have to break the analogy of moral laws to the unpromulgated laws of science.' I believe theists need not break any such analogy, but draw from it. Thus, just as we might rely on a teleological argument as part of an over-riding metaphysics in which to account for the ordered cosmos, a similar argument can be employed to account for the ordered, essential nature of *abstracta* and necessary ethical truths as well. For the theist, it would be misleading to think that 'Kepler's laws of planetary motion or Snell's laws on the diffusion rate of gas through a porous membrane . . . are perfectly good laws and yet they are not laid down by anyone.' For the theist, the laws of nature will themselves be seen as stemming from Divine agency. Alvin Plantinga's claim is representative: '[t]he very causal laws on which we rely in any activity are no more than the record of God's regular, constant and habitual dealing with the stuff of the universe he has created.'[19] Similarly, the very nature and pattern of necessary, objective moral truths is the record of God's essential, necessary creative activity.

The argument I propose, then, is a metaphysical argument, having to do with an explanatory account of a certain range of facts. In his chapter, Moore seems to shift at various points between addressing metaphysical and epistemic issues. He moves from 'must God exist for morality to be objective?' to '[w]ould the existence of God help at all in justifying our belief that morality is objective?' There are some important points that can be easily obscured here. If one wants to consider the epistemic side of the relation between God and the good, then Moore will presumably want to rephrase the question cited last. Thus, the question should be: would our having *justification* to believe that God exists help us in justifying our belief that morality is objective? When he says '[w]ould God's existence strengthen the case for morality's objectivity?' we need to think in terms of the epistemic justification of each. The metaphysical and epistemic issues are clearly distinguishable; something may be necessary metaphysically for a state of affairs to obtain and yet we may fail to appreciate this. Moreover there can be forceful evidence for false hypotheses. If the metaphysical argument sketched above that links the cosmological argument with neoCartesian accounts of Divine activity is plausible, would this provide additional reasons for thinking morality is objective? It might in several ways.

Some theists have argued that the truth of theism would provide good grounds for trusting our cognitive equipment that popular nontheistic schemes (such as evolutionary epistemology, Chisholmian internalism, virtue epistemology) lack.[20] Also, there is an obvious, uninteresting sense in which having justification for believing in God would assist my confidence in moral objectivism. I briefly note this only to set it aside. If I am unsure about the truth of moral objectivism—e.g., if a recent reading of Blackburnian projectivism has left me unsure—but I have independent reason to trust another person's judgements and *he* assures me moral objectivism is indeed true and that Blackburn is mistaken, then I have some justification to stick with moral objectivism. Of course, this would not be hearty, direct evidence of moral objectivism, but cases might arise when it is nontrivial. Imagine the case, then, where I am similarly unsure of objectivism but I have ample justification for believing and trusting God and evidence, too, that God is a moral objectivist. Well, under *those* conditions, surely I would have some further justification for objectivism. But I put these moves aside and address a slightly different point that concerns Moore.

If one were to accept the metaphysical dependence of moral objectivism on the will of God, does one run any moraly relevant risks? That is, do theists somehow make more precarious their grip on moral objectivity such that, if they were to abandon theism, they would be compelled to abandon moral objectivism? I do not see why this should be so.

The metaphysical argument advanced in this section is not exactly of the Doestoevskian kind that Moore reviews. From an Anselmian point of view, there is no possibility that God not exist. But, while I fully accept this, let me consider the following scenario. What if I were to change my mind about these claims concerning God's essential nature and become an atheist. Would this require my abandoning moral objectivism? Not at all. The above argument is advanced on the grounds of what is more reasonable to adopt, appealing to explanatory simplicity and a high order of intelligibility, not on the basis of a demonstrable proof. Having given up on theism, I might adopt G. E. Moore's schema or Platonism without God or any number of other options. It is crucial to appreciate that the cosmological-ethical argument contends that theism provides a rich, substantial theory according to which we can account for the existence of the cosmos *and* its objective moral features. Adopting it does not require ruling that all other accounts are *obviously* wrong. Hearkening back to the analogy of the first section concerning a debate over the analysis of knowledge claims, should I become a skeptic if I come to see that my analysis admits of counter-examples? There are other analyses in the neighborhood that can be wheeled out to avoid such an outcome. Developing a theistic moral argument of the kind articulated here no more courts moral skepticism, than developing a theistic cosmological argument invites skepticism or makes in any way precarious the belief that there is a cosmos. Recall, too, that the moral argument of this section is not an argument that is designed to explain the ethical in terms of things that are valueless, but ultimately in terms of a supreme value. Thus, we do not have to face the charge that 'an infinite amount of morally irrelevant attributes is still morally irrelevant'. This is why the God-good relation developed here is not a close ally with subjectivism.

I conclude by briefly noting two points Moore seems either to deny or neglect. Moore places most of his emphasis on the thesis that theism is not theoretically necessary, though he also wants to further the claim that it would be good to be without theism. I suggest two respects in which theism can play a helpful role in thinking about moral life.

III. IS IT GOOD TO BE WITHOUT THE IDEA OF GOD?

Even if it were good if there were no God, would it be so good if we were without the idea which God (or a God-like observer) plays in our moral reflection? I briefly sketch an argument to the effect that it would not be desirable.

Moore's realist objectivism is not based on person relative truths. 'States of affairs can be good or bad, better or worse, without reference to persons' wants, needs, or interests; we owe moral duties *tout court*, that is without owing them to some persons or person-like entity.' Even if this is right, does ethical realism entail person-relative truths?

In various places I have defended an ideal observer theory of ethics, revising an account advanced by Roderick Firth (but having some debts to Sidgwick, Hume, and Smith) according to which something's being right entails that it would be approved of by an ideal observer. The scheme I develop is one that ranges over not just moral judgements but aesthetic valuations as well.[21] In the version I adopt, the ideal observer is omniscient with respect to the nonmoral facts, impartial, and omnipercipient (that is, able to affectively appreciate the points of view of all involved parties). I believe that our moral disagreements often testify to the pivotal, regulative role of each of these features. Interlocutors in an ethical dispute will frequently accuse their opposites of failing to be impartial or truly appreciate the implications of actions on an affective level. What I refer to as nonmoral facts concern those facts that can be conceived without thereby explicitly conceiving their moral status, their ethical character. As Moore himself agrees, moral truths are largely grounded in what we might consider the nonmoral. Thus, a dispute about abortion might result, in part, from a disagreement about the empirical facts of the matter.[22] When we make moral judgements I believe we implicitly commit ourselves to holding that if there were an ideal observer (or IO) then the IO would make the same judgement.

The version of the ideal observer theory I adopt does not claim to be an analysis of moral judgements. If one can successfully advance the ideal observer theory as an *analysis* of moral truths, one will have made serious progress in advancing a robust theistic moral argument. Because I hesitate to think such an analysis is forthcoming, and also because I take the theory to be an account of moral judgements in terms of the hypothetical assessments of an ideal observer, I do not advance a Divine command theory in the spirit of Adams and Owen. But if not an analysis outlining the sufficient conditions for moral judgements, the theory may still be true, even necessarily true, according to which the goodness of a state of affairs such as 'there being friendships' entails that it would be approved of by an IO.[23] The IO, as described here, is not God, but it does suggest the idea of God; indeed, at various stages in its development the theory has been deliberately explicated in a way that suggests a 'God's eye point of view'. In light of this, it is not at all surprising that much of the contemporary case for skepticism is often articulated in terms of skepticism about a 'God's eye point of view'.[24] In its classical form, theism envisages God as impartial, omnipercipient, and omniscient of the nonmoral facts. This is not *all* God is; there are an array of other Divine attributes, but it does include these.

If plausible—and I have argued elsewhere that it is—one might at the least note that it would not be good to be without the idea of God or a God-like ideal observer. And, if morality is indeed so suited, then to think along the lines specified in the ideal observer theory is to try to think along God's lines. Moore writes that '[o]f course, if morality is God's will or thoughts we need God to know morality, that is, what is on his mind.' In this context, Moore's views may be reversed. If we have justification for believing that God exists and that God satisfies the conditions for the IO, then to know what God approves and disapproves of we need to think in ways that are captured (under idealized form) in the IO theory, aiming at impartiality, omnipercipience, and knowledge of the nonmoral.

IV. GOD'S ETHICS

Moore seems to think that if there is an all good God who wills the good, then this not only adds nothing to the objectivity of morality, but adds little of value at all. I draw this conclusion from Moore's comments about the implications of God's willing that people be good and that God's plans are moral. At most, Moore refers to the 'happy coincidence' and 'happy fate' that would be 'nice', should theism provide additional reasons for being moral. Moore asks '[w]hy should we think that participating in someone's plans is a good thing?' Such comments obscure some of the important implications for ethics if theism is true. Many issues could be brought to the fore here about how Divine commands may create obligations, about how God's ensuring an afterlife can bolster moral activity, and so on, but I shall focus briefly upon only two points. The first concerns the scope of values in general and the second the good of Divine-human accord.[25] In developing each I comment on how theists treat the affective dimension of God's relation to the world.

Moore acknowledges the effort of theologians to provide an expanded notion of God as present and affectively available to created persons.

Many theologians would add . . . another attribute of God, which is that he cares for us, loves us, or has the potential to be our friend. They do this in order to make what such a God could will closer to things that are good for us. That is, just as friendship, love, and altruistic concern between persons are constituted at least in part by caring for the good of another as one cares for one's own good, God too is conceived in these ways so that he must be concerned with our good.

This portrait of Divine-human accord is often articulated today in light of a passibilist version of theism. Traditionally, many theists have been impassibilists, believing that God is not at all subject to passions. This has formidable defenders today, but it is often attacked as well for its (supposed) failure to take seriously the claims of religious experience, the nature of the emotions, and a plausible understanding of the Divine love. I adopt a passibilist understanding of the Divine, according to which one may properly speak of God's sorrow over ill and delight in the good.[26] If there is such a being, affectively concerned about the cosmos He has created, what effect does this have upon the moral enterprise? I believe that it enlarges the scope of ethics, intensifying the values at stake.

Given the moral objectivism Moore and I share, certain states of affairs are clearly bad, such as the deliberate torturing of an innocent person. I am allowing that this would indeed be bad even if (*per impossibile*) there were no God. Imagine, however, that there is a God along the passibile lines I propose. The torturing of an innocent person remains profoundly wrong; it did not *become* bad just because God sorrows over it. But given God's existence the evil is even more evil than if there were no God. In a God-filled cosmos, the torture involves both the brutal wronging of the person as well as the destroying of a being created and loved by God, a being with whom God affectively identifies. The crime is one against humanity and it is also sacrilege. Moore's reference to 'a happy coincidence, no doubt'—if there is an all good God—'but not a coincidence that adds a whit of objectivity to morality' glosses over the way theism magnifies the scope of values that come under the heading of 'objective values'. Given a theistic outlook, there is an intensifying or magnification of values. This is a theme that runs throughout a great deal of the theology of values. Here I shall only cite Kierkegaard as summing up the point: '[b]ecause sin is against God, it is infinitely magnified.'[27] We might also add, when good occurs it, too, is infinitely magnified. Given the truth of a passibilist theism, the existence of good states of affairs (justice, courage, friendship) is the object of Divine pleasure, which is itself a good, following the principle that pleasure in the good is itself good, a view defended by G. E. Moore and Brentanno, among others. I close with highlighting a further dimension of value that theism provides in the way of Divine-human concord.

If theistic passibilism is true and God is disclosed to us in religious experience, there is the added good value that moral action can involve something affectively and volitionally shared. Christian theological tradition speaks of the good of Divine-human harmony as something that involves more than the conformity of distinct wills, but as a communion or union between persons, a communion which has affective and cognitive dimensions as well as connative. In the *Summa Theologica* Aquinas goes so far as to speak of this in terms of friendship with God. The renewed interest in friendship in moral theory allows us to appreciate it as a fundamental good comprised of other goods (a constellation that might include generosity, play, knowledge, kindness, compassion) and yet more than any of their parts taken alone.[28]

If plausible, theism offers reasons for understanding the moral cosmos (or 'the ethical garden' in Moore's phrase) as more expansive on both ends than Moore's: it contains more ill (the cruel wrongdoing against creatures involves a wronging of God) and good (there is the good of Divine-human concord or friendship).

Moore comments on how theism might comfort in a limited way—'[y]et this kind of comfort, possible only if God exists, in no way supports or gives value to objective values. Such values have precisely the same objectivity in a theistic world that they have in a godless world.' But in a God-filled cosmos of shared life there is something present that would be missing in a world without God, the added value of Divine-human friendship, a friendship that may or may not be very comfortable. (Judging the religious literature on this theme, divine friendship is not always very 'comfortable'.)

I note at least two reasons why Moore may underestimate the positive role of theism in its expanded role in ethics on this front.

The first is that he fails to take seriously the passibilist outlook sketched above. If the expanded moral life is understood only in terms of the added good of fulfilling Divine commands, this seems remote from what religious philosophers like Aquinas, Bonaventura, William of Auxerre, and Peter Lombard refer to as the good of Divine human communion and shared life. The latter involves more than a creature responding to 'a divine requester, a divine promiser, a divine commander' (Moore's terms), but a religious sense of the abiding, affective presence of God. The context of duties and rights is not the sole terrain for locating the good of an affectively shared life of friendship.[29]

Secondly, Moore places a peculiar restriction on what he thinks is accessible to us in our having desires. He thinks the only objects of our desires are inanimate objects and activities.

Why should it be the case that our desires are only ultimately responsive to the desires of another like being? Isn't our experience just the opposite, namely, that what we desire and will is not the object of anyone else's desire or will but is some inanimate object or action? My desire to eat ice cream, my desire to be a more courageous person, my desire never to harm others unnecessarily, are not experienced as desires reflective of other persons' desires; rather, the objects of those desires are experienced as desirable *tout court*, for their own sake, not as desired by someone else.

I can desire things (states, events, processes, actions) without experiencing such desire as 'reflective of other persons' desires', but why should this always be so? Surely desires can be shared with the same object in mind (we desire to dance) and it would be odd to construe all desires as directed upon either inanimate objects or actions. When I desire that you be relieved of pain, your being relieved of pain seems neither an inanimate object nor an action.[30] In the religious literature that explores the good of Divine-human accord there is a rich portrait of shared, mutually reflective desire that serves to deepen human yearning to do good and avoid evil.

These final observations do not show that positing God's existence is essential for *objective morality*, but they are designed to highlight the way belief in God can augment, extend, and deepen one's ethical outlook and practice. The net effect of appealing to the basic value of divine-human friendship is not to motivate right action as something to be done solely for the sake of a friendship. Rather, I have sought to make explicit the religious framework in which right action unfolds, a framework that houses a great good not found in a nontheistic cosmos.

NOTES

1 All citations from Moore are from his chapter 'Good Without God'.
2 A useful survey of the material here is brought out in the collection of papers *Being and Goodness* edited by Scott Macdonald (Ithaca, Cornell University Press, 1991). For a contemporary articulation of Divine perfection and an outline of its role in philosophical theorizing see T. V. Morris's 'Perfect Being Theology,' *Nous*, vol. 21, 1987, at pp. 19–30.
3 A good example of how the analysis and example, counter-example method is carried out in epistemology *and* philosophy of religion is Alvin Plantinga's *Warrant: The Current Debate and Warrant and Proper Function* (both published by OUP, 1993). Much of construction of arguments for and against competing analyses involves the reliance upon thought experiments, an issue I explore in some detail in *Consciousness and the Mind of God* (Cambridge, CUP, 1994). See also Roger Sorensen's *Thought Experiments* (Oxford, OUP, 1992).
4 It is not at all obvious when one begs the question, and there is a substantial debate over precisely what is wrong with it. See Douglas Walton's *Begging the Question* (New York, Greenwood Press, 1991).

5 Some Christian theologians are quite reluctant to use the term 'person' to describe God, unless in a credal context of referring to the trinity. See, for example, Brian Davies's contribution to *Language, Meaning, and God* edited by Davies (London, Geoffrey Chapman, 1987), 'Classical Theism and the Doctrine of Divine Simplicity', especially pp. 62–5. I defend the coherence of theism at length in *Consciousness and the Mind of God*. See also Richard Swinburne's *The Coherence of Theism* (Oxford, OUP, 1979).

6 An articulate development of this understanding of Anselmian philosophical theology is heralded in T. V. Morris's *Anselmian Explorations* (Notre Dame, University of Notre Dame Press, 1987). Adopting these necessitarian theistic claims need not commit one to the ontological argument. A carefully constructed defence of the Anselmian understanding of God is developed by Paul Tidman in 'The Epistemology of Evil Possibilities', *Faith and Philosophy* 10:2, 1993, at pp. 181–197.

7 T. V. Morris and Christopher Menzel defend a more radical version of *causa sui* than I can accept. See their paper 'Absolute creation', *American Philosophical Quarterly* 23, 1986, at pp. 353–62, and my 'The Limits of Power' in *Philosophy and Theology*, vol. 2, 1990, at pp. 115–24.

8 A. C. Ewing highlights some of the difficulty of defining idealism in light of a theistic metaphysics in his *Idealism: A Critical Study* which, despite its age, is still a superb introduction to this school of philosophy (London, Methuen & Co. Ltd., 1933).

9 The argument to be developed below will be neutral with respect to a variety of moral theories. My chief concern is only that the characterization of morality used in arguments for and against theism not be loaded from the outset in a way that unfairly rules out of court either position. In a note Moore claims he has 'no sleight-of-hand in mind' with begging the question against the theist. His gloss 8 is curious. 'If God creates moral qualities whose existence is independent of *our* beliefs in their existence, these qualities are objective, by my notion of objectivity' (emphasis Moore's). But in his chapter he defines moral objectivity in terms of being independent of what 'any person or group of persons believes about them' and given that Moore's theism casts God as a person, this appears to preclude the dependence of morality upon God from the outset. In reply to Moore's note I nowhere contend that 'no question' Moore wishes to ask would be begged if he altered his strategy in the ways I propose. Moore might wish for all kinds of things. My point against Moore is that his insistence at the beginning that 'God' cannot be defined with explicit ethical content and that objective morality be defined in a way that (I believe) excludes theistic dependence are illicit moves in a fair debate. I am not, then, urging Moore to be 'more generous' (as he puts it) but fair. My effort in this chapter is to show how an atheist (or any opponent) can allow provisionally the notion that God is essentially good and then use this to mount an attack on a moral theistic argument. There is plenty of room for objections including fundamental criticism of whether the initial provisional assumption is coherent. Obviously the result is nothing like Moore's analogy in his note ('the assumption that there are objective values would help the argument that there are objective values') which I believe is much more plausibly read as a compressed version of his argument

(the assumption that ethics cannot have a personal ground helps the argument that ethics cannot have a theistic personal ground).

10 For a more extended treatment of this and other theistic arguments, see my *Contemporary Philosophy of Religion* (Oxford, Basil Blackwell, forthcoming).

11 See, for example, *Metaphysics* by Richard Taylor (Englewood Cliffs, Prentice-Hall, 1963), *The Cosmological Argument* by William Rowe (Princeton, Princeton U.P., 1975), *The Intelligible Universe* by Huge Meynell (Totowa, Barnes and Noble, 1982), *The Cosmological Argument* by Bruce Reichenbach (Springfield, Ill., Charles Thomas, 1972), *The Cosmological Argument from Plato to Leibniz* by William Craig (New York, Barnes and Noble, 1980) and *The Kalam Cosmological Argument* also by Craig (New York, Barnes and Noble, 1979), *The Existence of God* by Richard Swinburne (Oxford, OUP, 1979) *Beyond the New Theism* by Germain Grisez (Notre Dame, University of Notre Dame Press, 1975). The aim of these arguments is not to show 'how God is necessary' (Moore's phrase), but to provide reasons for thinking *that* there is a necessarily existing being whose activity enters into an overriding account of our contingent cosmos.

12 To indicate the proximity of my argument with Finnis's, but also to duck the responsibility of having to indicate at each place where we part ways, I call what follows 'a cosmological-ethical argument' as opposed to 'an ethical cosmological argument'.

13 The importance of developing cumulative arguments is underscored in much of Richard Swinburne's work. See also Basil Mitchell's *The Justification of Religious Belief* (New York, Seabury, 1974).

14 In *Consciousness and the Mind of God* I defend the intelligibility of theism over against physicalist critics, both philosophical and theological. Moore seems to think a lot of things could be physical, 'numbers, kinds, properties, classes, and relations, may also be grudgingly admitted into such a macro-level, physicalist ontology.' These are items few strict physicalists admit, notwithstanding Penelope Maddy's brave attempt to develop physicalistic Platonism. See Bob Hale's discussion of the issues in 'Physicalism and Mathematics', *Objections to Physicalism*, Howard Robinson, ed. (Oxford, Clarendon Press, 1993), at pp. 39–59. Moore himself seems to think numbers are not spatio-temporal. On the difficulties facing materialism here, note William Lycan's comment: 'My appeal to sets . . . is indeed an embarrassment to physicalism, since sets et al. are nonspatiotemporal, acausal items . . . eventually set theory will have to be either naturalized or rejected, if a thoroughgoing physicalism is to be maintained.' *Consciousness* (Cambridge, Mass., MIT Press, 1987), at p. 90. As an aside, I note that, taken by itself, the questioner Moore cites from a Texan audience ('where do these moral laws come from') is not necessarily presupposing the source must have spatio-temporal location. I might well ask Moore where he got certain premises for an argument without assuming them to have some kind of spatial source. In the theistic moral argument mapped out in this chapter identifying a personal source for what Moore casts as 'impersonal' values, there is no assumption that the source is spatio-temporal.

15 Swinburne is the best known defender of the appeal to simplicity in theistic arguments. See his *The Existence of God* (Oxford, Clarendon Press, 1979). In this and other theistic arguments, Swinburne weighs evidence he believes provides

probative, evidential credibility on behalf of theism. There is therefore stress on what makes theism reasonable, not on what 'demands' a theistic explanation or makes a theistic account 'necessary'.

16 Descartes's stance is laid out succinctly in his letters. See especially *Descartes: Philosophical Letters*, translated and edited by Anthony Kenny (Oxford, OUP, 1970), at pp. 11, 14, 236, and 150.

17 See, for example, *Does God Have a Nature?* by Alvin Plantinga (Milwaukee, Marquette University, 1980); 'Absolute Creation' by Morris and Menzel; 'Theism, Platonism, and the Metaphysics of Mathematics' by Menzel in *Christian Theism and the Problems of Philosophy*, Michael Beaty, ed. (Notre Dame, University of Notre Dame Press, 1990); 'God, Creator of Kinds and Possibilities, *Requiescant universalia ante res'* by James Ross in *Rationality, Religious Belief and Moral Commitment*, R. Audi and W. Wainwright, eds. (Ithaca, Cornell University Press, 1986), 'The Necessity of Nature' by Alfred Freddoso in *Midwest Studies in Philosophy* X (Minneapolis, University of Minnesota Press, 1986) and 'Toward an Aristotelian Theory of Abstract Objects', by Michael Loux and 'Divine Necessity' by R. M. Adams, *Journal of Philosophy*, 80:11, Nov. 1983, at pp. 741–46. For an earlier development of this outlook, see Leibniz' *Monadology*, ss. 43 and 44.

18 'Absolute Creation', above at n. 17 at p. 357.

19 Plantinaga, *Does God Have a Nature?*, above at n. 17 at p. 3.

20 See, for example, Plantinga's *Warrant and Proper Functioning* (above at n. 3).

21 See two of my papers, 'The Ideal Aesthetic Observer', *British Journal of Aesthetics*, 30:1, 1990, at pp. 1–13, and 'Relativizing the Ideal Observer Theory', *Philosophy and Phenomenological Research* 49:1, 1988, at pp. 123–38.

22 Moore's way of putting the relation between the moral on the nonmoral is problematic. He writes that 'moral qualities . . . supervene upon, and in some sense are identical to, nonmoral (i.e., natural) properties'. At least in the way the term is used by most discussants in the philosophical literature (e.g. Kim, Sosa, Chisholm, and DePaul), the relation of supervenience is not an identity relation. In so far as Moore wishes to *identify* the moral with the nonmoral, he risks undermining his moral objectivism.

23 I try to clearly demarcate a version of the ideal observer theory that is distinguishable from a divine command theory in 'The Divine Command Theory of Ethics and the Ideal Observer', *Sophia*, 1983, at pp. 3–8. For an example of how a more ambitious theorist will critique the IO theory, see Peter Forrest's paper 'An Argument for the Divine Command Theory of Right Action', *Sophia* 28:1, 1989, at pp. 2–19.

24 This is brought out brilliantly by Roger Trigg in *Rationality and Science* (Oxford, Basil Blackwell Publishers, 1993).

25 I address the ethical and theological importance of the afterlife in 'Why We Need Immortality', *Modern Theology*, 6:4, 1990, at pp. 367–379, and the way in which Divine commands can give rise to obligations such as the prohibition against suicide in 'God's Estate', *Journal of Religious Ethics*, 20:1, Spring 1992, at pp. 69–92.

26 'The Passability of God', *Religious Studies* 25, 1989, pp. 217–24.

27 *The Sickness Unto Death*, trans. Howard and Edna Hong (Princeton, Princeton

U.P., 1980), p. 80. I defend this thesis in 'The Intensity of Theism', *Sophia*, 31:3, 1992, at pp. 61–73.

28 A book that spearheaded the new look on friendship is Lawrence Blum's *Friendship, Altruism, and Morality* (London, Routledge and Kegan Paul, 1980). Borrowing a term from G. E. Moore, I believe the good of friendship to be an organic whole. The intimate character of Divine-human friendship is brought out with great clarity and charm in the work of St Aelred of Rievaulx in *The Mirror of Charity* and *Spiritual Friendship* (12th century) (various translations and editions).

29 See, for example, St Bonaventura's *Itinerarius Menti's in Deum*, especially ch. II, William of Auxerre's *Summa Aurea*, II, ch. one, Peter Lombard's *Sentences*, Bk. I, and Duns Scotus' *Ouodlibet*. While these writers adopt the formal theological teaching of Divine impassibility, they did not think God incarnate was impassible. With theistic passibilism fully secured, there is considerable room for expanding the understanding of reported Divine-human union. For a philosophical treatment of this see William Alston's 'The Indwelling of the Holy Spirit' in *Philosophy and the Christian Faith*, T. V. Morris, ed. (Notre Dame, University of Notre Dame Press, 1985) at pp. 121–50. Of course many have little sympathy for the epistemic credentials of religious experience, but the philosophical defence of such reports is impressive. See, for example, Alston's *Perceiving God* (Ithaca, Cornell University Press, 1993). I defend the intelligibility of shared divine-human life in 'The Coinherence', *Christian Scholars Review*, 18:4, 1989, at pp. 333–45.

30 For some of the rich ways in which desire may be construed see the collection of papers, *The Ways of Desire*, Joel Marks, ed. (Chicago, Precedent Publishing Inc., 1986).

INDEX

abortion 17, 18, 45, 107, 108, 109, 110, 111
  n. 3, 199
absolutism 30, 244
activism 132, 169 n. 10
Adams, A. 190
Adams, J. Q. 183, 192 n. 25
Adams, R. M. 231, 248, 263 n. 18, 268 n. 83,
  269 n. 108, 282 n. 27, 288–9, 290, 294,
  300 n. 17
adjudication; *see* judicial reasoning
Aelred of Rievaulx, Saint 301 n. 28
afterlife 300 n. 25
agnosticism 288
alcoholism 143
Alien and Sedition Acts 147 n. 20
Allen, R. E. 25 n. 66
Alston, W. 228, 301 n. 29
Althusser, L. 89
American Law Institute 166
Angle, P. M. 112 n. 5
Anscombe, G. E. M. 264 n. 24, 266 n. 67
Anselm 286
anti-perfectionism 74
anti-realism 223, 276–7
anti-utilitarianism 53, 54, 55, 56, 57, 58, 59,
  65, 66, 67, 71, 72, 73, 74, 77, 78, 81, 89,
  90, 93, 94, 99
Aquinas, Thomas 1, 2, 4, 5, 7, 11, 18 nn. 1
  and 3, 19 nn. 9, 10 and 11, 21 n. 24, 22
  n. 31, 24 nn. 50 and 57, 107, 108, 170
  n. 22, 171 n. 31, 173 n. 39, 174 n. 42, 175
  n. 51, 182, 184, 185, 186, 195, 198, 200,
  201, 202, 208, 227, 228, 249, 250, 278
  n. 7, 282 n. 25, 284, 286, 296
Aristotle, 1, 2, 4, 7, 8, 12, 14, 18 n. 1, 20
  nn. 18 and 20, 21 n. 23, 22 n. 32, 24
  n. 61, 26 n. 80, 29, 30, 43, 51, 201, 217,
  218, 220, 237, 278 n. 7, 281 n. 20
Arrow, K. J. 70, 83 n. 35
Articles of Confederation 176 n. 61
atheism 298 n. 9
Augustine 13, 107, 170 n. 22, 201, 284
Austin, J. 228, 265 n. 54
authority 1, 2, 96, 123, 128 n. 2, 165, 171
  n. 25; *see also* government(s)
autonomy 113, 114, 116, 119, 120, 121, 128 n.
  10, 131, 132, 134–5, 136, 148 nn. 30 and 34

Bacon 186
Baker, Jr., J. S. 178 n. 68

Barksdale, E. 193 n. 38
Barnett, R. E. 168 n. 5, 170 n. 17, 172 n. 36,
  174 nn. 46 and 47, 175 nn. 55 and 57,
  179 n. 73, 188, 189
Barry, B. 81 n. 17, 83 n. 34
Beccaria 249, 250
behaviourism 203
Bell, D., 80 n. 5
Berger, R. 170 n. 16
Berlin, I. 30, 46 n. 9
Berns, W. 191 n. 7
Biden, J. 151, 152
bigotry 126, 142, 145, 150 n. 66
Bill of Rights 52, 165, 176 nn. 57 and 62, 177
  n. 70, 181, 183–4, 188, 189, 190
Black, C. 165
Black, H. L. 182, 183, 187
Blackburn, S. 292
Blum, L. 301 n. 28
Bonaventura, Saint 284, 296, 301 n. 29
Bork, R. 151, 152, 168 nn. 6, 7 and 9
Boswell, J. 47 n. 41
Boyd, R. 263 n. 19
Boyle, J. 11, 19 nn. 12 and 14, 20 n. 19, 30,
  196, 209 n. 3
Brentanno 295
Brink, D. 263 n. 19
Brown, P. 223
Buchanan, A. 80 n. 8, 83 nn. 33 and 37, 84
  n. 42
Buchanan, P. 149 n. 64
burdens of judgement; *see* judgemental
  toleration
Bush, President 151

Caiaphas 275
Callicles 17, 79
Calvin, J. 72, 73, 94
Catholicism 184, 236
causal order 203, 204, 205, 206, 291
causation 204, 224, 230, 232, 252, 253, 254,
  255, 289
Chase, S. 181
Chisholm 300 n. 22
Christianity 200, 274–5, 280 n. 17, 282 n. 25
Christlieb, T. 282 n. 25
Cicero 182, 200
citizenship 68, 71, 85 n. 55, 124, 125, 126,
  127, 129 n. 17, 131, 139, 140–1, 142–3,
  144, 145, 146

civil law 179 n. 72, 186
civil rights 187
Clarke 284
coercion 6, 7, 8, 10, 62, 120, 121, 122, 123,
  127, 128 n. 9, 131, 133, 134, 135, 138, 145,
  147 n. 27, 148 nn. 30 and 38, 154–5, 184
coercive paternalism 123, 126, 127, 128, 129
  n. 12, 131, 135–6, 137, 138, 139, 145, 146;
  see also paternalism
cognitive capacity 249
Coke, E. 18 n. 3
common good 1, 4, 5, 6, 7, 8, 13, 15, 16, 18,
  20 n. 17, 21 n. 26, 29, 140, 149 n. 64, 282
  n. 25
common law 165–6, 178 nn. 68 and 71, 179
  n. 72
Common Law, The (Holmes) 132
common principles 126
community 6, 17, 21 n. 26, 29, 125, 134, 141,
  142, 190, 208
consequentialism 199, 245, 246, 279 n. 15
constitutional adjudication; *see* judicial
  reasoning
constitutional amendment 167
constitutional law 22 n. 37, 151, 165, 179 n.
  73, 181
constitutional legitimacy 119, 128 n. 7, 139,
  146, 171 n. 34
constitutional rights 117, 118, 119, 161–2,
  164, 185, 187; *see also* rights
constitutionalism 186
constitutionality 177 n. 65
conventionalism 228
conversational fixation 96, 98
co-operation 66, 67, 68, 75, 91, 96, 108–9,
  111
co-ordination 123, 139
Copleston, Father Frederick 254
cosmological argument 288, 292, 295, 299 n.
  12
cosmology 225, 252, 253, 254, 255, 258, 284,
  287, 288, 291, 296, 297, 299
Council of Trent 13
Craig, W. 288, 299 n. 11
Croly, H. 77

Davidson, D. 237
Davies, B. 230, 250, 298 n. 5
De Bono Coniugali (Augustine) 13
de Coulange, F. 47 n. 41
de Tocqueville, A. 50, 80 n. 6, 87, 95, 96, 97,
  99
Decalogue 11
Declaration of Independence 181, 183, 184,
  185, 186, 192 n. 25
della Volpe, G. 81 n. 14
Demand of Justice; *see* justice

deontology 51, 241, 242, 243, 244, 245, 246,
  266 nn. 65 and 67
DePaul 300 n. 22
Descartes 290, 300 n. 16
descriptive jurisprudence 228, 260
desert 69, 80, 82 n. 26, 90, 91, 92, 93, 100,
  101, 102, 200, 201, 202, 204, 207, 208, 219
determinism 203
Dewey, J. 29, 46 n. 6
Difference Principle; *see* distributive justice
Dionysius 284
distributive justice 51, 52, 53, 54, 55, 59, 60,
  65, 70, 71, 79, 82 n. 26, 87, 88, 89, 90, 91,
  92, 93, 94, 95, 97, 98, 100, 101, 102, 103,
  104 nn. 1, 4 and 6
divine command theory 294, 296, 300 nn.
  23 and 25
divine impassibility; *see* theistic passibilism
divine law 249, 273
divine will 271, 286
Dosteovsky 221
Douglas, S. 110, 111
Douglas, W. O. 181
Dover, Sir Kenneth 24 n. 60
Due Process Clause 188
Durkheim, E. 72
Dworkin, G. 81 n. 12, 84 n. 43
Dworkin, R. 9, 10, 23 n. 42, 45, 48 n. 47, 80
  n. 7, 196, 197, 198, 209 nn. 5, 6 and 8,
  212 nn. 32 and 35, 214

efficiency 133–4
egalitarian liberalism 49, 50, 51, 52, 53, 55,
  56, 57, 59, 60, 61, 65, 71, 75, 79, 80, 87,
  88, 93, 95, 96, 97, 98, 99, 103, 104 n. 4,
  131, 132, 169 n. 10; *see also* liberalism
egalitarianism 50, 52, 56, 60, 87, 96
employment 114
enactment 153, 154, 157, 158, 159, 163, 166, 167
enlightenment 63, 105 n. 8, 184
entitlement 105 n. 6
envy 84 n. 51
Epicurus 278 n. 7
epistemology 227, 241, 291–2, 297 n. 3, 301
  n. 29
equal opportunity 52, 61
equality 50, 71, 77, 78, 95, 96, 98, 100, 101
espionage 20 n. 17
ethical cosmology; *see* cosmology
ethical naturalism 232; *see also* naturalism
ethical realism 293
ethics 246, 251, 252, 257, 261, 271, 293, 294,
  295, 299 n. 9; *see also* theological ethics
Ethics (Aristotle) 1
euthanasia 138, 148 n. 40
Ewing, A. C. 298 n. 8
existentialism 209, 221

fairness 59, 65, 66, 79, 103
federalism 134
Federalist, The 77, 134, 186, 188
Feinberg, J. 212 n. 32
Festugiére, A. J. 24 n. 62
Fields, W. C. 27
Fifth Amendment 175 n. 54
Finnis, J. 11, 19 nn. 12 and 14, 20 nn. 18, 19
    and 22, 21 nn. 24 and 25, 23 n. 42, 24
    nn. 50 and 60, 27, 28, 29, 30, 31, 32, 33,
    34, 35, 36, 37, 38, 39, 40, 41, 43, 44, 45, 46
    n. 16, 47 n. 31, 83 n. 32, 147 n. 17, 196,
    198–9, 209 n. 3, 210 nn. 15 and 20, 215,
    217, 222, 223–4, 229, 232, 235, 251–3,
    254, 255, 256–7, 258, 262 n. 3, 265 nn. 41,
    47 and 48, 269 n. 95, 279 n. 14, 282 n. 25,
    288, 299 n. 12
First Amendment 161, 184, 187
First Principle; *see* egalitarian liberalism
Firth, R. 276, 293
Fisher, C. 281 n. 25
Foot, P. 279 n. 17, 281 n. 20
Forrest, P. 300 n. 23
Fortescue, Sir John 18 n. 3
Fortin, E. L. 192 n. 29
founding fathers 213; *see also* framers'
    intentions
Fourteenth Amendment 161, 166, 175 n. 51,
    178 n. 70, 188
framers' intentions 159, 160, 161, 172
    n. 35, 175 n. 51, 176 n. 57, 179 n. 72,
    182, 186, 187, 188; *see also* founding
    fathers
Fredosso, A. 290, 300 n. 17
free markets 104 n. 1
freedom; *see* liberty
freedom of speech 52, 115, 145, 169 n. 12,
    179 n. 72
Friedman, B. 179 n. 74
friendship 5, 13, 14, 15, 32, 36, 39, 42, 297,
    301 n. 28
Fugitive Slave Act 209 n. 6
Fuller, L. L. 151, 168 n. 4, 210 n. 9
Fumerton, R. 268 n. 74
fundamental rights 55, 99, 115, 131, 149
    n. 54, 177 n. 65, 187, 190; *see also* rights

Galston, W. A. 59, 81 nn. 12 and 13, 83
    nn. 33, 35 and 39, 84 nn. 40 and 43, 94
Garcia, J. 262 nn. 11 and 12, 264 n. 39, 278
    n. 9, 279 n. 14, 286
Garner 264 n. 27
Geach, P. T. 266 n. 67, 268 nn. 72 and 73,
    269 n. 109, 270 n. 111, 281 n. 20
George, R. P. 11, 20 n. 19, 21 n. 22, 24 n. 60,
    146 n. 2, 148 n. 28, 149 n. 62, 198, 210
    n. 16

Gibson, A. B. 267 n. 70
Glaucon 246, 268 n. 74
Glover, J. 263 n. 22
God 183, 185, 186, 187, 200, 221, 222,
    223–5, 226, 227, 228, 229, 230–1, 232,
    233, 234–5, 238, 239, 241, 242, 244, 245,
    247, 249–50, 251, 252, 253, 254, 255,
    256–8, 259–60, 261, 262 nn. 12 and 13,
    263 n. 20, 266 nn. 64 and 67, 268 n. 72,
    269 n. 109, 270 n. 111, 271, 272–3, 274,
    276–7, 278 n. 3, 280 n. 17, 282 n. 25,
    283–4, 285–6, 287–8, 289, 290, 291,
    292, 293, 294–5, 296, 297, 298 nn. 5, 6
    and 9
Goldsworthy, J. 232
Goodrich, E. 172 n. 38
Gorgias (Plato) 15
Gourevitch, V. 82 n. 23
government(s) 7, 8, 107, 113–15, 119, 120,
    121, 122, 123, 124, 125, 127, 128 n. 2,
    131, 140, 190; *see also* authority; limited
    government
Granger, P. B. 175 n. 53
Grisez, G. 3, 11, 13, 19 nn. 12 and 14, 20
    n. 19, 21 n. 22, 25 n. 70, 26 n. 77, 27, 30,
    31, 32, 34, 35, 36, 38, 39, 46 nn. 16, 18
    and 20, 47 n. 27, 196, 209 n. 3, 217, 252,
    254, 288, 299 n. 11
Grotius, H. 221

Hale, R. 299 n. 14
Hamburger, P. A. 170 n. 16, 172 n. 35, 178
    nn. 67 and 72
Hamilton, A. 146 n. 10, 188
Hampton, 128 n. 4
Hare, R. M. 264 n. 29
Harman, G. 280 n. 19
Hart, H. L. A. 56, 57, 83 nn. 27, 28 and 29,
    151, 168 n. 3, 210 n. 9, 265 n. 54
Hegel, G. W. F. 280 n. 20
Henry, P. 189, 190
Heyd, D. 240, 255, 266 n. 58
Heyman, S. J. 170 n. 17, 174 n. 44, 175
    n.48
Hittinger, R. 46, 169 n. 13, 173 n. 39, 191
    n. 10, 282 n. 25
Hobbes, T. 72, 182, 185, 186, 187, 220, 268
    n. 74, 278 n. 7
Holmes, O. W. 132, 209 n. 4
Homer 25 n. 73
Hooker, R. 186
Hoose, B. 280 n. 18
human goods 4, 13, 14, 15, 16, 17, 19 n. 11,
    20 n. 22, 21 n. 26, 29, 30, 32, 38, 39, 40,
    44, 51, 57, 67, 73, 80, 85 n. 55, 93, 94, 97,
    99, 198, 199, 217, 218, 247, 250–1, 253,
    255, 256, 258, 283, 296

human rights 19 n. 13, 174 n. 45; *see also*
    rights
Hume, D. 78, 79, 232, 293

ideal observer theory 293–4, 300 n. 23
idealism 298 n. 8
immorality 200, 217
impersonalism 240
inalienable rights 163, 175 nn. 55 and 56,
    177 n. 70, 183, 184, 185, 190; *see also*
    rights
indemonstrabilia 217, 218, 219
independence 121, 122, 135, 136, 137, 148
    nn. 30 and 34
industrialism 95
injustice 99
internalism 291
Iredell, J. 181

James, W. 239, 241, 255
Jefferson, T. 77, 182, 184, 185, 186, 187, 213
Jocasta 203
John XXIII, Pope 19 n. 12
John Paul II, Pope 13, 26 n. 79, 280 n. 18
Johnson, W. 181
judgemental toleration 74, 75, 76, 97, 100,
    101, 107, 108, 111; *see also* toleration
judicial reasoning 152, 153, 169 n. 13, 181,
    197
judicial review 115, 131, 153, 169 n. 10, 177
    n. 65, 178 n. 67
jurisdiction 139, 178 n. 70
jurisprudence 162, 182, 197–8, 199, 213, 265
    n. 54
justice 44, 45, 51, 52, 53, 54, 55, 57, 59, 60,
    61, 62, 63, 64, 65, 66, 67, 68, 69, 71, 73,
    74, 75, 76, 77, 78, 79, 80, 82 nn. 25 and
    26, 84 n. 48, 87, 88, 89, 90, 91, 93, 94, 95,
    98, 102, 103, 104, nn. 2 and 4, 107, 109,
    110, 111, 128 n. 5, 154, 157, 186, 212 n.
    35, 220
justification 11, 211 n. 28, 217

Kant, I. 26 n. 80, 108, 202, 213, 215, 221, 243,
    247, 248, 250, 262 n. 8, 268 nn. 83 and
    86, 272–3, 276
Kennedy, A. 168 n. 7
Kennedy, J. F. 77
Kepler 227, 228, 229, 239, 291
Kierkegaard 295
Kim, 300 n. 22
King, M. L. 197
Koppelman, A. 36, 38, 47 nn. 30, 32 and
    41
Koresh, D. 155
Kramer, C. S. 169 n. 14
Kymlicka 128 n. 4

Lane, R. 85 n. 53
Larmore, C. 85 n. 55
law on the diffusion rate of gas 227, 291
Laws (Plato) 14
laws of planetary motion 227, 228, 229, 239,
    291
Lawson, G. 175 n. 53
legal philosophy 196
legal positivism 197, 214, 265 n. 54, 278 n. 3;
    see also positivism
legal rights 207; *see also* rights
legitimacy of conduct 159, 160
legitimacy of law 153–4, 155, 156, 157–8,
    159, 161, 162, 163, 167, 176 n. 60
legitimate authority; *see* constitutional
    legitimacy
Leibnitz 284, 300 n. 17
Letter on Toleration (Locke) 184
Levinson, M. H. 169 n. 14, 187
Lewis, D. 281 n. 24
Lewis, W. 177 n. 66
liberal fact 97, 98, 99, 101, 103, 105 n. 8
liberal toleration (non-judgemental) 107,
    108; *see also* toleration
liberal tyranny 145
liberalism 27, 28, 43, 44, 45, 50, 51, 54, 95,
    103, 131, 132, 133, 134, 147 n. 17, 150 n.
    65, 160, 174 nn. 43 and 46, 212 n. 35; *see*
    also egalitarian liberalism; minimalist
    liberalism; neutralist liberation;
    political liberalism; voluntarist
    liberalism
libertarianism 27, 79, 162, 175 n. 54
liberty 9, 52, 55, 56, 57, 59, 60, 62, 65, 70, 71,
    72, 73, 74, 77, 79, 85 n. 55, 87, 98, 100,
    105 n. 6, 113, 115, 116–17, 119, 120, 122,
    123, 128 nn. 5 and 6, 132, 134, 146 n. 8,
    149 n. 55, 150 n. 65, 159, 162, 164, 165,
    167, 169 n. 12, 176 n. 64, 177 n. 65, 178
    n. 71, 179 n. 72, 184, 200, 203, 206, 207,
    208; *see also* political liberty
liberty principle; *see* egalitarian liberalism
license 179 n. 72
limited government 1, 2, 4, 9, 11, 18 n. 1, 28,
    29, 30, 49, 50, 51, 52, 53, 56, 57, 58, 59,
    60, 61, 62, 63, 65, 75, 79, 80, 87, 88, 89,
    95, 96, 97, 98, 100, 102, 103–4, 115, 117,
    119, 131, 132, 133, 134, 169 n. 10; *see also*
    government(s)
Lincoln, A. 77, 110, 111, 150 n. 64
Locke, J. 29, 49, 58, 93, 177 n. 67, 184, 185,
    186, 187, 192 n. 25, 195, 208 n. 2, 213,
    218
Logos 200
Lombard, P. 296, 301 n. 29
Loux, M. 290, 300 n. 17
Luther, M. 72, 94

Lutz, C. E. 24 nn. 58 and 62
Lutz, D. S. 176 n. 57
Lycan, W. 263 n. 19, 299 n. 14
Lycophron 7, 22 n. 32

McAffee, T.B. 170 n. 16, 172 n. 35
McCarthyism 117
McCloskey, H. J. 212 n. 32
McConnell, M. 172 n. 35, 173 n. 39
Macedo, S. 10, 11, 12, 13, 17, 18, 22 n. 33, 23 n. 41, 25 n. 76, 26 n. 82, 156, 279 n. 14
Mach, E. 214
McIntyre, A. 63
Mackie, J. L. 221, 226, 229, 230, 270 n. 115
Mackinnon, C. 40
Maddy, P. 299 n. 14
Madison, J. 134, 147 n. 20, 159, 172 n. 37, 176 nn. 57, 59 and 62, 177 n. 70, 179 n. 75, 186, 188, 189–90
majoritarianism 162
majority rule 51
Making Men Moral: Civil Liberties and Public Morality (George) 10
manipulation 120, 129 n. 11, 135
Marshall, J. 188, 189
Marx, K. 50, 89
Massey, C. R. 170 n. 17, 175 n. 48
Masugi, K. 169 nn. 11 and 13, 173 n. 39
materialism 289, 299 n. 14
Mayer, D. N. 170 n. 17, 175 n. 48
meaning 261
Menzel, C. 290, 298 n. 7, 300 n. 17
Merquior, J. Q. 81 n. 14
meta-ethics 225, 226, 231, 241–2, 260, 270 n. 109, 281 n. 20
metaphysics 64, 75, 109, 203, 212 n. 35, 214, 227, 229, 230, 231, 232, 241, 254, 259–60, 276, 286, 288–91, 292, 298 n. 8
methodology 172 n. 35, 283
Meynell, H. 288, 299 n. 11
Michael, H. K. 170 n. 16
Miller, F. D. 81 n. 19, 82 nn. 23 and 26, 83 n. 34
minimalist liberalism 108, 109, 110, 111 n. 4; *see also* liberalism
Mitchell, B. 299 n. 13
modal realism 240, 281 n. 24
moira 200, 203
Montesquieu 186
Moore, A. W. 268 n. 86
Moore, G. E. 241, 281 n. 20, 292, 295, 301 n. 28
Moore, M. S. 211 n. 24, 262 n. 10, 263 n. 19, 265 nn. 42, 43, 46, 52 and 53, 266 nn. 55, 64 and 65, 268 nn. 74 and 85, 269 n. 101, 271, 273, 275–6, 277, 278 nn. 3, 5 and 11,

280 n. 20, 282 n. 28, 283, 285, 286–7, 288–9, 290–1, 292–3, 294–5, 296, 298 n. 9, 299 nn. 11 and 14, 300 n. 22
moral certainty 196, 197, 208, 214, 251, 268 n. 72, 278 n. 11
moral disagreement; *see* moral diversity
moral dissensus 93
moral diversity 102, 144, 162, 198, 262 n. 13, 283, 284, 285, 287, 292, 293
moral facts; *see* rights
moral knowledge; *see* moral realism
moral judgement 38, 46, 78, 107, 110, 199, 211 n. 24, 212 n. 35, 240, 241, 245, 246, 248, 257, 258, 270 n. 109, 293, 294
moral justification 273
moral law 149 n. 62, 173 n. 38, 214–15, 218, 221, 222, 224–5, 226, 227, 228, 229, 230, 231, 232, 234, 236, 239, 240, 241, 242, 243, 244, 245, 247, 248, 250, 251, 252, 255, 257, 258, 260–1, 262 n. 11, 263 n. 20, 271, 272, 273, 275, 276, 278 nn. 5 and 11, 280 n. 17, 283, 286–7, 290, 291, 292, 294, 295, 297
moral life 30, 217, 279 n. 17
moral necessity 215, 277
moral norms 19 n. 12, 234, 235, 242, 243, 244, 245, 267 n. 69, 273, 279 n. 11
moral objectivity; *see* moral law
moral obligation 128, 153, 154, 155, 156, 157, 158, 160, 215–16, 234, 235, 236, 237, 238, 239, 240–1, 242, 260, 271, 275, 276, 293, 296
moral order 252, 253, 277, 282 n. 25
moral paternalism 123, 127, 128, 129, 131, 135, 138, 139, 145–6; *see also* paternalism
moral philosophy; *see* moral realism
moral powers 67, 68, 70, 71, 72, 73, 74, 77, 78, 99; *see also* reasonableness; rationality
moral prescriptions 198
moral principles 16, 156, 196, 197, 201, 202, 208, 212 n. 35, 214, 215–16
moral qualities; *see* moral realism
moral realism 183, 196, 197, 199, 200, 201–2, 208, 211 n. 24, 212 n. 35, 213, 215, 222, 223, 225, 226, 228–9, 231, 232, 233, 234, 235, 238, 239, 240, 241, 242, 246, 248, 249–50, 251, 252, 253, 254, 255, 256, 259–60, 261, 262 n. 11, 263 nn. 19 and 39, 270 n. 112, 271, 275, 276, 278 nn. 5 and 11, 279 n. 17, 282 n. 28, 283, 287, 289, 290, 291, 293, 298 n. 9, 300 n. 22; *see also* anti-realism
moral reason; *see* moral judgement
moral right 174 n. 45, 238, 253, 296; *see also* rights
moral science 217

moral skepticism 209, 216, 223, 225, 246, 248, 249, 261, 268 n. 74, 270 n. 115, 271, 275, 277, 286; *see also* skepticism
moral sovereignty 236
moral theory 78, 95, 196, 202, 212 n. 35, 268 n. 73, 296, 298 n. 9
moral truth; *see* moral realism
morality 3, 7, 28, 109, 111, 120, 145, 149 n. 64, 150 n. 66, 160, 198, 199, 201, 202, 210 n. 20, 215, 221, 225, 229, 232, 233, 234, 237, 241, 242–3, 244, 245, 247, 248, 249, 250, 251, 253, 255, 256, 258, 260–1, 263 n. 20, 266 n. 64, 267 n. 69, 268 n. 72, 268 n. 83, 271–4, 276, 277, 278 nn. 3, 7 and 11, 279 nn. 14 and 17, 280 n. 17, 287, 294, 297, 298 n. 9; *see also* sexual morality
Morris, T. V. 290, 297 n. 2, 298 nn. 6 and 7, 300 n. 17
Mother Teresa 58, 93, 95
motivation 225
Murdock, I. 270 n. 112
Murray, J. C. 183–5, 186
mutable law 182
mutable rights 182; *see also* rights

Nagel, T. 23 n. 40, 30, 46 n. 9, 58–9, 80 n. 9, 81 nn. 11 and 18, 83 nn. 35, 38 and 39, 94, 120, 128 nn. 4 and 8, 211 n. 27, 256
natural law 1, 2, 3, 5, 6, 7, 10, 11, 27, 28, 29, 30, 31, 32, 33, 34, 35, 36, 37, 38, 39, 40, 42, 43, 44, 49, 51, 151, 152, 159–60, 169 nn. 11 and 13, 170 n. 22, 173 n. 39, 174 n. 41, 175 n. 56, 177 n. 65, 179 n. 72, 181, 182, 183, 184–5, 186, 187, 188, 195, 196, 197, 198, 199, 200, 201, 202, 203, 208, 209, 212 n. 35, 213, 214, 216, 217, 218, 219, 221, 226, 228, 229, 249, 271, 277 nn. 2 and 3, 270 n. 17, 282, n. 25, 290–1; *see also* natural rights
Natural Law and Natural Rights (Finnis) 29, 196, 222
Natural Right and History (Strauss) 3, 29
natural rights 99, 151, 152, 153, 159–60, 161, 162–3, 164, 165, 166–7, 173 n. 39, 174 nn. 41 and 45, 169 n. 10, 172 nn. 35 and 38, 175 nn. 54 and 57, 178 n. 71, 179 n. 72, 182, 183, 185, 186, 187, 195; *see also* natural law; rights
natural theology; *see* theology
naturalism 252, 281 n. 20; *see also* ethical naturalism
Nazism 195, 197, 200
Necessary and Proper Clause 161, 164
Neibuhr, R. 262 n. 12
neutralist liberalism 47 n. 44, 110; *see also* liberalism

neutrality 9, 10, 58, 83 n. 33, 108, 110, 111
Newton, I. 186
Niebuhr, R. 77
Nielsen, K. 80 n. 2, 81 nn. 11 and 17, 221
Nietzsche, F. 187, 259
Ninth Amendment 151, 159, 160, 161, 168 nn. 6, 7 and 8, 169 n. 9, 175 n. 50, 178 n. 70, 181, 182, 188, 189, 190
nomos 208, 220
non-cognitivism 228
normative legal philosophy 151
normative legal positivism 170 nn. 22 and 23
normative natural order 200, 202, 206
normativity 155, 156, 157, 200
Norton, B. N. 170 n. 17, 175 n. 48
Nowell-Smith, P. H. 245, 266 nn. 66 and 67
Nozick, R. 49, 55, 81 nn. 17 and 21, 87, 104 n. 1, 105 n. 6, 120, 128 n. 9, 177 n. 66
nuclear weapons 29, 30
Nussbaum, M. C. 24 n. 60, 46 n. 16

objectivism 240, 286, 287, 291–2, 293, 295, 300 n. 22
Oedipus 203
Olsen, G. 277 n. 2
On Princely Government (Aquinas) 7
ontology 202, 212 n. 35, 225, 226, 229, 231, 286–7, 289, 298 n. 6, 299 n. 14
Original Position; *see* anti-utilitarianism
Orwin, C. 84 n. 43
Owen, H. P. 228, 270 nn. 110, 113, 114 and 115, 288, 294

Pangle, T. L. 192 nn. 21 and 28
parent-positivism 214; *see also* positivism
Parfit, D. 238–9
Parker, R. B. 85 n. 53
paternalism 135–6, 138, 145; *see also* coercive paternalism; moral paternalism
Patterson, R. B. 191 n. 5
Paul, J. 81 n. 19, 82 nn. 23 and 26, 83, n. 34
Paul, Saint 251, 280 n. 17
Paul VI, Pope 26 n. 79
per se nota 217, 218, 219; *see also* self-evidence
perfectionism 57, 58, 74, 113, 122, 128, 131, 134, 144, 145
Perry, R. B. 240
Philo 47 n. 41
philosophia perennis 195
philosophical theology; *see* theology
physicalism 288, 299 n. 14
physis 200
Pius XI, Pope 13
Pius XII, Pope 13

Plantinga, A. 276, 290, 291, 297 n. 3, 300 nn. 17 and 20
Plato 12, 13, 14, 15, 19 n. 11, 24 n. 62, 25 n. 66, 26 n. 79, 43, 72, 246, 265 n. 50, 278 n. 7
Platts, M. 263 n. 19
Plummer, C. 19 n. 3
pluralism 9, 62, 63, 74, 75; *see also* value pluralism
Plutarch 13, 14, 16, 24 n. 62, 25 nn. 73 and 75
political culture 76, 77, 78
political liberalism 95, 97, 101, 107; *see also* liberalism
Political Liberalism (Rawls) 50, 56, 61, 62, 63, 64, 65, 66, 67, 68, 69, 70, 71, 72, 73, 74, 75, 76, 77, 78, 79, 87, 88, 89, 93, 95, 96, 98, 99, 100, 101, 103
political liberty 52, 61, 76, 115, 116, 117, 131, 133, 134; *see also* liberty
political principles 125
political theory 4, 9, 11, 75, 212 n. 35
Politics (Aristotle) 1, 2
Pollock, Sir Frederick 213
positivism 197, 214; *see also* legal positivism; parent-positivism; vintage-positivism
Posner, R. 33, 41
Post, G. 277 n. 2
post-modern dissensus 97, 98, 99, 101, 103, 105 nn. 8 and 9
Pound, R. 182
powers of Congress 164
practical reasonableness 218, 222, 251, 257
practical reasoning 4, 10–11, 215, 217, 235, 242, 252, 261, 265 n. 52
Prager, D. 263 n. 22, 265 n. 45, 269 n. 108
prescriptive laws 226, 228, 260–1
prescriptivity 225, 228, 229, 230, 231, 235
Price, A. W. 24 n. 60, 26 n. 79
primary goods 57, 58, 59, 65, 69, 70
Principia Ethica 275
privacy 183
private rights 166, 178 n. 71; *see also* rights
Privileges or Immunities Clause 161, 178 n. 70
projectivism 291
Providence 200, 201, 203, 206
psychology 225, 237, 248
public culture 78, 88, 89
punishment 260

Railton 263 n. 19
Randolph, E. 189
rationality 74, 215, 217, 247; *see also* moral powers
Rawls, J. 9, 10, 11, 22 n. 39, 44, 47 n. 43, 50,
51, 52, 53, 54, 55, 56, 57, 58, 59, 60, 61, 62, 63, 64, 65, 66, 67, 68, 69, 70, 71, 73, 74, 75, 76, 77, 78, 79, 80, 81 nn. 16, 17 and 22, 82 nn. 23, 25 and 26, 83 nn. 33 and 36, 84 nn. 39, 43, 45, 48 and 51, 85 nn. 55 and 56, 87, 88, 89, 90, 91, 93, 94, 95, 96, 97, 98, 99, 100, 101, 102, 103, 104 nn. 1, 2 and 4, 105 n. 8, 107, 111 n. 4, 116, 120, 128 nn. 4 and 8, 212 n. 35, 276, 281 n. 23
Raz, J. 9, 22 n. 39, 131, 132, 133, 134, 135, 136–43, 144, 145–6, 148 nn. 30, 34 and 38, 149 n. 63, 150 n. 65, 236, 265 n. 49
realism; *see* ethical realism; legal realism; modal realism; moral realism
Reardon, B. 262 n. 8
reasonableness 73, 74, 97, 198, 199, 279 n. 17; *see also* moral powers
reasons for actions; *see* practical reasoning
reciprocity 73
Reese, G. H. 193 n. 37
Reichenbach, B. 288, 299 n. 11
Reiman, J. 80 nn. 7 and 10, 81 nn. 15 and 16, 82 nn. 22, 25 and 26, 83 nn. 26, 36 and 39, 84 nn. 45, 46, 48 and 51, 85 nn. 52, 54 and 56, 104 n. 4, 162, 171 nn. 26, 28 and 34, 175 n. 52, 176 n. 60
relativism 223
religious belief 6, 221, 225, 237, 257, 258, 284
religious experience 288
religious freedom 6, 28, 64
religious traditions 285
Republic (Plato) 246
respect 139
responsibility 202, 203, 204, 205, 206, 207, 208, 219, 251, 260
restatements of the law 166
Richards, D. A. J. 81 n. 12, 197, 198
right over good 51, 59, 60, 88, 89, 93, 95, 97, 98, 99, 100, 108
rights 169 n. 12, 172 n. 37, 175 n. 57, 181, 183, 184, 187, 189, 190, 203, 206, 207, 208, 219; *see also* constitutional rights; fundamental rights; human rights; inalienable rights; legal rights; moral rights; mutable rights; natural rights; private rights
Roman Catechism 13
Rommen, H. A. 192
Roosevelt, F. D. 77
Rorty, R. 63, 81 n. 20, 84 n. 45, 111 n. 4
Rosen, J. 175 n. 57
Ross, J. 290, 300 n. 17
Rousseau, J.-J. 50, 72
Rowe, W. 299 n. 11
Rufus, M. 4, 12, 13, 14, 24 nn. 58 and 62

rule of law 1–2, 28, 51
rule utilitarianism 213
rules 207
rules of good conduct 29
Russell, B. 254, 257, 275

Sabl, A. 38, 47 nn. 32 and 41
sanctions 8, 154
Sandel, M. 28, 47 nn. 43 and 45, 81 n. 22,
    82 nn. 23 and 25, 83 n. 34
Santayana 275
Scanlon, T. M. 56, 81 nn. 20 and 21, 82 n. 23,
    83 nn. 29 and 31
Schaefer, D. L. 83 nn. 33 and 34, 84 n. 41
Schauer, F. 168 n. 3, 177 n. 64
Scheffler, S. 278 n. 7
scholasticism 236
Schopenhauer 272
Scotus, D. 301 n. 29
scrutiny of legislation 164, 178 n. 71
second class citizens 141, 142
Second Inaugural 150 n. 64
Second Treatise (Locke) 195
seduction 150 n. 66
self-evidence 218, 219; *see also per se nota*
self-interest 272, 278 n. 7
self-preservation 187
self-respect 125, 136, 141, 142, 149 n. 55
Sen, A. 70, 83 n. 35
sex 40
sexual liberation 27
sexual morality 15, 28, 30, 32, 33, 34, 39, 40,
    42, 44, 150 n. 67, 199; *see also* morality
sexual relations 9, 12, 13, 14, 15, 16, 17, 28,
    30, 32, 33, 34, 35, 36, 37, 38, 39, 40, 41,
    42, 43, 126, 143–4, 149 nn. 60 and 64,
    282 n. 26
sexuality 35, 36, 39, 41, 42, 43, 142, 145, 150
    n. 66
Shakespeare, W. 191 n. 6
Sherman, R. 173 n. 39
Sherry, S. 151, 152–3, 163, 170 n. 17, 175 n.
    48, 178 n. 68
Sidgewick, H. 241, 255, 273, 293
Sixteenth Amendment 175 n. 54
skepticism 157, 215, 216, 292, 294; *see also*
    moral skepticism
slavery 66, 107, 108, 110, 111, 150 n. 64, 209
    n. 6
Smart, J. J. C. 254, 266 n. 67
Smith 276, 293
Snell 227, 291
social goods 55
Socrates 12
Solon 25 n. 73
Sophocles, 211 n. 26
Sorensen, R. 297 n. 3

Sosa 300 n. 22
Souter, D. 168 n. 7
sovereignty 110, 189, 190
Spinoza 271
statism 174 n. 43
Stevens, W. 51, 52, 61, 75, 177 n. 65
Stoner, J. 84 n. 43
Storing, H. 189
Stout, J. 264 n. 23
Strauss, L. 3, 4, 19 n. 15, 20 nn. 16, 17 and
    18, 21 n. 22, 29, 30, 46 n. 12, 63, 84 n. 45,
    105 n. 8, 174 n. 39, 192 n. 31
Strawson, P. F. 211 nn. 27 and 29
Sturgeon 263 n. 19
Suarez, F. 236–7
subjectivism 228
subsidiarity 6, 29, 119, 133, 134, 147 n. 17
suicide 199
Sullivan, A. 47 n. 42
Summa Theologiae (Aquinas) 296
Sunstein, C. R. 111 n. 3
Supreme Court 8, 31, 52, 151, 167, 178 n. 70,
    181, 183, 188
Swinburne, R. 288, 289, 298 n. 5, 299 nn. 11,
    13 and 15
Symposium (Plato) 13

Taliaferro, C. 262 nn. 11, 12 and 13, 264 nn.
    30 and 39
Tannsjo, T. 263 n. 19
Taylor, R. 288. 299 n. 11
teleological ethics 37
teleology 46 n. 11, 57, 288, 289, 291
theism 253, 270 n. 115, 276, 283, 288,
    289–90, 293, 294, 296, 298 nn. 5 and 9,
    299 n. 14, 300 n. 15
theistic moral argument 223, 225, 227, 230,
    248, 251, 254, 258, 260–1, 271, 277,
    283–4, 285, 286–7, 288–93, 298 nn. 6, 8
    and 9, 299 nn. 10, 14 and 15
theistic passibilism 295, 296, 301 n. 29
theological argument 109, 223, 224, 261, 263
    n. 20, 285, 286, 295, 298 n. 5
theological ethics 226, 262 n. 3, 280 n. 18; *see
    also* ethics
theology 13, 225, 251, 257, 259, 265 n. 45,
    288–9, 296, 297 n. 3, 298 n. 6, 301 n. 29
theory of justice 53
Theory of Justice, A (Rawls) 50, 51, 52, 53, 54,
    55, 56, 57, 58, 59, 61, 62, 63, 65, 67, 68,
    69, 70, 71, 73, 74, 75, 76, 78, 79, 87, 88,
    89, 90, 91, 95, 98, 99, 100, 103
Thomas, C. 151, 152, 168 n. 7, 169 nn. 10, 11
    and 13, 177 n. 65, 197
Thomson, J. J. 207, 212 n. 34, 281 n. 20
Thoreau 58, 93, 95
Thrasymachus 79

Tidman, P. 298 n. 6
toleration 108, 109; *see also* judgemental toleration; liberal toleration
torture 266 n. 65
totalistic theory 29
Trethowan, I. 270 nn. 112 and 115
trial by jury 172 n. 37
Tribe, L. H. 111 n. 3, 169 n. 11
Trigg, R. 300 n. 24
Trump, D. 58, 93
trust 122, 123, 124, 126, 127, 128, 129 nn. 12 and 17, 131, 137, 138–9, 146, 148 n. 38

Ulysses 121, 136, 137, 146 n. 8
unalienable rights; *see* inalienable rights
Uniform Commercial Code 166, 171 n. 32
unjust law (legal injustice) 19 n. 10, 170 nn. 21 and 22, 179 n. 72
Untimely Meditations (Nietzsche) 259
US Constitution 101, 110, 118, 151, 152, 153, 154, 155, 156, 159, 160, 161–3, 165, 166, 167, 169 n. 10, 170 n. 23, 171 n. 25, 172 n. 35, 174 n. 44, 175 nn. 52 and 54, 176 nn. 57 and 59, 181, 182, 183, 185, 186, 187, 188, 189, 190, 192 n. 25, 197
utilitarianism 30, 53, 54, 55, 63, 220

valid law 154, 170 n. 20, 177 n. 65
value limitation 96, 98
value pluralism 30; *see also* pluralism
value theory 240, 241, 252, 253, 256, 257, 258, 261, 263 n. 13, 275, 276, 283, 285, 295, 296, 297, 298 n. 9
Veatch, H. B. 174 n. 40, 175 n. 56
Veil of Ignorance; *see* justice
Vendler 281 n. 20
verifiability 216

verificationism 214
Veritatis Splendor (Pope John Paul II) 3, 280 n. 18
vintage-positivism 214; *see also* positivism
Virginia Resolutions (1798) 147 n. 20
virtue 244, 247, 248, 251, 268 n. 83, 277, 278 n. 11
Vitoria 235, 236
Vlastos, 24 n. 62
volitional capacity 249, 251
voluntarism 278 n. 4, 280 n. 17
voluntarist liberalism 108; *see also* liberalism
von Bismarck, O. 158
Von Leydon 209 n. 2

Waldron, J. 128 n. 8, 211 n. 24
Walton, D. 297 n. 4
Weber, M. 244–5
Weinreb, L. L. 210 nn. 16 and 21, 211 n. 30, 213–14, 215, 216, 217, 218, 219, 220
Werner 263 n. 19
West, R. 156, 157
will theory of obligation 235, 237, 265 n. 54
William of Auxerre 296, 301 n. 29
Williams, B. 30, 46 n. 9, 266 n. 67, 279 n. 17, 282 n. 27
Wilson, J. 186
witch-hunts 31, 109
Wolf, S. 282 n. 27
Wolff, R. P. 56, 81 n. 17, 147 n. 17
Wood, A. 262 n. 8
Wythe, G. 165

Zuckert, M. P. 81 nn. 18, 21 and 22, 82 n. 26, 87, 88, 89, 90, 91, 93, 94, 95, 98, 99, 100, 101, 102, 103, 104 nn. 2, 4, 5, 6 and 8

Printed in the United Kingdom
by Lightning Source UK Ltd.
9467600001B